ANNUAL EGYPTOLOGICAL BIBLIOGRAPHY
BIBLIOGRAPHIE ÉGYPTOLOGIQUE ANNUELLE

INTERNATIONAL ASSOCIATION OF EGYPTOLOGISTS
ASSOCIATION INTERNATIONALE DES ÉGYPTOLOGUES

ANNUAL EGYPTOLOGICAL
BIBLIOGRAPHY

BIBLIOGRAPHIE ÉGYPTOLOGIQUE
ANNUELLE

1974

COMPILED BY/COMPOSÉE PAR

JAC. J. JANSSEN

WITH THE COLLABORATION OF/AVEC LA COLLABORATION DE

INGE HOFMANN

LEIDEN
E. J. BRILL
1978

The editor acknowledges the financial assistance of UNESCO in collecting the material for this volume; subvention UNESCO 1975 (CA. 2/9) under the auspices of the International Council for Philosophy and Humanic Studies (ICPHS).

Other grateful acknowledgment must be made of the financial contributions for the same purpose kindly given by the following institutions:

Ægyptologisk Institut, Københavns Universitet,
Centre d'Études Orientales, Genève,
Durham University, Durham,
Egypt Exploration Society, London,
The Griffith Institute, Oxford,
The Metropolitan Museum of Art, New York,
Museum of Fine Arts, Boston, Mass.,
Oosters Genootschap in Nederland, Leiden,
The Oriental Institute, The University of Chicago, Chicago, Ill.,
Schweizerisches Institut für Ägyptische Bauforschung und Altertumskunde, Cairo,
Société française d'Égyptologie, Paris,
University of Liverpool, Liverpool,
Kon. Vitterhets-, Historie- och Antikvitetsakademien, Stockholm.

Adres van de redacteur / Editor's address
Adresse du rédacteur / Anschrift des Schriftleiters:

Dr. Jac. J. JANSSEN

Nederlands Instituut voor het Nabije Oosten
Noordeindsplein 4-6
LEIDEN

ISBN 90 04 05608 4

Copyright 1978 by E.J. Brill, Leiden, The Netherlands
All rights reserved. No part of this book may be reproduced or translated in any form, by print, photoprint, microfilm, microfiche or any other means without written permission from the publisher

PRINTED IN BELGIUM

TABLE OF CONTENTS

List of abbreviations IX
Alphabetical list of authors and titles 1
Necrologies 236

DEDICATED
to the memory of
Dieter MUELLER

LIST OF ABBREVIATIONS

1) *periodicals*, Festschriften *and serials*:

XVIII. Deutscher Orientalistentag: XVIII. Deutscher Orientalistentag vom 1. bis 5. Oktober 1972 in Lübeck. Vorträge. Herausgegeben von Wolfgang Voigt, Wiesbaden, Franz Steiner Verlag, 1974 (14.5 × 22.5 cm; XXVIII + 711 p., 2 plans, 18 fig., 10 pl.) = Zeitschrift der Deutschen Morgenländischen Gesellschaft. Supplement II.

Actes premier congrès de linguistique sémitique: Actes du premier congrès international de linguistique sémitique et chamito-sémitique. Paris, 16-19 juillet 1969. Réunis par André Caquot et David Cohen, The Hague-Paris, Mouton, 1974 (18.5 × 26 cm; 416 p.) = Janua linguarum. Series Practica, 159.

Aegyptus: Aegyptus. Rivista Italiana di Egittologia e di Papirologia, Milano 54 (1974).
 Address: Università Cattolica (Scuola di Papirologia), Largo A. Gemelli 1, 20123 Milano, Italia.

AJA: American Journal of Archaeology, [New York] 78 (1974).
 Address: General Secretary, Archaeological Institute of America, 260 West Broadway, New York, N.Y. 10013, U.S.A.

Akten des XIII. Internationalen Papyrologenkongresses: Akten des XIII. Internationalen Papyrologenkongresses. Marburg/Lahn, 2.-6. August 1971. Herausgegeben von Emil Kießling und Hans-Albert Rupprecht, München, C.H. Beck'sche Verlagsbuchhandlung, 1974 (15.2 × 22.7 cm; XX + 501 p., 8 pl.) = Münchener Beiträge zur Papyrusforschung und Antiken Rechtsgeschichte, 66; rev. *ZDMG* 127 (1977), 77-78 (Hans Georg Gundel).

Antiquity: Antiquity. A Quarterly Review of Archaeology, [Cambridge] 48 (1974).
 Address: Heffers Printers Ltd, 104 Hills Road, Cambridge, CB2 1LW, Great Britain.

Archaeology: Archaeology. A Magazine Dealing with the Antiquity of the World, [New York] 27 (1974).
 Address: Archaeology, 260 West Broadway, New York, N.Y. 10013, U.S.A.

BASOR: Bulletin of the American Schools of Oriental Research Number 213 (February, 1974), 214 (April, 1974), 215 (October, 1974) and 216 (December, 1974).
 Address: American Schools of Oriental Research, Publications Office, 126 Inman Str., Cambridge, Massachusetts 02139, U.S.A.

BIFAO: Bulletin de l'Institut français d'Archéologie orientale, Le Caire 74 (1974).
 Address: Imprimerie de l'Institut français d'Archéologie orientale, 37 Rue el-Cheikh Aly Youssef (ex-rue Mounira), Le Caire, Égypte (R.A.U.).

BiOr: Bibliotheca Orientalis, Leiden 31 (1974).
 Address: Noordeindsplein 4-6, Leiden, Nederland.

BSAC: Bulletin de la Société d'Archéologie Copte, Le Caire.
 Address: Société d'Archéologie Copte, 222 Av. Ramsès, Le Caire, Égypte (R.A.U.).

BSFE: Bulletin de la Société française d'Égyptologie. Réunions trimestrielles. Communications archéologiques No 69 (Mars 1974); Nos 70-71 (Juin-Octobre 1974).
Address: Mme. F. Le Corsu, Cabinet d'Égyptologie, Collège de France, 11 Place Marcelin-Berthelot, Paris 5ᵉ, France.

CdE: Chronique d'Égypte. Bulletin périodique de la Fondation égyptologique Reine Elisabeth. Bruxelles XLIX, n° 97-98 (1974).
Address: Fondation égyptologique «Reine Elisabeth». Musées Royaux d'Art et d'Histoire, Parc du Cinquantenaire, B 1040 - Bruxelles, Belgique.

CRIPEL: Études sur l'Égypte et le Soudan anciens, Lille, Université de Lille III, Éditions Universitaires, [1974] = Cahier de Recherches de l'Institut de Papyrologie de Lille, 2.

Enchoria: Enchoria. Zeitschrift für Demotistik und Koptologie. Herausgegeben von E. Lüddeckens, H.-J. Thissen, K.-Th. Zauzich, in Kommission bei Otto Harrassowitz, Wiesbaden 4 (1974).
Address: Otto Harrassowitz, Taunusstrasse 5, Postfach 349, 6200 Wiesbaden, Bundesrepublik Deutschland.

Encyclopaedia Britannica: The New Encyclopaedia Britannica in 30 volumes. Macropaedia. Knowledge in Depth, Chicago / London / Toronto / Geneva / Sydney / Tokyo / Manila / Seoul / Johannesburg, Encyclopaedia Britannica, Inc. William Benton, Publisher, 1943-1973. Helen Hemingway Benton, Publisher, [1974].

Festschrift Ägyptisches Museum Berlin: Festschrift zum 150jährigen Bestehen des Berliner Ägyptisches Museums, Berlin, Akademie-Verlag, 1974 (21 × 29.7 cm; 522 p., 88 pl., 83 fig. [5 folded], including 4 plans) = Mitteilungen aus der Ägyptischen Sammlung, Band 8. At head of title: Staatliche Museen zu Berlin.

Forschungen und Berichte: Forschungen und Berichte. Archäologische Beiträge, Berlin 16 (1974).
Address: Staatliche Museen zu Berlin, Bodestr. 1-3, 102 Berlin.

GM: Göttinger Miszellen. Beiträge zur ägyptologischen Diskussion, Göttingen Hefte 9, 10, 11, 12, 13, 14 (1974). [Heft 12 = Wissenschaftsgeschichte und theoretische Grundlegung der Ägyptologie. Materialien und Einschätzungen; Heft 14 = Beiträge zu einer Zeichenliste der Hieroglyphen. Arbeitsberichte, Diskussionen und Ergebnisse eines Symposions "Das hieroglyphische Schriftsystem vor allem der Spätzeit", das vom 25. bis 27. Juli 1974 auf der Burg Reichenstein bei Basel abgehalten wurde, herausgegeben von Erik Hornung und Erich Winter].
Address: Seminar für Ägyptologie der Universität, 34 Göttingen, Prinzenstrasse 21, Bundesrepublik Deutschland.

The Gustavianum Collections: From the Gustavianum Collections in Uppsala, 1974. [To Torgny Säve-Söderbergh on his 60th Birthday 29th June 1974], Uppsala, 1974 (18 × 26.5 cm; 119 p., frontispiece, 4 fig., 25 ill., ill. on wrapper) = Acta Universitatis Upsaliensis. *Boreas*. Uppsala Studies in Ancient Mediterranean and Near Eastern Civilizations, 6.

Idö és történelem: Idö és történelem: A Marót Károly emlékkonferencia előadási, [Zeit und Geschichte. Vorträge der Karl Marót Gedenkkonferenz] — Az Eötvös Loránd Tudományegyeten Ókori Történeti Tanszékeinek Kiadványai 7, Budapest, 1974,

JAOS: Journal of the American Oriental Society, New Haven, Connecticut 94 (1974).
  Address: American Oriental Society, 329 Sterling Memorial Library, Yale Station, New Haven, Connecticut 06250, U.S.A.

JARCE: Journal of the American Research Center in Egypt, Princeton, New Jersey 11 (1974).
  Address: J.J. Augustin Publisher, Locust Valley, New York 11560, U.S.A.

JEA: The Journal of Egyptian Archaeology, London 60 (1974) [= Volume dedicated to Raymond O. Faulkner].
  Address: Honorary Treasurer of the Egypt Exploration Society, 2-3 Doughty Mews, London WCIN 2PG, Great Britain.

JNES: Journal of Near Eastern Studies, Chicago, Illinois 33 (1974).
  Address: University of Chicago Press, 5801 Ellis Avenue, Chicago, Illinois 60637, U.S.A.

MDAIK: Mitteilungen des Deutschen Archäologischen Instituts Abteilung Kairo, Wiesbaden 30 (1974).
  Address: Verlag Philipp von Zabern, P.O.B. 4065, Mainz/Rhein, Bundesrepublik Deutschland.

MNL: Meroitic Newsletter. Bulletin d'Informations meroitiques, [Paris] N° 14 (Février 1974), N° 15 (Octobre 1974).
  Address: Jean Leclant, 77 rue Georges Lardennois, F-75019 Paris, France.

Mundus: Mundus. A Quarterly Review of German Research Contributions on Asia, Africa and Latin America. Arts and Science, Stuttgart.
  Address: Wissenschaftliche Verlagsgesellschaft mbH, Postfach 40, 7000 Stuttgart 1, Bundesrepublik Deutschland.

Newsletter ARCE: Newsletter of the American Research Center in Egypt, Princeton, N.J. Nos 88 (Winter 1974), 89 (Spring 1974), 90 (Summer 1974).
  Address: 20 Nassau Street, Princeton, N.J. 08540, U.S.A.

Newsletter SSEA: Newsletter (of) The Society for the Study of Egyptian Antiquities, Toronto Vol. 4, No. 3 (March 1974) and No. 4 (May 1974); Vol. 5, No. 1 (September 1974) and No. 2 (December 1974).
  Address: 30 Chestnut Park, Toronto, Ontario M4W 1W6, Canada.

OLZ: Orientalistische Literaturzeitung, Berlin 69 (1974).
  Address: Akademie-Verlag GmbH, Leipzigerstraße 3-4, 108 Berlin.

OMRO: Oudheidkundige Mededelingen uit het Rijksmuseum van Oudheden te Leiden (Nuntii ex museo antiquario Leidensi), Leiden 55 (1974).
  Address: Rijksmuseum van Oudheden, Rapenburg 28, Leiden, Nederland.

Oriens Antiquus: Oriens Antiquus. Rivista del Centro per le Antichità e la Storia dell' Arte del Vicino Oriente, Roma 13 (1974).
  Address: Centro per le Antichità e la Storia dell' Arte del Vicino Oriente, Via Caroncini 27, 00197 Roma, Italia.

Orientalia: Orientalia, Commentarii trimestres a facultate studiorum orientis antiqui pontificii instituti biblici in lucem editi in urbe, [Roma] Nova Series 43 (1974).
  Address: Pontificium Institutum Biblicum, Piazza del Pilotta 35, I-00187 Roma, Italia.

RdE: Revue d'Égyptologie, Paris 26 (1974).
  Address: Librairie C. Klincksieck, 11 rue de Lille, Paris 7ᵉ, France.

Recent Advances in Science and Technology of Materials: Recent Advances in Science and Technology of Materials. Volume 3. Edited by Adli Bishay, New York and London, Plenum Press, [1974] (16.3 × 25 cm; XVI + 391 p., numerous tables, fig. and ill.) [= The Proceedings of the Second Cairo Solid State Conference Held in Cairo, Egypt, April 21-26, 1973, Volume 3].

Rivista: Rivista degli Studi Orientali, Roma 48 (1974).
Address:: Dott. Giovanni Bardi editore, Salita de crescenzi 16, Roma, Italia.

SAK: Studien zur Altägyptischen Kultur, Hamburg 1 (1974).
Address: Helmut Buske Verlag, Hamburg, Bundesrepublik Deutschland.

Studia Aegyptiaca I: Studia Aegyptiaca I. Recueil d'études dédiées à Vilmos Wessetzky à l'occasion de son 65ᵉ anniversaire, Budapest, 1974 (17 × 24.5 cm; XXI + 433 p., frontispiece = portrait, several ill. and fig.) = Az Eötvös Loránd Tudományegyetem Ókori Történeti Tanszékeinek Kiadványai, 9.

Tel Aviv: Tel Aviv. Journal of the Tel Aviv University Institute of Archaeology, Tel Aviv 1 (1974).
Address: Israel Exploration Society, P.O.B. 7041, Jerusalem, Israel.

Textes et langues III: Textes et langages de l'Égypte pharaonique. Cent cinquante années de recherches. 1822-1972. [Volume III.] Hommage à Jean-François Champollion, [Le Caire], Institut français d'Archéologie orientale du Caire, [1974] (20.2 × 27.3 cm; 308 p.) = Bibliothèque d'étude, 64/3.

ВДИ : Вестник Древней Истории, Москва 1 (127)-4 (130), 1974.
Address: Москва В-36, ул. Дмитрия Ульнова. Д. 19, Комн. 237, Институт всеобщей Истории, АН СССР.

WZKM: Wiener Zeitschrift für die Kunde des Morgenlandes, Wien.
Address: Selbstverlag der Wiener Zeitschrift für die Kunde des Morgenlandes, Universitätsstraße 7/V, A-1010 Wien 1, Österreich.

ZÄS: Zeitschrift für ägyptische Sprache und Altertumskunde, Berlin 100, 2 (1974) and 101 (1974) = Gedenkschrift für Siegfried Morenz. Teil IIb and III.
Address: Akademie-Verlag GmbH, Leipzigerstraße 3-4, 108 Berlin.

ZAW: Zeitschrift für die alttestamentliche Wissenschaft, Berlin 86 (1974).
Address: Walter de Gruyter & Co., Postfach 110240, 1000 Berlin 11.

ZDMG: Zeitschrift der Deutschen Morgenländischen Gesellschaft, Wiesbaden 124 (1974).
Address: Franz Steiner Verlag GmbH, Bahnhofstrasse 39, Postfach 743, 62 Wiesbaden, Bundesrepublik Deutschland.

2) *other abbreviations*:

AEB :	*Annual Egyptological Bibliography/Bibliographie égyptologique annuelle.*	km :	kilometre(s).
		m :	metre(s).
		p. :	page(s).
		pl. :	plate(s).
cfr :	*confer*, compare	publ. :	publication(s).
cm :	centimetre(s)	pr. :	price.
col. :	column	rev. :	review *or* summary.
etc. :	*et cetera*	⌐ :	above a numeral, this hieroglyph indicates a monograph.
fig. :	figure(s).		
ill. :	illustration(s).		

ALPHABETICAL LIST OF AUTHORS AND TITLES

74001 ABD EL-RAZIK, Mahmud, The Dedicatory and Building Texts of Ramesses II in Luxor Temple. I: The Texts, *JEA* 60 (1974), 142-160, with 1 plan.

This article is a preliminary to the study of the statues of Ramesses II in the first court of the Luxor temple. All the buildings texts are listed on the plan and hieroglyphic copies given of them, the translations and commentary being scheduled for the next volume of this journal. See *JEA* 61 (1975), 125-136.

E. Uphill

74002 ABITZ, Friedrich, Die religiöse Bedeutung der sogenannten Grabräuberschächte in den ägyptischen Königsgräbern der 18. bis 20. Dynastie, Wiesbaden, Otto Harrassowitz, 1974 (18 × 25.4 cm; 122 p., 2 plans, 6 fig., 9 pl. containing 10 plans) = Ägyptologische Abhandlungen herausgegeben von Wolfgang Helck und Eberhard Otto, 26; rev. *BiOr* 33 (1976), 17-18 (L. Kákosy); *JEA* 61 (1975), 295-296 (J. Gwyn Griffiths); *Mundus* 11 (1975), 3-4 (Hellmut Brunner). Pr. DM 48

The author studies the problem whether indeed the so-called "tomb-robber shafts" in the royal tombs from the XVIIIth to the XXth Dynasty have been intended, as usually stated, to protect the tombs against robbers or the influence of rain water, reaching the conclusion that they actually belong the religious scheme on which the plan of the tombs is based.

The introduction deals with the working methods and the material to the study. Since tombs KV 10 (Amenmesse) and KV 18 (Ramses X) could not be entered the study is based on 21 tombs, of which KV 62 (Tutankhamon) and KV 55 (Smenkhkare) are not specially investigated.

In chapter 2 the author discusses the plans of the tombs, the shafts and their side rooms, the walls barring the entrance to and exit from the shaft-rooms (room E), and the blocking up of the three entrance corridors in the earlier tombs. In the summary to this chapter (p. 47-50) he argues that shafts are an essential element in all tombs until Ramses III, but that, since in some instances the barrier walls to room E had doors, they cannot be intended to keep out the robbers. Nor could the wish to keep out the infiltration water be their explanation, since the entrance of the tomb was in some instances well closed. The only explanation is, therefore, a religious function.

Chapter 3 is devoted to the decoration of the tomb walls. In the conclusion (p. 79-80) the author states that the scenes and texts on the walls follow a fixed order, every room and corridor having a special function, the shafts included. Chapter 4 discusses the royal epithets accompanying royal figures and cartouches in room E; chapter 5 the position of the hours of *Amduat* in the tomb. Short chapters follow on the relation between shaft room and shaft, on particularities in the tombs of Sethi II and Tausert, and on the problem of religion and its expression in plan and decoration.

In the last chapter the author summarizes the results of his study, concluding that in the royal tombs from Tuthmosis III to Ramses III, which show a uniform scheme, the shaft symbolizes the 5th hour of *Amduat*, namely the tomb of Sokaris, over the upper half of which leads the road of the bark of Re, symbolizing the funeral procession of the king, possibly in the meantime the 6th hour, namely the tomb of Osiris. In this respect it stands in parallel to the sarcophagus hall.

el-ACHIRIE, Hassan, see our number 74259.

74003 ADAMS, Barbara, Ancient Hierakonpolis. With an Introduction by Professor H. S. Smith, Warminster, Aris & Phillips Ltd, [1974] (20.8 × 29.5 cm; XX + 88 p., 48 pl. containing ill. and fig., plan on endpapers); series : Modern Egyptology Series; rev. *BiOr* 33 (1976), 24-25 (Winfried Barta); *CdE* XLIX, No. 98 (1974), 282-286 (Gérard Godron); *JEA* 61 (1975), 259-260 (Joan Crowfoot Payne).
Pr. bound £ 12.50 [together with the Supplement : £ 13.50]

In his Preface Smith demonstrates the importance of the present publication for the understanding of the history of the site and the date of the "Main Deposit", which is of exceptional value for our knowledge of the Early Dynastic Period.

The Introduction by the author discusses the Petrie Collection at University College and the history of the present study. Most of the objects of the catalogue have been either inadequately published or not at all. Of the utmost value has been the discovery in Cambridge of the Green manuscripts relating to the excavation at Hierakonpolis, which provided the key to most of the site numbers noted on the objects. The introduction further presents a general discussion of the types of objects in the catalogue : mace-heads, statuettes, animal figures, ivories, etc.

The main part of the book consists of the catalogue itself, arranged by type, of the 388 objects at present in University College, among which the most important may be two fragmentary mace-heads, here called the King's and the Dearer mace-head (nos 1-2 = UC 14898 and 14898 A), and some of the ivories with representations of animals.

Each object is separately described and discussed, with mention of all available data, while all are reproduced in drawing and some also in photograph on the plates. The objects are : 3 great and 78 undecorated mace-heads, either disk- or pear-shaped; 8 statuettes, 7 inscribed objects, among which a faience plaque with the name of Tuthmosis III and the rim of an alabaster vase with that of Necho; 48 animal figures and fragments of them, numerous other models, beads, plaques, tiles, vessels and tools, and the important group of 61 ivories, probably all from the Main Deposit. The treatment of the latter is described by the author, the identification of their material by Miss Sandford (p. 59-60). At the end three objects from Group 315. There follows a list of objects already published by Brunton in the *Studies Presented to F. Ll. Griffith* (London, 1932), 272-276, arranged after their UC numbers (27469-27565). On p. 83-86 the index of all UC numbers discussed, with references to catalogue numbers and plates.

74004 ADAMS, Barbara, Ancient Hierakonpolis. Supplement, [Warminster], Aris & Phillips Ltd., [1974] (20.8 × 29.8 cm; [VI +] 169 p., numerous fig, frontispiece, plan on endpapers); series : Modern Egyptology Series; rev. *BiOr* 33 (1976), 24-25 (Winfried Barta); *CdE* XLIX, No. 98 (1974), 282-286 (Gérard Godron); *JEA* 61 (1975), 259-260 (Joan Crowfoot Payne). Pr. £ 2.50

The introduction describes the Green manuscripts, notebooks and maps to the Hierakonpolis excavations (cfr also appendix 2, p. 125-126), as well as drawings, a distribution list of the objects, three pages of outline flint drawings and a register of pottery types. It appears that Green has paid attention to what, at that time, may have been considered unimportant detail, since he made careful notes on the most insignificant finds, many of which may have never left the site. He also noted in his records opinions about the site different from those given in the publications, which may be of importance particularly for the dating of the objects in the "Main Deposit". These now have appeared, after cleaning the ivories, not to be Archaic but Old or perhaps Middle Kingdom in date.

The book mainly consists of the Green Manuscript Analysis Register, arranged according to the sites, with sketches of some deposits, buildings, etc., and of the objects there found. To them have been added all known museum numbers.

In Appendix 1a are listed the site numbers mentioned in *Hierakonpolis* I and II, those published in other works, those on the objects which are not published, and those in the Green manuscripts. Appendix 1b gives a key to the arrangement of the Ms. Analysis Register showing the proportion of unidentified site numbers.

Appendix 3a contains the distribution list from *Hierakonpolis* II (pls XLVIII a and b) with the present museum numbers, and 3b the distribution lists of the objects in the museums which cannot be identified in the preceding list, arranged after the museums in which they are preserved.

At the end an index giving the provenance of the objects not included in the Ms. Analysis Register; an index of unidentified site numbers, and one of unprovenanced objects.

ADAMS, B., see also our number 74099.

ADAMS, William Y., see our number 74580.

74005 ADAMSON, D., J.D. CLARK, and M.A.J. WILLIAMS, Barbed Bone Points from Central Sudan and the Age of the "Early Khartoum" Tradition, *Nature*, London 249, No. 5453 (May 10, 1974), 120-123, with 1 map and 1 fig.

Die Knochenspitzen mit Widerhaken ("Harpunen"), die typisch sind für die frühe holozäne Siedlung in Khartum ("Early Khartoum") wurden in drei weiteren Siedlungen am Weißen Nil südlich von Khartum entdeckt, und zwar in Tagra, Guli und Shabona. Die in Guli gefundene Keramik ähnelt der von Esh Shaheinab und der Khartoum Variant-Ware vom 2. Katarakt, die ebenfalls in Kashm el Girba am oberen Atbara belegt ist. Die Knochenspitzen mit Widerhaken kommen am Nil sonst nur noch im Fischercamp von Cat Fish Cave in Oberägypten vor, wo jedoch die Keramik fehlt. *Inge Hofmann*

AHLQUIST, Richard, see our number 74338.

74006 AIGNER-FORESTI, Luciana, Schardana — Schakruscha — Turuscha : Italische Stämme?, *in* : Franz Hampl und Ingomar Weiler, *Kritische und vergleichende Studien zur Alten Geschichte und Universalgeschichte*, Innsbruck, Herausgegeben von der Innsbrucker Gesellschaft zur Pflege der Geisteswissenschaften, 1974 (= Innsbrucker Beiträge zur Kulturwissenschaft, 18), 25-45.

The author, evidently not an Egyptologist (some transcriptions are wrong, references to more recent Egyptological literature almost absent) discusses the problem of the origin of the Sea-Peoples, particularly the *Šrtdtnt*, *Twrwšt* and *Škrwšt*. She deals with the philological interpretation of the names and their occurrences from the Amarna Letters to the Cairo stela of Ramses XI, attempting to establish their historical implications. The conclusion is that there is no proof for any connection between these peoples and the Sardinians, Etruscans and Sicels. The similarity of the names may be due to migration of the names themselves, which does not imply migration of the peoples.

ALBERT, Jacques, see our number 74781.

74007 ALLAM, S., An Allusion to an Egyptian Wedding Ceremony?, *GM* Heft 13 (1974), 9-11.

A reply to our No. 74360. The restoration ḫ[mȝ]y in Pap. Turin 2070 is not certain, and the context does not necessarily imply that the two persons involved were married or even living together.   *Dieter Mueller*

74008 ALLAM, Schafik, Vom Stiftungswesen der Alten Ägypter. Die Tübinger Grabkammer, *Das Altertum*, Berlin 20 (1974), 131-146, with 4 ill.

Proceeding from the scenes on the walls of the funerary chamber of the tomb of Seshemnefer III from Gizâ, at present in the collection of the Egyptological Institute at Tübingen and after having dealt with the funerary cult in general, among which the ḥm-kȝ priest, the author discusses the legal aspects relating to the institution of the funerary estate (ḏt) in the various periods of the Egyptian civilization.

The original moral duty to take care of the funerary cult of a person by members of the family was replaced by the institution of a funerary estate, in which there existed a legal obligation to guarantee the continuation of a person's funerary cult since its fund was connected with a purpose by a private action of the will. Because the funerary estate had no corporate capacity, the fund could be challenged.   *L.M.J. Zonhoven*

74009 ALLAM, Schafik, Zur Adoption im pharaonischen Ägypten, *XVIII. Deutscher Orientalistentag*, 1-7.

Summary of our number 73022.

74010 ALLAM, Schafik, Zur Tempelgerichtsbarkeit zur Zeit des Neuen Reiches, *ZÄS* 101 (1974), 1-4.

Das Gerichtswesen des Neuen Reiches enthält priesterliche und profane Rechtsprechungsorgane. Koordiniert in diesem einen System unterliegen beide der Kontrolle des Wesirs.
      M. Heerma van Voss

74011 ALLEN†, Thomas George, The Book of the Dead or Going Forth by Day. Ideas of the Ancient Egyptians concerning the Hereafter as Expressed in their own Terms. Prepared fo Publication by Elizabeth Blaisdell Hauser, Chicago, Illinois, The University of Chicago Press, [1974] (23 × 29.5 cm; X + 306 p.) = The Oriental Institute of the University of Chicago. Studies in Ancient Oriental Civilization, No. 37.   Pr. $20

According to the preface this volume of translations of the *Book of the Dead* has been completed by the late author in May 1968, which means that he did not make use of Barguet's translation (our number 67052). It has been prepared for publication by Mrs. Hauser, who added the footnotes through Spell 144b as well as the indexes.

Apart from the preface and an introduction the volume consists of translations of all 192 spells as well as the Spells Pleyte 166-174 (p. 215-223). The translation is based on New Kingdom manuscripts. For each spell the author mentions in a note the version(s) underlying his translation, while for some of them he presents variants, e.g. Spells 6, 15 A and B, and 65. The notes also point to the vignettes accompanying the spell. A few notes contain explanations of the translation.

There follow two appendices, one mentioning the correlations between places in the *Book of the Dead* and those in the *Coffin Texts* and the *Pyramid Texts* (p. 225-241), and one listing the documents cited.

Two indexes, one to names, epithets and subjects and one to the more significant and the unusual or uncertain Egyptian words and those not in the *Wb*, on p. 249-306.

74012 ALMAGRO BASCH, M., Die ägyptischen Tempel von Debod in Madrid, *Antike Welt*, Küsnacht-Zürich 5, Heft 4 (1974), 25-35, with 13 ill. and 1 plan.

Der Tempel von Debod wurde 1968 von der ägyptischen Regierung Spanien übergeben und in einem Park von Madrid wiedererrichtet. Nach einer Ausführung über die wechselvolle Vergangenheit des Tempels, seine Vergabe an Spanien und seiner Rekonstruktion in Madrid, folgt eine Beschreibung der Tempelbauten und ihrer Reliefs. *Inge Hofmann*

74013 ALTENMÜLLER, Hartwig, Bemerkungen zur Kreiselscheibe Nr. 310 aus dem Grab des Hemaka in Saqqara, *GM* Heft 9 (1974), 13-18, with 2 fig.

The author examines an unusual representation of a bird-trap holding two cranes, and concludes that cranes were still trapped in the Archaic Period, but raised in poultry farms in later times; a similar representation in the tomb of Mehu in Saqqara must be considered an archaism. *Dieter Mueller*

74014 ALTENMÜLLER, Hartwig, Gräber unter der Prozessionsstrasse. Neue Entdeckungen in Saqqara (Ägypten), *Antike Welt*, Küsnacht-Zürich 5, Heft 2 (1974), 20-34, with 20 ill. (9 in colour).

The author deals with the tombs of lower officials from the Vth Dynasty originally built in the quarry S.E. of the Djoser complex and later covered by the causeway of Unas. He describes the wall decoration of the rock tomb of Neferherenptah, already discovered in 1940, and the more recently discovered tombs, particularly the painted decoration of the tomb of Niankhkhnum and Khnumhotep, the blocks of the free standing part of which have been found in the foundation of the causeway.

74015 ALTENMÜLLER, Hartwig, Zur Ritualstruktur der Pyramidentexte, *XVIII. Deutscher Orientalistentag*, 8-17.

The reconstruction of the original order of collections of religious texts is of importance for the knowledge of the rites to which they belonged. These rites are represented in the tombs, but the scenes show a similar disorder as the texts. Still they may have been derived from a model which contained the original order. The author discusses the methods by which it may be reconstructed and by which the texts can be paired with the scenes. An example is the "late redaction" of the burial ritual represented in XVIIIth Dynasty tombs, which belongs to the "early redaction" of the *Pyr. Texts* (Unas). The author elucidates his argument by a discussion of *Pyr. Texts* Spell 306-312.

74016 ALTENMÜLLER, Hartwig, Zur Vergöttlichung des Königs Unas im alten Reich, *SAK* 1 (1974), 1-18.

Proceeding from two Middle Kingdom monuments attesting the cult of Unas (cfr our number 71417) the author discusses the evidence for it from the Old Kingdom. He mentions various indications, e.g.: personal names composed with *Wnis* and texts from 7 tombs of people who were in the service of his pyramid, all laying around it and dating from the VIth Dynasty. They call themselves *imȝḥw ḫr Wnis*, in two instances even in parallel to similar indications mentioning gods. Moreover, in one tomb, that of a *Ḥnw*, an inscription (translated and discussed in an excursus, p. 14-18) calls the owner *bȝk n Wnis*. Possibly Unas' pyramid was situated near a now destroyed sanctuary of Ptah-Sokar, which may have stimulated the deification of the king. Another reason will be the large personnel attached to his mortuary cult.

74017 ALTENMÜLLER, Hartwig und Ahmed M. MOUSSA, Eine wiederentdeckte Statue des Vezirs Rahotep, *MDAIK* 30 (1974), 1-14, with 1 pl.

Publication of a naophore statue of rose granite originally discovered by Zakaria Goneim near the monastery of St.

Jeremias and now at the main entrance to the Saqqara necropolis. It represents a vizier Rahotep, and may have come from his tomb. Its owner was probably the vizier (Pa)Rahotep from Abydos who lived during the early years of Ramesses II, and must be distinguished from the younger vizier (Pa)Rahotep from Sedment, whose term of office falls into the later years of this pharaoh. *Dieter Mueller*

AMICO, Bernardino, see our number 74780.

74018 el-AMIR, Mustapha, Varia Demotica, *Akten des XIII. Internationalen Papyrologenkongresses*, 111-116.

The author deals with five different points :
1. The circumstances in which Demotic family archives have been found (in jars) indicate the existence of the custom of παρακαταθήκη, i.e. deposit of money or property entrusted to one's care. 2. The unpublished Demotic Pap. Philadelphia XXX, an account from the year 4 of Ptolemy I, indeed belongs to Pap. Phil. V and VI on the sheet of which it has been written. 3. Cfr our number 69019. 4. The author argues that Egypt was the real Law Giver to the world, demonstrating his point by the law of contract as it appears from actual contracts. 5. Some Demotic words and expressions persisting in colloquial Arabic of Egypt.

74019 AMIRAN, Ruth, An Egyptian Jar Fragment with the Name of Narmer from Arad, *Israel Exploration Journal*, Jerusalem 24 (1974), 4-12, with 2 fig. and 1 pl.

Publication of a shoulder fragment of a jar found at Arad in 1973, bearing an incised *serekh* with the name of Narmer and upon which a Horus hawk stands. The catfish of the name is schematically drawn, the *mr*-sign is lacking. A similar inscription has been found at Tel 'Erani, but this one without the hawk.
In this connection the author gives a survey of the Egyptian pottery finds in Greater Canaan from the EBA I-II and discusses the historical conclusions which can be drawn from them. She i.a. states her doubt whether they indicate an Egyptian domination in southern Canaan, as has been suggested.

74020 AMIRAN, Ruth, The Painted Pottery Style of the Early Bronze II Period in Palestine, *Levant*, London 6 (1974), 65-68, with 5 pl.

The author, briefly discussing the painted pottery of the EB II Period found in Egypt (Abydos, Abû Sîr and Saqqâra) and in Palestine, deals with three points : the characteristics of the style, its development within the period, and echoes of the style in the pottery of the EB III Period and in that of the Old

Kingdom. At the end some remarks about the origin of the style, which is still uncertain.

74021 Ancient Art. The Norbert Schimmel Collection. Edited by Oscar White Muscarella, Mainz, Verlag Philipp von Zabern, [1974] (24 × 26.5 cm; 342 unnumbered p., 375 ill. [53 in colour], 4 fig., colour ill. on cover); rev. *AJA* 80 (1976), 317-319 (William Kelly Simpson). Pr. DM 98

This is the catalogue of an exhibition in honour of John D. Cooney held in the Cleveland Museum of Art (November-December 1974).
The book begins with a dedication to Cooney, followed by his bibliography. The catalogue itself consists of 265 numbers, of which the numbers 169-265 are objects of Egyptian art. The last 25 are Amarna reliefs.
Each piece of art is briefly described, the Egyptian objects by Cooney himself. Technical data and bibliography of each are added, and all are represented by one or more splendid photographs.
For the famous Schimmel collection, see our numbers 64231, 65121 and 67546.

74022 Anonymous, [Mustafa el-Amir], *BSFE* No 70-71 (Juin et Octobre 1974), 9.

Obituary notice. Compare our number 74840.

74023 Anonymous, [J. W. B. Barns], *BSFE* No 69 (Mars 1974), 4.

Obituary notice. Compare our number 74841.

74024 Anonymous, [Henri Chevrier], *BSFE* No 70-71 (Juin et Octobre), 7-8.

Obituary notice. Compare our number 74843.

74025 Anonymous, [Bryan G. Haycock], *BSFE* No 69 (Mars 1974), 4.

Obituary notice. Compare our number 74844.

74026 Anonymous, Jahresbericht 1972 des Deutschen Archäologischen Instituts Abteilung Kairo, *Archäologischer Anzeiger*, Berlin (1973), 1973/74, 750-754.

Report of the activities of the DAI in Cairo, mentioning i.a. the excavations of Elephantine, in ʿAsâsîf and in the Sethi I temple, and the work in Saqqâra.

74027 Anonymous (M.G.), Das Museum Calouste Gulbenkian in Lissabon, *Du*, Zürich 34, no. 395 (Januar 1974), 2-37, with 27 ill. and 7 colour ill.

We mention among the objects in the Gulbenkian Museum, Lisbon, here described, a New Kingdom incense spoon with a quite fantastic decoration of figures around the shaft which in itself represents a fruit-tree (p. 4).

74028 Anonymous, [Eberhard Otto], *BSFE* No 70-71 (Juin et Octobre 1974), 8.

Obituary notice. Compare our number 74845.

74029 Anonymous, [Marie-Thérèse Picard-Schmitter], *BSFE* No 70-71 (Juin et Octobre 1974), 9-10.

Obituary notice.

74030 Anonymous, Rätselhafte Mumie einer ägyptischen Pharaonin, *Antike Welt*, Küsnacht-Zürich 5, Heft 4 (1974), 54.

A short notice about three mummies recently examined, although originating from the find in the tomb of Amenophis II. One of the three belongs to one of the great queens of the New Kingdom, possibly Teje or even Hatshepsut. *L.M.J. Zonhoven*

74031 Anonymous, [Ramadan Saad], *BSFE* No 70-71 (Juin et Octobre 1974), 9.

Obituary notice. Compare our number 74846.

74032 Anonymous, Table des Matières des No 1 à 15 du Bulletin d'Informations Méroïtiques, Meroitic Newsletter, *MNL* No 15 (Octobre 1974), 31-38.

Zusammenstellung der Artikel und meroitistischen Tagungsberichte, die bisher in den *MNL* erschienen. *Inge Hofmann*

74033 Anonymous, Edward L. B. Terrace. 1936-1973, *Newsletter ARCE* No. 88 (Winter 1974), 1-3.

Obituary notice. Compare our number 74848.

74034 ANTHES, Rudolf, Die Bericht des Neferhotep und des Ichernofret über das Osirisfest in Abydos, *Festschrift Ägyptisches Museum Berlin*, 15-49, with 5 fig.

The author studies the inscription of King Neferhotep about the festival of Osiris in Abydos. The stela, published by Maspero (*Abydos*, II, pl. 28-30), has become lost; it was translated already by Pieper in 1929.
The author gives a new translation of parts of the text, with textual comments, as well as a transcription after Maspero (by Ulrich Luft). There follows an extensive analysis of the events during the festival as related by Neferhotep, which is compared with the famous text of Ikhernofre in the Berlin Museum.

Some conclusions are: it is the king himself who relates here the events, which occur down to line 21 in the actual order of the festival; Osiris was represented by the so-called emblem of This, the Ennead of Abydos by nine sacred staffs. The author points out differences between the M.K. stelae and attempts to explain them.

From line 22 onwards there follow a hymn and a personal hymn of the king to Osiris, which i.a. relates the return from Abydos.

Summary on p. 40-41.

In an appendix the author discusses three Ramesside texts concerning the festival, from the inscription of Wennofre (Louvre A 66), a hymn to Abydos (cfr our number 59133), and from the inscription of Kha (Louvre A 65) and Siese (Metr. Mus. of Art 17.2.5.). Of all three there are given a transcription of the relevant part, with translation and comments, followed by remarks on their informations about the festival.

A supplement deals with the question of place and time of the dressing of the emblem during the festival; another points out the representation of emblem and staffs on a XXIIIrd Dynasty statue (Berlin Inv. Nr. 17 272).

For a correction see *ZÄS* 102 (1975). 78.

74035 ANTHES, Rudolf, Harachti und Re in den Pyramidentexten, *ZÄS* 100, 2 (1974), 77-82.

In unserer Nummer 71033, S. 55f., hat Verfasser dargelegt, wie Re, die Sonne, als Himmelsherrscher Horus, den Stern, den Himmelskönig ablöste. Anthes untermauert hier seine Darstellung. *M. Heerma van Voss*

74036 Antik kunst i dansk privateje, et udvalg af oldtidskunst fra Middelhavsområdet og de tilgrænsende lande. Udstilling i Ny Carlsberg Glyptotek 16. maj-31. august 1974, København, 1974 (18.5 × 23 cm; 72 p., numerous ill.).

"Ancient art in Danish private collections, a selection of the art of antiquity from the Mediterranean area and the neighbouring countries".

The Egyptian part of the exhibition consisted of 66 items, all of which are illustrated. We mention especially Nos. 7 (a sculptor's trial piece, 4th century B.C.), 8 (a knob of a stick, on which Akhenaten and Nefertiti are represented) and 49 (a sitting baboon, Ramesside). *Torben Holm-Rasmussen*

74037 Antinoe (1965-1968). Missione Archeologica in Egitto dell' Università di Roma, Roma, Istituto di Studi del Vicino Oriente-Università, 1974 (22.4 × 31.4 cm; 155 p., 70 pl. with plans and fig. [5 folding], 83 pl. with ill.) = Università degli Studi di Roma. Serie archeologica, 21.

The report on the excavations at Antinoe begins with an introduction by Sergio Donadoni, containing a survey of the history of the excavations.
The first chapter, by Adriana Spallanzani Zimmermann, is devoted to the proto-dynastic cemetery S. of the Ramses temple. The 13 tombs are briefly described, with their contents. Some general conclusions precede the description.
The second chapter, by Luisa Bongrani Fanfoni, discusses the excavations in the area of the temple of Ramses II, which were concentrated on the area in front of the destroyed pylon.
The other chapters deal with the Graeco-Roman remains of the city.

ARMELAGOS, George J., see our number 74118.

74038 ARNETT, William Samuel, The Predynastic Origin of Egyptian Hieroglyphs: Evidence for the Development of Rudimentary Forms of Hieroglyphs in Upper Egypt in the Fourth Millennium B.C., *Dissertation Abstracts International A*, Ann Arbor, Mich. 34, no. 11 (May 1974), 7139/40-A.

Abstract of a doctor's thesis Ohio State University, 1973 (Order No. 74-10, 908; 181 p.).
The purpose of this thesis is to show that, at least so far as the beginning of hieroglyphs is concerned, their origin antedates the arrival of the Dynastic Egyptians into the Delta, and lies in Upper Egypt. *L.M.J. Zonhoven*

74039 ARNOLD, Dieter, Bericht über die vom Deutschen Archäologischen Institut Kairo im Winter 1972/73 in El-Târif durchgeführten Arbeiten, *MDAIK* 30 (1974), 155-164, with 2 plans, 1 fig. and 9 pl.

Continuation of our No. 73044.
Two further campaigns established that the royal tomb in the Saff el-Kisasija is older than that in the Saff el-Baqar; the former must therefore belong to Inyotef II, the latter to Inyotef III. The so-called East Mastaba may have been built in the IVth Dynasty on top of an older tomb whose equipment was usurped in the process. *Dieter Mueller*

74040 ARNOLD, Dieter, Der Tempel des Königs Mentuhotep von Deir el-Bahari. Band I. Architektur und Deutung [und] Band II. Die Wandreliefs des Sanktuares. Zeichnungen von Wolf-Günther Ledge und Reginald Coleman, Mainz am Rhein, Verlag Philipp von Zabern, [1974] (26.8 × 36.3 cm; Band I: 99 p., 39 fig. including plans, 43 pl. [2 folding] including plans,

1 loose folding plan; Band II : 59 p., colour frontispiece, 7 fig. including 2 plans, 62 pl. [3 folding, 1 in colour]) = Deutsches Archäologisches Institut. Abteilung Kairo. Archäologische Veröffentlichungen, 8 [und] 11.; rev. *Die Welt des Orients* 8 (1975-1976), 320-323 (Ingrid Gamer-Wallert). Pr. DM 120

Der Verfasser veröffentlicht die Ergebnisse der Reinigung und Neubearbeitung des Tempels durch das Deutsche Archäologische Institut Kairo von 1968 bis zum Winter 1971/72.
Das 1. Kapitel, Baubeschreibung, behandelt nacheinander die verschiedenen Bauteile des Tempels (1.1 Die untere Halle, 1.2 die Rampe, 1.3 die Tempelterrasse und obere Halle, 1.4 das Ambulatorium, 1.5 den Kernbau, 1.6 den Mittelhof, 1.7 die hypostyle Halle, 1.8 das Sanktuar, 1.9 das Königsgrab, 1.10 das Bab el-Hosan, 1.11 das Grab der Königin *Tm* und 1.12 Einzelfragen.). Nach einer Beschreibung des gegenwärtigen Zustandes wird jeweils ein Rekonstruktionsvorschlag gemacht. Kapitel 2 schildert die Geschichte des Tempels von seiner Erbauung bis in die neuere Zeit. Im 3. Kapitel, "Zur Deutung des Tempels", wird die Funktion einzelner Teile des Tempels besprochen anhand der nachweisbaren Kulte des Königs, des Month-Re, des Amun-Re, des Osiris und der Hathor und die Beziehungen zum Hebsed aufgezeigt. "Der vordere, durch seine monumentale Form eindrucksvollere Teil des Tempels muß ... als ein dem Sonnenfalken Month-Re geweihtes, urhügelhaftes Denkmal des Königs verstanden werden". Abhandlungen über die Namen des Tempels (Kapitel 4), seine Priesterschaft und posthume Nennungen des Königs (Kapitel 5) sowie ein Sachindex und ein Index erörterter Probleme schließen den Textteil des 1. Bandes.
Der 2. Band beginnt mit allgemeinen Bemerkungen zum Erhaltungszustand der Reliefs und zur Aufnahmemethode. Es folgt eine Besprechung der Rekonstruktionsvorschläge und anschließend eine zusammenfassende Darstellung des Bildprogramms und der Funktion des Sanktuars, dessen Dekoration vor allem seine Eigenschaft als Kultstätte des Königs, als Amun-Re-Kapelle und als Opfertisch-Saal betont. Die Kapitel 4 bis 8 umfassen eine Beschreibung der einzelnen Fragmente, eine Liste der im Sanktuar vorkommenden Hieroglyphen, eine Liste der sich außerhalb des Tempels befindlichen Fragmente, ein Verzeichnis der im Sanktuar genannten Götter und den Index.
E.M. Wolf-Brinkmann

74041 ASSMANN, Jan, Ägyptologie und Linguistik. Bericht über ein Heidelberger Kolloquium zwischen Ägyptologen und Sprachwissenschaftlern im Wintersemester 73/74, *GM* Heft 11 (1974), 59-76.

Report about a colloquium on the application of modern linguistic techniques to the study of Egyptian grammar; preliminary results of the discussion of the Egyptian verbal system are described in some detail.   *Dieter Mueller*

74042 ASSMANN, Jan, Der literarische Text im Alten Ägypten. Versuch einer Begriffsbestimmung, *OLZ* 69 (1974), 117-126.

Review article to our number 70243.
The author first lists a variety of meanings of the term "literature" in Egyptology, arguing that the aesthetic and the functional aspects do not coincide. He then discusses the problem of the genres (Gattungen) in Egyptian literature. He argues that for part of the texts the "Sitz im Leben" is decisive, while from these groups the actual literary genres are developed.

74043 ATZLER, Michael, Einige Erwägungen zum *srḫ*, *Oriens*, Leiden 23-24 (1974), 406-432.

The author argues that the *serekh* does not represent, as has been suggested, the facade of a palade (*'ḥ*), but a court with a panelled girdle wall. Its prototype was not a construction of mats but a brick construction. The panelling is symbolic and indicates the structure as being a royal building, which may or may not contain a palace. Panelling occurs on various objects, tombs, coffins, etc. indicating that they belong to the royal sphere. It is not merely a decorative element.

74044 AUBERT, Jacques-F. [and] Liliane AUBERT, Statuettes égyptiennes, Chaouabtis, ouchebtis, Paris, Librairie d'Amérique et d'Orient Adrien Maisonneuve, 1974 (16 × 24.7 cm; 341 p., frontispiece [map], 1 fig., 2 maps, 68 pl., ill. on cover).
Pr. NF 140

This study on the shawabti is based not only on the figurines in various museums but also on a large number of statuettes seen with antiquities dealers since 1950. These are represented in photograph on the plates, with a list of technical data on p. 289-298.
The book consists of three parts, dealing successively with the period from 1800 B.C. to the end of the New Kingdom, the Third Intermediate Period, and the Late Period until the Christian Era.
Part I begins with the most ancient shawabtis occurring c. 1800 B.C., which certainly represent the mummified dead. Two types, with and without hands in relief, are mentioned, as well as the appearance of the text (*BD* ch. 6). A special section deals with the figurines from the XVIIth Dynasty.

Chapter II, on the XVIIIth Dynasty, argues in the introduction that from this period onward the statuettes begin to represent substitutes of the defunct. The sections discuss royal and private shawabtis from the various reigns, followed by a section on exceptional forms: grinding figures representing the defunct and the servant at the same time, double figures and those lying on a funerary bed. The conclusions (p. 73-74) stress the differences between royal and private shawabtis.
Chapter III is devoted to the Ramesside Period, with special sections i.a. on shawabtis from the Serapeum, those of high and lower functionaries, and those of the poor. The conclusions (129-131) state that the heterogeneity in this time was even wider than before, e.g. the difference between large wooden and fine faience "commanders of the troop" and small wooden or alabaster servant figures with hardly any detail indicated. The inscription of Khaemwast's shawabtis has exceptional details.
Part II is also divided into 3 chapters. Chapter I, on the royal family of the XXIst Dynasty, contains i.a. sections on the statuettes from the royal cachette of Deir el-Bahri and the Rogers and McCullum tablets; chapter II, on the royal families of the XXIInd and XXIIIrd Dynasties, with sections on the princes and high priests and on the God's Wives of Amun; chapter III, on private persons, with i.a. a section on the second cachette of Deir el-Bahri. Among the conclusions (179-181) one finds the statement that shawabtis in this period were both more numerous and more uniform than before. The colour enables to distinguish various workshops. Unfortunately, by negligence of the excavators we do not know whether indeed 37 or 38 overseers to the troop were added to the 365 servants. For the XXIst and XXIInd Dynasties a headband along the forehead is characteristic.
Part III first deals with the Ethiopian Dynasty, discussing the shawabtis from the royal Nubian cemeteries as well as those from Egypt itself. In the second chapter we find sections on the period from the XXVIth to the XXXth Dynasties, including i.a. one on the rare statuettes of Persian officials and one on the local clergy of the Late Period. A short section is devoted to the subsequent era, and a last one to fakes (see the list on p. 273-275).
General conclusions on p. 275-283. Index on p. 323-338.

74045 Baedeker's Egypt 1929, Newton Abbott, David and Charles, [1974] (10.5 × 15.9 cm; [6+]CCVIII+ 495 p., 106 plans and maps [18 folding], 56 fig.) = [Reprint of] Egypt and the Sûdân. Handbook for Travellers by Karl Baedeker. Eighth Revised Edition, Leipzig, 1929; rev. *JEA* 62 (1976), 201 (E.P. Uphill).
Pr. £ 6

Reprint of the last pre-war edition of Baedeker's handbook for Travellers to Egypt. A preface, by I. Masser, briefly discusses the eight English editions listed on p. 6.
The maps are not in colour and rather faint.

BAER, Klaus, see our number 74782.

74046 BAINES, John, The Inundation Stela of Sebekhotpe VIII, *Acta Orientalia*, Copenhagen 36 (1974), 39-54, with 4 pl.

This fragmentary stela, which was found in the third pylon, is dated in year 4 of Sebekhotpe VIII, 4 *šmw*, the epagomenal days. The text on the verso mentions a great inundation, which flooded the *wsht*-hall of the temple in Karnak. The king went to the temple (probably to take precautions) and was seen wading in the water. The co-incidence of date and flood allowed a full re-enactment of creation : by wading in the flood in the temple the king was coming as near as he could to imitating the creator god. A relief on the recto shows the king wearing the flat cap with uraeus and two tall feathers, i.e., he is to some extent identified with Amun.
See also No. 74276, in which L. Habachi deals with the same stela plus an additional fragment. A second article by J. Baines will appear in *Acta Orientalia* 37. *Torben Holm-Rasmussen*

BAINES, John, see also our number 74648.

74047 BAKIR, Abd-El-Mohsen, A Further Re-Appraisal of the Terms: *Nḥḥ* and *Ḏt*, *JEA* 60 (1974), 252-254.

The writer expresses surprise that his previous views should have been the subject of controversy, and here gives the meaning of the two words as 'infinity' and 'everlastingness'. *E. Uphill*

74048 BAKRY, Hassan S.K., The Discovery of a Sarcophagus of Sat-Reʿ at Heliopolis, *Studi classici e orientali*, Pisa 23 (1974), 70-78, with 2 plans, 1 fig. and 7 ill. on 8 pl.

Publication of a red granite sarcophagus of the priestess of Atum of Tjeku Satre, from the New Kingdom, discovered in a tomb at Matarîya in 1967. The author translates the texts, with comments.

74049 BALLA, L., A propos des périodes de l'Iseum de Savaria, *Studia Aegyptiaca I*, 1-12.

The author discusses the history of the Iseum at Savaria, the date of its building and of the inscriptions and reliefs.

74050 BAQUÉS ESTAPÉ, Lorenzo, Galería de personajes en las piezas egipcias de los Museos Catalanes y Museo Balear. V, Museo Bíblico del Seminario Diocesano de Palma, Mallorca

(MBSP), *Información Arqueológica*. Boletín Informativo del Instituto de Prehistoria y Arqueología de la Diputación Provincial de Barcelona No 13 (enero-abril 1974), 11-15, with 1 ill.

Sequel to our number 73062.

An Aegyptiaca besitzt die Sammlung 1 Osiris aus Bronze, 1 Horus- und ein *wḏ3t*-Amulett aus weißer Fritte und 6 Skarabäen, zudem 1 anthropoiden Holzsarg mit gut erhaltener Bemalung, der angeblich aus dem Museum von Kairo nach Palma gelangte. Die Mumie des Sargs, eines Mannes namens *Jrt-n(t)-Ḥr-jr.w*, Sohnes der *Šp-n-Spdt* und des *Ḏd-B3stt-jw.f-ʿnḫ*, der etwa 25 Jahre alt wurde, ist ebenfalls erhalten. *I.Gamer-Wallert*

74051 BAQUÉS ESTAPÉ, Lorenzo, Galería de personajes en las piezas egipcias de los Museos Catalanes y Museo Balear. Resumen, *Información Arqueológica*. Boletín Informativo del Instituto de Prehistoria y Arqueología de la Diputación Provincial de Barcelona No 14 (mayo-agosto 1974), 31-37.

Verfasser gibt Zusammenstellung der Namen und Titel der ehemaligen Besitzer der 20 heute auf 5 katalanische Museen vertreuten ägyptischen Gegenstände, die in vorausgegangenen Artikeln (unsere Nr. 73060, 73061, 73062, 74050) behandelt worden waren. *I. Gamer-Wallert*

74052 BAQUÉS-ESTAPÉ, Lorenzo, Galería de Personajes en las Piezas Egipcias de los Museos Catalanes y Museo Balear, [no place, no publisher, no date] (20.8 × 27.4 cm; 48 p., colour ill. on cover, 13 ill.).

A separately edited booklet containing our numbers 73060, 73061, 73062, 74050 and 74051.

74053 BARGUET, Paul, Le Livre des Morts, *Textes et langages III*, 47-52.

The author successively deals with the publications, the text and the interpretation of the *Book of the Dead*. As regards the latter, he raises the question whether it is a double text, that is, a funerary ritual (cfr our number 60477) expressed in solar images, like the *Am-Duat*.

BARNES, I.L., see our number 74099.

74054 BAROCAS, Claudio, Ägypten. Vorwort von Oscar Niermeyer, Wiesbaden, Ebeling Verlag, [1974] (24 × 32.5 cm; 192 p., 1 map, 15 plans, 2 fig., 116 colour ill.). Series: Monumente grosser Kulturen.

This book on ancient Egypt is intended for the general public. The colour photographs, not of exceptional quality, represent the usual views of the monuments. Selected passages from older German translations of Egyptian texts are printed in small characters on various pages. The text of Barocas gives a survey of Egyptian history, while the last chapter is devoted to architecture.

We have not seen the original Italian version: "Egitto", Milano, Mondadori, 1970.

74055 BAROCAS, Claudio, Les statues "realistes" et l'arrivée des Perses dans l'Égypte saïte, *in* : *Gururājamañjarikā*. Studi in onore di Giuseppe Tucci, Napoli, Istituto Universitario Orientale, 1974, 113-161.

This important article investigates the position of the so-called "realistic portraits" of the Saite Period in the history of Egyptian art. Their superficial resemblance to Hellenistic and Roman portraits is enhanced by the fact that most of them are preserved as busts or solitary heads; but an examination of extant examples shows that the respective bodies have been deliberately cut off and discarded, either in ancient times or in the 18th Century. This is doubtless an indication of the taste of the respective collectors, who considered the statues as a whole too Egyptian, and thus too alien to their concepts of art. The assumption that this type of statuary is firmly embedded in Egyptian traditions is confirmed by the resemblance of the Saite heads to statues of the 13th Dyn. such as that of Sobekemsaf; their "realism" does not result from a faithful reproduction of individual features, but from the imitation of stylistic peculiarities of the late MK. In this respect, they are merely another example of the Saite "Renaissance", which is marked not by a slavish imitation of earlier models, but by the eclectic search for means of creating a new style.

It is remarkable that the Saite statues of priests and officials are not patterned after the royal statuary of that period. This may be explained as a symptom of the loss of the old identity of king and state caused by the policies of the Saite pharaohs who considered Egypt and its resources merely as a means to further their aims on the international scene. The refusal of the upper strata of Egyptian society to identify with the king facilitated the integration of Egypt into the Persian Empire, because the political institutions and the art acquired already in the Saite Period the new functions demanded by the role which Egypt was to play as part of a larger whole.   *Dieter Mueller*

74056 BARTA, Winfried, Das Gespräch des Ipuwer mit dem Schöpfergott, *SAK* 1 (1974), 19-33.

Accepting most of the conclusions of Fecht in his *Der Vorwurf an Gott in den "Mahnworten des Ipu-wer* (our number 72227) Barta discusses the ideas of Ipuwer in his Reproach. He argues that the aim of the discussion between Ipuwer and the Creator-God has been to offer the god an opportunity to defend himself. Referring i.a. to *CT* spells 181 and 1130 he demonstrates that the god answers to the reproach that he is guilty of the existence of evil in the world by pointing out man's own freedom of will. In its original version the discussion may have dealt with the problems of predestination and man's responsability for his character. The ambivalent attitude of Ipuwer occurs also in other texts.

At the end Barta points to close connections between the *Admonitions* and the *Dispute of a Man and his Ba*.

74057 BARTA, Winfried, Der Terminus *twt* auf den Grenzstelen Sesostris' III. in Nubien, *Festschrift Ägyptisches Museum Berlin*, 51-54, with 2 pl.

The author, studying the meaning of the word *twt* as it occurs on the parallel stelae of the year 4 of Sesostris III from Semna (Berlin 1157) and Uronarti (Khartum 451), refutes Kaplony's translation as "example" (cfr our number 66333). He suggests that the stelae themselves are thus called since they bear the royal name, and refers to statues of Pepy I (Brooklyn No. 39.120) and Ramses II representing the names of the pharaohs.

74058 BARTA, W., Zur Stundenanordnung des Amduat in den ramessidischen Königsgräbern, *BiOr* 31 (1974), 197-201, with 5 plans.

The author, studying the rules according to which the twelve hours of the Amduat are placed on the walls and corridors of the royal tombs from that of Tuthmosis III onwards until that of Ramses III, argues that, despite apparent differences, they follow until that of Ramses II the same principle, namely a spirality reflecting the continuous cyclic repetition of the revolution of the sun. Whether this principle is also reflected by the laying out of the tombs is a matter of more study. From Merenptah onwards the principle has been abandoned and the hours are placed in a straight line.

74059 BARUCQ, André, Les études d'hymnologie égyptienne, *Textes et langages III*, 53-64.

The author understands hymnology as the study of the style as well as of the contents of hymns. He first discusses various types of hymns, according to their elements. Then he presents a list of the major publications, arranged after the date of the texts. He also discusses the attempts to regroup the hymns, e.g. the Sun hymns, and some studies on hymnology, especially on prosody. In a last section possible future researches in this field of studies are mentioned.

BAUX, Jean-Pierre, see our number 74663.

74060 BECKER-COLONNA, Andreina Leanza, Ancient Egypt. An Exhibition of the Sutro Egyptian Collection, [San Francisco], San Francisco State University, Spring 1974 (18 × 22 cm; 88 p., 1 map, 4 fig., 14 ill.).

The collection bought by Mr. Sutro in Egypt, probably in 1884, consists of a large number of minor objects the provenance of which is unknown.
The introduction to this catalogue contains sections on the country, history and religion, with special sections on the Judgment of the Soul (and a translation of the Negative Confession) and on Canopic Jars, as well as lists of raw materials and their provenance and of the principal gods.
The catalogue itself consists of 331 numbers, all merely mentioned, mostly in one line, without any data. They are mainly vessels, shawabtis, scarabs, coffins and mummy masks, and suchlike. A few may be of more than ordinary importance, such as two model boats and the shawabti chest of the overseer of the stable Tja-ʿo.

74061 BEDELL, Ellen Dailey, Criminal Law in the Egyptian Ramesside Period, *Dissertation Abstracts International A*, Ann Arbor, Mich. 34, no. 7 (January 1974), 4127-A.

Abstract of a doctor's thesis Brandeis University, 1973 (Order No. 73-32, 367; 374 p.).
Based on the extant records of criminal proceedings this dissertation studies criminal law in the Ramesside period in a broad context, comprising i.a. court structure, methods of procedure in courts on different levels, and trial by oracle as an alternative to state courts.

BEEK, M.A., see our number 74824.

BEGELSBACHER, Barbara, see our number 74348.

BELLOD, A., see our number 74743.

BENITEZ, Jaime T., see our number 74465.

74062 BER, Arthur, Was de god Bes een hypothyreoïde dwerg?, *Organorama*, Oss 10, 4 (1973-1974), 25-30, with 7 ill. (4 in colour).

The author rejects the theory that Bes represents an achondroplastic dwarf, and suggests that the characteristics rather indicate a hypothyreoid dwarf.

74063 BERGER, Cathérine, Journées Internationales d'Études méroïtiques. 2ème session, Paris, 10-13 Juillet 1973, *Orientalia* 43 (1974), 424-425.

Short report on the second Meroitic congress, mentioning the lectures.

74064 BERGMAN, J., Horus und das Pferd, *Studia Aegyptiaca I*, 13-26.

Proceeding from the answer of Horus to Osiris in Plutarchus, *De Iside*, ch. 19, 358 B-C that the horse is the most useful animal in a battle the author first argues that the dialogue here mentioned belongs to the Wisdom Literature. He also points out that in Ptolemaic temples *nfr* ("useful") is in some instances written with a horse. In the second section Bergman discusses the role of the horse in Egypt, mentioning Ptolemaic scenes of Pharaoh on a horse-back. The idea expressed by Horus belongs to the sphere of Ptolemaic thought : Horus is the youth (*nfr*) and the foal (*nfr*), and a young horse is the most useful (*nfr*) animal.

74065 BERGMAN, Jan, Isis auf der Sau, *The Gustavianum Collections*, 81-109, with 4 ill. and 2 fig.

Proceeding from a rough terra cotta figure of a nude woman on a pig (Victoriamuseet No. 1716), which is compared with similar figures and explained as a representation of Isis, the author first deals with negative and positive appreciations of the pig in ancient Egypt. He discusses the relation between the white sow (= Isis, according to the Metternich stela) and the white female hippopotamus. Pig and hippopotamus are often not distinguished. The author then deals with the half anthropomorphic, half theriomorphic representations of Opet, and suggests that this figure, interpreted as a sow, was the prototype of the statuette here discussed, the two aspects after the Alexandrinian fashion being divided into a separate woman on a sow. Nakedness occurs in Egypt only with Nut, and is sometimes combined with frontality in order to show the pregnancy, as in the statuette. At the end the author mentions as a parallel the representation of Isis on a dog, and a vignette of the woman upon the beast from a mediaeval manuscript, illustrating *Apocalypse* 17,3.

74066 BERLANDINI-GRENIER, Jocelyne, Le dignitaire ramesside Ramsès-em-per-Rê, *BIFAO* 74 (1974), 1-19, with 2 fig. and 4 pl.

Publication of a fragment of a wall relief from the tomb of a Ramses-em-per-Re seen with an antiquities dealer in Cairo. Seven more documents of the same man, among which two stelae, as well as a mention in an ostracon are listed. The author also lists variant writings of his name, the names of members of his family, and his titles.

Ramses-em-per-Re was a Semite, originally called Banazen, from Ziri-Bashan. He acted as royal butler under Ramses II and Merenptah and controlled the building of the latter's tomb. The exact position of his tomb, from which came six of the documents, is unknown; it may be the Memphite region.

In an addendum the author also publishes a stela of another Ramses-em-per-Re, a *ḥry-sȝwty*, namely the stela Brit.Mus. 796. It dates from the same period and came from the Abydos region.

74067 BERLEV, Oleg, A Contemporary of King Sewaḥ-en-Rēʿ, *JEA* 60 (1974), 106-113, with 3 pl.

The author cites an important tomb discovered at Thebes nearly a century ago, that helps to throw light on the reign of this little-known king. This tomb included two sarcophagi CM 28028 and CM 28059, as well as other objects belonging to an official Sonb-nay and his wife Khons or *Mri.s*, among which was an inscribed staff, Moscow I 1a 1801, a, b, bearing the name of this Pharaoh. *E. Uphill*

74068 BERLEV, O. D., Стела вюрцбургского университетского музея (XIII династия), *Палестинский Сборник*, Ленинград 25 (88), 1974, 26-31, with 1 ill., and an English summary on p. 31.

"A Thirteenth Dynasty Stela in the Würzburg University Museum".

First publication of a stela from the XIIIth Dynasty. It shows that the vizier ʿAnkhu was related to the royal family through Queen Ay, which is indicative of the concentration of power in the hands of the vizier and his legitimate successors.

L.M.J. Zonhoven

74069 BICKNELL, Peter J., Santorini Tephra, Acid Rain, and Exodus, *Parola del Passato*, Napoli 29 (1974), 244-250.

The author connects the plagues of Egypt described in *Exodus*, which he dates in the reign of Ramses III, with the Thera paroxysm.

74070 BIDOLI†, Dino, Eine Stele des Königs Sethnacht aus Elephantine, *XVIII. Deutscher Orientalistentag*, 18.

Brief summary of the lecture by E. O[tto].

74071 BIEGER, Claus und Peter MUNRO, mit einem Beitrag von Jürgen BRINKS, Das Doppelgrab der Königinnen *Nbt* und

Ḥnwt in Saqqara. 1. Vorbericht über die Arbeiten der Gruppe Hannover im Herbst 1973, *SAK* 1 (1974), 34-54, with 2 plans and 2 fig.

After a general description of the cemetery between the enclosure wall of the Step Pyramid and the Unas causeway by Munro the double tomb of the queens *Nbt* and *Ḥwnt* is carefully described by Bieger. The complex appears to be architecturally a unity, although the eastern (*Ḥnwt*) part is now largely destroyed. Then Munro studies the various rooms, their reliefs and texts, mentioning several obscure points, e.g. the mysterious representation of an anonymous man.

At the end remarks on the painting by Brinks.

74072 BIETAK, Manfred und Eugen STROUHAL, Die Todesumstände des Pharaos Seqenenre' (17. Dynastie). Vorbericht, *Annalen des Naturhistorischen Museums in Wien*, Wien 78 (1974), 29-52, with 1 map, 4 fig. and 10 pl.

The authors study the question whether Seqenenre Taʿo II has been killed in a battle. They first discuss the Austrian excavations at Tell ed-Dabʿa and the MB II weapons found in the Eastern Delta, particularly a special type of battle-axe. They then present a survey of what is known about the king, arguing that there is no definite historical proof of a war against the Hyksos in his time. There follows an extensive discussion of the king's mummy and the injuries its head shows, leading to the conclusion that he was killed when standing higher than his attackers (on a war-chariot). Two of the wounds are due to the Asiatic axe, one other was inflicted by an Egyptian battle-axe, so that he possibly fell in a war against the Egyptian vassals of the Hyksos.

74073 BIMSON, Mavis, Glass in the Tutankhamun Treasure, *in: Annales du 6ᵉ Congrès de l'Association Internationale pour l'Histoire du Verre*. Cologne 1-7 Juillet 1973, Liège, 1974, 291-294, with 2 ill.

The author lists a number of occurrences of glass as inlay on objects from the tomb of Tutankhamun, as well as a glass scarab and beads. The pair of earrings (The Treasures of Tutankhamun = our number 72716, pl. 39) has buttons of colourless transparent glass on the clasps, not of quartz, as the catalogue states.

74074 BINGEN, Jean, Rapport du Directeur, *CdE* XLIX, No. 97 (1974), 8-10.

74075 BIRKSTAM, Bengt, Given Life Like Re Eternally — A Royal Epitheton, *The Gustavianum Collections*, 15-35, with 2 ill.

Proceeding from two fragments containing i.a. cartouches of Tuthmosis III (No. 131) and the god Aton (No. 17), here briefly published, the author amply discusses the meaning of the formula *di ʿnḫ mi Rʿ ḏt* in the XVIIIth Dynasty, quoting a large number of occurrences. Life, stability, dominion and durability are gifts handed over by the gods to the king at the occasion of his coronation, at the Sed festivals and when he officiated in the temple; they belong to him in his functions as king and are connected with his divine nature. The epitheton is used with Aton in the Amarna Period since there existed an identity between the divine nature of the king and this god.

74076 BJÖRKMAN, Gun, A Funerary Statuette of Hekaemsaf, Chief of the Royal Ships in the Saitic Period, *The Gustavianum Collections*, 71-80, with 2 ill. and 1 fig.

Study on account of a shawabti of Hekaemsaf (Victoriamuseet No. D 185), a chief of the royal ships from the Saite Period. Compare our number 69217. The author presents information about Hekaemsaf and his function, and about shawabtis in general, particularly about their number of 401.

74077 BJÖRKMAN, Gun, Neby, the Mayor of Tjaru in the Reign of Tuthmosis IV, *JARCE* 11 (1974), 43-51, with 2 pl.

A study of the career of *Nby* (c. of Tuthmosis IV) from his titles on four monuments: two canopic jars (Ronneby College, Sweden, and Musée Municipal, Sens, no. 327, both illustrated) and two stelae (Leiden V 43 and Sinai no. 58, both: *Urkunden IV*, 1634-5). Neby, educated at the court (as a *ḥrd n kȝp*) held a military post in Nubia (as a *wr n Mdȝy.w* and a *mr-ḫtm n tȝ n Wȝwȝ.t*, 'fortress commander of the land of Wawat'); perhaps he was of Nubian descent. The crown of his career were important functions in the frontier town of Tjaru (as a *ḥry-pd.t n Ṯȝrw* and a *ḥȝty-ʿ n Ṯȝrw*), whose role in this period is outlined. Neby also had the 'northern' title *mr-ḥn.t*, 'overseer of the *ḥn.t*-water' and he had some commission in the queen's household as well (as a *mr-pr n ip.t ḥm.t-nsw*). He may have been the owner of the Theban tomb no. 91. There are serious chronological objections against identifying a son of his, Haremhab, with the later king. *J.F. Borghouts*

74078 BLEEKER, C.J., Einige Bemerkungen zur religiösen Terminologie der alten Ägypter, *in*: *Travels in the World of the Old Testament. Studies Presented to Professor M.A. Beek on the Occasion of his 65th Birthday. Edited by M.S.H.G. Heerma van Voss, Ph.H.J. Houwink ten Cate, N.A. van Uchelen*, Assen/Amsterdam, van Gorkum, 1974, 12-26.

Proceeding from Morenz' remark that the Egyptian had no words for "religion", "piety" or "belief" the author investigates the Egyptian ways of expressing religious concepts. He discusses expressions concerning the nature of the gods, e.g. *nṯr, nfr, ḫpr, smȝ-tȝwy*; concerning man and his fate, e.g. "soul", "sin" and "death"; relating to the cult, e.g. *štȝ, prt, wṯs nfrw*; and concerning the conception of the world. It appears that the terms originated spontaneously, were plastic and free of conceptual reflexion.

BLAISDELL HAUSER, Elizabeth, see our number 74011.

74079 BLUMENTHAL, Elke, Eine neue Handschrift der "Lehre eines Mannes für seinen Sohn" (P Berlin 14374), *Festschrift Ägyptisches Museum Berlin*, 55-66, with 1 ill. on a pl. and 2 fig.

The author publishes an ostracon from the Berlin collection (P. 14374) containing five lines of "The Instruction by a Man for his Son" (for the latest publication, see our number 69329). The text is presented in photograph, facsimile and transcription, with an annotated translation.
In the second part the author deals with the question whether the principal person is the king or a god (as Goedicke has defended; see our number 67226). She concludes that it is probably the pharaoh, arguing that the central themes of the text are connected with the king's ideology of the Middle Kingdom.

BLUNT, Henry, see our number 74781.

74080 BOGOSLOVSKY, E.S., Два памятника сподвижника Аменхотпа III. *ВДИ* 2 (128), 1974, 86-96, with 4 pl. and an English summary on p. 95-96.

"Two Monuments Relating to an Associate of Amenhotep III". The author publishes a shawabti and the lid of a sarcophagus in the Hermitage (Nos 905 and 999), belonging to the Great Steward in Memphis Amenhotep (= Huy). For this person, cfr Helck, *Zur Verwaltung* (our number 58284), 483-485. Bogoslovsky provides a facsimile and transcription of the texts of the objects, discusses their style, and deals with the biography and genealogy of that Amenhotep.

74081 BOGOSLOVSKY, E.S., О вокализации имен собственных в современных трудах по египтологии, *ВДИ* 3 (129), 1974, 155-161, with an English summary on p. 161.

"On the Vocalization of Proper Names in Modern Egyptological Works".
In answer to an article of Korostovtsev (our number 73412)

the present author sets forth the inconsistency of the usual system of vocalizing Egyptian names by Soviet authors, defending the system of Perepelkin and Berlev as being based at least on our present knowledge of Egyptian sounds.
For a reply by Korostovtsev, see our number 74409.
Compare also our number 73545.

74082 BOGOSLOVSKI, Evgeni S., Die Wortverbindung śḏmw ꜥš in der ägyptischen Sprache während der 18. Dynastie, ZÄS 101 (1974), 81-89.

Verfasser kennt 213 Belege dieser Verbindung, unter denen 39 Beispiele der Abkürzung śḏmw. Er erörtert die Schreibweisen und gibt eine chronologische und topographische Übersicht.

M. Heerma van Voss

74083 BORGHOUTS, J.F., Egyptische sagen en verhalen, Bussum, Fibula-van Dishoeck, [1974] (14.6 × 21 cm; 198 p., 13 fig., colour ill. on cover); rev. BiOr 32 (1975), 346-347 (Michel Malaise).

The book contains Dutch translations of various works from the Egyptian literature and is intended for the general reader; it makes no claim to scientific value.
In the introduction the author i.a. offers short comments to the contents of each of the translated texts. They are, apart from the main Middle- and Late-Egyptian stories, a few poems (e.g., the Song of the Four Winds from the *Coffin Texts*), myths (e.g., the Destruction of Mankind), the two stories of Setne and two Demotic fables (e.g., The Mouse and the Lion), and two Coptic texts (e.g., Apa Makedonios and the Worshippers of the Falcon of Pilak). At the end an index of frequent words and concepts.

74084 BORGHOUTS, J.F., Magical Texts, *Textes et langages III*, 7-19.

After discussing the difficulties in defining the genre the author offers a short survey of the sources. The main part of the article is devoted to a discussion of the publications of various types of magical texts, those on stelae and statues, e.g. horuscippi, and those on papyri. Some are to be found in medical texts, while oracular decrees and execratory texts constitute special categories. Short sections deal with Demotic magical texts and spells in foreign languages. At the end an evaluation of the present state of our knowledge about the subject and some desiderata. The notes contain a valuable bibliography.

74085 BORKOWSKI, Zbigniew, Roger Rémondon†, *Archiv für Papyrusforschung und verwandte Gebiete*, Leipzig 22-23 (1974), 403.

Obituary notice.

74086 BOTHMER, Bernard V., The Karnak Statue of Ny-user-ra (Membra Dispersa IV), *MDAIK* 30 (1974), 165-170, with 6 pl.

The O.K. royal head in the Rochester Memorial Art Gallery (acc. no. 42.54) and the inscribed torso Cairo 42003 belong together and are part of a statue of King Ni-user-ra that once stood in Karnak. The statue is minutely described, and the problem of O.K. royal statuary of Theban provenance discussed in detail.   *Dieter Mueller*

74087 BOTHMER, Bernard V., Numbering Systems of the Cairo Museum, *Textes et langages III*, 111-122.

A corrected and amplified version of an article originally published in the *Newsletter* of the American Research Center in Egypt No. 22 (1956).
The author discusses the various systems of numbering in the Cairo Museum, explaining the qualifying prefixes to the numbers. K. refers to objects found in the Karnak cachette, T. to those from the tomb of Tutankhamon. Most of these objects have now also proper registration numbers. Bothmer then deals with the Journal d'Entrée (J.E.), the Temporary Register, that is, the Yardbook, used for objects the original number of which is unknown (T.R.), the Catalogue Général (C.G.), and the Special Inventory numbers (S.) referring to ledgers kept by the curators of the galleries and sections.

74088 BOTHMER, Bernard V., Pehenuka Reliefs in Brooklyn and Berlin, *Festschrift Ägyptisches Museum Berlin*, 67-69, with 1 pl.

Publication of a relief fragment from the second half of the Vth Dynasty belonging to the tomb of Pehenuka, at present in the Brooklyn Museum (No. 64.147). It shows animals in the desert and certainly belongs to the same wall as Berlin No. 1132, though the pieces do not adjoin.

74089 BOTHMER, Bernard V., The Publication of Texts in the Brooklyn Museum, *Textes et langages III*, 195-197.

Survey of the publications of texts in the Brooklyn Museum, New York. Apart from the hieroglyphic inscriptions published by James (our number 74356) the author mainly deals with editions of papyri.

BOTHMER, Bernard V., see also our numbers 74255 and 74500.

74090 du BOURGUET, P., Les quatre types de la phrase égyptienne et leur rôle pour une approche d'ordre linguistique de l'égyptien, CdE XLIX, No 98 (1974), 254-263.

Communication de congrès (Congrès Intern. Orientalistes, Paris 1973) dans laquelle l'auteur justifie l'usage qu'il fait dans sa Grammaire Egyptienne (notre No. 71078) des schémas empruntés à la grammaire générative et transformationnelle d'un point de vue tant scientifique que pédagogique.
On verra aussi notre No 74760 (Vergote, Une Nouvelle Grammaire du Moyen Egyptien). *Ph. Derchain*

74091 BOYAVAL, B., Découverte de Papyrus à Lille, *CRIPEL* 2 (1974), 9-10.

Ungefähr zweihundert Papyrusfragmente kamen in den Besitz des Institut de Papyrologie et d'Egyptologie de l'Université de Lille; sie stammen aus einer Mumienmaske und einem Vorderteil und kommen von einer Nekropole der hellenistischen Zeit in der Nähe von Medinet-en-Nahas im Süden des Fayum. Der größte Teil sind griechische Fragmente aus dem 3. vorchristlichen Jahrhundert; 20 Fragmente sind demotisch in einem allerdings schlechten Zustand. *Inge Hofmann*

74092 de BRAGANCA, Miguel, A Relief Fragment from the Tomb of Queen Nofru at Deir el Bahri in Boston, *AJA* 78 (1974), 163.

Summary of a paper.

74093 BRASSEUR CAPART, A.M. and A., Jean Capart ou le rêve comblé de l'Égyptologie, [Bruxelles], Éditions Arts et Voyages, Lucien de Meyer Éditeur, [1974] (14.5 × 22 cm; 235 p., 16 pl., 3 ill. on cover).

A vivid biography of the great Belgian scholar, written by his niece and her husband (for obituaries of Capart, see our volume 1947, p. 86).
The description of his life is full of anecdotes and memories of the authors themselves and of collaborators of Capart, as well as quotations from his letters, diaries and lectures.
The preface is by Pierre Gilbert, a "postface" by Arpag Mekhitarian, followed by a bibliography composed by Baudouin van de Walle (p. 201-229) and a "notice nécrologique faite par Jean Capart lui-même".

BRÉANT, Marie-Thérèse, see our number 74100.

74094 BRÉMOND, Gabriel, Voyage en Égypte. 1643-1645. Texte établi, présenté et annoté par Georges Sanguin†, [Le Caire, Institut français d'Archéologie orientale du Caire, 1974] (16.5 × 19.5 cm; XVIII + 185 p., 1 folded map) = Collection des voyageurs occidentaux en Égypte, 12.

The present volume is published by Jean-Claude Goyon after a manuscript discovered and prepared for publication by the late Georges Sanguin. Gabriel Brémond, probably from Marseille, a man about whose life almost nothing is known, travelled through the Near East and visited Egypt between 1643 and 1645, staying in Alexandria and Cairo. His description of Egypt written with didactic aims dates from 1668. An Italian translation has been published in 1673 and 1677. Brémond heavily relies on the "Description de l'Afrique" by Jean Léon l'Africain, from which source descriptions of towns and monuments are drawn which Brémond himself never visited. From his own additions we mention descriptions of a sarcophagus at Matarîya and the necropolis of Gîza as well as of his excavation of a tomb at Saqqâra.

74095 BRENTJES, Burchard, Studien zum Bewässerungsackerbau des Vorderen Orients, *Altorientalische Forschungen*, Berlin 1 (1974), 43-54.

In this rather general study of the subject a few remarks to ancient Egyptian irrigation on p. 49.

74096 BRENTJES, Burchard, Zum Problem von Humanismus und Menschenbild im Orient, *Wissenschaftliche Zeitschrift der Friedrich-Schiller-Universität*. Gesellschafts- und Sprachwissenschaftliche Reihe, Jena 21 (1972), 795-825, with 12 ill.

After sections on Humanism and the West, and Humanism in History, the author turns to the Origin and Development of the image of man and humanism in the Ancient Orient. Egypt is dealt with several times. The *Admonitions of Ipuwer* are discussed from the point of view of class struggle. In the *Eloquent Peasant* a representative of the lower social class is seen triumphant over his superiors. *L.M.J. Zonhoven*

74097 BRESCIANI, Edda, I testi letterari demotici, *Textes et langages III*, 83-91.

The author discusses in a historical order the more important editions and studies of Demotic texts, beginning with Brugsch' edition of *Setne I*. The notes contain a valuable bibliography of this field of researches.

74098 Brief Guide to the Department of Egyptian and Classical Art, Brooklyn, N.Y., The Brooklyn Museum, 1974 (15.5 × 23 cm; XVI + 116 p., 2 folding tables, 4 maps, 55 ill. [3 in colour], frontispiece in colour, colour ill. and plan on cover). Pr. $ 4

This is a new and revised edition of our number 70007. Two objects from the Near East are not anymore included, while the department has been renamed in 1972.

74099 BRILL, R.H., I.L. BARNES and B. ADAMS, Lead Isotopes in Some Ancient Egyptian Objects, *Recent Advances in Science and Technology of Materials*, 9-27, with 2 fig., 7 ill. and 1 table.

Since determination of isotope ratios in lead is useful for determining the geographical origin of the materials the authors investigated some XVIIIth Dynasty glass vessels and samples of kohl from early pots. They conclude that the leads used for making the pigment and kohl are similar to one another, but definitely different from leads from other parts of the Ancient World. Clearly the Egyptians used locally occurring ore. Glass specimens from the Graeco-Roman period, however, contain lead from different sources.

BRINKS, Jürgen, see our number 74071.

BRONGERS, H.A., see our number 74822.

74100 BROWN, Edward, Voyage en Égypte. 1673-1674. Traduit de l'anglais par Marie-Thérèse Bréant. Avant-propos, notes et index de Serge Sauneron, [Le Caire, Institut français d'Archéologie orientale du Caire, 1974] (16.5 × 19.6 cm; XXIV + 224 p., 1 folded map) = Collection des voyageurs occidentaux en Égypte, 10.

The identity of the author of this book is unknown, Brown being the name of his mother. He travelled in Egypt in 1673-1674 in order to acquire precious stones, visiting Alexandria, the Delta, Cairo and Suez, and making a trip through the Eastern Desert. In the Preface Sauneron points out that the editor of the book, which appeared in 1739, long after the death of its author, has borrowed for the description of Egypt in part II from Prosper Alpin's book "Historia Aegypti Naturalis", published in 1735. On the other hand, Brown's own observations are certainly genuine, and he differs from other travellers in his open attention for the people and customs of Egypt.

74101 BROWNE, Gerald M., The Martyrdom of Paese and Thecla (P. Mich. inv. 548), *CdE* XLIX, No. 97 (1974), 201-205.

Publication of P. Mich. inv. 548, a fragment of a sheet from a parchment codex with a few lines from the martyrdom of Apa Paese and his sister Thecla (cfr our number 73602) with the text, a translation and a commentary.

74102 BRUNNER, Hellmut, "Der Bekannte des Königs", *SAK* 1 (1974), 55-60, with 1 fig.

The author publishes the offering basin Tubingen Inv. 370 (cfr our number 68324), which may date from a period between the mid Vth to the mid VIth Dynasties, and derives from it evidence that already during the Old Kingdom the title 𓂋𓐍𓈖𓇓 was understood as *rḫ (n) nswt*, and that, therefore, *rḫ* cannot be a relative form.

74103 BRUNNER, Hellmut, *Dbt* "Kasten", *ZÄS* 100, 2 (1974), 150.

Same article as our number 72113.

74104 BRUNNER, H., Djedefhor in der Röm. Kaiserzeit, *Studia Aegyptiaca I*, 55-64.

In the *Embalmment Ritual* there occurs a passage (VII, 3-4; see Goyon, our number 72270, p. 58) which is a quotation from the *Instruction of Djedefhor*. The author lists and discusses the six quotations of these sentences at present known (cfr Brunner, our number 63079), adding remarks concerning knowledge and way of quoting of traditional texts in ancient Egypt.

74105 BR[UNNER], H[ellmut], Hieroglyphic Writing, *Encyclopaedia Britannica*. Volume 8, 853-857.

The author presents a survey of the decipherment, the development and the characteristics of hieroglyphic writing, with short sections on the hieratic and Demotic scripts.
For the Egyptian language see the above edition. Micropaedia. Vol. III, and for other references to the hieroglyphic writing, o.c. Vol. V. *L.M.J. Zonhoven*

74106 BRUNNER-TRAUT, Emma, Altägyptische Sprache und Kindersprache. Eine linguistische Anregung, *SAK* 1 (1974), 61-81.

The author studies the question whether there can be established a parallel between the development of children's language and the Egyptian language, that is, whether the theory of universals in the ontogenesis of grammar can be supported by evidence from the Egyptian.
Following the stages of development of children's speech she demonstrates that there are strong correspondences with the practice of the Egyptian language, e.g. in the use of auxiliaries and particles expressing mood and in the use of virtual interrogative sentences without transformations. She concludes that the Egyptians hardly passed the contemplative-concrete phase of intelligence (the phase of children between 7 and 12 years), and connects this difference between the Egyptian language and, e.g., Latin with the relation aspective-perspective in art.

74107 BRUNNER-TRAUT, Emma, Die Alten Ägypter. Verborgenes Leben unter Pharaonen, Stuttgart-Berlin-Köln-Mainz, Verlag W. Kohlhammer, [1974] (21 × 24.5 cm; 272 p., 62 fig., 3 maps, 80 pl., 16 colour pl., map on endpapers); rev. *Antike Welt* 6,

Heft 1 (1975), 55 (anonymous); *BiOr* 33 (1976), 14-15 (E.P. Uphill); *JEA* 61 (1975), 296 (J. Gwyn Griffiths); *Universitas* 29 (1975), 204-205 (H.W. Bähr); *ZDMG* 126 (1976), 193 (J.v. B[eckerath]). Pr. DM 78

This book, written for both the general public and the Egyptologist, is devoted to the hidden aspects of the Egyptian civilization, namely the personal everyday life in the houses and families. The various subjects are vividly described, with translations from all kinds of texts, and illustrated by a wealth of drawings and photographs. several of which showing less well known objects.

After an introduction characterizing the Egyptian civilization the 16 chapters deal with the following subjects: human aspects of pharaoh's daily life; relations between man and animal; pregnancy and child-birth; education; courtship, love and love-poetry; relaxation and games, feasts and festivals; fables told and drawn; traces of personal piety; disease and hygiene, medicine and corporal punishment; lucky and unlucky days, and dream-reading; the fear of the dead; ostraca used for drawings and for texts; life in the settlement of the necropolis workmen; crimes in this village; the Strike Papyrus; tomb robberies.

A chronological table (p. 244-246), a short bibliography, notes (249-262) and an index to names (269-272) at the end of the book.

A second edition has appeared in 1976.

74108 BRUNNER-TRAUT, Emma, Noch einmal die Fürstin von Punt. Ihre Rasse, Krankheit und ihre Bedeutung für die Lokalisierung von Punt, *Festschrift Ägyptisches Museum Berlin*, 71-85, with 10 ill. on 4 pl. and 11 fig.

Incited by Herzog's book on Punt (our number 68282) the author once more studies the physical appearance of the queen of Punt (compare our number 57082), using as material the (lost) representation of the queen and her daughter, the famous relief in Cairo (No. 34419), and a Berlin ostracon (No. 21442). She argues that the woman cannot belong to the Khoisanid race (Hottentots and Bushmen); that she in fact does not show the characteristics of steatopygia, but only those of pathological lordose; that she very probably belonged to the Aethiopid race, but was extremely fat. This may be due to fatty degeneration (adipositas).

In an addition the author deals with suggestions of Leca (cfr our number 71352).

See also our number 74311.

74109 BRUNNER-TRAUT, E., Der Tübinger Kultlöffel, *Studia Aegyptiaca I*, 65-73, with 4 ill.

Publication of a bronze "cosmetic spoon" with a handle ending in a duck's head and a lotus flower between handle and bowl. The object, at present in a private collection at Tübingen, is probably to be dated to the Ptolemaic Period. The author argues that it belongs to the equipment of the temple and was used to strew grains of incense on the altar.
In an addentum two parallels are mentioned, depicted in our number 74698, p. 47.

BRUNNER-TRAUT, Emma, see also our number 74648.

74110 BRYCE, T.R., The Lukka Problem — and a Possible Solution, *JNES* 33 (1974), 395-404, with 1 table.

The remarks of the specialist F.J. Tritsch are quoted on the difficulty of defining who the Lukka people were and localizing their original homeland accurately. Bryce believes, however, that certain texts have a "definite bearing on Lukka's location" while others probably do not. Thus by elimination the problem would be made less formidable. Several Egyptian texts constitute important references, notably the hieroglyphic inscription on an obelisk in the "Temple of Obelisks" at Byblos, dated c. 2000 B.C., honouring *Kwkwn* son of *Rwqq*. Albright equated the latter with Lukk and the former with Kukunnis, a Lycian name. More important for location is an Amarna letter from the king of Alasiya to Akhenaton referring to a raid on the Egyptian coast by the Lukki. Again this is uncertain, but Hittite sources suggest there were two main groups, one on the vicinity of Lycaonia, the other in Caria. The author also believes Alasia is definitely Cyprus. *E. Uphill*

74111 BUHL, Marie-Louise, A Hundred Masterpieces from The Ancient Near East in the National Museum of Denmark and the History of its Ancient Near Eastern Collections, [Copenhagen], The National Museum of Denmark, 1974 (18 × 24.5 cm; 123 p., frontispiece and numerous ill.); rev. *Syria* 51 (1974), 348-349 (A. P[arrot]).

Part I (p. 9-62, 60 ill. of which 16 are in colour) deals with the Egyptian antiquities and their history. The Department of Ancient Near Eastern and Classical Antiquities (the *Antiksamling*) was officially founded in 1851, but the nucleus of the collection goes back to the Royal Art Cabinet of Frederik III (1648-1670). During the history of the collection there have been several periods of expansion : in the middle of the 18th century (object from Niebuhr's expedition to Egypt and Arabia), at the beginning of the 19th century (antiquities sent to Copenhagen by the Danish consul in Alexandria), and from 1892 to 1916, when the classical archaeologist Chr. Blinkenberg was head of the Department.

Objects of particular interest are nos. 12 (a "pseudogroup" of *'Iti-sn*, Vth dyn.), 15 (a colossal royal head probably of Amenemhet III [sic]), 21 (a statuette of Amasis), 23-25 (three mummy portraits, 2nd-3rd cent. A.D.), and 50 (a relief of the judge *Sndm-ib*, perhaps a son of the vizier *Sndm-ib Mḥi*, Vth dyn.).   *Torben Holm-Rasmussen*

BURNEY, Ethel W., see our number 74583.

74112 BURRI, Carla M., Bollettino d'informazioni. Sezione archeologica. Istituto Italiana di Cultura del Cairo, No 32 (Novembre 1973 - Gennaio 1974), 19 p.

Sequel to our number 73128.
In this bulletin i.a. reports on the Italian activities at Sheikh Abada Antinoupolis, the Austrian excavations at ʿAsâsîf, various activities of the Germans and of the IFAO, the work of the Franco-Egyptian Centre at Karnak, etc.

74113 [BURRI, Carla M.], Bollettino d'Informazioni. Sezione archeologica. Istituto Italiano di Cultura del Cairo, No 33 (Febbraio-Maggio 1974), 30 p.

Sequel to our preceding number.
This number i.a. contains reports on the activities of the Organization of Antiquities at a large number of sites, the Polish work at Deir el-Bahari, the French work on the Pepy pyramid, etc. From p. 20-30 reports on the Italian, the French and the Polish activities in the Sudan.

74114 [BURRI, Carla M.], Bollettino d'informazioni. Sezione archeologica. Istituto Italiano di Cultura del Cairo, No 34 (Luglio-Ottobre 1974), 18 p.

Sequel to our preceding number.
After a long report on various researches by the CEDAE, i.a. at the Ramesseum and in the Valley of the Queens, and short ones on the work by the Franco-Egyptian Centre and on the third colloquium on ceramics of Ancient Egypt the bulletin contains reports on the Polish, the American and the Austrian activities as well as those of the Service des Antiquités.

BURRI, Carla M., see also our number 74780.

74115 BUTTERY, Alan, Armies and Enemies of Ancient Egypt and Assyria. 3200 BC to 612 BC, [Goring by Sea, Sussex, Wargames

Research Group, 1974] (19 × 24.7 cm; 83 p., 117 p., colour fig. on cover) = A War Games Research Group Publication. 4.

The first part of this book (p. 3-34) is devoted to Ancient Egypt. Chapter 1 lists the major battles and wars, each with their date and a very brief description. Chapter 2 deals with tactical methods, mainly during the New Kingdom, comparing them with tactics of Canaanite and Syrian and of Hittite armies. Two chapters briefly discuss the organization of the Egyptian army, its composition and its formations. The main chapter (18-34) is devoted to dress and arms, illustrating the argument by drawings which, although based on Egyptian representations, are made in a modern style.

There are no notes nor references either to the sources or to Egyptological literature.

74116 BUTZER, Karl W., Modern Egyptian Pottery Clays and Predynastic Buff Ware, *JNES* 33 (1974), 377-382.

The old view that Predynastic buff ware is evidence of large-scale trade along the Nile Valley, because it could have only been manufactured in one or two specific areas, is here challenged. The study of clay sources at Qena and Fustat casts serious doubt and suggests the necessary examination of clay sources. The Qena one was therefore investigated 1962-63, as well as the Fustat kilns in Cairo, thus showing that as the sources for buff-firing clays are not truly unique, ancient ware of this type could have been made from a variety of lime muds throughout most of Upper and Middle Egypt. *E. Uphill*

74117 CAMINOS, Ricardo A., The New-Kingdom Temples of Buhen, Volume I [and] II, [London], Egypt Exploration Society, 1974 (25 × 31.3 cm; [Vol. I:] XVI + 96 p., 1 fig., 105 pl. [4 double, 7 folding] containing a map, 2 plans, fig. and ill.; [vol. II:] X + 139 p., 5 fig., 95 pl. [36 double, 36 folding] containing 2 plans, fig. and ill.) = Archaeological Survey of Egypt Edited by T. G. H. James, 33rd [and] 34th Memoir.

The two volumes contain part of the final report on Emery's excavations at Buhen between 1957 and 1960, dealing with the inscriptions and reliefs of the Southern and Northern Temples. The S. Temple, built by the XVIIIth Dynasty and repeatedly rebuilt and restored, has at present been removed to the Sudan National Museum at Khartûm (see vol. I, pl. 7-8).

Vol. I. In part 1 (Introduction) the author presents a general survey of the setting of the temples and the history of their study. He also explains the scope of the present volumes and makes remarks concerning the colours of the temple reliefs.

In part 2 (p. 11-89), after preliminary considerations, the elements of the Court of the S. Temple are discussed in detail: the gateway, pilasters, pillars and columns. The texts are translated and annotated upon. At the end a catalogue of 21 miscellaneous fragments inscribed with texts and designs which have been found scattered in the court. In an appendix (90-91) M.F. Laming Macadam studies a Meroitic graffito on the outer gate.

A conspectus of records of the S. Temple (92-96) enables the reader quickly to determine where texts and names are to be located and where they are discussed and depicted.

Vol. II. Part 3 deals with the Main Building of the S. Temple (3-99). After a general description there follows a detailed study of the facade and the outer walls, the vestibule, the three rooms and the inner sanctuary. On p. 100-102 a conspectus of records similar to that in vol. I.

Part 4 (105-113) is devoted to the scanty remains of the Northern Temple, built by Ahmosis and rebuilt by Amenophis II. The remains in situ and miscellaneous findings are described and discussed.

Extensive indexes to both volumes on p. 115-139.

The plates of the vols bear photographs and/or line drawings of every single scene.

74118 CARLSON, David S., George J. ARMELAGOS and Dennis P. van GERVEN, Factors Influencing the Etiology of Cribra Orbitalia in Prehistoric Nubia, *Journal of Human Evolution*, London 3 (1974), 405-410, with 2 pl.

The authors examined 285 crania from Meroitic, X-Group and Christian culture horizons which revealed a concentration of cribra orbitalia, that is, lesions on the superior surface of the eye orbit, suggesting chronic iron deficiency anemia as its most likely causal factor.

74119 CASSON, Lionel, Travel in the Ancient World, London, George Allen & Unwin Ltd, [1974] (13.5 × 21 cm; 384 p., 4 maps, 14 pl.); rev. *BiOr* 33 (1976), 9-12 (H.W. Pleket).
Pr. £ 5.75

Ancient Egyptian travellers are mentioned in chapter 1 (In the Beginning: 3000-1200 B.C.), e.g. Harkhuf (p. 28-29) and Wenamon (39-43). On p. 32-33 remarks on Egyptian tourists of the New Kingdom visiting the pyramids.

CASTELA, Henry, see our number 74780.

74120 CASTIGLIONE, L., Das wichtigste Denkmal der Sarapis-Füsse im British Museum wiedergefunden, *Studia Aegyptiaca I*, 75-81, with 4 ill.

In addition to his article in *ZÄS* 97 (our number 71113) about the feet of Sarapis the author mentions that one of the instances of a bust of the god upon a votive foot, the whereabouts of which were said to be unknown, is at present in the British Museum (Inv. No. ES 983). The object is described and represented by photographs.

74121 CASTIGLIONE, László, Zwei verschollene Reliefs aus der Römerzeit, *Festschrift Ägyptisches Museum Berlin*, 465-472, with 5 pl.

Publikation von zwei bisher unveröffentlichten Denkmäler aus Berlin die während des Krieges verschwunden sind : ein römisches Relief mit der Darstellung einer Szene aus dem Isis-Mythos (Inv. Nr. 21490), und eine Reliefdarstellung des *Twtw* (Tithoes; Inv. Nr. 20914), in klassischem ägyptischem Stil. *V. Wessetzky*

74122 CASTILLOS, Juan Jóse, Further Remarks on Fayûm A and B Settlements, *Newsletter SSEA* 5, No. 2 (December 1974), 3-4.

Some additions to our number 73137.

74123 ČERVÍČEK, Pavel, Felsbilder des Nord-Etbai, Oberägyptens und Unternubiens, Wiesbaden, Franz Steiner Verlag GmbH, 1974 (21 × 28.5 cm; X + 229 S., 2 maps, 23 plans, 518 fig., 32 ill. on 16 pl.) = Ergebnisse der Frobenius-Expeditionen, Band 16; rev. *BiOr* 32 (1975), 208-210 (Inge Hofmann); *ZDMG* 126 (1976), 193-194 (J.v. B[eckerath]). Pr. DM 112

Es handelt sich um die Publikation der durch die VIII. DIAFE unter Leitung von Leo Frobenius 1926 im Nord-Etbai aufgenommenen über 500 Felsgravuren; dazu kommen noch 62 Felsbilder, die von Klaus Ruthenberg und Uwe Topper 1961 im mittleren Unternubien fotografiert wurden. Auf eine Einleitung mit einem Abriß der Geschichte und des jetzigen Standes der Erforschung der Felsbilder des Nord-Etbai und der angrenzenden Gebiete folgt ein Katalog der Funde mit den authentischen Expeditionsangaben der Fundumstände und Angaben über bisher veröffentlichte Bilder aus dem Material. Im zweiten Hauptteil der Arbeit werden die Darstellungen nach Motiven zusammengestellt (Schiffsdarstellungen, anthropomorphe Darstellungen, zoomorphe Darstellungen, Symbole und Ornamente) und zu datieren versucht. *Inge Hofmann*

74124 CHARLTON, Nial, Some Reflections on the History of Pharaonic Egypt, *JEA* 60 (1974), 200-205.

A highly subjective article on sculpture of the Amarna age and postulated royal characters derived therefrom, the validity of the letter of the Egyptian queen to the Hittite king, the quantity and origin of the gold in Tut'ankhamūn's tomb, the question of transporting cedar wood from Lebanon across the Nile Delta, the Pharaonic irrigation system and Egyptian place-names. *E. Uphill*

74125 CHRÉTIEN, J., La métaphore dans un extrait du Roman de Sinouhé, *Annuaire. École Pratique des Hautes Études.* V[e] section-sciences religieuses, Paris 82 (1973-1974), 116.

Report of a lecture.
Proceeding from *Sin*. B 200 ff. the author discusses the metaphoric use of the names of parts of the body. He also points out the similar use of the metaphor in African languages.

CLERC, Gisèle, see our number 74440.

74126 COCHE-ZIVIE, Christiane, Les colonnes du "Temple de l'Est" à Tanis. Epithètes royales et noms divins, *BIFAO* 74 (1974), 93-121, with 1 fig.

Study of 10 columns from the Eastern Temple of Tanis, based on material from the Mission Montet, the site being at present inaccessible.
The author describes the columns, which may be older than their decoration by Ramses II, usurped by Osorkon II. The texts are published, with translation and extensive comments. They contain epithets of the king, which are discussed, as well as the divinities mentioned. The function of the building of Osorkon and that of the original one of Ramses II remains obscure, but the texts shed light upon the Ramesside theology and royal ideology.

COLEMAN, Reginald, see our number 74040.

74127 de CONTENSON, Henri, Jacques-Claude COURTOIS, Élisabeth LAGARCE, Jacques LAGARCE, Rolf STUCKY, La XXXIVe campagne de fouilles à Ras Shamra en 1973. Rapport préliminaire, *Syria*, Paris 51 (1974), 1-30, with 5 ill.. 2 plans and 2 pl.

In the "maison aux albâtres", in the immediate vicinity of the Great Palace at Ugarit, there were found, among other objects, a bronze statuette of Ba'al wearing a crown which reminds of the Upper Egyptian white crown, an Egyptian (?) steatite statuette on an alabaster base, which is discussed in some detail and attributed to the end of the XVIIIth or the XIXth Dynasty, as well as an alabaster fragment probably bearing the cartouche of Ramses II, seemingly the first monument of the XIXth Dynasty found outside a palace or temple.
There is so much material pointing to Egypt that the proprietor

of the house may have been an Egyptian living at Ugarit. In this connection the authors trace the relations between Egypt and Ugarit in various periods.   *L.M.J. Zonhoven*

74128 CONTI, Giovanni, Egiziano *3sḫ* "tagliare col falcetto" etiopico '*3zḫ* "pietra focaia", *Rivista* 48 (1973-74), 29-35.

Proceeding from a connection between Eg. *3zḫ*, "to reap with the sicle", and Eth. (Ge'ez) '*3zḫ* suggested by Albright (*AJSL* 34, [1918], 216), the author briefly discusses the theories explaining an African component in the Egyptian language (substratum or parastratum). Adducing arguments for a cultural influence on Africa from the direction of the Mediterranean in the Neolithic Period the author suggests that a prehistoric common culture of Egypt and Ethiopia is not improbable.

74129 COONEY, John D., Way Stations on the Primrose Path, *The Bulletin of the Cleveland Museum of Art*, Cleveland 61, Number 7 (September 1974), 241-246, with 8 ill. (one on cover).

On p. 245-246 remarks on drinking and wine in ancient Egypt.

COONEY, John D., see also our number 74021.

74130 COUROYER, B., Les Aamou-Hyksôs et les Cananéo-phéniciens, *Revue Biblique*, Paris 81 (1974), 321-354 and 481-523.

In the first part of his article on the origin and nature of the ethnic group called '*3mw* by the Egyptians, the author concentrates on the texts that provide information on the geographic location of their territory and their relations with Egypt. Quoting from historical texts mainly of the Old and Middle Kingdoms, he concludes that the '*3mw* inhabited not only Palestine as far north as Byblos and Ullaza, but also most of the Eastern Desert from the Wadi Hammâmât in the south to the Sinai in the north. Their relations with Egypt were often hostile during the older period, but improved early in the Middle Kingdom.

Having established that the '*3mw* in later times also inhabited the territory known as Canaan, the author argues in the second part of the article that this enigmatic ethnic group is identical with the Canaanites of the Old Testament, and as such responsible for the introduction of the god '*êl* into Palestine and Syria. They also constitute the bulk of the so-called Hyksos, who more or less peacefully penetrated northern Egypt after the decline of the Middle Kingdom. It is at least very likely that they are connected with the Amorites mentioned in cuneiform sources. Originating from somewhere in the South Arabian Peninsula, the '*3mw*-Amorites-Hyksos-Canaanites would have migrated to the Red Sea desert at the dawn of history, made their way north in the course of the third millennium B.C., and established the flourishing Middle Bronze Age civilization of Canaan after the completion of their conquest. *Dieter Mueller*

COURTOIS, Jacques-Claude, see our number 74127.

74131 COWELL, M.R. and A.E. WERNER, Analysis of Some Egyptian Glass, in: *Annales du 6ᵉ Congrès de l'Association Internationale pour l'Histoire du Verre*. Cologne, 1-7 Juillet 1973, Liège, 1974, 295-298, with 1 table.

The technique of atomic absorption spectophotometry has been applied in the analysis of 7 glass fragments from the XVIIIth Dynasty in order to determine their composition. The results are in agreement with the findings given by Lucas-Harris, "Ancient Egyptian Materials and Industries" (our number 62392), chapter X.

74132 CRAIGIE, P.C., The Comparison of Hebrew Poetry: Psalm 104 in the Light of Egyptian and Ugaritic Poetry, *Semitics*, Pretoria 4 (1974), 10-21,

The author investigates the parallels between *Ps* 104 and the Aton hymn of Akhnaton, stating that a direct link between them is unlikely. The general similarities will have to be explained from a common background.

74133 CROWFOOT PAYNE, Joan, An Early Amethyst Vase, *JEA* 60 (1974), 79-81, with 1 pl.

This amethyst vase now in the possession of Mrs G.G. Medlicott was bought in London in 1966. It measures 7.7 cm. in height and has the rim encased in gold foil. Comparisons are made with other examples of similar type and although generally not archaeologically datable these are certainly of Gerzean rather than First Dynasty origin. *E. Uphill*

74134 CROZIER-BRELOT, Claude, L'ordinateur remplacera-t-il le scribe?, *Textes et langages III*, 301-306.

The author discusses the possibilities which the use of the computer may offer to future researches, as well as the results already obtained, mentioning particularly her index to the *Pyramid Texts* (see our numbers 71135 and 73165). At the end a bibliography to the subject.

74135 CULICAN, W., A Phoenician Seal from Khaldeh, *Levant*, London 6 (1974), 195-198, with 2 pl.

Publication of a limestone scaraboid seal found at the Phoenician site of Khaldeh, with on the face some hieroglyph-like figures in Phoenician style. For this type of seals cfr our number 67594.

74136 CURTO, Silvio, L'Egitto antico. Storia e archeologia, Torino, G. Giappichelli Editore, [1974] (17.5 × 25 cm; 271 p., 52 pl. containing plans, fig. and ill., 1 loose map).   Pr. L. 7000

This handbook of the history and archaeology of ancient Egypt is not so much a continuous narrative as an enumeration of our present knowledge and the way it has been obtained. Each chapter consists of a number of short sections dealing with one subject, clearly indicated by the underlining of the first words. A second characteristic is that the study covers the entire period from the prehistory to the Arab conquest, while also the Nubian history of that time is included.

After two introductory chapters the author deals in the first part with the geography (topography and climate, fauna, communications, economy, etc.), followed by a survey of the relevant literature. The second part is devoted to the "historical vicissitudes", that is, the history within the framework of the evolution of mankind. This concept is discussed in the first chapter, which is followed by chapters on the prehistory and the various historical periods to the end of the Byzantine Period. At the end a chapter on Nubia. Where possible, e.g. for the Middle and New Kingdoms, the discussion consists of sections on the main rulers. There follows a chapter on modern historiography of Egypt.

The third and longest part (p. 113-226) deals with arts: architecture, statuary, reliefs, etc. The various sub-categories are briefly discussed, e.g. various types of mastabas (120-134), elements of architecture (164-171), or types of statues (178-183). The next chapter, on archaeology, deals with the destruction of the monuments, the exploration (with mention of the major publications), art criticism, and the major museums, institutes and libraries.

In the last part (227-263) the written documents are dealt with: language, writing, alphabet, production and destruction of the documents, the instruction, etc., followed by a last chapter on philology.

The plates mostly contain plans and drawings to the chapter on architecture.

74137 CURTO, Silvio, Ernesto Scamuzzi, *Aegyptus* 54 (1974), 203-205.

Obituary notice, with a bibliography. Compare our number 74847.

74138 CURTO, S., [Scavi nel Museo di Torino.] I. Un naos di Sethi I, *Oriens Antiquus* 13 (1974), 40, with 2 pl.

Brief report on the reconstruction of a granite naos of Sethi I from a few fragments found by Schiaparelli at Heliopolis in 1903.

74139 CURTO, Silvio e Alessandro ROCCATI, L'edizione dei testi del Museo egizio di Torino, *Textes et langages III*, 141-150.

After a brief mention of the origin of the Turin collection and its first publications the authors discuss the major editions, dividing them into the following categories: epigraphic documents, funerary papyri and other texts, non-funerary papyri, ostraca and tablets, Demotic, Greek and Coptic texts. The last section deals with the general catalogue.

CURTO, Silvio, see also our numbers 74526 and 74616.

74140 DANNESKIOLD-SAMSØE, Irene, Die Statue eines ägyptischen Würdenträgers Berlin 15789, *Festschrift Ägyptisches Museum Berlin*, 473-482, with 5 pl.

Publication of the statue Berlin Inv. No. 15789, representing a man wearing the so-called "serrated scarf". On account of its style, which is extensively discussed and compared with that of several other statues, the piece is dated to about A.D. 310.

74141 DAUMAS, François, Le temple de Dendara. Publications et études, *Textes et langages III*, 267-273.

The author sketches the importance of the temple complex and discusses its descriptions prior to Champollion as well as those by Dümichen, Mariette and Chassinat. He also describes his own work on the temple and the problems connected with it. At the end a bibliography of recent books and articles on Dendara.

74142 DAUMAS, François, Les textes bilingues ou trilingues, *Textes et langages III*, 41-45.

Proceeding from the Stone of Rosetta the author discusses the bilingual, or in fact, since Demotic is almost a separate language, trilingual decrees from the Graeco-Roman Period, of which that by Cornelius Gallus is written in Greek, Latin and hieroglyphs. He also mentions Greek translations of Egyptian originals, e.g. the text of an obelisk translated by Hermapion.
Daumas then deals with the role of the bilinguals and trilinguals in the decipherment of the hieroglyphs, and their importance for the study of the Egyptian language.

74143 DAUMAS, François, Y eut-il des mystères en Égypte?, *Les Conférences de 'l'Atelier d'Alexandrie'*, Alexandria no. 8 (1972), 37-52, with 1 ill.

The celebration of certain divine mysteries by the Egyptians is attested by Greek authors (e.g. in Herodotus, Book II, 170-1) and corroborated by native Egyptian evidence from the Middle Kingdom onward. This concerns especially the celebration of the death, resurrection and final victory of Osiris, alluded to in the Berlin Ikhernofret stela. Rubrics in certain chapters of the *Book of the Dead* (where the desire of the deceased to become osirianized transpires everywhere) point to their use on earth by a limited group of initiated persons. Further evidence may be gathered from passages in biographies (e.g. that of Paheri at El Kab) and from representations in tombs (Petosiris, reproduced here). Even temples, hardly investigated for this particular purpose, provide indications: the unique psychostasy scene in the Hathor temple at Deir el-Medîna and a small tribune near the sacred lake of the Dendera temple where (following Herodotus) mysteries could be celebrated. Other evidence comes e.g. from festival rites in the Hathor cult, where sacral drunkenness enabled the participants to penetrate into the sphere of the divine. This is alluded to in temple inscriptions (cf our number 68156) and in the (Ptolemaic) biography of Wennofer (Cairo). A new investigation of all the material might perhaps throw light on the question of the influence of Egyptian mystery rites on Greek practices. *J.F. Borghouts*

74144 DAVIES, W.V., John Wintour Baldwin Barns, *JEA* 60 (1974), 243-246, with portrait.

Obituary article. Compare our number 74841.

74145 DAVIES, W.V., An Inscribed Axe Belonging to the Ashmolean Museum, Oxford, *JEA* 60 (1974), 114-118, with 2 pl.

This object, Ashm. Mus. 1927.4623, presented to the Museum by Sir Arthur Evans in 1927, formerly belonged to his father. Its earlier provenance is uncertain and Budge in 1892 misattributed it to Ka-mes, whereas it actually bears the two cartouches of king Amosis, while the linking of it with the Aḥ-ḥotpe treasure further bedevilled the issue. A detailed description is given and it is suggested that although of the period it did not come from the Aḥ-ḥotpe find.

DAVIES, W.V., see also our number 74478.

71146 DEAKIN, G.B., A Note on two New Instances of the Rare Proper Name *Mrjw-Mrjw*, *ZÄS* 100, 2 (1974), 150.

This rare name is also attested on a shawabti in the Fitzwilliam Museum in Cambridge (E 269-40), and on a heart-scarab in the Sheffield City Museum (J II.5.81-291).

Dieter Mueller

74147 DECKER, Wolfgang, Bemerkungen zum Agon für Antinoos in Antinoupolis (Antinoeia), *in* : *Kölner Beiträge zur Sportwissenschaft 2*. Jahrbuch der Deutschen Sporthochschule Köln, 1973, Schondorf, Hofmann-Verlag, 1974, 38-56.

Discussion of a passage from the inscription of the so-called Barberinus obelisk on the Monte Pincio in Rome, erected by Hadrianus on the tomb of Antinoos (cfr Erman in *Abh. der Preuss. Akad. der Wiss.* 1917, 4, 10-17 and 28-47). The sentences dealing with the agon are given in transcription with a translation and extensive comments. The author argues that the text is a translation from a Greek original, which appears from the difficulties to render technical terms in Egyptian.
For a "Nachtrag", see *Kölner Beiträge zur Sportwissenschaft 4*. Jahrbuch der Deutschen Sporthochschule Köln, 1975, 213-214.

74148 DECKER, Wolfgang, La délégation des Éléens en Égypte sous la 26ᵉ dynastie (Hér. II 160–Diod. I 95), *CdE* XLIX, No 97 (1974), 31-42.

Étudiant les conditions historiques dans lesquelles a pu se dérouler l'ambassade des Éléens en Égypte dont parlent les deux auteurs mentionnés dans le titre, pour soumettre aux Égyptiens leur réglement des jeux olympiques, Decker pense que le récit est authentique et que cette ambassade est réelle. On aurait toutefois tort de croire que les Grecs auraient reconnu pour cela une compétence spéciale en matière agonistique aux Égyptiens. Au contraire, plusieurs traits rapportés suggèrent que les jeux sportifs devaient être inconnus dans l'Égypte de la 26ᵉ dynastie. C'était simplement à leur grande réputation de sagesse en général et de justice qu'on avait fait appel. *Ph. Derchain*

74149 DECKER, Wolfgang, Einige Bemerkungen zum Thema "Frau und Leibesübungen im Alten Ägypten", *in* : *Beiträge zur Geschichte der Leibeserziehung und des Sports*. Internationales Seminar für Geschichte der Leibeserziehung und des Sports. Hispa-Seminar. Wien, 17.-20. April 1974. Referate Band 1, Wien, Institut für Leibeserziehung der Universität Wien, [1974], [1-12], with summaries in German, English and French on 3 unnumbered p.

The author, discussing the connections between woman and sport in Egypt, first mentions types of sports typical for girls : three kinds of ball games and swimming. He then deals with the tomb scenes of fishing and fowling with their religious and erotic traits, in which women are depicted. In the *Story of the Doomed Prince* a princess occurs as the prize of a contest. Some goddesses are mentioned as patronesses of special types of sport, e.g. Sekhet of hunting and Astarte of riding on horseback.

74150 DECKER, W., Kenden de Egyptenaren sport?, *Spiegel Historiael*, Bussum 9 (1974), 550-559, with 1 plan and 8 ill.

The author discusses for the general reader the problem whether there has existed sport in ancient Egypt. He i.a. translates the Sphinx stela of Amenophis II and deals with various aspects of the function of physical exercises within the Egyptian civilization. Compare our number 71144.

74151 DECKER, Wolfgang and Jürgen KLAUCK, Königliche Bogenschießleistungen in der 18. ägyptischen Dynastie. Historische Dokumente und Aspekte für eine experimentelle Überprüfung, *in*: *Kölner Beiträge zur Sportwissenschaft 3*. Jahrbuch der Deutschen Sporthochschule Köln, 1974, Schondorf, Hofmann-Verlag, 1974, 23-55, with 7 fig. and 7 ill.

The first author presents a survey of our knowledge concerning sportive archery by the kings of the XVIIIth Dynasty, discussing pertinent texts (with translations), representations and equipment. He argues that for Amenophis II the reports will be historically correct; afterwards they became a topos, which finds a place within the Egyptian conception of history. That archery was indeed a sport in Egypt may be concluded from the frequent copper "oxhide-shaped" ingots, as e.g. from the ship sunk near Cape Gelidonya (see our number 67060).

The second author discusses technical investigations into the problem whether royal archers could indeed have perforated the copper targets. Experiments prove that with the ancient equipment this is improbable, although not absolutely impossible.

74152 DERCHAIN, Philippe, Miettes, *RdE* 26 (1974), 7-20, with 1 fig.

Cinq notules:
1. Les nombres 77 et 777 que l'on rencontre dans certains textes religieux et magiques du Nouvel Empire et de la Basse Époque servent à exprimer un nombre indéterminé (comme le français 36).
2. le mot ḫh (*Wb.* 5, 66, 11) doit désigner cette espèce d'entrave que l'on voit souvent aux mains des prisonniers dans les bas-reliefs de Medinet Habou et d'ailleurs. On le retrouve avec le même sens à Edfou, dans le mythe d'Horus.
3. Dans le mythe d'Horus d'Edfou apparaissent des traces d'emprunts au conte néo-égyptien d'Horus et de Seth: *Edfou* 6, 120, 1-2 + 4-5 = P. Chester Beatty I, 15, 9-12.
4. Le traitement infligé par Horus à Seth après sa victoire à Oxyrrhynchos est inspiré de celui que fit subir Achille au cadavre d'Hector (*Edfou* 6, 120- 6-8). En outre, il semble que l'usage grec de la répartition des chairs de la victime d'un

sacrifice ait servi de modèle à la rédaction du passage *Edfou* 6, 116, 8—117, 1.

5. Une page du récit du voyage de Jean Thévenot au Levant (1658) décrit la découverte d'intailles antiques à Alexandrie qui semble avoir été totalement pillée à cet égard avant l'époque des fouilles modernes. Ph. Derchain

74153 DERCHAIN, Philippe, Les temples secondaires des époques ptolémaïque et romaine, *Textes et langages III*, 275-277.

The author draws the attention to the large number of minor temples from the Graeco-Roman Period, local ones as well as secondary sanctuaries surrounding the major temples, such as mammisis. He sketches the importance of studying them, indicating what still has to be done.

74154 DERCHAIN-URTEL, Maria-Theresia, Ein ptolemäisches Schriftspiel, *GM* Heft 11 (1974), 17-18.

The hieroglyphic group *Dendera* V, 53, 6 is to be read '*Isdn nb Ḥmnw*. Dieter Mueller

74155 DERCHAIN-URTEL, Maria Theresia, Die Schlange des "Schiffbrüchigen", *SAK* 1 (1974), 83-104.

The author studies the figure of the snake in the story of the *Shipwrecked Sailor* in order to discover the impression it made on its hearers.

The snake with its body of gold and its eyebrows of lapis lazuli clearly bears solar characteristics, its long beard pointing to Atum. The figure 74 (his brothers, sisters and children) is to be connected with the 74 (75) shapes (*ḫprw*) of Re, together constituting the god in his various aspects. As the divinities connected with Re in their functions within his "constellation" can assume the traits of relatives, so the 74 relatives of the snake are part of him in the absolute harmony formerly reigning on the island.

The supposition that the snake was Re(-Atum) is confirmed by the description of his approach. The reference (line 128-9) to his "little girl" the author translates as : "Dabei will ich dir nicht eine kleine Tochter erwähnen, welche ich als Wissender (dessen, war geschehen ist) hinweggebracht habe", identifying the girl as Maat. For *ḫt ḥr gmgm* (line 59) she proposes the translation : "er splitterte das Unterholz", which points to an exotic landscape. The Island of the *K3* belongs to the Golden Age, the sailor surviving its destruction like Osiris survived in his son.

74156 DERCHAIN, Maria-Theresia und Philippe, Zur ägyptischen Wortforschung, *ZÄS* 101 (1974), 5-12.

Anhand von drei Beispielen versuchen die Verfasser zu zeigen, daß man eine bessere Klassifizierung der Eintragungen der Wörterbücher erreichen kann. Dazu müssen einige allgemein anerkannte Sprachgesetze auch für das Ägyptische akzeptiert werden.
Zusammenfassung in unserer Nummer 73184.

M. Heerma van Voss

DERRY, Douglas E., see our number 74172.

74157 DESANGES, J., Un point de repère dans la chronologie du royaume de Méroe à la fin de l'époque tétrarchique, *in* : *Mélanges d'Histoire Ancienne*. Offerts à William Seston, Paris, 1974 (= Publications de la Sorbonne, Série "Études", Tome 9), 161-165.

Der Dodekaschoinos wurde von Diokletian 298 n.Chr. (wahrscheinlich richtiger als das meist angenommene Datum von 297 n.Chr.) aufgegeben. Für die meroitische Chronologie haben wir dadurch jedoch nichts direkt gewonnen. Die Episode in *Apostelgeschichte* VIII, 27 vom Schatzmeister der äthiopischen Kandake wurde immer wieder von den Kirchenvätern kommentiert. Besondere Bedeutung gewinnt Eusebius in seiner Kirchengeschichte (zuerst wohl 312 n.Chr. publiziert) mit der Bemerkung, daß gemäß alter Sitte auch jetzt noch das äthiopische Volk von einer Frau beherrscht sei. Da Eusebius sich vor 311 n.Chr. in der Thebais aufhielt, kommt seiner Bemerkung historische Bedeutung zu. Daß es im 3. und 4. nachchristlichen Jahrhundert Kandaken bzw. herrschende Königinnen gab, wird durch archäologische Zeugnisse erhärtet.

Inge Hofmann

74158 DESANGES, Jehan et Serge LANCEL, Bibliographie analytique de l'époque antique VIII (1971), Paris, Editions E. de Boccard, 1974 (21 × 27 cm; 32 p.).

In der vorliegenden Arbeit werden die Bücher und Artikel über das antike Afrika vorgestellt, die 1971 erschienen sind. Die erste Folge dieser chronologischen Aufschlüsselung umfaßt die Arbeiten von 1961-62 und erschien im *Bulletin d'Archéologie Algérienne* I, 1962-1965.
Das Material ist aufgegliedert nach: 1. Sources et Répertoires. 2. Bibliographies et Bilans, Ouvrages généraux. 3. Géographie historique, Études du substrat, Faits généraux de civilisation(s) 4. Afrique punique. 5. Royaumes indigènes. 6. Période romaine. 7. Christianisme africain, archéologie et épigraphie chrétiennes, Afrique vandale et byzantine.

Inge Hofmann

74159 DESROCHES NOBLECOURT, Ch., Nouvelles acquisitions. Musée du Louvre. Département des Antiquités égyptiennes, *La Revue du Louvre et des Musées de France*, Paris 24 (1974), 43-54, with 21 ill.

We mention the six acquisitions of 1973 here discussed: 1. A fragmentary bust of Tuy mother of Ramses II (Inv. No. E 27.132); 2. A terra cotta model boat from the Thinite Period (Inv. No. E 27.136); 3. A terra cotta statuette of an adult and a young monkey facing each other, possibly from the First Intermediate Period (Inv. No. E 27.137); 4. A wooden toy representing a man standing in a cart drawn by two horses, probably from the Coptic Period (Inv. No. E 27.134); 5. An important false door from the Old Kingdom, belonging to a Sheshi (Inv. No. E 27.133); 6. A torso of Queen Neferu-Sobek, who acted shortly as reigning pharaoh after the death of her (half-)brother Amenemhat IV (Inv. No. E 27.135).
One other acquisition is mentioned on p. 347 of the same periodical. *L. M.J. Zonhoven*

74160 DESROCHES-NOBLECOURT, Ch., La statue colossale fragmentaire d'Aménophis IV offerte par l'Égypte à la France (Louvre E. 27112), *Monuments et mémoires. Fondation Eugène Piot*, Paris 59 (1974), 1-44, with 27 ill., 3 fig., 3 plans and 1 colour pl.

The description of the monumental bust of Akhnaton is followed by a discussion of the temple East of the Karnak girdle-wall, suggested to be the Gem-pa-Aton from the representation of the king with Nefertiti in the Window of Appearances in Ramose's tomb. The author also deals with Akhnaton's early art and the role of the sculptor Bek, the alleged diseases of the king, etc.
Cfr also our number 72180.

DESROCHES-NOBLECOURT, Christiane, see also our number 74259.

74161 DEWACHTER, Michel, Un bloc du "temple haut" de Karnak Nord au Musée de Grenoble, *CdE* XLIX, No 97 (1974), 52-58, with 1 fig. and ill.

Le musée de Grenoble possède un bloc de grès jaune (Inv. No 15) rapporté d'Égypte par le comte Louis de Saint Ferriol, attribué jusqu'ici aux ruines d'Erment, mais qui provient en réalité du temple haut de Karnak Nord. Il représente l'accueil de Nectanébo II par une déesse. *Ph. Derchain*

74162 DEWACHTER, Michel, Une nouvelle statue du vice-roi de Nubie Ousersatet à Khartoum, *Archeologia*, Paris No. 72 (Juillet 1974), 54-58, with 1 fig. and 4 ill.

Publication of a statue in the museum at Khartûm (Inv. no. 32), found by Budge in the temple of Uronarti and ascribed by him to a Tcha-ib, bei Steindorff to a User. Actually it bears the name of the vice-roy User-satet as well as a cartouche of Amenophis II. The author presents a description of the piece and a facsimile and translation of its inscriptions He also gives a list of representations of the vice-roy (stelae, statues, a shawabti and graffiti). The present statue is by far the best known of User-satet.

74163 DIEM, Werner, Das Problem von *ṯ* im Althebraïschen und die kanaanäische Lautverschiebung, *ZDMG* 124 (1974), 221-252.

Study of the phonetic value of the Hebraic *śin*. The common conception of it hardly suits what we know about other Canaanite dialects ($\acute{s} > \check{s}$), or Aramaic ($\acute{s} > s$). The author defends a development $\underline{t} > \acute{s} > \check{s}$, that is, the concurrence of $\acute{s}$ and $\check{s}$ as a later, secondary phenomenon. For his argument he adduces evidence from Egyptian spellings of Canaanite names and words, warning, however, not to overstress their meaning since the Egyptians may have had no exact equivalents to Canaanite sibilants and were used to write words according to the historical orthography. It appears that in M.Eg. texts Canaan. $\check{s}$ = Eg. $\check{s}$, as in early N.Eg. texts, where old Canaan. $\acute{s}$ and $\underline{t}$ = Eg. $s/\acute{s}$. That means that in the middle of the 2nd mill. B.C. Caan. $\check{s}$ and $\acute{s}/\underline{t}$ were still distinguished. A few exceptions may point to the later concurrence of $\acute{s}$ and $\underline{t}$ with $\check{s}$.

74164 DINKLER, E., Deutsche Ausgrabungen im Sudanischen Niltal 1967-1969, *Heidelberger Jahrbücher*, Heidelberg 18 (1974), 1-21, with 16 ill. and 8 fig.

Es handelt sich um einen Bericht über die Arbeiten des Deutschen Archäologischen Instituts in Nubien zwischen 1960 und 1970. Ein kurzer Geschichtsabriß vom Untergang des meroitischen Reiches bis zum Ende der christlichen Epoche wird gegeben, sowie einige wichtige Grabungsstätten (Qasr Ibrim, Faras, Alt-Dongola, Jebel Barkal, Wadi Ghazali) genannt. Die deutschen Grabungsobjekte lagen auf den Inseln Sunnarti und Tangur sowie in Kulb; die Burg des letztgenannten Ortes könnte möglicherweise ein Kloster gewesen sein.

Inge Hofmann

74165 DIXON, D. M., Timber in ancient Egypt, *Commonwealth Forestry Review*, London 53, No. 157 (September 1974), 205-209.

Survey of the kinds of timber, indigenous as well as imported, used in ancient Egypt, and the technics applied to wood, which were partly due to its scarcity.

74166 DONADONI, Sergio, L'edizione dei testi dei musei egizii d'Italia, *Textes et langages III*, 151-158.

The author presents a survey of the catalogues and some of the more important publications of collections and monuments in various Italian cities : Turin, Florence, Bologna, Naples, Rome, Trieste, Padua, Como, Milan, Parma, Pisa, Cortona, Benevento and Palermo.

74167 DONADONI, Sergio, La Missione Archeologica in Egitto della Università di Roma, *Newsletter ARCE* No 88 (Winter 1974), 20-21.

Sequel to our number 73197.
The work of the Archaeological Mission of the University of Rome in Tomb No 27 (Sheshonq) at ʿAsâsîf was continued in 1973.
The antechamber of the lower room and the court itself were studied. The back wall of the antechamber revealed two large false doors. *L.M.J. Zonhoven*

74168 D[ONADONI], S[ergio], Scavi nel Museo di Torino, *Oriens Antiquus* 13 (1974), 39.

Introduction to a series of articles. Compare our numbers 74138, 74169, and 74617.

DONADONI, Sergio, see also our number 74037.

74169 DONADONI ROVERI, A. M., [Scavi nel Museo di Torino]. III. Una stele di Heka-ib al Museo di Torino, *Oriens Antiquus* 13 (1974), 53-56, with 1 pl.

Publication of a stela (Turin No Suppl. 18130) of a certain *Wnmỉ*, who is depicted with his wife while the names of 7 children occur below the couple. The stela dates from the XIIIth or the XIVth Dynasty, its main particularity being the mention, besides Osiris, of Hekaib, the deified prince of Elephantine.

74170 DONNER, Herbert, Die Beschwörung des Großen Gottes, *ZÄS* 100,2 (1974), 82-95, with 2 ill.

Bearbeitung der magischen Gemme 460 aus unserer Nummer 64105. Verfasser beschreibt den Text als mixtum compositum zum Zwecke des Schutzzaubers, des Offenbarungszaubers und des Namenzaubers. Donner schliesst mit einigen Überlegungen zur Stelle des Zaubers in der Religion. *M. Heerma van Voss*

74171 DOWNES, Dorothy, The Excavations at Esna 1905-1906, Warminster, Aris & Phillips Ltd, [1974] (21 × 30 cm; XII + 136 p., 3 plans, numerous fig. and ill., maps on endpapers); rev. *BiOr* 33 (1976), 178-179 (Michel Valloggia); *CdE* LI, No. 101 (1976), 111-112 (Herman de Meulenaere).

The excavations at Esna by John Garstang in 1905-1906 (actually conducted by the unexperienced Harold Jones) have never been published in a proper way. For a preliminary report, see *ASAE* 8 (1907), 132-145. The present author, Mrs Downes (née Slow) has taken on the difficult and ungrateful task to present the material from the incomplete and inadequate field records, while she has also attempted to trace the widely dispersed objects.

The tombs discovered in the area mostly date from the early XVIIth to the mid XVIIIth Dynasties, though many have been reused in later times. An other group belongs to the XXth to XXIInd Dynasties. From the findings from the first period it appears that it was a comparatively poor provincial cemetery. Hardly any traces of Hyksos influence have been discovered.

In the introduction Mrs Downes describes the two campaigns and the records and museum sources she has consulted. There follows a discussion of all material, divided into ten categories and preceded by a description of the site. Chapter 2 contains the discussion of individual tombs and object groups. There follow chapters on : pottery (with a corpus of types drawn on p. 29-49); beads and amulets (drawings on p. 52-55); scarabs, seals and inscribed shells (drawings p. 60-66); 22 funerary stelae, mostly represented in photograph and line drawing, all of fairly rough workmanship; human statuettes and figurines; various objects of clay and terra cotta; stone vessels; metal objects (toilet articles, rings, etc.); objects of faience, of ivory, etc. Basketry and textiles have not been found in consequence of the humidity of the soil.

Most objects are represented by photographs and/or drawings. A brief section on the conclusions on p. 113.

The last part of the book consists of an inventory, arranged after the numbers of the object groups, based on the lists of small finds and the corpus of pottery made in the field, listing all major information as to dates, types of pottery and other objects, etc. Index of names and titles on p. 133-136.

74172 DUNHAM, Dows and William Kelly SIMPSON, The Mastaba of Queen Mersyankh III. G 7530-7540. Based upon the excavations and recordings of the late George Andrew Reisner and William Stevenson Smith. Museum of Fine Arts—Harvard

University Expedition, Boston, Department of Egyptian and Ancient Near Eastern Art. Museum of Fine Arts, Boston, 1974 (26.5 × 33.7 cm; VI + 26 p., 1 map and 4 plans [on unnumbered p.)], 22 pl., 17 [unnumbered] pl. with drawings [7 folding], frontispiece [colour photograph]) = Giza Mastabas. Edited by William Kelly Simpson, Volume 1; rev. *AJA* 78 (1974), 433 (John D. Cooney); *BiOr* 33 (1976), 25-27 (Rosemarie Drenkhahn).

The publication of Queen Mersyankh's tomb consists of two chapters. The first one, by Simpson, contains general comments. The tomb is notable for the situation of the underground chapel, cut out of the rocks beneath the N. end of the mastaba, and even more so for its remarkable reliefs of which the vivid colours are well preserved. The author mentions several earlier references to the chapel and its reliefs, and discusses the superstructure and its offering chapel (now largely destroyed), the relief fragments here found, the exterior chapel on the SE corner of the mastaba (probably never finished), the entrance of the substructure and the three underground chambers.

Chapter two, written by Dunham with additions by Simpson and Henry G. Fischer, contains a description of the reliefs preceded by remarks on the queen and her family relations. She was the daughter of Prince Kawab and Queen Hetepheres II, and the wife of Chephren. There are also remarks on the building history of the tomb. The reliefs are described and all texts transliterated and translated. At the end notes on Mersyankh's sarcophagus (Cairo JdE 54935) and her mummy (by Douglas E. Derry).

Two appendices contain a list of the moveable objects found during the excavations of the tomb (p. 23) and a list of the persons represented in the reliefs, with their titles (25-26).

The plates contain photographs of the reliefs as well as of the sarcophagus, the mummy, and several statuettes and fragments of them, among which a pair-statuette of the queen with her mother. On the unnumbered plates line drawings of the reliefs, the sarcophagus and some objects.

74173 DZIERŻYKRAY-ROGALSKI, Tadeusz, Kadero II — The Archaeological Site in the Sudan to be Investigated, *Africana Bulletin*, Warszawa 20 (1974), 169-172, with 4 ill.

Sequel to our number 72202.
Short survey of the excavation on two Neolithic sites at Kadero, Sudan.

DZIEWANOWSKI, Andrzej, see our number 74506.

74174 EDEL, Elmar, Hans Bonnet. 22. Februar 1887 — 27. Oktober 1972, *ZÄS* 100, 2 (1974), VI.
Obituary article. Compare our number 74842.

74175 EDEL, Elmar, Neue Identifikationen topographischer Namen in den konventionellen Namenzusammenstellungen des Neuen Reiches, *GM* Heft 11 (1974), 19-21.
The ending -ḥ in the toponyms *P3b3ḥ*, *Sgrwrḥ*, *H3brḥ*, and *'rtpḥ* represents the Hurrian suffix -ḥi "land of", e.g. Khaburkhai "land of the Khabur river". A number of other toponyms are also discussed.   *Dieter Mueller*

74176 EDEL, Elmar, Zwei Originalbriefe der Königsmutter Tūja in Keilschrift, *SAK* 1 (1974), 105-146 and 295, with 1 fig.
The author studies a cuneiform letter of queen Tūya, the mother of Ramses II, to Ḫattušiliš, found at Bogazköy (= KUB XXXIV, 2), as well as another (fragmentary) letter of the same queen to the Hittite queen Tuduḫepa (426/W). The latter is here published for the first time, while it is of the former the first transliteration and translation with comments. Apart from wishes it mentions presents from the queen to Ḫattušiliš, among them garments the names of which the author attempts to identify with Egyptian words.
The author demonstrates that the letters have been written in the year 22, shortly after the Treaty (cfr also our numbers 444 and 1293). Very probably Queen Tūya has died in this same year. Other letters found at Bogazköy and sent in the same year come from Nefertari and Sethhikhopshef. Since the same people occur in the temple of Abu Simbel its building has also begun in the year 22. Still an other letter was sent by the vizier *P3-sjrw* (= Pesiūr), who thus still held the office in that year.
The author makes several remarks as to linguistic matters. In an appendix (p. 135-146) he studies two lists of garments, mentioned in a letter of Amenophis III to Taḫundaradu, the king of Arzawa (VBoT 1) and in one of Amenophis IV to Burnaburias (EA 14 III).
See also the Nachtrag on p. 295.

74177 EDEL, Elmar and Steffen WENIG, Die Jahreszeitenreliefs aus dem Sonnenheiligtum des Königs Ne-user-Re, Berlin, Akademieverlag, 1974 (Tafelband: 29.7 × 40 cm; portefolio containing 6 colour pl. + 48 pl. [9 folded]; Textbeilage: 21 × 29.8 cm; 47 p.) = Staatliche Museen zu Berlin. Mitteilungen aus der ägyptischen Sammlung, 7; rev. *JEA* 62 (1976), 196-197 (C.H.S. Spaull).   Pr. DM 86.

In this volume drawings and some photographs are published of all reliefs which may be supposed to belong to the representations in the Room of the Seasons in the sanctuary of Neuserre at Abû Ghurâb. Parts of the fragments preserved in the Ägyptisches Museum, Berlin (Inv. Nos. 20035-36 and 20038-39) are represented in colour photographs, while a colour drawing of Cairo JE 34193 is to be found on pl. D.
Discussion of the reliefs will follow in a separate volume still to be published. For a provisional study by the second author, cfr our number 67603. See also, by the first author, our numbers 61199, 64128 and 65154.
The added textbook relates the history of the publication and contains a technical description of the plates with measures, bibliography, etc. of each relief fragment, as well as a list of the present whereabouts of the pieces, several of which have been destroyed during the last world war.

74178 EDWARDS, I..E.S., The Collapse of the Meidum Pyramid, *JEA* 60 (1974), 251-252.

The views of Mendelssohn in the previous number of the journal are questioned here, the evidence of the New Kingdom graffiti on the walls of the mortuary temple being critical as to the question of when and if it was buried in Pharaonic times. It is suggested that the May graffito, dated to the reign of Amenophis III, suggests that the pyramid was still in good condition at that period, and then its eventual ruin was subsequent, due perhaps to an earth-tremor rather than to heavy rainfall. *E. Uphill*

EDWARDS, I.E.S., see also our number 74270.

74179 EGGEBRECHT, Arne, Frühe Keramik aus El-Târif, *MDAIK* 30 (1974), 171-188, with 1 fig. and 10 pl.

A survey of the pottery discovered by the German Archaeological Institute during recent excavations at El-Târif (Saff el-Kisasîya and Saff el-Baqar) in Western Thebes. Especially the O.K. mastabas and their surroundings yielded material from the Naqada II Period, the Early Dynastic Period, and the Old Kingdom. *Dieter Mueller*

74180 EGGEBRECHT, Arne, Überlegungen zur Härtebestimmung. Plädoyer für eine technologische Untersuchung altägyptischer Keramikerzeugnisse, *SAK* 1 (1974), 147-177.

In the first part of the article the author explains a system of exactly establishing the hardness of ceramic products. The so-called scale of Mohs i.a. has the disadvantage of very irregular and in some instances very large intervals between the ten degrees of hardness. Various other systems and methods of establishing hardness are discussed, particularly an apparatus called durimet, which appears useful in that it produces more detailed results.

The second part is devoted to a large number of problems in the prehistory and history of Egypt and of Nubia to which a study of the material of the various types of ware and their method of production may bring definite results, more objective than the study of shapes and decoration. Each of these historical problems is well explained, and some sections constitute a nice summary of our present knowledge, as, for example, that on the Pan-Grave people (p. 174-176).

74181 Egyptian Antiquities in the Hermitage. Памяатники Искусства Древнего Египта в Эрмитаже, Leningrad, Aurora Art Publishers, [1974] (21 × 28.5 cm; 20 p., 139 colour ill. on 117 pl., colour ill. on title page).

The picture book, edited by B. Piotrovsky, is compiled and introduced by N. Landa and I. Lapis. The text is throughout in English and Russian.

The introduction offers a survey of the history of the collection and the major pieces. 139 illustrations represent a large number of them, covering the whole range of Egyptian antiquities: palettes, alabaster vessels, statues and statuettes, stelae and reliefs, coffins, glass flasks, etc. They are arranged in a chronological order, each object accompanied by some technical data and literature.

74182 EISSA, N.A., H.A. SALLAM, S.A. SALEH, F.M. TAIEL and L. KESTHELYI, Mössbauer Effect Study of Ancient Egyptian Pottery and the Origin of the Colour in Black Ware, *Recent Advances in Science and Technology of Materials*, 85-98, with 6 fig. and 5 tables.

An exploratory survey of sherds from different periods carried out by Mössbauer effect spectroscopy shows differences for the periods which may be due to variations in the clay-baking processes. The black colour in the interior of predynastic pottery is probably not caused by carbon alone, as Lucas has suggested, but also by reduction of ferric oxide to ferrous compounds.

74183 EKSCHMITT, Werner, Paměť Národů. Hieroglyfy, písmo a písemné nálezy na hliněných tabulkách, papyrech a pergamenech, Praha, Orbis, [1974] (15.5 × 22.5 cm; 253 p., 40 pl., 7 plans, 12 fig., 3 tables).

Czech translation of our number 64135.

74184 ELANSKAYA, A. I., Происхождение предыменного формата ере в системе коптского спряжения, *Палестинский Сборник*, Ленинград 25 (88), 1974, 81-86, with an English summary on p. 86.

"The Origin of the Grammatical Element ере in the Coptic Conjugation System".
The grammatical element of Fut. III second and circumstantial tenses ере prefixed to a nominal subject is here explained as being derived from the Part. Pass. of *iri*, meaning "done", "made", and, therefore, "existing", "present"; this in analogy to its pre-pronominal correlate є(< *iw*), denoting "presence", "existence".
Thus ере пр̄ωме сωт̄м̄ is to be explained as "what exists, (namely) the man, on (= while) hearing" > "here is the man on hearing". Either ере is the principal member of the nominal sentence, пр̄ωме being an apposition and сωт̄м̄ the adverbial adjunct to it, or ере is taken as a non-enclitic particle denoting existence and ере пр̄ωме as the principal member of the nominal sentence.

74185 ENGLUND, Gertie, Propos sur l'iconographie d'un sarcophage de la 21e dynastie, *The Gustavianum Collections*, 37-69, with 1 fig. and 11 ill.

Discussion of a wooden sarcophagus from Deir el-Bahri (Victoriamuseet No. 228) belonging to the priest of Mut and scribe of the temple of Amon Khonsumose (= Daressy, Les cercueils des prêtres d'Ammon, *ASAE* 8, [1907], No. 82).
After a general introduction the author studies the scenes on the outside of the sarcophagus and the representations on its lid. There follow translations of the texts between the scenes, remarks on the conception "offerings", on the symbols (*imy-wt*, plants, *wḏЗt*-eye, unguents, etc.) and on the orientation, that is, the apparently wrong place of the scenes on the sarcophagus. At the end some remarks on the reception of a man with a lunar name in the solar world of Osiris-Re.

74186 The Facsimile Edition of the Nag Hammadi Codices. Codex II. Published under the Auspices of the Department of Antiquities of the Arab Republic of Egypt in Conjunction with the United Nations Educational, Scientific and Cultural Organization, Leiden, E.J. Brill, 1974 (24 × 33 cm.; XIX p., 160 pl.); rev. *Biblica* 56 (1975), 257-259 (H. Quecke); *BiOr* 32 (1975), 370-372 (Robert Haardt); *CdE* XLIX, No. 98 (1974), 418 (Jean Bingen); *WZKM* 67 (1975), 253-256 (Robert Haardt).
Pr. cloth fl. 224

Fortsetzung unserer Nummer 73219.

Photographische Publikation — zur Erstveröffentlichung vgl. unsere Nummer 4683 — des meistbehandelten Codex des koptischen Handschriftenfundes von Nag Hammadi mit einem kurzen Vorwort in Arabisch und Englisch. Es werden die verschiedenen Numerierungen des Codex angeführt, sowie die Haupteditionen und Erstübersetzungen der einzelnen Teile. Diese, in stark subachmimisch gefärbtem Sahidisch geschrieben, beinhalten im einzelnen : 1-32, 9 Apokryphen des Johannes, 32,10–51,28 Thomas-Evangelium, 51,29–86,19 Philippos-Evangelium, 86,20–97,23 Hypostase der Archonten, 97,24–127, 17 und 127,18–137,27 titellose gnostische Schriften, und 138,1–145,19 Buch des Athleten Thomas. 145,20-23 ist die Aufforderung des Schreibers, seiner im Gebet zu gedenken mit dem Segenswunsch. Ausführlich werden Einband und Verschnürung des Codex beschrieben. Den Hauptteil des Buches nehmen die auf 160 Tafeln hervorragend reproduzierten Photos ein. Außer den einzelnen, in Originalgröße, mit Angabe der Faserrichtung, wiedergegebenen Seiten und Fragmenten werden auf den Tafeln 1-8, jeweils mit Maßstab, Photos des Einbandes und ältere Aufnahmen des unverglasten Codex gegeben.

Karl Martin

74187 FAIRMAN, H.W., The Triumph of Horus. An Ancient Egyptian Sacred Drama. With a Chapter by Derek Newton and Derek Poole, London, B.T. Batsford Ltd., [1974] (14 × 21.5 cm; X + 150 p., 1 map, 2 plans, 17 fig., 4 pl.); rev. *BiOr* 32 (1975), 200-201 (L. Kákosy); *CdE* XLIX, No. 97 (1974), 105-107 (Dieter Kurth); *JARCE* 12 (1975), 112-113 (Dieter Mueller).

Pr. £ 3

After a Preface in which the author explains aims and method of the book chapter 1 deals with the drama in ancient Egypt. The author quotes several texts, i.a. concluding that the Osiris mysteries were mimed actions rather than a play; that texts such as on the Shabaka Stone and the Ramesseum Dramatic Papyrus contain elements of a ritual drama; that of the actual plays which Drioton has listed only "The Birth and Apotheosis of Horus" is possibly indeed a genuine play.

Chapter 2 is devoted to the background of the only certain play we know at present, the "Triumph of Horus". It deals with its position on the inner side of the enclosure wall of the Edfu temple and its date (c. 110 B.C.); the relation between the reliefs and the texts; the reason why Fairman conceives it as a play, its story and significance (the renewal of the victorious power of the reigning king); its age (the text may at least date from the New Kingdom, while the harpoon ritual is already depicted on a seal of the 1st Dynasty); the principles on which its reconstruction is based and some details of interpretation; the setting and history of Edfu temple, the place where the play was performed (probably in front of the pylons) and the atmosphere in which it was presented; the present translation, an adapted and slightly improved version of a former by Blackman and Fairman (*JEA* 28-30), but combining relief captions and main texts, and being in verse form; the language of the texts ("Temple Egyptian") and that of the translation.

Chapter 3, by Derek Newton and Derek Poole, describes the production of the play by Padgate College in 1971 and a second performance at Lancaster.

There follows the translation, divided into a Prologue, three acts with five, two and three scenes respectively, and an Epilogue, each accompanied by a drawing of its relief. After that a glossary.

In Appendix A Fairman presents second thoughts on the Edfu stage, drawing attention to the pedestals on which the king and/or other persons are standing. They may give indications as to the way in which the original play was performed. Occurrence of pedestals in the reliefs of the "Legend of the Winged Disk" depicted above the Triumph of Horus may indicate that this too was a play.

Appendix B, by Jennifer Etherington, reports about an earlier and independent performance at Cheltenham in 1969.

Notes on p. 145-147; bibliography p. 149-150.

There is also an American edition, Berkeley and Los Angeles, University of California Press, 1974 (Pr. $ 9).

74188 FAKHRY, Ahmed, The Oases of Egypt. Volume II. Baḥriyah and Farafra Oases, Cairo, The American University in Cairo Press, [1974] (16.5 × 24 cm; XVI + 189 p., 7 maps, 14 plans, 19 fig., 49 ill., ill. on endpapers, fig. on cover).

Sequel to our number 73221.
In the Preface John A. Wilson sketches the life and person of Ahmed Fakhry.
The introduction relates the author's travels through the desert. Chapters I and II are devoted to the geography and population of the Bahrîya oasis, while chapter III deals with its history. Whether the oasis, in Egyptian called *Ḏsḏs*, has been inhabited during the Old Kingdom is uncertain. From the Middle Kingdom onwards we know of relations with the Nile Valley, but only during the XVIIIth dynasty the prosperity of the area begins, lasting till the end of the New Kingdom, possibly even longer, when during the Third Intermediate Period it was occupied by the Libyans. It also greatly flourished during the XXVIth Dynasty, from which period several monuments date. The

author also relates its subsequent history, mentioning some famous travellers from the 19th century such as Cailliaud, Wilkinson and Steindorff.

Chapter IV describes the antiquities of Bahrîya : tombs, e.g. that of Amenhotep, the governor of the oasis in the late XVIIIth to early XIXth Dynasties; a tomb with ibis burials from the Ptolemaic and Roman Periods; Libyan inscriptions, etc.

Chapter V discusses some decorated rock tombs near al-Bawiti, which are described and illustrated by photographs, drawings and plans.

Chapter VI and VII are devoted to the Farafra oasis (= *tꜣ iḥt*, "Land of the Cow"). Ancient sites here are listed on p. 163-164. Index on p. 181-189.

FANFONI-BONGRANI, Luisa, see our number 74037.

74189 FAY, Biri, Egyptian sculpture, *DAI Bulletin*, Dayton, Ohio Vol. 32, Number 1 (Dec. 1973), 10-15, with 9 ill.

Publication of four pieces of Egyptian art from the collection of the Dayton Art Institute. They are : a relief fragment representing the head of a man (No. 72.49), from the Vth or VIth Dynasty and probably from Saqqâra; the wooden torso of a girl (No. 71.253), from the XIIth Dynasty; a painted relief fragment representing a seated couple (No. 72.48), from the Ramesside Period and probably from Thebes; and an alabaster vessel (No. 71.248), from the Saite Period.

74190 FECHT, Gerhard, Die Königs-Insignien mit *s*-Suffix (1. Teil), *SAK* 1 (1974), 179-200.

In order to adduce material to the subject the author deals in this first part with *Pyr. Texts* Spell 263 (W), §§ 337-341, for which he offers a translation with comments on its meaning, metric and on the translation itself. Particularly relevant is the discussion proceeding from the word *ḏsr*, which he suggests to be, like *sḏr*, a causative of *ḏrì*, with metathesis of the sibilant. For this phenomenon he adduces several more examples, such as *sšp — špsì* and *sšm — šmsì*.

In an excursus called "Einige Bemerkungen zur Entwicklungsgeschichte von Nominalbildungstypen" (p. 195-200) the author discusses problems of the formation of nouns in relation to the development of the vocalisation, quoting the study by Osing: Die Nominalbildung des Ägyptischen, Mainz, Verlag Philipp von Zabern, 1976.

74191 FERRON, J., La statuette d'Harpocrate du British Museum, *Revista di Studi Fenici*, Roma 2 (1974), 77-95, with 6 pl.

Study of a Harpokrates statuette in the British Museum (Inv. No. 132908), which is a parallel to that in Madrid published by the author in *Trabajos de Prehistoria*, Madrid 28 (1971), 359-379, with the differences that in the latter instance the Horus child wears the *pshent* and that the former bears an inscription in hieroglyphs beside one in Phoenician characters. For this Phoenician inscription, see Röllig, our number 70464.

The author mainly agrees with Röllig's translation, except for the reading of the name of the engraver, which he reads as NN. He makes some remarks concerning the origin of the veneration of Harpokrates in Egypt as well as in Phoenicia and Carthago and studies the Phoenician writing, concluding that the object dates from the early 5th century B.C. and that it has been made and engraved in Egypt.

FEUCHT, Erika, see our number 74445.

FILIP, Jan, see our number 74486.

74192 FINKENSTAEDT, Elizabeth, The Internal Chronology of Egyptian Predynastic Black-topped Ware, *AJA* 78 (1974), 165.

Report of a lecture.

74193 FISCHER, Henry G., The Ideographic Use of 𓀀 in a Group of Old-Kingdom Names, *JEA* 60 (1974), 247-249, with 1 fig.

Ranke read a name using this writing as Kay-en-nebef and is followed by Moussa and Altenmüller. The writer suggests a variant reading $K3$-$(.i)$-ny-$nb.f$ is more likely.   *E. Uphill*

74194 FISCHER, Henry G., *Nbty* in Old-Kingdom Titles and Names, *JEA* 60 (1974), 94-99, with 3 fig.

The writer discusses six variants in the titulary of the Old-Kingdom queens, and questions Gauthier's reading of *mry* without the *t* as 'beloved'. If, however, this is taken as a masculine participle referring to the king, then the translation would be 'consort of him who is beloved of the Two Ladies'.

E. Uphill

74195 FISCHER, Henry G., Redundant Determinatives in the Old Kingdom, *Metropolitan Museum Journal*, New York 8 (1973), 1974, 7-25, with 22 fig. and 6 ill.

Usually in the Old Kingdom name-determinatives are omitted in the inscriptions, while the statue or two-dimensional representation itself may be regarded as an enlarged determinative. In studying the evidence from statues, reliefs, lintels and architraves the author demonstrates that there is a distinction between masculine and feminine names; the latter usually do have a (redundant) determinative. Names of other people than the tomb-owner also show a tendency to end with determinatives, while the name of the owner may be absent from a statue when placed in his tomb. The custom to omit name-determinatives seems to have been dropped in later ages, though the author is able to mention at least one instance from the XVIIIth Dynasty.

74196 FISCHER, Henry G., Les textes égyptiens du Metropolitan Museum de New York, *Textes et langages III*, 199-202.

The author briefly mentions the texts found during the museum's excavations at Deir el-Bahari, and those on the numerous stelae, reliefs, statues, etc. in the collection. The notes refer to the most important publications.

FISCHER, Henry G., see also our number 74172.

FISHER, R. M., see our number 74541.

74197 FODOR, A., The Solar Bark in a Muhammedan Mi'rāj Text, *Studia Aegyptiaca I*, 83-87.

The solar bark is mentioned in a Turkish text of the 17th century A.D.

74198 FORDE-JOHNSTON, J., History from the Earth. An Introduction to Archaeology, London, Phaidon, 1974 (21 × 24.5 cm; 256 p., 200 ill. and fig., including numerous maps and plans, 16 colour pl., frontispiece).

In this work on archaeology for the general reader ancient Egypt is dealt with on p. 113-128, less than ten pages of text in which the entire Egyptian history from the Predynastic Period to the Ptolemaic Age is sketched, with special sections on domestic architecture and writing.

74199 FOSTER, Herbert J., The Ethnicity of the Ancient Egyptians, *Journal of Black Studies*, Beverly Hills, Calif. 5, No. 2 (December 1974), 175-191.

The author, relating the history of the "Hamitic hypothesis", that is, the theory that the Egyptians were Caucasians as their intellectual superiority proves (sic!) and that the main cultural acquirements of Africa were due to the white race, defends the thesis that the Negro element in the Egyptian population and civilization has been preponderant. He refers only to secondary literature (e.g., Leonard Cottrell!) and nowhere to recent anthropological studies.

74200 FOSTER, John L., Love Songs of the New Kingdom, New York, Charles Scribner's Sons, 1974 (18 × 24.5 cm; 120 p., 14 ill.); rev. *JARCE* 12 (1975), 113-114 (David Lorton). Pr. $ 10

Es wird der Versuch gemacht, in der Sprache moderner amerikanischer Schriftsteller wie Ezra Pound, William Carlos Williams u.a. eine neue Übersetzung der altägyptischen Liebeslieder zu liefern, wobei sich Verf. die Freiheit vorbehält, kleinere Lücken zu ergänzen. Die Lieder finden sich zusammengefaßt unter Überschriften wie: "Some Rather Lively Lines. Songs Inscribed on an Earthern Vessel. Songs of the Garden. Songs of the Great Heart's Ease. Songs from a Faded Papyrus. Stanzaic Love Song. Song of the Orchard. Songs of the Birdcatcher's Daughter". Zugrunde liegen Originale aus Pap. Chester Beatty I Recto und Verso, Ostrakon Kairo 25218, ergänzt durch Ostrakon Dêr el-Medîne 1266, Papyrus Harris 500 und Papyrus Turin 1966. Als Illustration dienen Reproduktionen von Tafeln aus dem Werk von Nina M. Davies und A. H. Gardiner, "Ancient Egyptian Paintings" (Chicago, 1936). *I. Gamer-Wallert*

74201 FOSTER, John L., Ostracon Cairo 25218 augmented by Ostracon Deir el Medineh 1266, *Newsletter ARCE* No. 88 (Winter 1974), 19.

A translation of two lyrics from Ostraca Cairo 25218 and Deir el-Medîneh 1266.
Compare our number 73244. *L. M. J. Zonhoven*

74202 FÓTI, L., Bibliographie des ouvrages de Vilmos Wessetzky, *Studia Aegyptiaca I*, XIV-XX.

The bibliography consists of 120 numbers.

74203 FÓTI, L., Le "Faust Hermétique", *Studia Aegyptiaca I*, 89-96.

Remarks concerning the origin of the alchemic Hermetism and its relation to the motif of Faust.

74204 FÓTI, László, Hermész Trismegistosz a "varázshegy"-ben, *Helikon*, Budapest 20 (1974), 246-257.

"Hermes Trismegistos im 'Zauberberg'".
Für das im ersten Teil des Aufsatzes gesagte, vgl. unsere Nummer 74203.
Im zweiten Teil eine detaillierte Besprechung des gnostisch-hermetischen Dualismus des Zauberbergs von Thomas Mann.
V. Wessetzky

74205 FÓTI, László, Moiris és Ménés, *Idö és történelem*, 53-63.

"Moiris und Menes".

In der Prophetie des Neferti ist der Pharao 'Imnj mit Amenemhat I. zu identifizieren. In der weiteren Geschichte der Dynastie ist die grossartige Regelung des Fayums eng mit Moiris-Amenemhat III. verknüpft. 'Imnj könnte man aber auch mit dem mythischen Namen des Menes identifizieren. Die thebanische Amon-Ideologie hat diesen "südlichen" Aspekt in der Vordergrund gestellt, während im Norden 'Imnj-Menes mit dem Moiris-Amenemhat in Verbindung gebracht wurde.

V. Wessetzky

74206 FÓTI, László, Zur Frage des ägyptischen Labyrinths, *Annales Universitatis Scientiarum Budapestiensis de Rolando Eötvös Nominatae. Sectio historica*, Budapest 15 (1974), 3-15.

The author first translates and discusses various reports about the labyrinth in Egypt by classical writers, stating that there is no ancient Egyptian evidence to it. He then briefly deals with the labyrinth of Minos and the symbolism expressed in it, which is not so much the difficulty to find the way in it, but rather to subdue the monster hiding in a foreign element. For the story of the labyrinth by Diodorus he refers to the end of the story of the *Doomed Prince*. The conclusion is that the mythos of the labyrinth is a late reflection of the activities in the Faiyûm by Amenemhat III : the hero who subdues, with the help of the well-disposed crocodile, the power of the lake. The actual building was certainly the tomb and funerary temple of the king. For other studies about the labyrinth, cfr our numbers 68412 and 70356.

74207 FRANDSEN, Paul John, An Outline of the Late Egyptian Verbal System, Copenhagen, Akademisk Forlag, 1974 (21.5 × 30 cm; XIX + 329 p.). Pr. D.kr. 120

In the Introduction (p. VII-X) the author delimits his source material. Only non-literary, hieratic texts chiefly dating from the end of the 19th Dyn. to the first part of the 21st Dyn. and *Wenamun*, which is a genuine non-literary document, have been included in the investigation (p. VII). Then follows a definition of linguistic terms used in the book (VIII-X). The book is divided into four main sections.

I. Conjugation patterns (1-152). The author first treats the initial conjugation patterns, which are defined as being capable of functioning as initial main sentences and contracting syntagmatic relationship with the converter iw (p. IX in the Introduction). According to their nature as sentence conjugations this group consists of the perfect active $sdm.f$ (1-9), $bwpw.f$ sdm (9-14), the prospective $sdm.f$ (14-26), the perfect passive $sdm.f$ (27-31), the negative aorist (31-38), bw $irt.f$ sdm

(39-41), the third future (41-50), the first present (51-78). Also belonging to the group of initial conjugation patterns are the imperatives (78-84). The second part of this section is made up of the non-initial conjugation patterns, viz., the sentence conjugation *iw.f ḥr sḏm* (84-104) and the clause conjugations "until" (106-108) and preposition + *p3y.f sḏm/p3 sḏm iir.f* (109-112). The conjunctive (112-152) closes this group.
II. The that-form (153-170).
III. *wn/wnn* (171-193).
IV. The converter *iw* (194-224).
After these four main sections follows a Recapitulation, which consists of I. Statements (226-227); II. Conditional Sentences (227-232); III. Temporal Clauses (233-235); IV. Relative Clauses (236-239).
At the end notes, a bibliography, lists of references, and additions and corrections. *Torben Holm-Rasmussen*

74208 FREEMAN, G.E., The Osiris-Shoshenq Hypocephalus, *Newsletter SSEA* 5, No. 2 (December 1974), 4-9, with 6 pl.

Short discussion of a hypocephalus from the collection which Joseph Smith bought in 1835. It appeared to have been restored by Smith for his publication in "Pearl of the Great Price".
For an addition to note 21, see *Newsletter SSEA* 5, No. 3 (February 1975), 5-6.

74209 FREND, W.H.C., The Podium Site at Qaṣr Ibrîm, *JEA* 60 (1974), 30-59, with 12 fig., 2 plans, 1 section and 6 pl.

This structure excavated in 1963-4 has posed a problem as regards its date and purpose. It is a fine mass of sandstone masonry rising 4 m above the surrounding *gebel* and remained unfinished on the west, while being 80 m above the Nile it cannot have served as a quay. The writer describes different occupational levels, and concludes the podium was originally built in the 1st century B.C., being adapted in the Meroitic period and later covered by Christian houses. Three long appendices list the small finds, graffiti and ceramic finds. *E. Uphill*

74210 GAÁL, E., Osiris-Amenophis III in Ugarit (*Nmry.mlk.'lm*), *Studia Aegyptiaca I*, 97-99.

In an Ugaritic text (RS 20.08:9), a list of dieties, *Nmry mlk 'lm* occurs, that is, Amenophis (III) "the king of eternity". For an Egyptian parallel to this deification of the king as Osiris, see our number 73582.

74211 GABALLA, G.A., Two Dignitaries of the XIXth Dynasty, *MDAIK* 30 (1974), 15-24, with 2 pl. and 6 fig.

Publication of a block statue of the famous vizier Paser, found in the Karnak Cachette in 1905 (Cairo JdE No. 38062), and of a statue of the High Priest of Ptah Pahemneter, discovered in 1950 in the ruins of the monastery of St. Jeremias at Sakkara (Cairo JdE No. 89046). *Dieter Mueller*

74212 GABRA, Gawdat, Hemen and Nectanebo I at Moʿalla, *CdE* XLIX, No 98 (1974), 234-237, with 1 fig.

Des fouilles occasionnelles ont mis au jour à Moʿalla un bloc provenant d'un temple consacré par Nectanébo Ier, sur lequel le roi offre Maât au dieu local Hemen. Dans les notes, on trouvera l'essentiel de la bibliographie consacrée à ce dieu.
Ph. Derchain

74213 GAMER-WALLERT, Ingrid, Spanische Ägyptologie, *GM* Heft 13 (1974), 7.

A brief report about the current position of Egyptological studies in Spain. *Dieter Mueller*

74214 GAMER-WALLERT, Ingrid, Die Statue des Harsomtus-em-hat in Madrid (MAN 2014), *Die Welt des Orients*, Göttingen 7 (1973-1974), 195-205, with 3 pl.

Publication of a block statue at present in the National Museum of Madrid (Inv. Nr. 2014). The piece is extensively described, while the texts are given in hieroglyphs and translation. On account of the style the statue is ascribed to the time of Psammetichus I. It holds a systrum and hence may be a temple statue, the original owner being Harsomtus-em-hat, of whom another statue is preserved in Cairo (Cat. gén. 888). The statue may come from Sais, but how it reached first Barcelona (cfr Porter-Moss VII, 420) is obscure.
See also our number 74559.

74215 GARDE-HANSEN, P., On the Building of the Cheops Pyramid, *Ingeniøren* 1/74, Transactions udgivet af Dansk Ingeniørforening [København, 1974] (21 × 29.5 cm; 36 p., 3 ill., 2 fig., 8 tables, 1 map and 5 diagrams); rev. *Antiquity* 49 (1975), 317-318 (I.E.S. Edwards). Pr. D.Kr. 46

The author, who is a civil engineer, states that there can never have been an earthen ramp to the very top of the pyramid, because the quantities of fill for this ramp "proved so enormous that to obtain and transport them would require too much man-power and/or time" (p. 15, calculations on p. 26-29). Instead he visualizes a ramp (made of desert sand and rubbish from quarries on the west side of the Nile) built at the northern side of the pyramid to a height of about 80 m. From this

level upwards the blocks were levered from tier to tier, as described in principle by Herodotus, Book II 125 (p. 18-19). See also our nos. 69345 and 71556.
The book is obtainable from the Danish Technical Press, Skelbaekgade 4, 1717 Copenhagen V, Danmark.
Torben Holm-Rasmussen.

GAUTIER, Achilles, see our number 74798.

74216 GELINSKY, Gerd, Ein heliakischer Frühaufgang bei Abu Simbel, *GM* Heft 9 (1974), 19-24, with 1 ill.

The first rays of the rising sun illuminate the inner chamber of the Great Temple at Abu Simbel on October 20 and February 20. The author concludes that these dates coincided under Ramses II with the first day of the first month of *prt*, and the first day of the first month of *šmw*. *Dieter Mueller*

74217 GEORGE, B., Die Bahn der Sonne am Tage und in der Nacht: altägyptische Sonnenuhren und Königsgräber, *Studia Aegyptiaca I*, 101-116, with 1 fig.

The author argues that a terminology related to sun-dials was reflected by the architectonic plan of the royal tombs, which represented the sun's course, that is, a clock for the course of the sun during the nightly hours. She translates and studies a text from the West side of the ceiling of the Sarcophagus Chamber in the Cenotaph of Sethi I at Abydos, with extensive comments to the technical terms.

74218 GEORGE, Beate, Ein Stockholmer Statuette des Gottes Osiris-Min, *Medelhavsmuseet Bulletin*, Stockholm 9 (1974), 13-18, with 4 fig.

Publication of a steatite Osiris figurine (height 10.5 cm) in the Medelhavsmuseet (NME 401), from the Ptolemaic Period. A badly legible inscription on the base; on the back pillar a frontal representation of Min.
The author studies the relations between Osiris and Min, particularly Min-Kamutef, arguing that Min sometimes replaces Osiris in the triad with Isis and Horus, while in other instances they are represented beside each other (as in this piece) or even in one figure. This may be explained from the conception that the creator-god and the god of the dead are two aspects of the same reality.

74219 GERU, M.A., Het Egyptische dodenboek. In het Nederlands vertaald. Inleiding B. van der Meer. Voorwoord van Edzina A. Rutgers, Deventer, Uitgeverij Ankh-Hermes b.v., [1974] (12.7 × 24.5 cm; 204 p., 2 ill. on endpapers, 26 ill. on 16 pl., 131 fig., colour ill. on cover).

After a Preface and an Introduction (based on translations of Wallis Budge), a short discussion of some terms (*khat* = body, *ka*, *khu*, etc.) and an equally short "Orientation" there follows a Dutch translation of 192 spells, several accompanied by a vignette. It is nowhere clear which copy of the *BD* is used, and the very short bibliography (p. 23) contains no references to recent studies or translations.

van GERVEN, Dennis P., see our number 74118.

74220 GEUS, F. and Y. LABRE, La Nubie au sud de Dal : exploration archéologique et problèmes historiques, *CRIPEL* 2 (1974), 103-123, with 2 maps.

Bericht über die Survey-Unternehmungen der Section Française de Recherche Archéologique du Service des Antiquités du Soudan zwischen Dal und Amara. Die Begehungsplätze ließen sich mehr oder weniger genau anhand der Keramik identifizieren (Khartum-Variante, geriefelte Ware der A-Kultur, Kerma-Ware); die Keramik zwischen dem Ende der ägyptischen Herrschaft in Kusch und der meroitischen Kultur ist am wenigsten bekannt. Waren der X- und der christlichen Kultur sind reich belegt. Zu jeder Periode wird ein kurzer historischer Abriß geboten. *Inge Hofmann*

74221 GHALIOUNGUI, P. et G. WAGNER, Terres cuites de l'Égypte gréco-romaine de la collection P. Ghalioungui, *MDAIK* 30 (1974), 189-198, with 7 pl.

Publication of 30 terracotta figurines from the collection P. Ghalioungui; they are divided into six groups (deities, cripples, grotesque figures, masks, lamps, and vases) and compared to similar pieces published elsewhere. *Dieter Mueller*

GILBERT, Pierre, see our number 74093.

74222 GILLINGS, R.J., The Recto of the Rhind Mathematical Papyrus. How Did the Ancient Egyptian Scribe Prepare It?, *Archive for History of Exact Sciences*, Berlin-Heidelberg-New York 12 (1974), 291-298.

The tables of Pap. Rhind rt. which give the values of 2 divided by the fifty odd numbers from 3 to 101 were needed by the Egyptian scribes because of the constant doubling usual in their arithmetics; doubling of even unit fractions (e.g., $1/18 \times 2$) is obvious, but doubling of the result ($1/9 \times 2$) presents difficulties the tables provided for. The author explains how in his opinion the tables have been constructed.

GILLINGS, Richard J., see also our number 74612.

74223 GILULA, Mordecai, An Offering of 'First Fruits' in Ancient Egypt, *Tel Aviv* 1 (1974), 43-44.

The author points out a parallel to the ancient Hebrew custom of the "offering of first fruits" in Egypt, quoting from the contracts of Hepdjefa with the priest of Wepwawet in Siut.

74224 GILULA, Mordechai, A *tm.n.f sḏm* Sentence?, *JEA* 60 (1974), 249-250.

A good example is yielded for the Middle Kingdom by the *Coffin Texts* and, although perhaps ambiguous, it at least provides the last piece in the jigsaw puzzle of negative structure of Second Tenses. *E. Uphill*

74225 GILULA, Mordechai, עִבְי in Isaiah 28,1 — A Head Ornament, *Tel Aviv* 1 (1974), 128, with 1 ill.

The author argues that עִבְי, "deer, gazelle", in *Is.* 28,1 indicates a head ornament, as worn by Reshef on the stela Brit. Mus. 191.

74226 GITTON, Michel, Ahmose Nefertari, sa vie et son culte posthume, *Annuaire. École Pratique des Hautes Études.* V^e section-sciences religieuses, Paris 82 (1973-1974), fasc. 2, 84.

Abstract of a thesis. Compare now : Michel Gitton, L'épouse du dieu Ahmes Néfertary, Paris, Annales littéraires de l'Université de Besançon, 172. Les belles lettres, 95, 1975 (= Centre de recherches d'histoire ancienne, volume 15).

74227 GITTON, Michel, Le palais de Karnak, *BIFAO* 74 (1974), 63-73, with 2 plans.

The author studies the localization of the *'ḥ' n 'Ipt-Swt* on account of some passages from the coronation text of Hatshepsut written on blocks of the Red Chapel (soon to be published, by Lacau and Chevrier with collaboration of the author). They describe the procession of the bark of Amon along various buildings and through the palace. Gitton argues that this palace was situated North of the lake of that time, that is, North of the present Hypostyle Hall, which corresponds to the place of the Ramesside palaces, and that it was actually inhabited by the queen.

74228 GIVEON, Raphael, Amenophis III in Athribis, *GM* Heft 9 (1974), 25-26, with 3 fig.

Publication of a scarab in the Dayan Collection describing Amenophis III as "loved by Horus-Khentikhety Lord of Athribis". *Dieter Mueller*

74229 GIVEON, Raphael, Determinatives of Canaanite Personal Names and Toponymns in Egyptian, *Actes premier congrès de linguistique sémitique*, 55-59.

The author quotes some Canaanite personal names and toponyms in the hieroglyphic writing where the correct use of the determinatives demonstrates that the Canaanite meaning was understood. The limitations of this knowledge of Canaanite appears from some "false etymologies" and from the use of determinatives which belong to Egyptian "homonyms".

74230 GIVEON, Raphael, Hyksos Scarabs with Names of Kings and Officials from Canaan, *CdE* XLIX, No. 98 (1974), 222-233, with 1 ill. and 2 fig.

En étudiant la répartition des scarabées portant des noms royaux Hyksos et des titulatures de hauts fonctionnaires égyptiens découverts en Palestine, l'auteur arrive à la conclusion que, pendant la Deuxième Période Intermédiaire, l'Égypte a dû continuer à exercer une certaine suzeraineté sur le sud de Canaan, spécialement sur les régions traversées par la route côtière, ainsi que les villes de Jéricho et Megiddo. Ainsi s'expliqueraient aussi les faibles difficultés de la 18e Dynastie au début de son règne dans ce pays où les oppositions que rencontra Thouthmosis III avaient toutes été fomentées par des adversaires dont la puissance était en fait située plus au nord.

Ph. Derchain

74231 GIVEON, Raphael, Investigations in the Egyptian Mining Centres in Sinai. Preliminary Report, *Tel Aviv* 1 (1974), 100-108, with 2 pl.

The author describes the clearing works executed at the temple of Serabît el-Khâdem and the preparation of a corpus of inscriptions. Some inscriptions were discovered which had not been seen by Černý and only collated by him from photographs, while others have even been unknown to him. No new royal names have turned up, but four representations of Hathor as a cow have been found, two of them indicating the animal between papyrus which proves her to be an Egyptian goddess. The article publishes 4 texts: inscription 71.122, a funerary text from the New Kingdom; inscription 68 A Ia, with a secondary text mentioning two charioteers (XIXth or XXth Dynasty); relief Z 247, with part of a purification scene; stela 71.93 from the time of Tuthmosis III, i.a. mentioning the high official Sennufer.

74232 GIVEON, Raphael, A Monogram Scarab from Tel Masos, *Tel Aviv* 1 (1974), 75-76, with 1 ill.

The author discusses a scarab found during the recent excavations at Tell Masos (for the excavations themselves, see the preceding article), depicting a pharaoh slaying a prisoner and accompanied by the signs *rʿ* and *ḫpr*. He proposes to read the name as *Wsr-ḫpr(w)-Rʿ* (= Sethy II), reading the figure as *wsr*, for which he quotes some parallels.

74233 GIVEON, Raphael, The Scarabs from Ginosar, *ʿAtiqot*, Hebrew Series, Jerusalem 7 (1974), 40-42, with 1 fig. and 1 pl., and an English summary.

A group of 12 Egyptian scarabs is described. Six of them come from the excavation proper, the others from the debris near the burial caves. All of them are of well-known types of the Hyksos Period. Two scarabs with plain bases are made of amethyst.
Author's own summary

74234 GIVEON, Raphael, A Second Relief of Sekhemkhet in Sinai, *BASOR* Nr. 216 (December, 1974), 17-20, with 2 ill.

Publication of a second, rediscovered relief of Sekhemkhet in the Wâdi Maghâra, very similar to Sinai Inscr. No. 1 and situated some 35 m North of it. The title of the officer in front of the royal figures (here at a lower level too) is slightly different, ending on *ḥtm nswt*, which hence may have to be restored in the middle of Inscr. No. 1b. The relief is unfinished and of inferior quality to No. 1.

74235 GIVEON, Raphael, עקבות פרעה בכנען. מאמרים על קשדי ארץ־ ישראל ומצרים העתיקה, תל אביב, הוצאת המדור לידיעה הארץ בתנועה הקיבוצית, [1974] (16.5 × 23.5 cm; 188 p., numerous fig. and ill. including plans, colour ill. on cover).

"Footsteps of the Pharaohs in Canaan. (Essays on the Relations between the Land of Israel and Ancient Egypt)".
A collection of articles, partly translations of those published elsewhere between 1961 and 1973 and recorded in our volumes (our Nos 62223; 63185; 64176-'177; 65199-'200; 67217-'220; 69207; 71205; 71208; 72254).
Some articles have especially been written for this volume, e.g. the introduction on the history of the relations between Israel and Egypt in Antiquity; chapter 9 on Serabît el Khâdim, a description of the Hathor temple, its discovery and its inscriptions; chapter 11 on scarabs, mainly dealing with pieces found in Palestine; chapter 17 on a seal of Isebel with Egyptian motifs.
For more extensive abstracts, see J. Agam, *GM* Heft 18 (1975), 51-55.

74236 GIVEON, Raphael, ツナイの石は語る, 東京都, 學生社, 昭和 49 年 [= 1974] (14.8 × 21.8 cm; 212 p., 2 maps, 5 plans, 41 ill. [1 colour ill. on cover]). Series: 歴史・考古学翻訳ツリーズ.
Pr. 1400 yen

"The Stones of Sinai Speak". Not seen.

74237 GIVEON, R. and A. GOREN, תבליט מצרי מימי הממלכה הקדומה בדרום ־סיני, *Qadmoniot*, Jerusalem 7, Nos. 3-4 (27-28) (1974), 98-101, with 1 map and 3 ill.

"An Egyptian Old Kingdom Relief in Southern Sinai".

74238 GODRON, Gérard, L'Elephantine-du-Sud, *CdE* XLIX, No 98 (1974), 238-253, with 1 map.

L'auteur ayant réuni 19 mentions du toponyme "Eléphantine du Sud" (*3bw rsyt*) examine les diverses tentatives de localisation qui en ont été faites et opte finalement pour Faras qui, dans l'antiquité, était une île comme l'Éléphantine par rapport à laquelle elle est nommée.   *Ph. Derchain*

74239 GOEDICKE, Hans, The Berlin Leather Roll (P Berlin 3029), *Festschrift Ägyptisches Museum Berlin*, 87-104, with 2 pl.

The Berlin Leather Roll, previously discussed by de Buck (*Studia Aegyptiaca* I = *Analecta Orientalia* 17, Roma, 1939, 48-57), is here studied anew. The author offers a new translation with extensive commentaries, while a photograph is published on the plates. The main conclusions (p. 103-104) are: the text was formulated after Sesostris I became sole regent, though describing an event of the early years of his coregency, clearly in order to claim exclusively the credit for the building up for Atum in Heliopolis. The literary qualities suggest a talented writer to be the author, the style, quoting several maxims and adages, being that of the later "Königsnovelle". As for the author Goedicke suggests the name Khety, so well known from that period.

74240 GOEDICKE, Hans, Die Geschichte des Schiffbrüchigen, Wiesbaden, Otto Harrassowitz, 1974 (17.5 × 25 cm; XII + 92 p.) = Ägyptologische Abhandlungen herausgegeben von Wolfgang Helck und Eberhard Otto, 30; rev. *BiOr* 33 (1976), 16-17 (Jesus Lopez).   Pr. DM 44

The study on the *Story of the Shipwrecked Sailor* mainly consists of a new translation with extensive comments in which the author defends his — partly new — renderings. For the sake of surveyability the author has divided up the story into 18 passages, dealing with each of them in a separate section.
The last section (p. 72-90) contains a summary. After presenting

once more the — now continuous — translation the author argues that the story is not a fairy tale but a moralistic treatise, the narrative merely being a means to express the intention of its author, who may perhaps be the famous Khety. The homeward bound journey is a metaphor for death. In the frame-story two human types are contrasted: the frightened, earth-bound, uncertain man against the man wise by experience. In order to defend this conception of the story Goedicke points at a large number of what he argues to be symbols, e.g.: the sea means life; the shipwreck is a metaphor for misfortune (*dpt*, "ship" — *dp*, "experience"); the snake symbolizes the immanent sphere, as against the transcendent whence the destruction has come, etc.

Index of Egyptian words on p. 91-92.

74241 GOEDICKE, Hans, The Inverted Water, *GM* Heft 10 (1974), 13-17.

Continuing the discussion of the meaning of *p3 ym '3 n mw qd* (see our Nos 73344 and 73720), the author proposes an entirely new solution: *mw pf qdw ḥdd m ḫnty* in *Urk*. IV 85, 14 is to be understood as "that water which turned the one sailing north into one sailing south", and refers to the Nubian defeat at the hands of Thutmose I near the Second Cataract. *P3 ym '3 n mw qd*, on the other hand, has a parallel in *p3 ym '3 n H3rw* (*Wenamun* 1,8), and means "the great sea of *Mw qd*" (prob. the Arabian Peninsula). The two occurrences of *mw qd* are therefore not connected, and neither refers to the Euphrates river or the Persian Gulf.

See also our No. 74585. *Dieter Mueller*

74242 GOEDICKE, Hans, Some Remarks Concerning the Inscription of Ahmose, Son of Ebana, *JARCE* 11 (1974), 31-41.

The following passages are discussed and re-interpreted: 1. *Urkunden IV*, 2,5-6 (p. 31-33; "the brave one rejoiced [*iw rn.n. kn*] about [*n*] what was done to him without ceasing in this country eternally"); 2. *Urk. IV*, 2,12-16 (33-35; "I commenced to act as a soldier — to replace him in the fleet — of (the ship) 'The Killer' while I was a lad, before I had taken a wife; I (always) spent the night at dressing the ropes"); 3. *Urk. IV*, 3,2-8 (35-37; a reconsideration of the interrelationship of the sentences); 4. *Urk. IV*, 3,9-11 (37-39; "and then I was selected for [the journey to/for] the coronation at Memphis. Then one fought on the water on that [water] called 'the other water of Avaris'"); 5. *Urk. IV*, 4,4-8 (39-40; "and then I brought in a life-prisoner — namely a man whom I attacked to that water; lo, he was brought in as a capture on that side of the water when I had crossed over the water with him — who was reported to the royal herald"); 6. *Urk. IV*, 4,14 (there is no implication of a continuous siege of Sharuhen).

J.F. Borghouts

74243 GOEDICKE, Hans, Zum Papyrus Berlin 9010, *ZÄS* 101 (1974), 90-95.

Neubearbeitung des im Titel erwähnten Textes aus dem Alten Reich. Sethe hat ihn *ZÄS* 61 (1926), 67-79, als Prozessurteil betrachtet. Goedicke bezeichnet ihn als Klageerwiderung und entwickelt neue Einsichten für das Erbrecht.

M. Heerma van Voss

74244 GÖRG, M., Die Gattung des sogenannten Tempelweihespruchs (1 Kg 8, 12f), *Ugarit-Forschungen*, Kevelaer/Neukirchen-Vluyn 6 (1974), 55-63.

The author draws a parallel between the poetic words of *I Kings* 8, 12-13 and Egyptian texts, namely the sun hymn of the architects Suty and Hor, and some passages from the Papyrus Harris I.

74245 GÖRG, Manfred, *mrk* (Wb II, 113) = kan. *mlg?*, *GM* Heft 13 (1974), 13-15.

The Semitic loanword *mrk*, translated by W. Helck as "royal gift", is probably derived from Akk. *mulūgu*, Ugaritic *mlg*, Aram. *mlwg* "a kind of dowry". *Dieter Mueller*

74246 GÖRG, Manfred, Untersuchungen zur hieroglyphischen Wiedergabe palästinischer Ortsnamen, Bonn, Selbstverlag des Orientalischen Seminars der Universität, 1974 (14.8 × 20.7 cm; [VII +]226 p., 3 pl.) = Bonner Orientalistische Studien, Neue Serie. Herausgegeben von Otto Spies, 29. Pr. DM 14

This study investigates the way in which Palestinian geographical names are rendered in Egyptian hieroglyphic writing. Since many of them have been written in the syllabic orthography the study contributes to the evaluation of the correctness and range of the usual interpretation of its vocalization. Moreover, the author has attempted to localize the places.
All together 19 names are studied. Apart from extensive geographical discussions the author makes remarks as to the vocalization, though a summary of his results is not given. See, however, the index of hieroglyphic signs and sign-groups on p. 211-214. In some excurses details are dealt with.

74247 GÖRG, M., Zum 'Skorpionenpass' (Num. XXXIV 4; Jos. XV 3), *Vetus Testamentum*, Leiden 24 (1974), 508-509.

The name from Edel's "Ortsnamenlisten" (our number 66181) B_N li. 11, *'qrb(w)t*, "Scorpion pass", may be the same name as *mqrp(w)t* in Šimon's "Handbook", I, 94. The error *m* for ʿ is to be explained from a hieratic model, since a Sem. *mem* can be written (wrongly) as an Eg. ʿ*ayin*.

74248 GÖRG, Manfred, Zur Valenz der Gruppe 𓏭𓇋, *GM* Heft 10 (1974) 19-20.

The author contests the proposed reading *la*₂, and suggests that the group may represent a double *n* as in cuneiform *ḫa-lu-un-ni*.
Dieter Mueller

74249 GÖRG, Manfred, Zur Zeichenkombination *jjj* in MR, *GM* Heft *11* (1974), 23-24.

The double and triple reed at the end of non-Egyptian names may be the result of a wrong transcription of hieratic *tỉ* or *ty*; hence *m(ʿ)kyy* = *mkty* "Megiddo". Dieter Mueller

74250 GOLTZ, Dietlinde, Studien zur altorientalischen und griechischen Heilkunde. Therapie—Arzneibereitung—Rezeptstruktur, Wiesbaden, Franz Steiner Verlag, 1974 (16.5 × 24 cm; XIV + 352 p.) = Sudhoffs Archiv. Zeitschrift für Wissenschaftsgeschichte. Beiheft, 16. Pr. DM 80

Although mainly devoted to Babylonian and Greek medicine, particularly pharmacotherapy, and their relations, a few sections deal with Egyptian medicine. On p. 247-251 remarks to the Egyptian receipt literature and its relation to its Babylonian and Greek counterparts. In the next section the author argues that at present nothing is known about Egyptian influence on Babylonian medicine or the reverse; influence on Greece is very probable but difficult to establish. On p. 278-280 the author compares Greek and Egyptian conceptions of disease, which may demonstrate a fundamental similarity.

74251 GOMAÀ, Farouk, Die libyschen Fürstentümer des Deltas vom Tod Osorkons II. bis zur Wiedervereinigung Ägyptens durch Psametik I., Wiesbaden, Dr. Ludwig Reichert Verlag, 1974 (17 × 24 cm; [X +]173 p.) = Beihefte zum Tübinger Atlas des Vorderen Orients. Reihe B (Geisteswissenschaften), Nr. 6; rev. *JEA* 61 (1975), 272-273 (K.A. Kitchen); *Welt des Orients* 8 (1975-1976), 325-326 (Erik Hornung). Pr. DM 24

The author discusses the history of the Delta in the second half of the Third Intermediate Period, from the death of Osorkon II (866/861 B.C.) to the beginning of the XXVIth Dynasty. The study will serve as basis for drawing a historical map of the area as part of the Tübinger Atlas but does not contain itself even a provisional map.

The material is divided into an introduction and six chapters. In the Introduction (chapter 1) the author presents a survey of the history of the Libyans in Egypt and mentions the main Egyptological literature, particularly the studies of Yoyotte (our number 61770) and Kitchen (our number 73405). It appears that in details Gomaà's reconstruction differs from that of the latter scholar.

Chapter 2 is devoted to the rulers of Memphis, first the dynasty of the Great Chiefs of the Mashwash from Sheshonq (D, according to Kitchen) to Harsiese (H), and then the later rulers, e.g. Tefnakht, the Kushite kings, and the Assyrians.

Chapter 3 discusses the Libyan princes in the Western Delta, first those of the region West of Rosetta (see the list on p. 35-36), than those East of it, and in the third section prince (later king) Tefnakht, his territory and his successors.

In chapter 4 the princedoms of the Middle Delta are dealt with: Busiris, Sebennytos and Mendes. The first two mainly from the conquest by Piye (Piankhi), since before that time little is known about them, while from Mendes we know under Sheshonq III the family of Hornakht and Smendes, the chronology of which the author attempts to reconstruct.

Chapter 5 is devoted to the Eastern Delta, first during the period before the XXVth Dynasty, then the princes of *Ḥsb*/Pharbaitos, of *Pr-Spdw*/Saft el-Hinna, and other princes. In chapter 6 the royal cities of the Delta are discussed: Leontopolis and the kingdom of Iuput II, Bubastis and the kingdom of Osorkon IV, and Tanis. The last chapter deals with the princes of Athribis and Heliopolis (see the list on p. 160-161).

Indexes on p. 165-173.

74252 GORDON, Cyrus H., "He Is Who He Is", *Berytus*, Beirut 23 (1974), 27-28.

The author discusses the Divine Name of *Ex.* 3,14, comparing with it the words of *Wenamun* 2,27-28 of which he only quotes *p3 nty wnw.f*, translating "The One Who Is Who He Is".

GOREN, A., see our number 74237.

74253 GOUDSMIT, S.A., An Illiterate Scribe, *AJA* 78 (1974), 78, with 1 pl.

Publication of a Late Period papyrus fragment with the text of the twelfth division of the *Book of Amduat* from which the author argues that the scribe was illiterate. Although the cols. of the text are to be read from left to right the scribe placed signs which he could not fit in at the bottom of a col. at top of the col. at the left instead of the right.

74254 GOYON, Georges, Kerkasôre et l'ancien observatoire d'Eudoxe, *BIFAO* 74 (1974), 135-147, with 1 map and 1 fig.

The author argues that Kerkasōre (*grg Wsr*), mentioned by some classical authors, is Ausîm/el-Zeidîya (Letopolis), where a Tower of Cheops (a sun-temple) had already been used as orientation-point for the building of the Great Pyramid. It was used in pharaonic times as observatory, and again by Eudoxus in 360 B.C.

74255 GOYON, Jean-Claude, Confirmation du pouvoir royal au nouvel an. [Brooklyn Museum 47.218.50]. Planches, The Brooklyn Museum et L'Institut français d'Archéologie orientale, 1974 (30 × 40.5 cm; III p., 15 double pl. containing photographs and hieroglyphic transcriptions) = Wilbour Monographs, 7; rev. *Aegyptus* 56 (1976), 300-301 (S. Curto); *Studia Aegyptiaca* 2 (1974), 215-218 (L. Kákosy). Pr. $ 5

Plate volume to our number 72269. After a foreword by Bernard V. Bothmer, the texts are presented in photograph, with the hieroglyphic transcriptions on the opposite page.

L.M.J. Zonhoven

74256 GOYON, Jean-Claude, La littérature funéraire tardive, *Textes et langages III*, 73-81.

The discussion of the funerary texts from the Late Period first mentions some major texts written in Demotic or in hieratic or hieroglyphs. The author then deals with some separate texts, e.g. the *Books of Respirations*, the bilingual Pap. Rhind I and II, and various rituals, particularly the four *S3ḥw* or Books of the *"Glorifications" of Osiris*. Many publications, recent as well as older ones, are mentioned in the notes.

74257 GOYON, Jean-Claude, Sur une formule des rituels de conjuration des dangers de l'année. En marge du papyrus de Brooklyn 47.218.50. II, *BIFAO* 74 (1974), 75-83.

Sequel to our number 71216.
In two passages of the ceremony described in the papyrus a refrain is mentioned with the words *Ḥr sp sn.nw w3d n Sḫmt ḥ3 iwf n Pr-'3 tm n 'nḫ*, "Horus, Horus, offshoot of Sekhmet, is behind the flesh of Pharaoh in the fullness of life". The formula is characteristic for prophylactic texts, from which the author lists 27 occurrences of these words, dating from the New Kingdom to Ptolemaic temples. They attempt to conjure a harmful intervention of the Eye of Re by assimilating the king with the son of Sekhmet, who alone is able to escape the fury of his mother.

74258 GOYON, J.-Cl., La véritable attribution des soi-disant chapitres 191 et 192 du livre des morts, *Studia Aegyptiaca* I, 117-127, with 2 p. of hieroglyphic text.

The author establishes that the so-called supplementary chapters 191 and 192 of the *Book of the Dead* found by Allen are actually extracts (§§ XV and VII) from an Osiris ritual which is still partly unpublished (see our number 70524) and from which a large number of copies are known (see the list on p. 120-121).

74259 GOYON, J.-Cl. et H. el-ACHIRIE, Le Ramesseum. VI. La salle des litanies (R), Le Caire, Centre de documentation et d'études sur l'ancienne Égypte, 1974 (21 × 27 cm; portefolio containing XIV + 48 loose p., 29 loose pl. [14 folding] with plan, drawings and photographs, frontispiece). At head of title: Collection scientifique.

Sequel to our number 73274.
This second volume that is published in the series on the Ramesseum consists of two parts: a description of the architecture of the "Room of the Litanies" (*PM* II², 441: "Inner Room") by el-Achirie, and of the scenes and texts by Goyon. Hieroglyphic copies of the texts on p. 21-39.
In the preface, by Dr. Moukhtar and Mme Desroches, there is i.a. stated that not a single proof has been found for the suggestion that this and the adjoining "Astronomical Room" held the library of the temple.
Index to the titles of the scenes on p. 40, concordances between texts, description and plates on p. 41-42.

GOYON, Jean-Claude, see also our number 74094.

74260 GRAEFE, Erhart, Nachtrag zum Index: P. MUNRO, Die spätägyptischen Totenstelen, in GM 5, 1973, S. 47 ff., *GM* Heft 10 (1974), 58.
An addition to our No. 73277.   *Dieter Mueller*

74261 GRAEFE, Erhart, Eine neue Schenkungsstele aus der 22. Dynastie, *Armant*, Köln 12 (1974), 3-9, with 2 pl.

Publication of a donation stela in a private collection at Cologne, of which the upper half with the representation and part of the first two lines are lost. The text is dated to a year 4 of a Shoshenq, who may be Shoshenq III, IV or V, and mentions a donation of 100 *arourai* by a *Nmrd-pd* to his daughter.
In an appendix the author presents corrections and additions to Schulman's list of donation stelae (our number 66537; cfr also 70316).

74262 GRAEFE, Erhart, Die vermeintliche unterägyptische Herkunft des Ibi, Obermajordomus der Nitokris, *SAK* 1 (1974), 201-206.

It has been suggested that Ibi, great steward of the God's Wife of Amon Nitokris, came from the Delta, but he himself states on the lid of his sarcophagus to have been born at Thebes.

Whether his father's title *mrì nṯr* points at the surroundings of the king is uncertain. In general there is no proof that Psammetichus I did not appoint to the offices his partisans from Upper Egypt.

74263 GRAEFE, Erhart, Zwei Konkordanzen zur Identifizierung von Gegenständen des Leidener Museums, *GM* Heft 10 (1974), 49-57.

A synoptic table of the Egyptian antiquities in the Leiden museum published in the *Beschreibung der aegyptischen Sammlung des Niederländischen Reichsmuseums der Altertümer in Leiden* and the *Description raisonnée des monumens égyptiens du Musée d'Antiquités des Pays-Bas, à Leide*.   Dieter Mueller

74264 GRANT, Michael, Mittelmeerkulturen in der Antike, München, C. H. Beck, 1974 (15 × 23 cm; XII + 354 p.); rev. *Antike Welt* 6, Heft I (1975), 55 (anonymous).   Pr. cloth DM 29.50

Deutsche Übersetzung unserer Nr. 69220. S. 40 - 62 (2. Kapitel) beschäftigt sich mit Ägypten.   Inge Hofmann

74265 GRATIEN, Brigitte, Les Nécropoles Kerma de l'Ile de Saï. II, *CRIPEL* 2 (1974), 51-74, with 1 map, 18 ill. and 3 fig.

Fortsetzung unserer Nr. 73279.
Es werden drei Ausgrabungsstellen (SKC2b, SKC3, SKC4) des großen Kerma-Friedhofes von Sai beschrieben. SKC2b ist vom klassischen Typ mit großen Tumuli, die Gräber von SKC4 erinnern mehr an diejenigen der Pfannengräber-Kultur, während SKC3 einen ganz neuen Typ zeigt. Die Keramik, die aus den Gräbern dieses Typs stammt, hat Beziehungen zu der der A-, C- und Kerma-Kultur; sie gehört einer bisher nicht bekannten Gruppe an, die der Kerma-Kultur voranging. Anklänge an den C-Gruppen-Friedhof von Faras sind vorhanden.

Inge Hofmann

74266 GREEN, Alberto Ravinel Whitney, The Role of Human Sacrifice in the Ancient Near East, *Dissertation Abstracts International A*, Ann Arbor, Mich. 34, No. 4 (October 1973), 1799-A.

Abstract of a doctor's thesis University of Michigan, 1973 (Order No. 73-24,575; 407 p.).
In Egypt the ritual of human sacrifice assumed three forms. 1. The murder of attendants at the passing of an important person. 2. The sacrifice of captive kings or princes at the accession of certain pharaohs. 3. The sacrificial offering of foreigners and animals to Egyptian deities at the mortuary cult of some members of the Egyptian nobility.

L.M.J. Zonhoven

74267 GRIESHAMMER, Reinhard, Die altägyptischen Sargtexte in der Forschung seit 1936. Bibliographie zu de Bucks The Egyptian Coffin Texts I-VII, Wiesbaden, Otto Harrassowitz, 1974 (21.5 × 30.7 cm; [VI+]179 p., 1 folded table) = Ägyptologische Abhandlungen, 28; rev. *BiOr* 32 (1975), 353 (Dieter Mueller); *JEA* 61 (1975), 283 (C.H.S. Spaull); *Mundus* 11 (1975), 110-111 (Waltraud Guglielmi); *ZDMG* 126 (1976), 192 (J. v. B[eckerath]). Pr. DM 56

This is a bibliography to publications about the *Coffin Texts*, listing them after the order in which the texts occur in de Buck's publication. It appears that there is at least one reference to the majority of the lines. A folded table at the end enables a quick consultation.
On p. 171-179 some references to the earlier publication of the *Coffin Texts* by Lacau, and some additions from recent studies. Compare also the "Index des Citations" by Claude Crozier-Brelot (our number 72161).

74268 GRIESHAMMER, Reinhard, Die Sammlung des Ägyptologischen Institutes, *Ruperto Carola*, Heidelberg 33 (1974), 35-38, with 2 ill.

A brief description of the Egyptian collection of the Egyptological Institute of the Heidelberg University. *Dieter Mueller*

74269 GRIESHAMMER, Reinhard, Zum "Sitz im Leben" des negativen Sündenbekenntnisses, *XVIII. Deutscher Orientalistentag*, 19-25.

The so-called Negative Confession familiar from *BD* Chapter 125 has parallels in Ptolemaic inscriptions regulating admission to the temples, in a Greek papyrus containing the oath sworn by candidates entering the priesthood, and in some Old Testament texts. There is good reason to believe that the *BD* version is derived from texts of this type, and was incorporated into Chapter 125 after it had been adapted to serve a funerary purpose (compare our Nos 68404 and 69412).
Dieter Mueller

74270 [GRIFFITHS, John Gwyn], Editorial Foreword, *JEA* 60 (1974), 1-4.

The Editorial Foreword contains short notes on the excavation seasons at Saqqara, by H.S. Smith and Geoffrey T. Martin, that at Qasr Ibrim, by J. Martin Plumley, and short obituary notices of John W.B. Barns by Hugh Lloyd-Jones, of Bryan Haycock by M.F. Laming Macadam, and of Jacques Vandier by I.E.S. Edwards.

74271 GRIFFITHS, J. Gwyn, The Egyptian Antecedents of the Isidis Navigium, *Studia Aegyptiaca I*, 129-136.

The rite of dedicating and launching the Ship of Isis, as described by Apuleius (*Metam.* XI, ch. 5), usually thought to be of Greek origin, may have been derived from various Egyptian religious conceptions, e.g. the ship of Osiris and Isis and the boat of Isis where she replaces Hathor.

GROSSMANN, Peter, see our number 74367.

74272 GUGLIELMI, Waltraud, Die Feldgöttin *Sḫ.t*, *Die Welt des Orients*, Göttingen 7 (1973-1974), 206-227, with 4 fig. and 1 pl.

Studying the field-goddess *Sḫt*, who was mentioned throughout the Egyptian history from the *Pyr. Texts* to the Greco-Roman Period, the author first states that she never was a goddess in the fullest sense, one who was "all in the act of worship" for the worshippers, and that she never had a cult.
There follows an extensive discussion of the name and the nature of the diety, her functions, i.a. as a mistress of fishing and fowling, her relations to other gods, her role in the hunt of the hippopotamus. From the XVIIIth Dynasty onwards she appears in the procession of the Nile-gods, frequently represented on temple walls since the XIXth Dynasty, but she also remained a field-goddess down to the Late Period.

74273 GURALNICK, Eleanor, The Chrysapha Relief and its Connections with Egyptian Art, *JEA* 60 (1974), 175-188, with 2 pl.

This archaic relief found in Laconia in 1877 is of blue-grey marble and 87 cm high. It is assumed to depict a dead husband and wife with two small worshippers bringing offerings. It is probable that it should be dated to c. 560 B.C. Egyptian influence is here discussed, especially with reference to the snake, mourning veil, cup, pomegranate, lotus, hen and egg, all funerary themes, and examples from Egyptian tomb scenes, papyri and temple reliefs are cited. The bearded snake and its link with the protection and resurrection of Osiris are significant, and literary references are included to show that both Greece and Egypt had separate traditions regarding the serpent as a chthonic deity. Thus the relief is not merely an imitation but a modification in some respects. *E. Uphill*

74274 GUTBUB, Adolphe, Kom Ombo: les textes et leur étude, *Textes et langages III*, 239-247.

After describing Champollion's work on the temple of Kom Ombo the author discusses a large number of recent publications devoted to various aspects, geography, history and epigraphy, as found in its texts. He mentions his own preparations to a complete edition. The last section deals with studies based on the texts : their epigraphy, their contents, the cult, gods, myths and theology of Kom Ombo.

74275 HABACHI, Labib, Aménophis III et Amenhotep, fils de Hapou, à Athribis, *RdE* 26 (1974), 21-33, with 1 fig. and 2 pl.

L'auteur réunit les documents qui évoquent les relations d'Amenhotep, fils de Hapou, avec Athribis, où il était resté titulaire d'un sacerdoce et montre que ce personnage, quoiqu'on en ait dit, n'a jamais fait de carrière militaire, car les allusions qu'on avait cru y trouver reposent sur de fausses attributions. Il réexamine également le bloc fameux où l'on a voulu voir la preuve d'une corégence d'Aménophis III et d'Aménophis IV, découvert à Athribis et montre qu'il n'y a aucune raison d'y restituer les noms des deux rois, mais qu'il s'agit d'un fragment de frise où les cartouches d'Aménophis III alternaient.

Ph. Derchain

74276 HABACHI, Labib, A High Inundation in the Temple of Amenre at Karnak in the Thirteenth Dynasty, *SAK* 1 (1974), 207-214, with 2 pl. and 3 fig.

Publication of a fragmentary stela of king Sekhemre Seusertaui Sebekhotep (VIII), of the XIIIth Dynasty, extracted from the Third Pylon in Karnak. The text is dated to the epagomenal days of the year 4 and mentions a high inundation ($\bar{H}py$ '3 or *wr*) which flooded the temple, or at least its hall (*wsḫt*). Compare our number 74046.

74277 HABACHI, Labib, Lids of the Outer Sarcophagi of Merytamen and Nefertari, Wives of Ramesses II, *Festschrift Ägyptisches Museum Berlin*, 105-112, with 3 pl. and 3 fig. (2 folded).

The author, in clearing Theban Tomb No. 271, has found a fragment of the lid belonging to the outer sarcophagus of Queen Merytamon, a large part of which is preserved in the Berlin collection (Inv. no. 15274). Both parts are here published, together with surviving portions of the outer sarcophagus of Queen Nefertari, now in Turin, which bears a similar decoration. The author translates the texts and makes remarks on the lives of their original owners.

74278 HABACHI, Labib, Psammétique II dans la région de la première cataracte, *Oriens Antiquus* 13 (1974), 317-326, with 4 fig. and 2 pl.

Two of the rock inscriptions from the Saite Dynasty, both of Psammetichus II and located on Elephantine, are here published (pl. 19). More important is the stela found at el-Shallâl (see our number 67047), to which the upper part of a stela already known to Lepsius and now in Cairo (pl. 20 a) is a parallel. The author discusses why these stelae, mentioning the campaign of year 3, have been erected at such a lonely place. Referring to other stelae put up at the beginning of desert roads (compare our number 68065) he suggests that it was the beginning of the route of the Nubian expedition.

At the end publication and discussion of a block from Edfu also referring to a Nubian campaign of a Psammetichus, who may be the first ruler of that name.

74279 HABACHI, Labib, Sethos I's Devotion to Seth and Avaris, *ZÄS* 100,2 (1974), 95-102, with 3 fig. and 2 pl.

The author re-publishes a quartzite stand for a sacred bark, dedicated to Seth and now in the Vienna Museum. It was erected by Sethos I in Avaris, in the area of Khatâ'na-Qantîr.
This king constructed a palace in the same district. From it came beautiful tiles in blue "faience" decorating lintels and jambs, at present in the Louvre and shown on a plate. Labib Habachi points out that the city was of importance before the Hyksos reign and still long after it. At the end of the Ramesside Period Avaris-Piramesses became a cursed town, and the capital was removed to Tanis - San el-Hagar. *M. Heerma van Voss*

74280 HABACHI, Labib, Three Large Rock-Stelae Carved by Ramesses III near Quarries, *JARCE* 11 (1974), 69-75, with 7 pl.

The following stelae in Middle and Lower Egypt locations are treated and translated: 1. at El-Babein (El-Sirîrîya in Porter-Moss, *Topographical Bibliography* IV, 126): the king with Sobk, lord of *S3* and the local Hathor (*nb.t 'ḥ.wy*). 2. At Tihna (Porter-Moss IV, 131 (3)): the king with Sobk, lord of *Š3n3* (= *'Inš(n)*?) and Amun *m3wt-ḥnt*. For the latter epithet, a translation is proposed which differs from the usual one: 'Amun of the Island of front'. 3. At Khâzındârîya (not mentioned as such in Porter-Moss V, 16): the king with Seth and *'nty-wy*, the lords of *Tbw*. Such large rock-stelae were carved near quarries wherefrom the stone was extracted for building activities in the local temples. Some of the gods associated with the locations are found in contemporary documents, like the Pap. Harris I. *J.F. Borghouts*

74281 HABACHI, Labib, Three Objects of Unusual Form, *Studia Aegyptiaca* I, 137-150, with 4 fig. and 5 ill.

The three objects here published are: 1. a red granite oblong plate (15.5 × 13 cm) with a figure of Amenophis II in high relief, surrounded by a bird (the head is lost). The object was preserved in the storeroom of the Luxor temple.

2. A small limestone dyad with roughly made figures of Amon and Mut, found in the Taharqa temple at Karnak and according to an inscription dedicated by a priest of Khnum called Neferronpet, possibly a man from the Cataract Region who visited Thebes in the Ramesside Period.

3. A cone-shaped bust (Hildesheim) with a text in which its owner is called chief steward at Memphis Ramesses-sma-khaset and unusual epithets of Ptah are mentioned. The text is translated, with commentary.

74282 HAENY, Gerhard, [Ägyptologie. Ein offener Brief], *GM* Heft 9 (1974), 53-62.

A passionate appeal to re-examine critically the operation of modern Egyptology. *Dieter Mueller*

HAENY, Gerhard, see also our number 74367.

HAEVERNICK, Thea Elisabeth, see our number 74632.

HAMPL, Franz, see our number 74006.

74283 HANEVELD, G. T., An Egyptian Mummy of the New Kingdom with an Ulceration of the Leg, *Archivum Chirurgicum Neerlandicum*, Wageningen 26 (1974), 103-107, with 4 ill.

Report of the examination of a well-preserved foot of a mummy from the New Kingdom which shows ulceration of the leg, possibly due to saphenous incompetence.

74284 HANKEY, Vronwy, A Late Bronze Age Temple at Amman : II. Vases and Objects Made of Stone, *Levant*, London 6 (1974), 160-178, with 2 plans, 1 table, 3 fig. containing drawings, and 6 pl.

In this second part of his report on the objects from the Late Bronze Age temple at Amman (part I, on p 131-159, deals with the Aegean pottery) the author describes in the catalogue two Predynastic Egyptian vessels, three from the XIIth Dynasty, and 38 from the XVIIIth Dynasty. Extensive notes on materials, manufacture, etc. precede the catalogue.

74285 HANKEY, Vronwy, Turmoil in the Near East, c. 1200 B.C., *Asian Affairs*, London 61 (1974), 51-59, with 1 map and 5 fig.

The author gives a survey of the facts known about the migrations of the Sea Peoples, stressing that the exact dates and causes of the turmoil are still uncertain but the consequences fairly well known.

HARARI, Ibram, see our number 74495.

74286 HARI, Robert, Les cônes funéraraires égyptiens du Musée de Genève, *Genava*, Genève 22 (1974), 255-264, with 4 ill. and 7 fig.

Publication of five funerary cones preserved in the Musée d'art et d'histoire at Geneva, with prosopographical notes. They are :
1. Nos MF 754 and 755, from the same matrix, belonging to a scribe Djehuty-nefer called Senu (cfr Corpus Nos 14 and 396). The owner is known from two stelae at Turin (153 and 157) and from the section of a door-jamb in the Metropolitan Museum (cfr *Scepter* II, 166), and is not identical with the Djehuty-nefer of Theban Tomb A6 and Cone No. 241.
2. No. MF 756 (= Corpus No. 2), of the priest Minnakht (cfr Cairo statue C.G. 624).
3. No. D 185 (= Corpus No. 395), of Amenemhat, an official of a God's Wife.
4. No. MF 753 (= Corpus No. 401), of Shepenmut, wife of the third prophet of Amon Pedamen-nebnesuttauy.

74287 HARI, Robert, Maya, ou la persécution, *Orientalia* 43 (1974), 153-161, with 1 table.

The author, studying the documents concerning the architect Maya, first mentions in passing an architect of this name from el-Kab, who cannot be identical with Horemheb's architect but may perhaps have been his father. He then lists the documents of the "Theban Maya", one of which (the royal cubit of Turin) actually does not mention him at all, and adds three possible occurrences from the Speos of el-Silsila. Then a list is drawn up of the documents of the "Memphite Maya", among which the Leiden statues. From comparison of the titles and the mothers and other evidence the author concludes that there were two Maya's, the later one in Memphis under Ramses II. In the last section the author discusses the alleged persecution of the Theban Maya, arguing that the name was only destroyed in el-Silsila during the XIXth Dynasty, possibly because of the connections of Maya with el Amarna.
For other views on Maya, see Schneider in *BSFE* No. 69 (1974), our number 74655, and Graefe in *GM* Heft 16 (1975), 9-15.

74288 HARI, Robert, Un Scarabée inédit d'Hatshepsout. Scarabées à légende architecturale, *JEA* 60 (1974), 134-139, with 1 pl. and 15 fig.

A number of specialized scarabs are listed, each detailing the erection of particular monuments such as obelisks by various rulers, and especially one recalling those of this queen at Karnak. *E. Uphill*

74289 HARRIS, J.R., Desiderata, *GM* Heft 11 (1974), 9-10.

A list of finds from el-Amarna whose present whereabouts are unknown. *Dieter Mueller*

74290 HARRIS, J.R., Kiya, *CdE* XLIX, No 97 (1974), 25-30.

L'auteur rassemble six documents certains et quatre autres probables de la reine Kiya, première épouse d'Akhenaton, qui paraît bien avoir été celle qu'il remplaça par la suite par Meritaten. Les monuments au nom de cette reine portent de nombreuses traces de mutilation intentionnelle.
Ph. Derchain

74291 HARRIS, J.R., Nefernefruaten regnans, *Acta Orientalia*, Copenhagen 36 (1974), 11-21.

Continuing the argument concerning Nefernefruaten/Smenkhkare (see our numbers 73313 and 73314) the author discusses four instances in which the cartouches of Akhenaten and Nefernefruaten occur together, as well as four others constituting the alleged marriage of Meritaten and Smenkhkare. Nowhere there is any proof that the person referred to as Nefernefruaten is male. Although Meritaten was obviously $ḥmt\ nsw\ wrt$ to Nefernefruaten, the title may well have been functional and permanent, without a necessary implication of marriage.

74292 HARRIS, J.R., A Note on the Ramessid text of 'Sinuhe', *GM* Heft 11 (1974), 25-28.

Graphical peculiarities in the Sinuhe text of the Ashmolean ostracon indicate that this text is derived from a version transcribed and emended in the Amarna Period.
Dieter Mueller

74293 HASSAN, Fekri A. and Fred WENDORF, A Sebilian Assemblage from El Kilh (Upper Egypt), *CdE* XLIX, No. 98 (1974), 211-221, with 2 maps and 1 table.

L'article présente les résultats de l'exploration d'un site situé près d'El Kilh, à quelques kilomètres au Nord d'Edfou, sur la rive occidentale. Il s'agit d'un ensemble sébilien typique malgré quelques variations (d'ordre stylistique, présence de nombreuses microlithes et de nucléi du type "levalloisien-discoide") qui marquent l'individualité locale de cette industrie plutôt qu'elles ne permettent de l'écarter chronologiquement du sébilien inférieur de Vignard (*BIFAO* 22 [1923], 1-76). *Ph. Derchain*

HASSAN, Fekri A., see also our number 74297.

74294 HAWKES, Jacquetta, Atlas of Ancient Archaeology, New York - St Louis - San Francisco - Toronto, Mc Graw - Hill Book

Company, [1974] (21.5 × 28 cm; 272 p., numerous plans, maps and fig).

This atlas contains maps and plans of a large number of archaeological sites all over the world, each accompanied by a short description and a bibliography, some also by one or more drawings.
The chapter to Ancient Egypt (p. 146-165) is due to Barry Kemp. After a general introduction there follow plans and descriptions of Sakkara, Giza, Beni Hasan, Karnak and Luxor, W. Thebes, Abydos, el-Amarna, Tanis, Abu Simbel, Edfu, Aswan and Philae, Semna, Kerma and Meroe, each on one or two pages. The plans are of a very high quality.
There is also an English edition, London, Heinemann, 1974 (Pr. £ 6.50).

74295 HAWKINS, Gerald S., Celestial Clues to Egyptian Riddles, *Natural History*, New York 83, No. 4 (April 1974), 54-63, with 1 plan and 5 ill. [4 in colour]).

With a mass of details, some irrelevant and others wrong ("Ra-Hor-Akhty" = "the sun-god of the two horizons") the author attempts to prove that the Egyptian temples were in alignment with the sun and the moon.

HAYNES, Vance, see our number 74798.

74296 HAYS, T.R., 'Wavy Line' Pottery: An Element of Nilotic Diffusion, *The South African Archaeological Bulletin*, Claremont, Cape 29, Nos. 113 & 114 (June 1974), 27-32, with 1 map and 2 fig.

The author examines the theory that Khartûm has been the centre of diffusion of the "Khartum Culture" during the Mesolithic and Neolithic Periods. Studying the lithic assemblage and particularly the so-called "Wavy Line" pottery found in the Dongola Reach and along the Second Cataract he reaches the conclusion that the idea of a homogenous "Khartum Culture Area" along the Nile must be disregarded. The similarities in the pottery style are to be explained by the "horizon-style" concept, that is, by a rapid spread of a new idea over a wide geographical area.

74297 HAYS, T.R. and F.A. HASSAN, Mineralogical Analysis of Sudanese Neolithic Ceramics, *Archaeometry*, Oxford 16 (1974), 71-79, with 3 fig., 3 tables and 2 pl.

An investigation into the petrography and mineralogy of Sudanic Neolithic ceramics led to the conclusion that, although all showing a similar "design style", the studied sherds were locally made in various places.

74298 HEATON, E.W., Solomon's New Men: The Emergence of Ancient Israel as a National State, London, Thames and Hudson, 1974 (14 × 21.5 cm; 216 p., 3 maps, 10 plans, 14 fig., 24 pl.). Series: Currents in the History of Culture and Ideas. Pr. £ 4.50

The thesis of this study is that Israel's rapid development in the age of Solomon owed much to the Egyptian civilization, so much indeed that the author calls Solomon "the Pharaoh of Israel". In order to prove the thesis the author throughout refers to Egyptian sources, although, not knowing Egyptian himself, he has to rely on the translations.
Chapter 1 deals with the annals of Solomon (*Kings* 3-11), arguing that their style as well as the policy they report about are imitations of the pharaonic tradition. Chapter 2 is devoted to the state which Solomon inherited, chapter 3 to the new bureaucracy created according to the Egyptian example (cfr our number 71415, but also Redford's rejection, our number 72589). In chapter 4 Solomon's public works and his court are discussed. Chapter 5, called "Education in Wisdom", deals with the Egyptian scribal schools and analyses the Instructions of Ptahhotep, Ani and Amenemope, comparing the latter with the *Book of Proverbs*. Chapter 6 is devoted to the literature of the time: the Joseph Story, the Succession Story, and the Yahwist's Story, indicating the numerous parallels with their counterparts in Egyptian literature.
In the last chapter the question is studied in how far Solomon's cultural milieu was directly or indirectly influenced, through older Palestinian or Phoenician mediation, by the Egyptians. The answer of the author is that Egypt's influence on arts and crafts was indirect, whereas the literature and the administration of Solomon's age were directly dependent on Egypt.
Notes on p. 179-203, a chronological table on p. 204-205, indexes on p. 212-216.

74299 HEERMA VAN VOSS, M., Een bezwering van het hart, [Den Haag], Sarva-Nederland, 1974 (14.3 × 21 cm; 6 p., 2 colour ill., colour ill. on cover).

Hieroglyphic text with translation and a general commentary of Spell 30 B of the *Book of the Dead*.
The pamphlet is published by a chemical firm and distributed among the Dutch physicians together with a model of a heartscarab.

74300 HEERMA VAN VOSS, Matthieu, Dodenboek 193, *ZÄS* 100, 2 (1974), 103-104, with 1 pl.

On spell 193 of the *Book of the Dead*. A philological commentary. For a translation and discussion one may consult our number 71258, for the original facsimile reproduction 71260, pl. 20.

M. Heerma van Voss

74301 HEERMA VAN VOSS, M., Een dodendoek als dodenboek, *Phoenix*, Leiden 20 (1974), 335-338, with 2 ill.

Publication of the fragment of a mummy shroud from the Wellcome Collection, Swansea (Inv. No. W 869) with scenes and texts from the *Book of the Dead*. The shroud has come from Deir Rîfa and belonged to a certain Hapy. The author dates it to the XIXth or XXth Dynasty.
For similar shrouds, compare our number 70105.

74302 HEERMA VAN VOSS, M., De gerichtsscene in het Egyptische Poortenboek, *in*: *Travels in the World of the Old Testament. Studies Presented to Professor M.A. Beek on the Occasion of his 65th Birthday*. Edited by M.S.H.G. Heerma van Voss, Ph.H.J. Houwink ten Cate, N.A. van Uchelen, Assen/Amsterdam, Van Gorkum, 1974, 80-90, with a fig.

The author discusses a scene in the *Book of Gates* in which Osiris is sitting on a platform, in front of him a pair of scales, and on the steps to the platform four figures approaching him. In the room here represented also occur four heads of antelopes, a bark with a pig and two monkeys, and the figure of Anubis. Heerma enumerates the occurrences of the scene, 6 in royal tombs of the New Kingdom and 3 on sarcophagi of the Late Period, and attempts to translate the difficult cryptographic texts, with comments as to their meaning.

74303 HEERMA VAN VOSS, M., Een mythologische papyrus in Den Haag, *Phoenix*, Leiden 20 (1974), 331-334, with 2 ill.

Description of some scenes in a mythological papyrus in the museum Meermanno-Westreenianum at The Hague. The author presents short interpretations of ten scenes, indicating relations to funerary literature.

74304 HEINEN, Heinz, Das Ptolemäische Alexandrien. Bemerkungen zu einem Werk P.M. Frasers, *BiOr* 31 (1974), 201-207.

Review article to our number 72238.

74305 HELCK, Wolfgang, Altägyptische Aktenkunde des 3. und 2. Jahrtausends v. Chr., München-Berlin, Deutscher Kunstverlag, 1974 (17.2 × 23.8 cm; [VI +]161 p., 26 fig.) = Münchner Ägyptologische Studien. Herausgegeben von Hans Wolfgang Müller, 31. Pr. DM 29

This is the first systematic study of the characteristics of records and charters in the Pharaonic Period until the end of the New Kingdom, Demotic documents having been excluded since they constitute a separate field of study.

The first chapter presents a survey of the material on which the records have been written, e.g. the sizes of the papyrus sheets in various periods. Then a long chapter (p. 10-52) follows devoted to the inner form of records, discussing i.a. the royal decrees of the Old Kingdom, the Abûsîr papyri, the Reisner papyri, and offering lists of the New Kingdom. The author indicates how the combinations of vertical and horizontal lines are to be understood, illustrating his argument with drawings.

The next chapter deals with the use of red ink, and contains i.a. a list of diacritical marks (p. 61-62). In the fourth chapter the internal order of the records is discussed, the way in which the data are arranged, e.g. the order of temples in New Kingdom documents and that of deliveries in the annals of Tuthmosis III. Then follow chapters on the registration of calculations, the fixed formulae in the records, the use of royal names and the mention of the names of officials.

Two chapters are devoted to the charters, dealing with their inner form and their phraseology, with an alphabetical list of phrases and terms on p. 125-132. The last chapters discuss the writings of cubic measures, the expression of value, and the way in which documents are converted into representations.

Throughout the book Helck stresses the development during the ages.

Three indexes (p. 146-161), to subjects, Egyptian words and texts.

74306 HELCK, Wolfgang, Die altägyptische Gaue, Wiesbaden, Dr. Ludwig Reichert Verlag, 1974 (17 × 24 cm; VIII + 216 p., 16 maps) = Beihefte zum Tübinger Atlas des Vorderen Orients. Reihe B (Geisteswissenschaften) Nr. 5; rev. *CdE* LI, No. 101 (1976), 96-102 (Alain-Pierre Zivie); *Mundus* 12 (1976), 26-27 (Karola Zibelius). Pr. DM 30

After a short introduction stating that the present book aims merely at exposing the material at present known in order to provide a basis for further study chapter II lists the sources, e.g. the nome-lists, processions of estates from the Old Kingdom, historical documents of various character and works of classical authors. These sources are systematically discussed in chapter III, with special attention i.a. to the kiosk of Sesostris I, town lists from the Middle and New Kingdom, Strabo's description of Egypt, etc. Section 16 lists the nomes of the Byzantine Period, section 17 arranges the main sources in chronological order.

In section 18 (p. 49-60) the author deals more extensively with the nome administration, mainly during the Old Kingdom, arguing i.a. that the nomes mostly originated from royal estates in the Thinite period.

The rest of the book mainly consists of a discussion of the separate nomes of Upper (chapter IV) and Lower Egypt (chapter V), each chapter opening with general remarks about the arrangement of the nomes. Moreover, section 2 of chapter IV deals with Upper Egypt in the Graeco-Roman Period, section 2 of chapter V with mouths and branches of the Nile. The oases occur at the end of chapter IV.

Chapter VI (199-203) presents a short survey of the history of the nome organization, from the Early to the Roman Period. There have been many detail alterations in size and number of the nomes and in their administration, but never a fundamentally new division of the country.

Thirteen maps at the end show the areas of the nomes in various periods. There is a list of abbreviated titles at p. 213-216, but no indexes.

74307 HELCK, Wolfgang, Die Bedeutung der Felsinschriften J. Lopez, *Inscripciones rupestres* NR. 27 und 28, *SAK* 1 (1974), 215-225.

The author discusses two rock inscriptions found North of the Khor el-Aquiba, on the east bank opposite Karanog, and published by Lopez (compare our number 66397). Contrary to Lopez the author dates them to the IVth Dynasty. One text states that 17,000 Nubians were caught. which Helck connects with a deficiency of population in Egypt during that period caused by the establishment of royal estates in order to provide the growing number of officials with food. The development is connected with the building of the pyramids. Helck amply sketches the religious, political and economic background of the development.

74308 HELCK, Wolfgang, Bemerkungen zum Annalenstein, *MDAIK* 30 (1974), 31-35.

The author argues that the fragments K1-K4 are all part of the Palermo Stone itself, and calculates the length of Dyn. I as recorded in lines 2-3 as 197 years, while that of Dyn. II in line 4 amounted to appr. 130 years. *Dieter Mueller*

74309 HELCK, Wolfgang, Die Handwerker- und Priesterphylen des Alten Reiches in Ägypten, *Die Welt des Orients*, Göttingen 7 (1973-1974), 1-8.

The author discusses Edel's conclusions about the phylae (see our number 69174), arguing that there were five of them (*wr* being an abbreviation of *imy-wrt*). Four of the names were indeed derived from those of ship's parts, as Kees has suggested (see our number 530). Every phyle consisted of two groups, each with a changing number of members, from 14 to 28 or even 35.

74310 HELCK, Wolfgang, Siegfried Schott. 28. August 1897-29. Oktober 1971, *ZÄS* 100,2 (1974), V, with portrait.

Obituary article. Compare our number 71652.

HELCK, Wolfgang, see also our number 74445.

HELMI, F.M. see our number 74634.

74311 HELWIN, Hellmut, Gehörte die Königin von Punt zu den chondrodystrophen Zwergen?, *Gegenbaurs Morphologisches Jahrbuch*, Leipzig 120 (1974), 280-289, with 6 fig. and 6 ill.

A new attempt to explain the physical deformation of the Queen of Punt (see also our number 74108). The author rejects the possibility that it was caused by chondrodystrophy. He suggests a bilateral luxation of the hip-joints, which may be increased by obesity following immobility.

74312 HENFLING, Edwin, Ägyptologie heute: unaufkündbarer Auftrag?, *GM* Heft 12 (1974), 89-113.

A slightly ironical summary of Serge Sauneron, L'Égyptologie (our No. 68524), and Wolfgang Helck, Ägyptologie an deutschen Universitäten (our No. 69246).   *Dieter Mueller*

HENFLING, Edwin, see also our number 74342.

74313 HERRMANN, Siegfried, Die "Wirklichkeit Gottes" in der ägyptischen Religion, *ZÄS* 101 (1974), 95-107.

Auseinandersetzung mit drei Arbeiten von Morenz und einem Buche von Hornung, unseren Nummern 60503, 64345, 64346 und 71282.   *M. Heerma van Voss*

74314 HERRMANN, Wolfram, Neue Belege für die Kuṯarāt, *ZÄS* 100,2 (1974), 104-108.

Verfasser beschäftigt sich mit den Kuṯarāt-Göttinnen aus Ugarit. Sie haben eine hervorragende Funktion als "Bildnerinnen", d.h. des ungeborenen und des aufwachsenden Kindes.
Herrmann bespricht zwei ägyptische Stellen, die (wahrscheinlich) ebenfalls die Kuṯarāt erwähnen, sei es im Singular. Es sind "The Cairo Calendar No. 86637", Recto XVII, 11 (unsere

Nummer 66037), und die Cairo Stele veröffentlicht von Leibovitz (unsere Nummer 560). Beide(?) gehören in die 19. Dynastie.

M. Heerma van Voss

74315 HERZOG, Rolf, Ägypten und das negride Afrika; Überprüfung einer bekannten Hypothese, *Paideuma*, Wiesbaden 19/20 (1973/74), 200-212.

Es wird die Frage untersucht, "ob man die Zugehörigkeit Ägyptens zu Afrika lediglich als Zufallsergebnis eines geographischen Gliederungsschemas oder auch als Indiz für anthropologische, völkerkundliche und kulturhistorische Zusammenhänge werten sollte". Dem Problem anthropologisch-rassensgeschichtlicher Zusammenhänge, dem genetischen Anteil der Negriden an der Bevölkerung des ägyptischen Niltales in vorislamischer Zeit, dem Anteil negrider Elemente beim Zustandekommen der frühen ägyptischen Kulturen und der Kontaktnahme der dynastischen Zeit mit dem negriden Afrika wird nachgegangen und die Fragestellungen innerhalb der Wissenschaftsgeschichte beleuchtet.

Inge Hofmann

74316 HEYLER, A. et J. LECLANT, Courte note sur les épitaphes méroïtiques du vice-roi Abratêye, *Actes premier congrès de linguistique sémitique*, 381-392.

The authors study a stela and an altar of the viceroy *Brtêye* (Cairo JE 90008 and 90009), found near Khôr Oba in the neighbourhood of Tomâs in 1961 (see our number 65307). Both pieces probably came from Karanog and bear funerary inscriptions in cursive Meroitic script. Other texts of the same viceroy date from the reign of Teqêrideamani (A.D. 246-266). The authors give a synoptic transcription of the texts, to which is added a transcription of a text of viceroy *Ḫwitrêr*, with an attempt to translation and comments to the title "viceroy" (*pestê*).
In an appendix a list of documents mentioning Meroitic viceroys.

74317 HEYOB, Sharon Kelly, The Cult of Isis among Women in the Graeco-Roman World, *Dissertation Abstracts International A*, Ann Arbor, Mich. 34, No. 3 (September 1973), 1262/3-A.

Abstract of a doctor's thesis The Catholic University of America, 1973 (Order No. 73-19,863; 195 p.).
This dissertation investigates the role of woman in the cult of Isis in the Graeco-Roman world.

L.M.J. Zonhoven

74318 HIEN, N.V., R.H. MARCHESSAULT und T.N. KLEINERT, X-Ray Identification of Ancient Egyptian Linen, *Holzforschung*, Berlin 27, No. 4 (1973), 136, with 3 fig.

Report of an investigation of two linen specimens from Egyptian tombs by X-raying.

74319 HINKEL, Friedrich, 2. Internationale Tagung für meroitistische Forschungen, Paris 1973, *Ethnographische-archäologische Zeitschrift*, Berlin 15 (1974), 323-325.

Report on the Meroitic Congress at Paris, July 1973.

74320 HINTZE, Fritz, Koptische Steuerquittungsostraka der Berliner Papyrus-Sammlung, *Festschrift Ägyptisches Museum Berlin*, 271-281, with 6 pl.

Publication of 27 tax receipts from the Berlin papyrus collection, with an introduction, photographs, transcription and translation with some comments.
The article is followed by some remarks by the late Paul E. Kahle, "Zu den koptischen Steuerquittungen" (p. 283-285), published by Hintze.

74321 HINTZE, Fr., Meroitische Verwandtschaftsbezeichnungen, *MNL* No 14 (Février 1974), 30-32, with 3 fig.

Die meroitischen Totentexte enthalten an Worstämmen, die eine verwandtschaftliche Bezeichnung beinhalten: *-dẖe-* "geboren von ...", *-rike-* "gezeugt von ...", *kdi-* "Schwester", *wil-* "Bruder", *šte-* "Mutter", *sm-* "Ehefrau". Im vorliegenden Artikel versucht Verf. den Ausdruck *yetmde-* als Angabe des Verwandtschaftsverhältnisses mit einem Bruder der Mutter zu erklären. Davon ausgehend wird auf eine mutterrechtliche Ordnung in der meroitischen Sozialstruktur geschlossen, die sich auch in der Erbfolge und bei der Übernahme von Ämtern und Funktionen widerspiegelt, indem diese durch die weibliche Linie vererbt oder weitergegeben werden. *Inge Hofmann*

74322 HINTZE, Fritz, Statistisches zu den Sargtexten, *GM* Heft 9 (1974), 63-74.

A statistical analysis of the incidence of 𓂞 and 𓏙 for *rdỉ* "give" in the *Coffin Texts*, on account of Junge's dissertation (our number 70287). *Dieter Mueller*

74323 HINTZE, Fr., Zur statistischen Untersuchung afrikanischer Orts- und Völkernamen aus ägyptischen Texten, *MNL* No 14 (Février 1974), 4-19, with 3 tables.

"The aim of this paper is to call attention to some problems which are connected with the utilization of numerical data in linguistic argumentation, and to show that such data may be misleading if they are used without statistical tests. The possibility to apply simple statistical methods is demonstrated by means of some examples, using data given by K. Zibelius in her paper "Statistical study of African place-names", *MNL* 5 (unsere Nr. 70611). Vgl. auch unsere Nr. 72807.

Author's own summary

74324 HIRSCHBERG, Walter, Die Kulturen Afrikas, Frankfurt a. Main, Akademische Verlagsgesellschaft Athenaion, 1974 (22.5 × 28.5 cm; X + 390 p., 163 ill., 15 maps, 2 pl.) = Handbuch der Kulturgeschichte, 2. Abteilung. Kulturen der Völker; rev. *Mitteilungen der anthropologischen Gesellschaft in Wien* 104 (1974), 183-185 (Karl R. Wernhart); *Mundus* 11 (1975), 313-314 (Eike Haberland). Pr. DM 170

In der vorliegenden Darstellung der afrikanischen Kulturen wird häufig Bezug genommen auf Ägypten, mehr noch auf die meroitische bzw. die christlich nubische Kultur, so bei der Behandlung der Felsbilder (S. 25ff.), dem sakralen Königtum (83ff.), der Erforschung Afrikas (310ff.). Kap. IV (65-82) "Altägypten — Napata und Meroe" gibt eine kurze Übersicht über die Beziehungen Ägypten-Sudan, über das meroitische Reich, die Bedeutung des Eisens, das christliche Nubien mit seinen angeblichen Ausstrahlungen auf das übrige Afrika (biblische Motive, "Basis-Dellen-Keramik"). Kap. XIII (220-225) behandelt die Frage "Altägypten in Schwarzafrika": Schädeldeformation, Mumifizierung, "Porträtstatuen" verstorbener Herrscher, stilistische Eigenheiten innerhalb der Kunst, Elemente höfischer Kultur: "Niemand denkt heute ernstlich daran, bei allen diesen Erscheinungen einen direkten altägyptischen Einfluß anzunehmen. Das große Tor, durch das der "pharaonische Gedanke" in Schwarzafrika Einzug hielt, war nicht Altägypten, sondern, wie bereits an zahlreichen Beispielen gezeigt werden konnte, Napata - Meroe bzw. die christlichen Nachfolgestaaten Nobatia, Makuria und Alodia" (222f.).

Inge Hofmann

74325 HODGE, C. T., Verbum mortuum est. Vivat verbum, *Language Sciences*, Bloomington, Indiana No. 29 (February 1974), 22-23.

The author argues that all historical Egyptian verb forms, the imperative excepted, are derived from nominal constructions, as is a considerable amount of the Semitic system.
See also our number 74487.

74326 HODJASCH, S., Skarabäen mit Pflanzendarstellungen, *Studia Aegyptiaca I*, 177-201, with 21 ill.

The author discusses plant motifs on scarabs, e.g. palm leaves, lotus flowers and papyrus bouquets, and the symbolic meaning of plant representations in general.

74327 HOFFMAN, Michael A., The Social Context of Trash Disposal in an Early Dynastic Egyptian Town, *American Antiquity*, Washington D.C. 39, No. 1 (January 1974), 35-50, with 1 table, 4 plans and 3 fig.

The author studies the trash disposal system of Early Dynastic Hieraconpolis, so far as it has been excavated. He distinguishes between three kinds of structures : non-elite, elite and industrial, and is able to suggest from the distribution of trash to a distribution of socio-economically defined zones in the town and their development.

74328 HOFFMANN-AXTHELM, Walter, Die Geschichte der Zahnheilkunde, Berlin, Buch- und Zeitschriften-Verlag, 1973 (not seen).

The first part of chapter 1 (p. 17-23, with 8 ill. and 1 fig.) gives a survey of the dentistry in Ancient Egypt, discussing i.a. passages from the Pap. Ebers and evidence for caries and dental surgery.
From the bibliography (p. 32) it appears that the author does not know the studies of F. Filce Leek.

74329 HOFMANN, I., Arensnuphis — ein meroitischer Gott?, *MNL* No 14 (Février 1974), 52-55.

Die Arensnuphis-Darstellungen in Musawwarat es Sufra (und nur dort ist der Gott eindeutig zu identifizieren) zeigen, daß der Gott die Tracht des ägyptischen Jägergottes Onuris trägt. Da sein Hauptkultort in Ägypten liegt und sein Name meroitisch nicht nachzuweisen ist, erscheint es zweifelhaft, daß Arensnuphis seinen Ursprung in Meroe gehabt haben soll (vgl. unsere Nr. 73780). Sehe auch unsere Nr. 74799.
Inge Hofmann

74330 HOFMANN, Inge, Die Artzugehörigkeit des syrischen Elefanten, *Säugetierkundliche Mitteilungen*, München 22, Heft 3 (September 1974), 225-232, with 1 fig.

Der syrische Elefant, der weder eine Zwergform noch eine Südform des Mammuts war, kam nach Inschriften, Darstellungen sowie Knochen- und Zahnfunden im Gebiet zwischen den Oberläufen von Euphrat und Tigris, vornehmlich am Ḥābur, und im Orontestal vor, in dessen Sümpfen noch am Ende des 1. vorchristlichen Jahrhunderts Herden gelebt haben mögen.
Inge Hofmann

74331 HOFMANN, I., Beitrag zu Paul van Moorsel : Zur Diskussion : Was ist "Nubologie"?, No 14 (Février 1974), 57-58.

"Nubologie" wird verstanden als Oberbegriff der Disziplinen, die sich mit den kulturellen Hinterlassenschaften des sudanischen Gebietes von der Frühzeit an beschäftigen. Ein Oberbegriff erscheint notwendig, um der Zersplitterung und dem Auseinanderleben unserer "Orchideen-Fächer" entgegenzutreten. Sehe auch unsere Nummer 74741. *Inge Hofmann*

74332 HOFMANN, I., Bemerkungen zur Funktion und Morphemgestalt des suffigalen Elementes -*yos* bzw. -*os* im Meroitischen, *MNL* No 14 (Février 1974), 48-51.

Eine Anzahl meroitischer Titel werden mit dem Suffix -*os* unbekannter Bedeutung gebildet, das nach einem Vokal -*yos* lautet. Eine Gleichsetzung des Einschränkungssuffixes -*s* mit -*yos* (bzw. -*os*) als freier Variante (vgl. unsere Nr. 73648) scheint verfehlt. *Inge Hofmann*

74333 HOFMANN, Inge, Satis in der meroitischen religiösen Vorstellung, *GM* Heft 10 (1974), 21-24.

The *interpretatio graeca* Satis = Hera, attested in Greek inscriptions from Aswan, explains her close association with Amon (= Zeus) in Meroitic sources. *Dieter Mueller*

74334 HOFMANN, I., Zu einigen Nominalausdrücken in den Deskriptionsphrasen der meroitischen Totentexte, *MNL* No 14 (Février 1974), 33-47.

Es wird versucht, den Nominalausdruck *yetmde-* mit "Günstling" wiederzugeben (vgl. unsere Nr. 74321), sowie einige meroitische Titel aus dem Ägyptischen herzuleiten. *Inge Hofmann*

74335 HOFMANN, Inge, Zur Datierung des Königs Adikhalamani, *GM* Heft 9 (1974), 27-32.

The Meroitic ruler Adikhalamani was perhaps a contemporary of Arqamani (Ergamenes) and Ptolemy IV, ruling over the Dodekaschoinos between Aswan and the Meroitic kingdom proper. *Dieter Mueller*

74336 HOLTHOER, R., Another Canope of Padihoremheb, *Studia Aegyptiaca I*, 203-210, with 2 fig. and 1 ill.

Publication of the plaster cast of a canopic jar made for Padihoremheb and now in the Finnish National Museum of Helsinki (Museum No. 14560:28). The original was once in the museum in Reval (Tallin), and is presumed to have been destroyed during the Second World War. Two other jars belonging to the same person have been published by W. Wessetzky (our No. 57545). *Dieter Mueller*

74337 HOLTHOER, Rostislav, An Uncommon Ušebtj-figurine from a Finnish Collection, Helsinki, 1974 (16.5 × 24.5 cm; 9 p., 4 ill., 1 fig.) = Studia Orientalia Edidit Societas Orientalis Fennica XLIII:10.

After a short survey of form and function of the shawabti figure in general the author publishes an example of the category in "costume des vivants", now in the private collection of Mr. Magnus Schwanck at Helsinki. The text mentions the overseer of the workshops of the temple Hr-nfr (once Nfr-Hr). The object may come from Medînet Habu and may date from the late XIXth or XXth Dynasty.

74338 HOLTHOER, Rostislav and Richard AHLQUIST, The "Roman Temple" at Tehna el-Gebel, Helsinki, 1974 (16.5 × 24.5 cm; 24 p., 4 fig., 4 ill.) = Studia Orientalia Edidit Societas Orientalis Fennica XLIII: 7.

Description of a decorated, but uninscribed temple at Tehna el-Gebel, on the east bank of the Nile appr. 6 km north of Minyeh (*Porter-Moss* IV, 129). Although called Roman, the temple clearly resembles the chapels of Tuna el-Gebel which date from the reign of Ptolemy V. *Dieter Mueller*

74339 HOOK, Donald, The Edwin Smith Surgical Papyrus, *The Bulletin of the Cleveland Medical Library*, Cleveland, Ohio 20 (1973), 23-25.

After a few words on Edwin Smith and the history of the publication of the papyrus bought by him and named after him the author gives an extensive and reliable survey of its methods and contents, quoting various examples after Breasted's translation.

74340 HORN, Jürgen, Herausgeforderte Ägyptologie. Geschichte einer Auseinandersetzung unter falschen Voraussetzungen, *GM* Heft 12 (1974), 55-87.

Between 1934 and 1938, H. Berve, W.F. Albright, W. Wolf, and R. Anthes engaged in a debate about the value of Egyptology. Their arguments are critically examined. *Dieter Mueller*

74341 HORN, Jürgen, Zum Wissenschaftsbegriff der Ägyptologie — eine Zusammenfassung der Diskussion, *GM* Heft 9 (1974), 51-52.

Report on a discussion on Egyptology as a discipline held in Göttingen on Febr. 17 and 18, 1974. See also Seibert (our No. 74665). *Dieter Mueller*

74342 HORN, J., in Zusammenarbeit mit E. HENFLING, U. KÖHLER, Ch. MÜLLER, W. SCHENKEL und B. SLEDZIANOWSKI, Wissenschaftsgeschichte und theoretische Grundlegung der Ägyptologie, *GM* Heft 12 (1974), 7-28.

The authors question the theoretical foundations of modern Egyptology and its position in society, and propose a thorough discussion of these issues. A bibliography of earlier books and articles on this topic is found on pp. 19-28.

Dieter Mueller

74343 HORNBOSTEL, Wilhelm, Erwerbungen der Antikenabteilung (1965-1973), *Jahrbuch Hamburger Kunstsammlungen*, Hamburg 19 (1974), 139-166, with 20 ill.

Among the recent acquisitions of the collection at Hamburg we mention a relief fragment with the representation of a queen or Isis (Inv. Nr. 1970.145) from the late Ptolemaic Period (p. 143).

74344 HORNUNG, Erik, Ergebnisse der Schlußdiskussion, *GM* Heft 14 (1974), 65-67.

A summary of the results of a symposium on "The Hieroglyphic Writing System Especially of the Late Period" held near Basel on July 25-27, 1974. *Dieter Mueller*

74345 HORNUNG, Erik, Seth. Geschichte und Bedeutung eines ägyptischen Gottes, *Symbolon. Jahrbuch für Symbolforschung*, Köln N.F. 2 (1974), 49-63, with 2 fig.

The author basing his arguments on te Velde's thesis (our number 67575), first presents a historical survey of the cult of Seth. Originally closely connected with kingship he was also feared as the murderer of Osiris, but in the meantime highly valued during the XVIIIth and XIXth Dynasties, and even afterwards. His actual outlawing only has begun after the Assyrian conquest.
These changes in appreciation are explained from a study of the nature of Seth as god of the foreign world, of the thunderstorm, of violence, etc. In the myth of Horus and Seth the conflict between violence and order is personalized, ending with compromise and reconciliation. Despite his character as trickster Seth belongs to the world-order, so that to acknowledge his existence means to acknowledge the actual structure of the world.

74346 HORNUNG, Erik, Die Totenbücher des Neuen Reiches, *Textes et langages III*, 65-71.

After a general survey of the study of various Books of the Netherworld the author briefly mentions each of them separately: The older Am-Duat and the Book of Gates, the younger ones, such as the Book of Caves and the Book of Earth. A third category constitute the books of the sky: the Nut-Book, the Book of Night and the Book of Day. All are mentioned with their major publications. Related texts, e.g. the sun-litanies, are briefly discussed, and the importance of this field of studies for our knowledge of ancient Egypt is stressed.

74347 HORNUNG, Erik, Zur Diskussion, *GM* Heft 14 (1974), 47-48.

Introductory remarks to a discussion about a hieroglyphic signlist at a colloquium devoted to the subject.
For the conclusions, see our number 74344.

74348 HORNUNG, Erik und Elisabeth STAEHELIN, unter Mitarbeit von Barbara BEGELSBACHER, Bertrand JAEGER und Christine SEEBER, Studien zum Sedfest, [Genève, Éditions de Belles-Lettres], 1974 (21.1 × 29.8 cm; 103 p.) = Aegyptiaca Helvetica, 1. Herausgegeben von/publié par Ägyptologisches Seminar der Universität Basel et Centre d'Études orientales de l'Université de Genève; rev. *BiOr* 33 (1976), 171-172 (Dieter Mueller); *CdE* LI, No 101 (1976), 107-109 (Dieter Kurth); *JEA* 62 (1976), 201 (J. Gwyn Griffiths).   Pr. Sw. Fr. 20

Gestellt wird die Frage nach der jeweils gesicherten Realität eines schriftlich oder bildlich tradierten Sedfestes. Es wird versucht, zwischen tatsächlicher, aktueller Verwirklichung und allzeit verbindlicher Norm zu trennen. Es zeigt sich, daß nur 13 der 50 mit Sedfesten in Zusammenhang gebrachten Könige dieses Fest mit Sicherheit realiter gefeiert haben. Haben sie es, so sprechen sie von ihrem "ersten", "zweiten", "dritten" u.s.w. Sedfest; meist wird dabei das Regierungsjahr mitgenannt, das Fest also geschichtlich verankert. Als Regel gilt, daß das Fest seit dem Mittleren Reich zum erstenmal im 30.Regierungsjahr des Königs gefeiert wird, dann im Neuen Reich in regelmäßigen Wiederholungen von 3 bis 4 Jahren; gelegentlich wird die Regierungszeit des voraufgehenden Herrschers in die 30-Jahresfrist einbezogen. Mit der sich vermindernden geschichtlichen Bedeutung des Königtums verliert während der Spätzeit auch das Sedfest mehr und mehr an Bedeutung und wird in die Akzentverschiebung vom König auf die Götter hineingezogen. Als Erneuerungsfest des Königs und damit der Welt, wobei die 30 Jahre einer Generation entsprechen, enthält es das Kernthema ägyptischen Jenseitsglaubens, die Hoffnung auf "Erneuerung" im Grab. So gehört es schon im Alten Reich fest zum Bildprogram der Totentempel, ohne deshalb als Zeugnis des wirklich gefeierten Festes des jeweiligen Königs gelten zu können.

I. Gamer-Wallert

HUBER, Peter, see our number 74782.

74349 HUGOT, H.-J., Le Sahara avant le désert, [Toulouse], Éditions des Hespérides, [1974] (16.5 × 21 cm; 343 p., numerous ill. and fig., 8 maps, 8 colour ill.); series: Collection archéologique, horizons neufs.

In this lavishly illustrated study on the Saharan Prehistory some sections are of importance to Egyptologists. Chapter 6 is entirely devoted to the Neolithic of Sudanic tradition, the race that was bearer of this tradition, its material and its spiritual culture.
In chapter 7, on the Tenere (a region S.E. of the Ahaggar), the author deals with the alleged Egyptian influences on the neolithic industries of this area (p. 181-184), a hypothesis which is strongly denied.
Chapter 9 deals with the Saharan rock drawings. Once more influence of Egyptian art is denied (245-247). The occurrence of representations of chariots drawn by running horses (278-283) is connected with the Libyans and Sea Peoples (284-290), an invasion of whom is hesitantly suggested.
See our number 74424.

74350 HUMBERT, Jean, Les obélisques de Paris: projets et réalisations, *Revue de l'Art*, Paris 23 (1974), 9-29, with 38 ill.

Study of some of the obelisks which once have been and in some instances still are erected in Paris. Two of them are genuine Egyptian monuments: the Luxor obelisk on the Place de la Concorde, and the obelisk Albani, once part of a monument of the general Desaix and now in Munich (Gl. Waf. 39).

74351 IRMSCHER, Johannes, Siegfried Morenz als Koptologe, *in*: *Studia Coptica*. Herausgegeben von Peter Nagel, Berlin, Akademie-Verlag, 1974 (= Berliner Byzantinistische Arbeiten, 45), 19-28.

An obituary article on Siegfried Morenz, particulary on his significance for Coptology.
Compare our number 70619.

74352 ISKANDER, Zaky, Some Restoration Problems in Egypt and their Treatment, *Recent Advances in Science and Technology of Materials*, 1-8.

The author deals with the technical side of the treatment of painted reliefs and of the cut-lines resulting from the removal of the temples of Abu Simbel; the removal of the paintings on the walls of Nubian churches and the Christian paintings in the temple of Abu Oda; and the restoration works in the tomb of Nefertari.

ISKANDER, Zaky, see also our number 74634.

74353 ISSERLIN, B.S.J., Report on the Third International Colloquium on Aegean Prehistory, *BiOr* 31 (1974), 348-349.

Since it is particularly interesting to Egyptologists, we mention that several papers were presented, having as topic Egyptian evidence about the "Sea Peoples", during a colloquium on Aegean Prehistory held at the University of Sheffield, from April 15-19, 1973.

74354 JACQUET, Jean, Fouilles de Karnak Nord. Sixième campagne 1972-1973, *BIFAO* 74 (1974), 171-181, with 1 folded plan and 4 pl.

Sequel to our number 73360.
This season the temple of Tuthmosis I with six chapels and a peristyle court has completely been excavated. In front of it an older building had been incorporated. The excavator also discovered the pylon of the temple, though he did not yet reach its central doorway. There are indications that blocks of the building have been reused in Karnak South.
Among the finds we mention a fragmentary lintel with the representation of the high-priest Amenhotep, son of Ramsesnakht (pl. 26) and blocks with the names Ahmose-Nefertari and Amenophis I. Possibly the latter belonged to a sanctuary for the divinities of the necropolis.

JACQUET-GORDON, Helen, see our number 74576.

JAEGER, Bertrand, see our number 74348.

JAKOBIELSKI, Stefan, see our number 74503.

74355 JAMES, Frances, Stone Knobs and Chariot Tracks, *Expedition*, Philadelphia, Penn. 16, Number 3 (Spring 1974), 31-39, with 1 map, 7 ill. and 6 fig.

During the excavations at Beth-Shan the author found a number of stone knobs of varying sizes and shapes, some of marble, others of alabaster or gypsum. She demonstrates that these are yoke terminals and saddle bosses belonging to the equipment of Egyptian chariots, as shown in the representations and on the chariots from Tutankhamon's tomb.

74356 JAMES, T.G.H., Corpus of Hieroglyphic Inscriptions in The Brooklyn Museum. I. From Dynasty I to the End of Dynasty XVIII, Brooklyn N.Y., The Brooklyn Museum, 1974 (21.5 × 27.8 cm; XXVI + 215 p., 1 fig., frontispiece in colour, 12 pl. + 76 pl. with hieroglyphic text); rev. *AJA* 79 (1975), 153-154 (William Kelly Simpson); *BiOr* 32 (1975), 347-348 (Robert Hari); *CdE* XLIX, No. 98 (1974), 269-271 (Herman de Meulenaere); *JARCE* 12 (1975), 111 (Dieter Mueller); *JEA* 62

(1976), 198 (C.H.S. Spaull); *Welt des Orients* 8 (1975-1976), 319-320 (Hellmut Brunner); *ZDMG* 126 (1976), 192 (J.v. B[eckerath]).　　　　　　　　　　　　　　　　Pr. $ 10

Band I ist den Inschriften der 1. bis zum Ende der 18. Dynastie im Brooklyn Museum gewidmet. Alle Texte, seien sie auch noch so fragmentarisch erhalten, sind aufgenommen und zeichnerisch wiedergegeben, die für ihre Epoche charakteristischsten zusätzlich in Photographie.

Das stattliche Corpus von 435 Objekten ist, so weit wie möglich, chronologisch geordnet. Es enthält zu jedem Stück eine detaillierte Beschreibung, Übersetzung des Textes, Inv. Nr., Maß-, Material- und Herkunftsangaben, und eine vollständige Bibliographie. Ein Kommentar erläutert nicht nur die Übersetzung, sondern gibt darüber hinaus Einzelheiten zu früherem Verbleib sowie Erwerbung. All dies und die Indizes zu Königs-, Privat-, Götter- und Ortsnamen, Titel und Herkunftsangaben und drei Konkordanzen machen den Band zu einem Nachschlagewerk weit über das gestellte Thema hinaus.

Ingrid Gamer-Wallert

74357 J[AMES], T.G.H., Egypt, History of. I. Egypt to the end of the 17th dynasty, *Encyclopaedia Britannica*. Volume 6, 460-471.

The author presents a survey of the Egyptian history from the Predynastic Period until the New Kingdom, after having made general remarks on the nature of the ancient Egyptian civilization, and on sources and chronology. For the period from the New Kingdom onwards see our number 74801.

For other references to the history of ancient Egypt see the above edition. Micropaedia, Vol. III.　　　*L.M.J. Zonhoven*

74358 JANKUHN, Dieter, Bibliographie der hieratischen und hieroglyphischen Papyri, Wiesbaden, Otto Harrassowitz, 1974 (17 × 24 cm; X + 114 p.) = Göttinger Orientforschungen. Veröffentlichungen des Sonderforschungsbereiches Orientalistik an der Georg-August-Universität Göttingen. IV. Reihe: Ägypten. Band 2.　　　　　　　　　　　　　　　　　Pr. DM 20

In this bibliography the author offers an alphabetical list of hieratic and hieroglyphic papyri with references to their publications and translations, at least insofar as they deal with the text as a whole. The author has included all different types of texts, religious, literary, medical, juridical, etc.

Each papyrus is mentioned under its usual name, with reference, if necessary, to its museum number. The author has largely used cross-references, e.g. under the heading "Amuns-Hymnus: → Berlin 3050; → KAIRO Boulaq 17; → Leiden I 350. Groups of texts preserved in the main museums (e.g., Berlin or the British Museum) are preceded by an entry "generell", some with several cross-references. With each text there is an indication as to its nature (TB, myth., Brief, etc.), and in some instances of its date.

For some economic texts the author refers to the Indices of Helck's Materialien zur Wirtschaftgeschichte (our number 70269).

In his introduction the author asks for corrections and additions since he intends to compose a later "Nachtrag".

74359 JANKUHN, Dieter, Das Verhältnis von Bildern und Texten der Horusmythen von Edfou, *XVIII. Deutscher Orientalistentag*, 26-32, with 8 fig.

Studying the relations between scenes and texts of the myth of the winged sun-disk on the inner side of the western girdle wall of the Edfu temple, the author argues, i.a. from the lack of harmonic relations in the second register and the mutilation of puns in the text, that the model was a papyrus. Its reconstruction is still full of problems.

74360 JANSSEN, Jac. J., An Allusion to an Egyptian Wedding Ceremony?, *GM* Heft 10 (1974), 25-28.

If the lacuna in Pap. Turin 2070 l.3 is to be restored as $h[m^3]y$ "salt", the phrase ("while she is eating her [salt] with Nekhmin") may contain a description of the marital status of a certain Merut who was apparently his second spouse. It is not clear, however, if they were actually legally married, or merely living together.

Compare our number 74007. *Dieter Mueller*

74361 JANSSENS, Paul A., Het radiografisch onderzoek van de mummie, *Antwerpen*. Tijdschrift der stad Antwerpen 20 (1974), 136-143, with 8 ill.

Report of the X-raying of a mummy in the Museum Vleeshuis at Antwerp. The author states that the mummy dates from the period between the early XIIth and late XVIIIth Dynasties and belonged to a woman of c. fifty years. For the sarcophagus in which the mummy has been placed, see our number 74425.

JARITZ, Horst, see our number 74367.

JOHANSEN, Flemming, see our number 74588.

74362 JOHNSON, Janet H., The Demotic Chronicle as an Historical Source, *Enchoria* 4 (1974), 1-17.

A re-examination of this important text has confirmed its historical reliability. The author suggests a number of new readings and interpretations which show that the Demotic Chronicle agrees in important details with other sources for the history of the last three dynasties of Egypt.

Dieter Mueller

74363 JUNGE, Friedrich, Linguistik und Ägyptologie, *GM* Heft 10 (1974), 59-75.

A general discussion of modern linguistics and their significance for the study of Egyptian grammar on account of our numbers 73132, 73151 and 73647. *Dieter Mueller*

74364 JUNGE, Friedrich, Mehrfach adverbielle Bestimmungen nach zweiten Tempora, *XVIII. Deutscher Orientalistentag*, 33-41.

In instances where a second tense is followed by more than one adverbial adjunct it is a problem which of them was intended to be emphasized. The author successively deals with the so-called incomplete verbs (such as *wrš* or *gmi*), which, since it is evidently the adverbial adjunct that is stressed, usually do not occur in the emphatic form; with verbs followed by both subject and object; and with verbs with two objects. With the latter it is the second object, expressed by an adverbial adjunct, which is stressed (e.g., "you may deliver Redjedet of [*m*] the three children"). It is the "free" condition which is emphasized by the second tense, the function of which it is to include it into the sentence.

74365 KÁDÁR, Z., Des scarabées chez Pline l'ancien, *Studia Aegyptiaca I*, 211-220.

The author argues that Plinius indicated by the word scarabeus not only genuine scarabs but various kinds of beetles (Coleoptera).

74366 [KADISH, Gerald E.], Editorial Foreword, *JARCE* 11 (1974), 5-7.

Contains a list of the research projects and fellowships sponsored by the American Research Center in Egypt for the years 1974-1975. *J.F. Borghouts*

KAHLE, Paul E., see our number 74320.

74367 KAISER, Werner, Peter GROSSMANN, Gerhard HAENY und Horst JARITZ, Stadt und Tempel von Elephantine. Vierter Grabungsbericht, *MDAIK* 30 (1974), 65-90, with 6 pl and 3 plans (1 folding).

Sequel to our number 72357.

The results of the 4th campaign of the German and Swiss Archaeological Institutes in the spring of 1972 have made it possible to draw up a preliminary survey of the history of the town of Elephantine from the Old Kingdom to the Roman Period. Its main feature is the remarkable continuity in the development and use of the site; the first major changes are introduced under Nectanebos II, and culminate in the reconstruction and enlargement associated with the Ptolemaic Period and the Roman occupation. *Dieter Mueller*

74368 KÁKOSY, László, Egyiptom és az aurópai irodalem, *Helikon*, Budapest 20 (1974), 167-176.

"Ägypten und die europäische Literatur".
Eine zusammenfassende Darstellung der Wirkung Ägyptens in den Themen der klassischen Literatur (Homeros, Aisopos, Horatius, Apuleius, Heliodoros, der Alexander-Roman, Hermetismus) und die Behandlung der Frage der Wechselwirkung (Petubastis, Setna-Siusire). Schilderung der Auffassung in der Renaissance und Erwähnung einiger moderner Romane mit dem Thema des Alten Ägyptens von den Autoren Thomas Mann, F. Werfel, B. Prus, Théophile Gautier, Anatole France, etc. *V. Wessetzky*

74369 KÁKOSY, László, Az egyiptomi időfogalom, *Idő és történelem*, 81-89.

"Der ägyptische Zeitbegriff".
Nach Anschauung des Neuen Reiches wird die Zeit von der Sonne in Bewegung gesetzt. Man hat sich aber auch vor dem Stehenbleiben der Zeit gefürchtet. Im Jenseits kann die Zeit auch reversibel sein : die Jahre des verstorbenen Königs können auch rückwärts fließen. Vergangenheit und Zukunft werden von Osiris und Re personifiziert. *V. Wessetzky*

74370 KÁKOSY, L., Isis Regina, *Studia Aegyptiaca I*, 221-230.

Proceeding from the invocation of the Regina caeli (Isis) in Apuleius' *Metamorphoses* (XI, 2) the author first discusses instances relating divinities to the power of Pharaoh. In Ptolemaic times Isis is considered to be royal mother and king's wife, with allusions to the kingship of Osiris, who receives royal titulary and is conceived as one of the primeval kings, or even as the genuine present king. In the Roman Period all gods became sovereigns of the country, or even of the entire earth.

74371 KÁKOSY, László, Ein Sarkophag aus der Ptolemäerzeit im Berliner Ägyptisches Museum, *Festschrift Ägyptisches Museum Berlin*, 113-118, with 3 pl. and 1 fig.

Publication of the limestone sarcophagus of a priest *Wnn-nfr*, probably from the 2nd or 1st century B.C. and preserved in the Berlin Museum (Inv. No. 46). The texts, taken from the *Book of the Dead*, ch. 72, are presented in photograph and transcription, with a translation and a commentary.

74372 KÁKOSY, L., Semitische Götternamen in einem unpublizierten magischen Text (Vorbericht), *GM* Heft 11 (1974), 29-32.

The magical papyrus Inv. No. 51.2168 in the Budapest Museum of Fine Arts contains two divine names of Semitic origin. One, *Ktr*, doubtless denotes the Ugaritic god Kotar; the other might be 'El or 'Ilum, but cannot yet be identified with certainty.
Dieter Mueller

74373 KÁKOSY, László, Ujév az ókori Egyiptomban, *Természet Világa* ["Die Welt der Natur"], Budapest 105 (1974), 548-549, with 3 ill.

"Neujahr im Alten Ägypten".
Zusammenfassung der kultischen Bedeutung des altägyptischen Neujahrsfestes. Die Fotos zeigen: eine Neujahrsflasche, das Relief mit Isis-Sothis aus dem Heiligtum von Savaria und die Kanne aus Egyed mit Darstellung von Neujahrssymbolen.
V. Wessetzky

74374 KÁKOSY, László, Vilmos Wessetzky a 65 ans, *Studia Aegyptiaca I*, XI-XIII.

Short biography of the scholar to whose honour the studies are published.

74375 KANAWATI, Naguib, The Financial Resources of the Viziers of the Old Kingdom and the Historical Implications, *Archaeological and Historical Studies*, Alexandria 5 (1974), 1-20, with 1 fig.

This is an attempt to establish the relative wealth of the Old Kingdom viziers as reflected by their expenditure on their tombs. After drawing up a list of 35 viziers and discussing their chronology the author compares the floor areas of their tombs (see graph on p. 16). It appears that from Cheops or slightly earlier until the early Vth Dynasty the tombs became smaller, while afterwards there were sudden, but temporary rises, mainly at the beginning of some reigns.

74376 KANAWATI, N., Notes on the Genealogy of the Late Sixth Dynasty, *Archaeological and Historical Studies*, Alexandria 5 (1974), 52-58.

After a few remarks on the marriages and children of Pepy I the author discusses those of Pepy II. He suggests that Nemtyemsaf (formerly read as Antyemsaf) was the son of Queen Neith and Pepy's first successor, possibly followed by two ephemeral kings, after whom came Neferkare, the son of Pepy's fourth wife Ankhenespepy.

KANTOR, Helene J., see our number 74486.

74377 KAPLONY, Peter, Das Büchlein Kemit, *Akten des XIII. Internationalen Papyrologenkongresses*, 179-197.

A translation of the so-called "Book of *Kmyt*", followed by lexicographical and grammatical notes. The commentary classifies this book as a literary letter comparable to the "Instruction of a Father for His Son", and discusses its philosophical background.   *Dieter Mueller*

74378 KAPLONY, Peter, Das Grab des Haremhab im Tal der Könige, *Orientalia* 43 (1974), 94-102, with 2 pl.

A review article of our number 71286.

74379 KAPLONY, Peter, Eine Spätzeit-Inschrift in Zürich, *Festschrift Ägyptisches Museum Berlin*, 119-150, with 1 pl.

The author publishes the inscription of a limestone relief from the Late Period, probably c. 750 B.C., now in a private collection in Zürich. He provides the few words, all titles of priests, with an extensive commentary, discussing with material from the entire Egyptian history the gods mentioned, i.a. Osiris of Mehenet and Horus of the Broad Court (*Ḥr šḥw*). A summary is given on p. 149-150.

74380 KAPLONY-HECKEL, Ursula, Ein neuer demotischer Brief aus Gebelēn (zusammengesetzt aus zwei Fragmenten in London und Berlin), *Festschrift Ägyptisches Museum Berlin*, 287-301, with 3 fig. and 3 pl.

Publication of three papyri from Gebelein, one of which at present preserved half in London (Brit. Mus. 040) and half in Berlin (P 13381). The others are PD Heidelberg 781a + 742b (cfr Spiegelberg, *ZÄS* 42, 1905, 50), which is a close parallel, and PD Heidelberg 781b. The latter dates from the year 110 B.C., the others from 103 and 102 B.C.

Of all three texts there are given a photograph, a facsimile, a transliteration and a translation with commentary. At the end (p. 300-301) a list of names from these texts.

74381 KAPLONY-HECKEL, Ursula, Schüler und Schulwesen in der Ägyptischen Spätzeit, *SAK* 1 (1974), 227-246, with 2 fig.

The author studies the last stage of the Egyptian schoolsystem and its contacts with the Greeks and their language. After stating that the Late Period was not at all sterile, that it begins with the reign of Psammetichus I, that the position of the Egyptian language was a very weak one as compared with the Greek, and that it is difficult to discern the subjects of the highest level of civilization, the author enumerates and discusses instances of grammatical exercises and lists of words in Demotic. She then studies the place of the schoolroom in the late temples, what we know about teachers and the results of teaching, and the penetration of the Greek in legal documents. At the end remarks on *B3k-3ḥw* in whose house in Tanis the famous "Sign-List" and the "Geographical Papyrus" have been found, one of the last admirers of a lost civilization.

In two appendices the author publishes DP Wien 6464, a Demotic grammatical exercise, and ostraca Bod. Eg. Inscr. 683 and 300, with a similar text and a list of month-names.

74382 KAPLONY-HECKEL, Ursula, Streitigkeiten zwischen Nachbarn. Lexikalische Beobachtungen am Rechtsbuch von Hermopolis, *Akten des XIII. Internationalen Papyrologenkongresses*, 199-205.

The article proceeds from three paragraphs of the still unpublished Codex from Hermopolis concerned with quarrels between neighbours, and studies the use of the words for friend/neighbour and for master/servant. The author points out that some, such as *hjnw*, "neighbour" and *nb*, "master" disappeared afterwards, while others remained in use. The lexical evolution is not at all clear.

For the codex, see now Girgis Mattha, The Demotic Legal Code of Hermopolis West, Le Caire, Institut français d'Archéologie orientale, 1975 = Bibliothèque d'étude, 45/1 and 45/2.

74383 KARAGEORGHIS, Vassos, Excavations at Kition. I. The Tombs (Text), Nicosia, Published for the Republic of Cyprus by the Department of Antiquities, Cyprus and Printed by Zavallis Press Ltd, 1974 (23 × 29.5 cm; X + 178 p., 7 ill., 10 fig., 1 colour pl.).

Appendix I of this report of the excavations at Kition (Cyprus), by E.J. Peltenburg, deals with the glazed vases and contains sections on Egyptian faience vases (p. 110-116), with a catalogue of faience rhyta found in various countries among which Egypt (126-127), and a section about inlaying and outlining polychrome faience in Egypt (130-135).

Appendix III, by Jean Leclant, describes three scarabs found in tomb 9.

74384 KASSER, R., Réflexions sur quelques méthodes d'étude des versions coptes néotestamentaires, *Biblica*, Roma 55 (1974), 233-256.

Critical discussion of our number 72495 and of some reviews of the author's book about the Gospel of St. John (our number 67309). The author lists the Greek text and translations in six Coptic dialects of *Joh.* 10, 1-18 (discussed by Mink) and deals with the methods according to which the text has to be analysed, illustrating his argument with remarks to differences in the versions.

74385 KASSER, R., Y a-t-il une généalogie des dialectes coptes?, *in*: *Mélanges d'histoire des religions* offerts à Henri-Charles Puech, Paris, Presses Universitaires de France, 1974, 431-436.

Discussing the historical relations between the Coptic dialects the author first presents a survey of the conceptions concerning this subject since the 18th century A.D. As the dialect of Lycopolis, usually called Sub-Akhmimic (*A2*), is not a sub-dialect of Akhmimic, he proposes the use of the siglum *L* for it.
Kasser states that all dialects known from written texts are more or less contemporaneous; they are "brothers", not "fathers and sons". Their appearance in writing coincides with the disappearance of a centralized state with uniform writing traditions. As the influence of the Church increased, once more one dialect began to dominate the others, at least between Aswân and Heliopolis, namely Sahidic. It was only when under the Arab rule the influence of the Church decreased that the dialects once more for a short period came to the fore.

74386 KEEL, Othmar, Die Weisheit spielt vor Gott. Ein ikonographischer Beitrag zur Deutung des Meṣaḥäqät in Spr. 8, 30f., Freiburg, Schweiz/Göttingen, Universitätsverlag/Vandenhoeck & Ruprecht, [1974] (16 × 23.5 cm; 79 p., 2 + 34 fig.).

In this study on the O.T. concept of Wisdom as it occurs in *Proverbs* ch. 8 the author pays much attention to scenes of amusing the gods in ancient Egypt (section 5) and to the "playing Maʿat" (section 6). In section 5 he discusses i.a. ball-games, sham fights, acrobatics with their erotic notion, music and dances, all performed in front of the gods. In section 6 he stresses the relation between Maʿat and Hathor, and deals with the representations of the king offering Maʿat to the god, in some instances accompanied by a queen (e.g., Ahmose-Nefertari). The argument is illustrated by scenes from tomb and temple walls.
The study has also appeared in: *Freiburger Zeitschrift für Philosophie und Theologie*, Freiburg/Schweiz 21 (1974), 1-66.

74387 KEEL, Othmar, Wirkmächtige Siegeszeichen im Alten Testament. Ikonographische Studien zu Jos 8, 18-26; Ex 17, 8-13; 2 Kön 13, 14-19 und 1 Kön 22, 11, Freiburg, Schweiz/Göttingen, Universitätsverlag/Vandenhoeck & Ruprecht, 1974 (17.5 × 25 cm; 233 p., 78 ill. and fig.) = Orbis biblicus et orientalis, 5.

The book contains four studies of powerful symbols of victory in the OT, for each of which the author finds parallels in ancient Egypt, although he is unable to indicate the way in which Israel derived them from the Egyptians. The well chosen fig. are an essential element in the author's argument.
Chapter 1 is devoted to the scimetar of Joshua (*Jos.* 8, 18 and 26). The author discusses the diffusion of scimetars as a weapon in the Near East and in Egypt, where it seems to occur for the first time during the XVIIIth Dynasty and disappears at the end of the New Kingdom. A section (p. 51-58) is devoted to the symbolic meaning of the scenes in which the king smites the enemies while a god offers him a scimetar, which occurs also in the egyptianized art of Palestine and Phoenicia. The scimetar is mostly not used to kill the enemies; that the god presents it to the king means that the latter will gain or has gained a victory with his mace.
Chapter 2 deals with the raised arms of Moses during the battle against Amalek, and discusses (95-103) the gesture of the raised arm in Egyptian iconography and (103-109) the way in which it has to be interpreted and was borrowed by Israel.
In chapter 3 the author deals with the rite of shooting an arrow (*II Kings* 13, 14-19), also a victory magic, which was performed during the Sed-festival. In chapter 4, on the horns of iron which Zedekiah made for himself (*I Kings* 22, 11), a parallel is drawn with the representations of Pharaoh as a bull trampling his enemies.
The summary (135-146) is followed by two appendices, one on the king presenting captives to a god, and one on the representations of the outstretched or raised hand (for Egypt, see 158-160).
A biblical index and an extensive bibliography are followed by two short additions.

74388 KELLEY, Allyn L., The Evidence for Mesopotamian Influence in Predynastic Egypt, *Newsletter SSEA* 4, No. 3 (March 1974), 2-11.

The author evaluates the various arguments for Egyptian-Mesopotamian contacts in the Predynastic Period: the invasion of a "Dynastic Race"; ceramic affinities; the Gerzean "foreign boat" pottery motif; predynastic construction techniques. He concludes that the evidence is scarce or even lacking, all Mesopotamian influence dating from dynastic times.

74389 KELLEY, Allyn L., Reserve Heads: A Review of the Evidence for their Placement and Function in Old Kingdom Tombs, *Newsletter SSEA* 5, No. 1 (September 1974), 6-12.

The statements concerning meaning and placement of reserve heads in Old Kingdom tombs are contradictory. The author presents a survey of the evidence about 31 heads, four of which have been recovered from the burial chamber and fifteen to sixteen from the burial shafts; the original placement of the others is unknown. Three explanations of the heads have been given : a "second head" as resting place of the soul, a transitional between moulded linen and plaster modelling, and a sculptor's model. Final conclusions are not yet possible.

74390 KEMP, Barry J., University Museum, University of Pennsylvania. Excavations at Malkata, *Newsletter ARCE* No. 88 (Winter 1974), 13-18, with 1 plan.

The work of the University Museum, Pennsylvania has been concerned with the Birket Habu area and Amenhotep III's palace complex at Malkata, which are quite contemporaneous. During the excavations in the palace sherds apparently identical to those of the Badarian culture were found, and an area of private housing was cleared, yielding a rich collection of organic debris.
The investigations of the Birket Habu presented considerable difficulties, as do the determination of its function and its identification with Tiy's pleasure lake. See our following number. *L.M.J. Zonhoven*

74391 KEMP, Barry and David O'CONNOR, An Ancient Nile Harbour. University Museum Excavations at the 'Birket Habu', *The International Journal of Nautical Archaeology and Underwater Exploration*, London 3 (1974), 101-136, with 2 maps, 6 plans (1 folding), 9 ill. and 10 fig. (2 folding); Addendum on p. 182.

In part I the second author, after discussing transport in general, presents a survey of what is known about harbours on the Nile, discussing the Egyptian words for quays and harbours, the pictorial and archaeological evidence, including that from Nubia. He particularly deals with what is known about artificial harbour basins.
Part II, by both authors, studies the Birket Habu, stating after Yoyotte (our number 59655) that it is not the pleasure lake for Queen Tiy but an actual harbour basin. There is an extensive discussion of the Birket Habu on account of the excavations of

the University Museum in 1971 and 1973, as well as of the Malkata palace. The basin appears to be contemporaneous with the palace. The dumping of the spoil has been part of a carefully planned enterprise. The (fairly large) dimensions of the lake and its approximate depth (5.9 m) are discussed, and it is calculated that the basin may have been more or less dry during low Nile. As for its history and function, the authors argue that the basin was excavated in two stages; that it served as the harbour for the fairly large town around the palace complex, as well as being used, in its unfinished state, for the ceremonial boat journey during the *sed*-festival; that major work on it ceased after the death of Amenophis III; that the size of the basin together with the associated buildings reflects the effort of the king to emphasize his unique status; and that its building implies the transfer of importance from eastern Thebes to the west bank, i.e., away from the national centre of Amon.

KEMP, Barry J., see also our number 74294.

74392 KEMPINSKI, A., Tell el-'Ajjûl — Beth-Aglayim or Sharuḥen?, *Israel Exploration Journal*, Jerusalem 24 (1974), 145-152.

The article discusses the identification of Tell el-'Ajjûl (near Gaza). Rejecting the identification with Beth-Aglayim and arguing that the floruit of the site (the largest city of the MBA) is to be dated from the excavated remains to the period between the XIIIth Dynasty and c. 1570 B.C., when the city was destroyed and lost most of its importance, the author suggests that it was Sharuhen, the last stronghold of the Hyksos. Other data, e.g. the presence of an Egyptian garrison under Tuthmosis III, point at the same conclusion.

KESTHELYI, L., see our number 74182.

74393 KHANJIAN, John, Wisdom in Ugarit and in the Ancient Near East with Particular Emphasis on Old Testament Wisdom Literature, *Dissertation Abstracts International A*, Ann Arbor, Mich. 35, No. 1 (July 1974), 568/9-A.

Abstract of a doctor's thesis Claremont Graduate School, 1974 (Order No. 74-14,883; 325 p.).
The Ugaritic Wisdom Literature is studied in a broader context, among which Egyptian Wisdom Literature which itself is placed within its historical, conceptual and literary settings and is concluded with a section on its typology.   *L.M.J. Zonhoven*

74394 KIRWAN, L.P., Nubia and Nubian Origins, *The Geographical Journal*, London 140, Part 1 (February 1974), 43-51, with 1 map.

Unter "nubischem Ursprung" wird das Kerngebiet dieser Bevölkerung im Niltal verstanden; an Hand antiker Literatur und Inschriften wird über das Wohngebiet der Nuba der griechischen und römischen Schriftsteller, der Noba der Aksumiten, der Nobades der späteren griechischen Inschriften berichtet, sowie die Auseinandersetzung mit den Bega und dem römischen Ägypten dargelegt, wobei Silko und seine Nubier als Verbündete der Römer angesehen werden, die in seinem Sieg über die Blemmyer die Hand mit im Spiel gehabt haben mögen. Als Kernland der Nubier wird das Herrschaftsgebiet des christlichen Königreiches Nobadia oder Nouba bis zum 3. Katarakt angesehen. *Inge Hofmann*

74395 KISCHKEWITZ, Hannelore, Fragmente eines Sarges der Spätzeit in Berlin und Paris, *Festschrift Ägyptisches Museum Berlin*, 151-157, with 1 pl.

Publication of a wooden coffin of which parts are preserved in the Louvre Museum (Nos. 2939 and 2940) and another in Berlin (Inv. No. 633). The author describes the fragments, translates the texts, and discusses office and person of the owner, an officer of the cavalry *Knš*, son of *Ns-sw-ist*. All evidence points to a date in the Saite Period.

74396 KISS, Zsolt, Les fouilles polonaises en Égypte et au Soudan en 1972, *Africana Bulletin*, Warszawa 19 (1973), 130-136, with 3 ill.

Short report of the Polish reconstruction works at Deir el-Bahari and the excavations at Kôm el-Dikka (Alexandria), Qasr Ibrîm, Dongola, and Kadero in 1972.

74397 KITCHEN, K.A., Nakht-Thuty — Servitor of Sacred Barques and Golden Portals, *JEA* 60 (1974), 168-174, with 2 fig.

An 'advance' edition of a tomb text to be published in *KRI* III. Nakht-Thuty, Superintendent of Carpenters and Chief of Goldworkers, made his two-roomed chapel in the outer court of the tomb of Kheruef, i.e. No. 189. Two large inscriptions are given here, one originally showing no less than twenty-six doorways and barques, together with translation and notes. An important date, year 58, shows that the tomb is to be placed at the end of Ramses II's very long reign when the owner did much work in Karnak and at Thebes on renewing wood and goldwork. Later Nakht-Thuty worked on portable barques for a whole series of Upper Egyptian deities. *E. Uphill*

74398 KITCHEN, K.A., *Prd > Ptr =* 'Mule' in New Kingdom Egypt?, *GM* Heft 13 (1974), 17-20.

The loanword *ptr* attested twice on Ostr. Gardiner 86 may be West-Semitic *prd* "mule". *Dieter Mueller*

74399 KITCHEN, K.A., Ramesside Inscriptions. Historical and Biographical. I. Fascicle 5, Oxford, B.H. Blackwell Ltd, [1974] (20.5 × 28.7 cm; 64 p. [= I, 129-192]); rev. *JARCE* 12 (1975), 117 (Hans Goedicke); *JEA* 62 (1976), 198-199 (C.H.S. Spaull).

A sequel to our number 73403.
The fascicle presents a continuation of the Royal Monuments — Geographical Series of Sethos I, containing inscriptions from the Great Temple at Abydos: the First and Second Hypostyle Halls; the dedications of the seven chapels of Sethos I himself, Ptah, Re, Amun, Osiris, Isis and Horus; the Suite of Osiris, and that of Sokar and Nefertem; the Gallery of the kings; and the Stairway corridor. *L.M.J. Zonhoven*

74400 KITCHEN, K.A., Ramesside Inscriptions. Historical and Biographical. I. Fascicle 6, Oxford, B.H. Blackwell Ltd, [1974] (20.5 × 28.7 cm; 64 p. [= I, 193-256]).

A sequel to our preceding number.
The inscriptions of the Great Temple at Abydos are continued with those of the Butcher's Hall and Annexe, and those of the Treasuries, Dependencies and Lesser Remains. The sections on the Royal Monuments, Geographical Series, and the Great Temple of Sethos I at Abydos are concluded by the texts from the Great Hypostyle Hall at Karnak, the temple of Qurna (mostly dedicatory texts) and various other places.
Next follow the Miscellaneous and Minor Royal Monuments (i.a. stelae and offering tables). The fascicle ends with Documents of the Reign and Period: Pap. Cairo 58057, Pap. Northumberland I-III, Palace Accounts from Memphis, Years 2-3 (several Pap. Bibl. Nat. and "Rechnungen"). *L.M.J. Zonhoven*

74401 KLASENS, Adolf, The Publication of Texts in the Leiden Museum, *Textes et langages III*, 181-194.

The author first deals with the history and general publications of the Leiden collection, explaining the different systems of reference. He then lists the more important objects with their recent publications, divided into "sections" according to the system of Leemans' *Monumens*, e.g. manuscripts (I), tombs (K), sarcophagi (L), stelae (V), etc.

KLAUCK, Jürgen, see our number 74151.

KLEINERT, T.N., see our number 74318.

KOBUSIEWICZ, Michal, see our number 74798.

74402 KOCHAVI, M., Tel Aphek, *Israel Exploration Journal*, Jerusalem 24 (1974), 261-262.

Noteworthy is the find of some sherds of Egyptian vessels from the First Dynasty.

KÖHLER, Oskar, see our numbers 74554 and 74556.

74403 KÖHLER, Ursula, Die Anfänge der deutschen Ägyptologie: Heinrich Brugsch. Eine Einschätzung, *GM* Heft 12 (1974), 29-41.

A review of Heinrich Brugsch's attitude toward ancient Egypt and Egyptology.
See also Spiegel, *GM* Heft 16 (1975), 55-68 and the reply by Ursula Rößler-Köhler, *GM* Heft 17 (1975), 67-71.

Dieter Mueller

KÖHLER, Ursula, see also our number 74342.

74404 KOELBING, Huldrych M., Thomas Young (1733-1829), die physiologische Optik und die Ägyptologie, *Gesnerus*, Zürich 31 (1974), 56-75, with a portrait and an English summary on p. 74-75.

Description of Thomas Young's life as a physician, with special attention for his contributions to the physiological optics (his theory of the undulatory nature of light), and to the decipherment of the hieroglyphs.

74405 KOMORZYNSKI, Egon, Die Erschliessung der inschriftlichen Denkmäler der Wiener ägyptischen Sammlung, *Textes et langages III*, 209-218.

After a survey of the history of the Egyptian collection in the Kunsthistorisches Museum at Vienna and the work of its directors, particularly Ernst von Bergmann and including the present author himself, with their publications, the author deals with the problem of neglecting the inventory numbers. He mentions his composition of an adequate inventory with concordances.
At the end a list of more important publications of inscriptional material arranged alphabetically after the author's name; when not mentioned in the publication the inventory number is added.

74406 KOROSTOVSTEV, M.A., Академик Борис Александрович Тураев (О стиле работы ученого), *ВДИ* 2 (128), 1974, 111-114.

"The Academian Boris Alexandrovich Turaev (On the Style of his Scientific Work)". Survey of the work of the well known Russian Egyptologist Turaev (1868-1920).

74407 KOROSTOVTSEV, M.A., Древний Египет и космогония древних иудеев, *Палестинский Сборник*, Ленинград 25 (88), 1974, 20-25, with an English summary on p. 25.

"Ancient Egypt and the Cosmogony of the Ancient Judaeans". The article supports and develops the thesis of Sayce of Egyptian influence on the Bible. In both worlds the means of creation is the divine word, not only exclusively in the Memphite theology, but in the Pap. Bremner-Rhind and other Egyptian cosmogonies as well. Notable is also the mention of God in many passages of the Bible as having large wings, just like the sky-god Horus is depicted as a winged solar disk.

L.J.M. Zonhoven

74408 KOROSTOVTSEV, M. A., Относительные (релятивные) формы глагола в египетском языке, *in: Основные проблемы африканистики. Этнография. история. филология.* К 70-летию члена-корреспондента АН СССР Д. А. Ольдерогге, Moscow, Издательство « Наука », 1973, 335-338.

"The Adjective (Relative) Verb Forms in Egyptian".
To determine the place of the so-called relative verb forms in the verbal system is no easy matter. They are typologically indistinguishable from other finite forms of the $sḏm=f$-type, and even share a common origin with the latter (a passive participle). Their contents are complex: they have a verbal predicate, an agent and an object reference. In course of time the relative forms, originating from passive verb forms with an agent of their own, were replaced by *nty*-headed constructions and gradually disappeared completely. Their complex character and their distributional equivalence to quite differently structured forms are good illustrations of what might be called 'incorporation': a sentence-like construction, embodied in one word which structurally is a unity.

J.F. Borghouts

74409 KOROSTOVTSEV, M. A., Снова о вокализации египетских имен собственных, *ВДИ* 3 (129), 1974, 162-165, with an English summary on p. 164-165.

"Once More on the Vocalisation of Egyptian Proper Names". Reply to our number 74081, repeating in the essence the arguments of the author's earlier study (our number 73412).

74410 KOROSTOVTSEV, Michel, Sur les textes égyptiens dans les collections soviétiques, *Textes et langages III*, 225-228.

The author briefly discusses the more important papyri and some stelae in the Museum of Fine Arts at Moscow and the Ermitage at Leningrad.

74411 KOSACK, Wolfgang, Alltag im alten Ägypten. Aus der Ägyptensammlung des Museums, Freiburg i.Br., Städtische Museen, 1974 (21 × 29.7 cm; XVIII + 50 p., 24 pl.) = Veröffentlichungen des Museums für Völkerkunde 1/1974. At head of title : Museum für Völkerkunde der Stadt Freiburg im Breisgau.

Publication of over three hundred Egyptian objects from the collections of the ethnological museum at Freiburg im Breisgau. The majority of them dates from the Coptic Period, some from pharaonic or Graeco-Roman times.
In the introduction the author relates the history of the collection, which comes from the German excavations at Qarâra and el-Hîba in 1913-14. Some conservation problems are mentioned. The author also offers a survey of the Coptic civilization and an evaluation of the collection's importance.
The catalogue itself is divided into eight sections : dress and ornament (97 numbers); musical instruments and toys (21); furniture and household equipment (16); tools and instruments (46); kitchen and household (mainly containers; 63 numbers); funerary cult (25); religion (43) and writing (19). Each object is briefly described, the more important pieces are represented by a photograph. Some texts on p. XVII.
From the objects from Pharaonic Egypt, mostly from the later periods, we mention : a wooden canopic chest (G 25); a stela (G 36); a bronze shovel (D 18) and a bronze model hoe (D 19); a coffin (F 1), part of a mummy case (F 5); two so-called concubine figurines (F 16-17). There are also amulets, bronze statuettes, etc.

74412 KOSACK, Wolfgang, Antike Touristen in Aegypten, *Armant*, Köln Heft 13 (1974), 3-20, with 8 fig. and 1 ill.

The author deals with classical, mainly Roman visitors to Egypt, amply quoting from the sources.   *L.M.J. Zonhoven*

74413 KOSACK, Wolfgang, Lehrbuch des Koptischen. Teil I : Koptische Grammatik. Teil II : Koptische Lesestücke, Graz, Akademische Druck- u. Verlagsanstalt, 1974 (18.5 × 27.3 cm; XVIII + 442 p., numerous fig. and ill., 2 tables [1 folding]); rev. *Armant* Heft 12 (1974), 30-33 (Helmut Birkenfeld); *Orientalia* 44 (1975), 454-456 (H. Quecke); *WZKM* 68 (1976), 187 (H. Satzinger).

As the title indicates, this is not a scientific grammar but a text-book, intended for those wishing to learn the language even without any knowledge of Egyptian or Greek. The didactic character appears from the arrangement of the subjects and from the numerous questions and exercises in the sections themselves. Moreover, the second part (p. 211-442) consists of 245 exercises, short bits of texts, mostly no longer than a page, taken from a very large variety of sources and arranged after their subjects

(e.g., biblical, monasticism, gnosticism, magic, letters, tomb and building incriptions, private documents, stories, historical texts, philology, philosophy, etc.).
Although the order in which the subjects are discussed — see, for instance, the relatively early discussion of Pres. I and II, even before that of the nomen — as well as the terminology (e.g., "tut"-Form for the Ist Present) — are clear evidence of the didactic aims the author has evidently made use of the most recent scientific publications.
After a chapter on Coptic writing and a very long one on grammar there is added a short discussion (p. 157-163) of vulgar Sahidic and the rendering of Greek and other words in Coptic script. Then follows a fourth chapter in which the characteristics of four other dialects are dealt with : Bohairic, Faiyumic, Akhmimic and Subakhmimic (called "Siutisch"). In accordance with its character the book contains no notes, but also no bibliographical references, nor as yet a list of words to the exercises; the latter is to be expected later (see p. V).

74414 KRAUSE, Martin, Die Koptologie im Gefüge der Wissenschaften, *ZÄS* 100,2 (1974), 108-125.

Antrittsvorlesung, am 3.XII.1966 in Münster, Philosophische Fakültat der Westfälischen Wilhelms-Universität, gehalten. Sie wurde angeregt von unserer Nummer 61508.
Für Verfasser ist die Koptologie ein Zweig der Orientalistik, philologisch zum grösseren Teil zur Ägyptologie, zum kleineren Teil zur Altertumskunde gehörig. Die koptische Kunst überschneidet sich mit der Archäologie. Der Zeitraum reicht in die altägyptische Epoche zurück und teilweise bis in die Gegenwart. Die Koptologie umfasst Ägypten und Nubien, mit Ausstrahlungen bis ins Abendland (S. 110).   *M. Heerma van Voss*

74415 KRAUSE, Martin, Nubische Grabungspublikationen : Ermenne West, *OLZ* 69 (1974), 533-539.

Review article of our numbers 67559, 67596 and 70534.

74416 KRAUSE, Martin, Walther Wolf. 24.11.1900–11.1.1973, *ZÄS* 101 (1974), V-VI.

Obituary notice. Compare our number 74849.

74417 KRAUSPE, Renate, Eine heute verlorene Stele der Leipziger Sammlung (Ägyptisches Museum der Karl-Marx-Universität Leipzig 5128), *Festschrift Ägyptisches Museum Berlin*, 159-161, with 1 ill. on a pl.

Publication of the Middle Kingdom stela Leipzig 5128 (destroyed during the war). Its importance is to be found in the mention of

Mut, Mistress of *Mqb* and *Nfrt* (= Hathor), Mistress of *Mint*, both places being located in the Xth Upper Egyptian nome.

74418 KRAUSPE, Renate, Ein Königskopf der 18. Dynastie in Leipzig, *ZÄS* 101 (1974), 107-109, with 2 pl.

Veröffentlichung eines kleinen Kopfes aus Marmor im Ägyptischen Museum der Sektion Kulturwissenschaften und Germanistik an der Karl-Marx-Universität Leipzig, Inv. Nr. 1640. Verfasserin identifiziert den mit dem 'Blauen Helm" dargestellten König mit Amenophis II. *M. Heerma van Voss*

74419 KREBS, Walter, Graffiti, *Das Altertum*, Berlin 20 (1974), 195-199, with 8 ill.

Viele der Graffiti, die im Altertum an Bauten und Denkmälern angebracht wurden (die angeführten Beispiele stammen aus Musawwarat es Sufra und Redesiah), legen aufgrund der Schreibfehler oder der verschieden ausgeführten Buchstaben die Annahme nahe, daß manche der Besucher selbst versuchten, ihren Namen in den Stein einzugraben. Prominente Reisende mögen für ihre Inschriften einen Fachhandwerker gefunden haben. Einige der Inschriften fallen durch ihre einfachen und geradlinigen, aber sehr gleichmässigen und korrekten Buchstaben auf, sodaß der Eindruck entsteht, als seien sie von der gleichen Hand oder nach einheitlichem Muster ausgeführt worden. Möglicherweise saß an frequentierten Stellen ein ausgedienter Steinmetz, der auf Wunsch der Besucher ihren Namen eingravierte. *Inge Hofmann*

74420 KRECHER, Joachim, In memoriam Eberhard Otto, *Saeculum*, Freiburg/München 25 (1974), 291-292.

Obituary notice. Compare our number 74845.

74421 KROMER, Karl, Weśer-ib-Chefren und die frühdynastische Siedlung in Giseh bei Kairo, *Antike Welt*, Küsnacht-Zürich 5, Heft 2 (1974), 53-54, with 2 fig.

Sequel to our number 73418 (see also our number 72394). From the campaigns of 1973 and 1974 the author mentions some seal-impressions with the name Weser-ib (= Khephren), which prove that the settlement did still exist in his reign. The occurrence of a sanctuary of Re on the impressions indicates that this god was already venerated in this area during the IVth Dynasty.

74422 KRZYŻANIAK, Lech, Pierwsza kampania badań wykopaliskowych w Kadero (Sudan), *Fontes Archaeologici Posnanienses*, Poznań 24 (1973), 1974, 217-223, with 1 map, 5 fig. and English and German summaries.

"First Excavation Campaign at Kadero (Sudan)".
Short report on the campaign of 1972. The settlement and the cemetery excavated belong to the Khartum Neolithic Culture and can be dated to the second half of the 4th millennium B.C.

74423 KÜHNE, Klaus, Frühgeschichtliche Werkstoffe auf silikatischer Basis. Chemie im Dienste der Archäologie, *Das Altertum*, Berlin 20 (1974), 67-80, with 7 ill. and 1 fig.

The article deals with a chemical analysis of ancient Egyptian frits, such as faience and pastes. As new names for respectively faience and paste are proposed silica frit (Kieselfritte) and copper silica frit (Kupferkieselfritte). *L.M.J. Zonhoven*

KUENTZ, Ch., see our number 74727.

74424 KUNZ, Jürgen, Neue Sahara-Felsmalereien, *Antike Welt*, Küsnacht-Zürich 5, Heft 1 (1974), 19-26, with 15 ill.

Der Tassili n'Ajjer erweist sich immer mehr als das Kerngebiet der saharanischen Felsbildkunst. Ein nordwestlicher Ausläufer des Tassili n'Ajjer ist das Sandsteinmassiv von Ifedaniouene, bei dessen Erforschung im Frühjahr 1971 zwei neue Felsbildstationen entdeckt wurden. Die Bildfunde entsprechen in den Grundzügen den bisher bekannten Felsbildern der Ostregion, die vier aufeinanderfolgende Kunstphasen und zugleich Zeitabschnitte erkennen lassen: 1. Epoche der Jäger, in der das Jagdwild monumental als Einzelwesen wiedergegeben wird. 2. Epoche der Viehzüchter mit dem domestizierten Rind als Leitbild. C 14-Analysen ergaben Daten zwischen 4000 und 2000 v.Chr. 3. Epoche der Garamanten mit Beginn um 1200 v.Chr., gekennzeichnet durch die Darstellung des Pferdes und 4. seit der Zeitwende als Hauptobjekt der Felskunst das Kamel.
Eine Streitwagen-Darstellung wird ausführlich besprochen, die Einführung von Pferd und Wagen im Saharabereich im Zusammenhang mit der Seevölkerbewegung angezweifelt und die Wagenszenen eher für Darstellungen aus dem sportlichen Leben als für Kampfdarstellungen gehalten. Man sehe unsere Nummer 74349. *Inge Hofmann*

LA BAUME, Peter, see our number 74632.

LABRE, Y., see our number 74220.

LAGARCE, Élisabeth and Jacques, see our number 74127.

74425 LAMBRECHTS-DOUILLEZ, Jeannine, De houten sarcofaag en haar mummie uit de verzameling van het Museum Vleeshuis Antwerpen, *Antwerpen*. Tijdschrift der stad Antwerpen 20 (1974), 129-135, with 6 ill.

Discussion of a sarcophagus preserved in the Museum Vleeshuis at Antwerp, which belonged to the chantress of Amon Neskhonsu of the XXIst Dynasty (not the wife of Pinodjem) and came to the collection about A.D. 1890. There are given photographs of the sarcophagus and of some details of its decoration. The mummy it contains does not belong to it (see our number 74361).

74426 LAMENDIN, H., Observation with SEM of Rehydrated Mummy Teeth, *Journal of Human Evolution*, London 3 (1974), 271-274, with 7 pl.

Observation with the scanning electronic microscope (SEM) of the teeth of mummies from Gebelein and Aswân after rehydration of the tissues appears to be a means to estimate the age of the mummies.

LANCEL, Serge, see our number 74158.

74427 LANDA, N.B., Стела *Jpj* (первая половина XIV в. до н.э.), *ВДИ* 2 (128), 1974, 97-104, with 1 pl. and an English summary on p. 104.

"The Stela of *Ipj* (First Half of the XIVth Century B.C.)".
Discussion of the stela of the great steward in Memphis Ipy, son of Amenhotep, in the Hermitage (No. 1072). For the father, see our number 74080.
The author studies Ipy's career from the reign of Amenophis III to that of Tutankhamon as well as style and iconography of the stela, from which he concludes that it is to be dated in the reign of the latter pharaoh. It probably came from the still unidentified tomb of Ipy in Memphis.

LANDA, N.B., see also our number 74181.

LAPIS, Irma Alexandrowna, see our number 74181.

74428 LASKOWSKA-KUSZTAL, Ewa, Uwagi na temat datowania kilku fragmentów architektonicznych z Edfu, *Rocznik Muzeum Narodowego w Warszawie*, Warszawa 18 (1974), 23-49, with 23 ill. and summaries in Russian and English on p. 48-49.

"Remarques sur la datation de quelques fragments architectoniques d'Edfou".
Fragments architectoniques ornés de bas-reliefs du Musée National de Varsovie ont été trouvés au cours des fouilles franco-polonaises à Edfou en 1936-39, et ils font partie d'un large ensemble de blocs décorés provenant du groupe de mammisi d'Edfou. L'exécution d'une négligence manifeste des reliefs et l'analyse iconographique indiquent que les sculptures datent d'une période de décadence des ateliers d'Edfou, ce qui eut lieu sous Ptolémée XII Neos Dionysos.   *A. Szczudlowska*

74429 LÁSZLÓ, P., Néhány megjegyzés II. Ramszesz fia, Khaemuaszet pályáját és történelmi szerepét illetően, *Studia Aegyptiaca I*, 243-262.

"Einige Bemerkungen zum Lebenslauf und der geschichtlichen Rolle des Khaemwaset, Sohn Ramses II.".
Nach einem Überblick und Versuch der Klärung der Frage der Thronfolge schildert Verf. die Rolle des Khaemwaset als Oberpriester des Ptah und untersucht er seine weitere Priestertitel. In diesem Zusammenhang verweist er auf die auffällige Übereinstimmung der Schreibung des Titels *sm-stm-stnj* (als Namengeber : Setna) mit dem Determinativ in demotischer Schrift und die *sntj-Ḥr* Titel des Khaemwaset.
Vgl. unsere Nummer 73271. *V. Wessetzky*

74430 LAUER, J.P., Le mystère des pyramides, Paris, Presses de la Cité, 1974 (13 × 20 cm; 378 p., 74 fig., 32 pl. [16 in colour)); series : Collection Coup d'œil; rev. *Syria* 51 (1974), 362-365 (A[ndré] P[arrot]).

An up-to-date revision of the author's earlier work 'Le problème des pyramides d'Égypte' (see our number 552). The chapter headings are the same, except that 'Les théories scientifiques' has been changed to 'Les théories pseudo-scientifiques'. Significant discoveries at pyramid sites since 1948 are summarized and recent speculations by pyramid theorists are refuted. Among the new features are a table showing the sizes, angles of incline and the proportions of the major pyramids and a Bibliography. The footnotes of the earlier version have been supplemented and transferred to the end. Text figures have been increased by approximately a half. All the illustrations in colour and many in black and white are new. *I.E.S. Edwards*

74431 LECLANT, Jean, Colloque : « Les syncrétismes dans les religions de l'antiquité ». Besançon, 22-24 Octobre 1973, *Orientalia* 43 (1974), 423.

Notice to a colloquium, with a list of the lectures.

74432 LECLANT, Jean, Deux colloques sur le déchiffrement des écritures, *Orientalia* 43 (1974), 418-420.

After mentioning several manifestations celebrating the 150th anniversary of Champollion's decipherment of the hieroglyphs the author reports on a colloquium on the decipherment of writings and languages at Paris (17-18 July, 1973) and another on undeciphered languages at London (24-28 July, 1973).

74433 LECLANT, Jean, Fouilles et travaux en Égypte et au Soudan, 1972-1973, *Orientalia* 43 (1974), 171-227, with 56 ill. on 36 pl.

Sequel to our number 73442.

In his yearly survey of the excavation activities and discoveries the author this time mentions 56 sites in Egypt, 18 in Sudan, and 14 places elsewhere.

The major entries for Egypt are those on Matarîya (a list of recent finds, from 1957 onwards), Gîza, Saqqâra (with a long section on the researches in and around the pyramid of Pepi I), Karnak, Western Thebes (many expeditions, i.a. those of the Deutsches Archäologisches Institut Kairo, the University of Vienna, the Polish Centre of Mediterranean Archaeology and the CEDAE), Aswân and Qasr Ibrîm.

From the expeditions in Sudan we mention the Survey South of the Dal Cataract (Vila), the excavations on Sai (Vercoutter) and at Tabo, and the Survey of Central Sudan (by the Universities of Berkeley and MacQuarie).

Among the finds in other countries there is particularly the discovery of a statue of Darius I at Susa (see our number 72794).

74434 LECLANT, Jean, Histoire de la diffusion des cultes égyptiens, *Annuaire. École Pratique des Hautes Études.* V^e section - sciences religieuses, Paris 82 (1973-1974), fasc. 3, 115-118.

Neben einer allgemeinen Übersicht über die Probleme, die die Ausbreitung der ägyptischen Kulte aufwerfen, wurde Gewicht gelegt auf das ägyptische bzw. ägyptisierende Material von Zypern und die jüngsten Entdeckungen in Italien und Spanien. Innerhalb der meroitischen Forschungen wurde am REM (Répertoire d'épigraphie méroitique) weitergearbeitet. Es folgt ein Überblick über Ausgrabungskampagnen und Tagungen sowie eine Bibliographie. *Inge Hofmann*

74435 LECLANT, Jean, Mise en place d'un inventaire systématique de la documentation concernant la civilisation méroïtique, *in*: *Banques de données archéologiques.* Marseille, 12-14 Juin 1972, Paris, Éditions du Centre National de la Recherche Scientifique, 1974 (= Colloques Internationaux du Centre National de la Recherche Scientifique, No 932), 267-275.

The Meroitic civilization, which developed in the Middle Nile steppes between the 8th century B.C. and the 4th A.D., constitutes a research field clearly limited in time and space. Thus optimal circumstances are gathered to perfect a documentary method, to set up a systematic inventory and construct a data bank.

Since 1960, an experiment is being carried out leading to the automatic processing of about 900 known Meroitic texts. In the Repertoire d'Épigraphie Meroïtique, texts are ordered according to their publication data. They are divided into syntagmatic units called "stiches". To each Meroitic sign corresponds one letter in the transliteration. The use of a double pack of cards serves the attempt to give a real analysis parallel to the transliteration.

The use of "separators" by the Meroits has made possible concordances and indexes which serve as an introduction to a lexicon of this language one still fails to know the nature of. But henceforth, for one of the most ancient African languages, linguists and historians have at their disposal implements for any sort of structural, statistic or comparative research till a bilingual text opens the way to a thorough knowledge of Meroitic.

74436 LECLANT, J., Osiris en Gaule, *Studia Aegyptiaca I*, 263-285, with 13 ill.

Wessetzky has suggested that the relatively high number of Osiris statuettes in Hungary as against those of Serapis is an indication for a progressive egyptianization of the Isis cult. The author investigates in how far this is correct for various parts of the Roman Empire, concluding that certainty is hard to achieve, but that it seems that the osiriazation of the Isis cult has not been detrimental to Serapis. He also assembles the pertinent data for France, where once more the explication of the relative multitude of Osiris statuettes is not clear.

74437 LECLANT, Jean, Third International Colloquium on Aegean Prehistory. Université de Sheffield, 15-19 Avril 1973, *Orientalia* 43 (1974), 421-422.

Notice to a colloquium. Among the lectures some deal with Egyptological evidence about the "Sea Peoples".

74438 LECLANT, Jean, Titres et travaux, [Paris, privately published, 1974] (21 × 29 cm; 61 p.).

Hierbei handelt es sich um eine Zusammenstellung der wichtigsten Daten des wissenschaftlichen Lebenslaufes von J. Leclant, seine Mitgliedschaften und Ehrungen. S. 4-50 beinhalten seine Publikationen auf den Gebieten der Ägyptologie, der Nubien- und Sudanforschung, der Untersuchungen über die Beziehungen zwischen Ägypten und Afrika, Forschungen über äthiopische Archäologie und Geschichte, Forschungen über Amun und die Ausbreitung des Isiskultes u.a.m. Darauf folgt eine Angabe über seine wissenschaftliche Tätigkeit an der Universität, in der Feldforschung, auf Kongressen und Kolloquien usw.

Inge Hofmann

74439 LECLANT, Jean, Jacques Vandier (1904-1973), *Journal Asiatique*, Paris 262 (1974), 11-18.

Obituary article. Compare our number 73828.

74440 LECLANT, J., avec la collaboration de Gisèle CLERC, Inventaire bibliographique des Isiaca (IBIS). Répertoire analytique des travaux relatifs à la diffusion des cultes isiaques. 1940-1969. E-K, Leiden, E.J. Brill, 1974 (15.7 × 23.8 cm; XII + 276 p., frontispiece, 28 pl., 2 folding maps) = Études préliminaires aux religions orientales dans l'empire romain publiées par M.J. Vermaseren, 18. Pr. fl. 112

Sequel to our number 72420.
This second volume contains the numbers 347-701, once more followed by extensive indexes (p. 170-272).

LECLANT, Jean, see also our numbers 74316, 74383 and 74663.

LEDGE, Wolf-Günther, see our number 74040.

74441 LEPROHON, Ronald J., The Wages of the Eloquent Peasant, *Newsletter SSEA* 5, No 1 (September 1974), 4-6.

In the *Eloquent Peasant*, B I 84 a daily ration of 10 loaves of bread and 4 jugs of beer is said to be allotted to the peasant, which from other instances appears to be a normal workman's ration of bread in the Middle Kingdom, but a higher quantity of beer than usual.

74442 LESKO, Leonard H., Brief Report on the Computer Printing of Hieroglyphs, *GM* Heft 14 (1974), 17-20.

A discription of the Berkeley project to produce with the help of a computer a dictionary of Late Egyptian, starting with a concordance of the Late Ramesside Letters.
Dieter Mueller

74443 LEWIN, Peter, A.J. MILLS, Howard SAVAGE and John VOLLMER, Nakht. A Weaver of Thebes, *Rotunda*, Toronto 7, no. 4 (Fall 1974), 14-19, with 4 ill. and 1 fig.

Report of the unwrapping and autopsy of a mummy formerly on display in the Royal Ontario Museum, Toronto. The mummy was found in its coffin at Deir el-Baḥri in 1905 and belonged to the weaver Nakht of the funerary cult of Sethnakht, to be dated to the XXth-XXIst Dynasty. The linen wrappings and bandages were well preserved, as were the organs, including the brains since they were not removed, Nakht being a relatively poor man. The bandages consisted i.a. of a large and a small (child's?) tunic. Some torn strips were of white linen patterned with blue stripes. Nakht may have been about 15 years old when he died, possibly from malaria.

74444 LEWIS, Naphtali, Papyrus in Classical Antiquity, Oxford, At the Clarendon Press, 1974 (13.7 × 21.5 cm; VIII + 152 p., 8 pl.);

rev. *BiOr* 33 (1976), 29-30 (H. Leclercq); *CdE* XLIX, No. 98 (1974), 404-405 (Georges Nachtergael). Pr. £ 5.50

Although outside the scope of the *AEB* it seems useful to mention this study — a revised and enlarged version of the author's thesis ("L'industrie du papyrus dans l'Égypte gréco-romaine", Paris, 1934) — because of the detailed discussion of the manufacturing process according to classical sources (p. 34-69) as well as the chapter on cultivating and harvesting the papyrus-plant (p. 103-114).

74445 Lexikon der Ägyptologie. Herausgegeben von Wolfgang Helck und Eberhard Otto. Unter Mitwirkung von Erika Feucht. Band I, Lieferung 6 [and] 7, Wiesbaden, Otto Harrassowitz, 1974 (20 × 28 cm; 320 col. [= col. 801-1120], 2 fig., 1 map, 2 plans, 3 ill.).

Sequel to our number 73455.
The two fascicles contain the lemmata from "Bildhauer" (first lines in fasc. 5) to "Domestikation". Only a few are longer than four columns, e.g. "Brief" (cols 855-864, followed by "Briefe an Tote", 864-870), "Chenti-irti" (926-930), "Deir el-Bahari" (1006-1025), "Dekret" (1037-1043) and "Delta" (1043-1052).
The number of authors is regularly increasing, as indicated on the endpaper. It is evident that by the progress of the publication of its fascicles (fasc. 8, completing vol. I, has appeared in 1975) the *LdÄ* becomes a significant source of information for the Egyptology.

74446 LILYQUIST, Christine, Early Middle Kingdom Tombs at Mitrahina, *JARCE* 11 (1974), 27-30, with 3 pl.

Record of a short investigation in 1971 of a group of Middle Kingdom burials at Kom el-Fakhry, to the south of Mît Rahîneh. Use is made of the notes of a preliminary excavation by Abdul Towal el-Hitta in 1954 (see our number 3988). There is at least one mud-brick mastaba with multiple burials inside; the burial chambers were decorated. A dating to the IXth-XIth Dynasty seems probable. *J.F. Borghouts*

74447 LINDSAY, Jack, Blast-Power and Ballistics. Concepts of Force and Energy in the Ancient World, New York, Harper & Row Publishers, Inc., [1974] (14 × 21.5 cm; 509 p., 87 fig.).

Although mainly dealing with the classical antiquity the author refers on some pages to ancient Egypt (cfr the Index s.v. Egypt, p. 503). We mention p. 207-212, in the chapter on the sources of Greek scientific thinking, where the author discusses the Egyptian concept of a creator-god, and p. 351-353, where in the discussion of blast power the author refers to the *Book of Gates* and the *Book of Amduat*.

74448 LIPIŃSKA, Jadwiga, Rozwój egiptologii w Polsce, *Rocznik Muzeum Narodowego w Warszawie*, Warszawa 18 (1974), 401-416.

"The Development of Egyptology in Poland".
Extensive survey of the history of Polish Egyptology, from the earliest times prior to Champollion until today. The author describes the work of all Polish scholars in our field of studies, referring to their publications in the notes.

74449 LIPIŃSKA, Jadwiga, Studies on Reconstruction of the Hatshepsut Temple at Deir el-Bahari — A Collection of the Temple Fragments in the Egyptian Museum, Berlin, *Festschrift Ägyptisches Museum Berlin*, 163-171, with 12 ill. on 6 pl. and 7 fig. (2 folded).

The author studies 12 pieces of walls from the temple at Deir el-Bahri now in the Berlin Museum, divided into four groups: I. 5 fragments of the eastern wall of the Upper Court (pieces of the "Feast of the Valley" representations); II. fragments of slabs from the niches in the Outer Sanctuary; III. 2 fragments of inscriptions; IV. 3 miscellaneous fragments.
Of each block is given a photograph, the relevant technical data such as measures, inventory number and bibliography, while the author discusses its original place in the temple.

74450 LIPIŃSKI, Edward, אשיהו and אשבעל and Parallel Personal Names, *Orientalia Lovaniensia Periodica*, Leuven 5 (1974), 5-13.

The name אסחור, frequently occurring in the Elephantine papyri, is a transcription of the Egyptian proper name '*Iś-ḥr* "Belonging to Horus", a late form for *Nś-ḥr*.   *L.M.J. Zonhoven*

74451 van LITH, S. M. E., Index of Articles Volumes 1-50 of Aegyptus. 1920-1970, Amsterdam, Adolf M. Hakkert, 1974 (15 × 22.3 cm; VI + 183 p.) = Studia Amstelodamensia ad epigraphicam, ius antiquum et papyrologicam pertinentia, 2.

The first part (p. 1-57) of this index volume consists of an index of the articles which have appeared in *Aegyptus* vols. 1-50, arranged in the alphabetical order after the names of the authors.
The second part consists of systematic indexes to various subjects, papyri, grammar, law, history, etc. For Egyptology and Egyptian documents see particularly p. 142-144, for Coptology p. 140-142. Articles pertaining to Egyptology occur also, however, under other headings, such as medicine, religion, magic, orientalia and archaeology.

74452 LITTAUER, Mary Aiken, An element of Egyptian horse harness, *Antiquity* 48 (1974), 293-295, with 2 fig. and 1 pl.

Publication of a slender wooden rod topped by a spindle-whorl-like disk from which bronze spikes protrude, rod and disk being inlaid with coloured bark in patterns. It has been found in a private house at Amarna. The author argues that it is a "goad", an element of the horse harness, mentioning seven more examples from Tutankhamon's tomb. The "goad" was used, like the modern "head pole", for keeping the horse from turning his head to his team mate.

LLOYD-JONES, Hugh, see our number 74270.

74453 LÖHR, Beatrix, Aḥanjāti in Heliopolis, *GM* Heft 11 (1974), 33-38.

Under Akhenaton, Heliopolis regained its former importance: a new temple of Re called *wts-rˁ m 'Iwnw* was erected between year 5 and year 10 of this king, and its cult and architecture served as a model for the other sun temples of this period.

Dieter Mueller

74454 LONG, Ronald D., A Re-examination of the Sothic Chronology of Egypt, *Orientalia* 43 (1974), 261-274, with 1 table.

L'auteur recommande la prudence à propos de la méthode de datation par observations astronomiques, que l'on a tendance à considérer comme définitive. Elle dépend de la précision, voire de l'écriture des documents. Le plus ancien jalon, XIIe dynastie, reste fort douteux : la lecture du cartouche royal que porte le papyrus Ebers, dans une annotation toujours inédite, ne sera peut-être jamais une certitude. Même la référence à Thoutmosis III de l'inscription d'Eléphantine se serait pas inattaquable. Dans Théon, l'ère "apo Menophréôs" peut s'appliquer à un roi, mais pourrait aussi bien se rapporter à Memphis. La rédaction du calendrier de Médinet-Habou pourrait dater aussi bien de Ramsès II que de Ramsès III. Bien au contraire, le Décret de Canope attesterait fermement le rattachement au cycle sothiaque, qui a été observé tout au long du premier millénaire av.J.-C. Censorinus et d'autres anciens tendent à confirmer la date-repère de +139.

J. Custers

74455 LOPEZ, J., Rapport préliminaire sur les fouilles d'Hérakléopolis (1966), *Oriens Antiquus* 13 (1974), 299-316, with 1 map, 1 plan, 6 fig. and 10 pl.

Report of the first Spanish campaigns at Ihnâsya (Herakleopolis) in 1966. Of four trial trenches dug in the neighbourhood of the Herishef temple one led to the discovery of a necropolis from the Late Period (XXIInd Dynasty to the Roman Era). The researches in the court of the temple yielded blocks and a statue of Ramses II (or, possibly, usurped by him). The discoveries in

74456 LÓPEZ, Jesús, Une stèle ramesside de la collection Aubert, *RdE* 26 (1974), 115-117, with 1 ill.

Publication d'un fragment de stèle attestant un culte de statue royale nommée *Ḫʿw Rʿ*, érigée à Hérakléopolis Magna, connu par d'autres monuments que l'auteur signale. *Ph. Derchain*

74457 LORTON, David, The Juridical Terminology of International Relations in Egyptian Texts Through Dyn. XVIII, Baltimore and London, The Johns Hopkins University Press, [1974] (17.5 × 25.5 cm; X + 198 p.); series: The Johns Hopkins Near Eastern Studies; rev. *BiOr* 33 (1976), 18-21 (Raphael Giveon).

This study, originally a doctoral dissertation at the Johns Hopkins University, deals with the terminology used to indicate Egypt's relations with foreign countries down to the XVIIIth Dynasty.

The Introduction discusses the problem how to establish which lexical items contain a technical meaning. Most words and phrases here studied originate from the administrative or religious terminology, and hence their development from the earliest times has to be studied. Correspondences and differences between Egyptian terms and those of the Asiatics have also been pointed out.

Part I (p. 7-69) discusses a large number of terms indicating the Pharaoh as ruler of foreign lands and princes, such as *ity*, *mȝỉ*, *nb*, *nswt*, *Rʿ*, *ḥqȝ* and *ḫʿw*, most of them followed by various adjuncts, e.g. *n ḫȝswt nbt*, *n psḏt-pḏwt*, etc. The author defends some new translations, such as "ruler of those who are ruled" for *ḥqȝ ḥqȝw*. The second chapter deals with words for foreign rulers, *wr*, *ḥȝty-ʿ* and *ḥqȝ*.

Part II is devoted to 42 words and phrases by which the relations with foreign countries and the effecting of these relations are expressed, arranged in alphabetical order. We mention: *inỉ ḏr* ("to acquire the limits"), *ʿrq* ("to swear"), *wʿf* ("to bow down"), *bȝk* ("to work [for pay]", "to trade", etc), *mỉ nty n ḫpr* ("like him who had not been"), *ḥm* ("not to have relations"), *šfyt* ("legitimate rights/power/rule"), etc.

The author concludes (p. 176-182) that technical terms regarding international relations are first attested in and after the Hyksos Period, due to Egypt's exposure to the system of international relations. However, whereas the Asiatics recognized parity relationships as a form of partnership, the Egyptians represented these relations as gifts of the Pharaoh. Most terms had Semitic equivalents, but the concept of the king as *ḥqȝ*, holder of *de facto* political power is foreign to the Asiatic system.

The author also argues that one is entitled to speak of international law in the period, notwithstanding the lack of enforcement.

The Addendum (183-184) briefly deals with three more occurrences of terms discussed. There follow a bibliography (185-195) and limited indexes.

74458 LORTON, David, Terminology Related to the Laws of Warfare in Dyn. XVIII, *JARCE* 11 (1974), 53-68.

Five XVIIIth Dynasty text corpora (biographies of Ahmose, son of Ebana, Ahmose of Pennekhbet and Amenemheb; annalistic reports of Tuthmosis III and Amenophis II) as well as related random passages referring to the theme 'battle-plunder-official allotment of spoil (recompense)' form the source material for the study of the following terms: *ini m mḥ*, 'to bring as a captive'; *isy-ḥȝk*, 'legal plunder', *ḥȝk*, 'plunder', *ḥȝk.t*, 'spoil'; the variants *ḥ(ȝ)f* and *kf* (of the same root), 'taking' (of living enemies); *skr ʿnḫ*, here considered a term for a 'captured wounded soldier, *still* alive', by extension 'captive' in general.
J.F. Borghouts

74459 LÜDDECKENS, Erich, Ein demotischer Urkundenfund in Tuna el Gebel mit einer genealogischen Skizze, *Akten des XIII. Internationalen Papyrologenkongresses*, 235-239, with a table.

Preliminary report on a collection of Demotic documents recently discovered at Tûna el-Gebel (Hermopolis). They date from 191-162 B.C. and belonged to two families with fairly intricate relations. Moreover, the texts contain new formulae and mention, for the first time in Demotic documents, the names of eponymous priests of the cult of the Ptolemies.

74460 LUFT, Ulrich, Ein Amulett gegen Ausschlag (*srf.t*), *Festschrift Ägyptisches Museum Berlin*, 173-179, with 1 pl. and 3 fig.

The author publishes Pap. Berlin 15749, an amuletic text against *srft*-rash consisting of 13 lines. Below is drawn a row of seven divinities and two *wadjet*-eyes. Under the gods, very small, a crocodile and a man hunting a hippopotamus. The text, in Middle Egyptian with some Late Egyptian influences, is presented in photograph, facsimile and translation with commentary. On p. 178 some rare hieratic signs are listed. The author mentions several similar texts, though no close parallels are known except P. Deir el-Medîna 36 (see our number 70483).

74461 LUFT, Ulrich, Aus der Geschichte der Berliner Papyrus-Sammlung. Erwerbungen und Ankäufe orientalischer Papyri zwischen 1828 und 1861, *Archiv für Papyrusforschung und verwandte Gebiete*, Leipzig 22-23 (1974), 5-46.

A well-documented history of the Berlin collection of hieratic and demotic papyri in its formative years under G. Passalacqua and R. Lepsius. The article includes lists of the papyri acquired at that time, each entry being followed by a brief bibliography.

Dieter Mueller

74462 LUFT, Ulrich, Siegfried Morenz. 22.11.1914–14.1.1970, *Archiv für Papyrusforschung und verwandte Gebiete*, Leipzig 22-23 (1974), 401-402.

Obituary notice. See our number 70619.

LUFT, Ulrich, see also our numbers 74034 and 74809.

74463 LUNSINGH SCHEURLEER, Robert, Quelques terres cuites memphites, *RdE* 26 (1974), 83-99, with 3 pl.

L'auteur publie quatre terres cuites inédites appartenant à la même classe que celles trouvées par Petrie dans le quartier des étrangers de Memphis. Il reprend le problème des œuvres égyptiennes d'influence achéménide et aboutit à la conclusion qu'il devait y avoir à Memphis au 5ᵉ siècle a.C. des ateliers de coroplastes dont les œuvres reflètent le caractère cosmopolite de la grande ville.

Ph. Derchain

74464 LURKER, Manfred, Götter und Symbole der alten Ägypter. Einführung und kleines Lexikon. [zweite, überarbeitete und erweiterte Auflage, Weilheim], Otto Wilhelm Barth Verlag, [1974] (12.5 × 20.5 cm; 221 p., 1 map, 3 tables, 69 fig.); rev. *Mundus* 11 (1975), 320-321 (Emma Brunner-Traut).

Pr. DM 19.80

Second, revised and enlarged edition of our number 64310.
Compared with the first edition the length of the book has increased by more than one fourth, as the result of the inclusion of 46 new lemmata and a large number of minor additions and corrections.

74465 LYNN, George E. and Jaime T. BENITEZ, Temporal Bone Preservation in a 2600-year Old Egyptian Mummy, *Science*, Washington D.C. 183, No. 4121 (18 January 1974), 200-202, with 2 ill.

Examination of the mummy unwrapped by Cockburn (see our number 73153) demonstrated that the eardrums were perforated, suggesting an acute middle ear infection which probably resulted in a defective hearing. A beetle larva of the Staphylinidae found in the ear canal will have entered it during the mummification process.

MACADAM, M.F. Laming, see our numbers 74117 and 74270.

74466 McCALL, Daniel F., The Prevalence of Lions: Kings, Deities and Feline Symbolism in Africa and Elsewhere, *Paideuma*, Wiesbaden 19/20 (1973/74), 130-145.

Within the context of a discussion of lion symbolism in connection with kingship in various societies the author also deals with lions in ancient Egypt. His remarks are somewhat uncommon. He states, for example, that Sekhmet is a form of Hathor, and that the latter's "real name" was something like Nit or Neith, or even Nut.

74467 McHUGH, William P., Late Prehistoric Cultural Adaptation in Southwest Egypt and the Problem of the Nilotic Origins of Saharan Cattle Pastoralism, *JARCE* 11 (1974), 9-22, with 1 map.

In the Gilf Kebir and the Gebel 'Uweinat massifs (in the southwest of Egypt) prehistoric occupation is mainly attested by rock-art, while artefacts are more rare. These settlements by comparison with material from i.a. the Wadi el Akhdar and the Wadi el Bakht are probably datable to the early and mid-holocene periods. The ecological conditions for some of the fauna depicted can be inferred from comparison with modern conditions; probably a minimum rainfall of 250 mm *per annum* prevailed, the geological structure of the areas allowing the preservation of water in the dry season. Two modes of life in chronological succession can be deduced: a hunting phase and a cattle herding phase, with the cattle imported from elsewhere.
The two areas are strategically situated to cast light on the various hypotheses of a westward spread of cattle pastoralism from the Nile valley into the Sahara. This is countered with the following arguments: 1. prehistoric pastoralism in the Nile valley is attested much later; 2. the ecological conditions of the intermediate areas between the Nile valley and the massifs is unsuitable to provide 'way-stations' for a cattle-raising migratory population; 3. the material remains for cattle-pastoralism in this intermediate zone are absent (while hunter-gatherers are attested indeed); 4. the faunal inventory of the massifs and of the late prehistoric Sudanic is different in essential points; 5. there are no linguistic traces to support the hypothesis of a 'Hamitic' spread from the Nile valley into the Sahara. To the contrary, people of the ancient Saharan languages themselves may have been responsible for the production of the cattle rock-art. The desiccation of the Sahara necessitated retreating southwards and thus contributed to the ramification of the Nilo-Saharan languages.

J. F. Borghouts

74468 MADDIN, Robert and James D. MUHLY, Some Notes on the Copper Trade in the Ancient-Mid-East, *Journal of Metals*, New York 26, No. 5 (May 1974), 24-30, with 1 fig., 11 ill. and 7 tables.

Report of analyses of one of the oxhide copper ingots from the Cape Gelidonya shipwreck (cfr our number 67060). On account of the impurities, particularly 0.2% cobalt, the authors conclude that the metal came from SE Turkey, not from Cyprus. The island's importance for the copper production may have been exaggerated. No site has yet been identified on Cyprus which is likely to have been the production centre of the large amount of copper found in the shipwreck. This may be of consequence for the identification of Alashiya. More investigation is necessary, however.

74469 MAJEWSKA, Aleksandra, Życie idziałalność naukowa Jeana Françoisa Champolliona, *Rocznik Muzeum Narodowego w Warszawie*, Warszawa 18 (1974), 395-400.

"Life and Work of Jean François Champollion".
Paper about life and work of Champollion presented at the meeting in honour of that scholar in Warsaw in 1973.

A. Szczudłowska

74470 MALAISE, Michel, La traduction de Sinouhe B 160, *GM* Heft 10 (1974), 29-34.

Discussing the difficult passage Sinuhe B 160, the author suggests "c'est un au-secours pour qu'un heureux événement se produise". Compare our No. 68635. *Dieter Mueller*

74471 MALAMAT, A., Megiddo, 609 B.C. : The Conflict Reexamined, *Acta Antiqua Academiae Scientiarum Hungaricae*, Budapest 22 (1974), 445-449.

Short version of our number 73471.

74472 MÁLEK, Jaromír, Names of the Estates of Senedjemib Inti (Gîza Tomb G 2370), *GM* Heft 13 (1974), 21-24.

The recovery of squeezes made by A. and R.Th. Lieder in the mastaba of Senedjemib in 1850 has made it possible to improve the reading of some of the names of his estates listed in the doorway (*PM* III^2, 86, 3a and b). *Dieter Mueller*

74473 MÁLEK, Jaromír, Two Monuments of the Tias, *JEA* 60 (1974), 161-167, with 2 pl. and 2 fig.

There are five monuments of the Overseer of the Treasury Tia in the reign of Ramesses II, and another four of his wife who was possibly the king's sister. To these are added here descriptions of monuments of two further members of this family, Amenemḥab Pekhoir's stela in the Gulbenkian museum in Durham, and a pyramidion of Tia brought back by William Lethieullier and at present no longer located. Further monuments from the tomb of the Tias will be published later, thus bringing the total to fifteen. The stela previously copied by Birch and Wilkinson is a standard one here translated again, the pyramidion copied by Gordon is also of normal form and being of granite may have come from Saqqâra rather than Thebes. *E. Uphill*

MÁLEK, Jaromír, see also our number 74583.

74474 MALININE, Michel, Une vente de prébendes sous la XXXe dynastie (Pap. Moscou No 135), *RdE* 26 (1974), 34-41, with 3 pl.

Le document publié ici date de l'an 12 de Nectanébo II (366 a.C.). Il provient d'Eléphantine et se rapporte aux prébendes d'une famille de fonctionnaires du temple de Khnoum. L'intérêt majeur en est de mentionner un revenu affecté au culte de Khnoum et Arensnouphis associés, comme ils le sont aussi dans un document daté d'Artaxerxes Ier. Ces documents contiennent ainsi les plus anciennes mentions du dieu nubien en Égypte, de plus d'un siècle et demi antérieures à la date admise jusqu'ici pour l'introduction de son culte (Winter, *RdE* 25, 235-250 = notre No 73804).

L'auteur reconstitue le texte complet du document grâce aux copies des divers témoins qui figurent dans le papyrus et en fait un commentaire philologique détaillé. On retiendra spécialement la longue liste des graphies d'Arensnouphis. *Ph. Derchain*

MARCHESSAULT, R.H., see our number 74318.

74475 MARCINIAK, Marek, Deir el-Bahari. I. Les inscriptions hiératiques du Temple de Thoutmosis III, Varsovie, PWN — Éditions scientifiques en Pologne, 1974 (20.5 × 29.3 cm; [IV +]266 p., 92 double pl.); at head of title : Centre d'archéologie méditerranéenne de l'académie polonaise des sciences et centre polonais d'archéologie méditerranéenne dans la République Arabe d'Égypte au Caire sous la direction de Kazimierz Michałowski; rev. *BiOr* 33 (1976), 173-176 (S. Allam).

This volume, completely written by hand, contains the publication of the graffiti occurring on the columns of the temple of Tuthmosis III at Deir el-Bahri discovered by the Polish excavations.

In the introduction the author describes his material, 142 graffiti written in ink by visitors and pilgrims. He mentions similar texts at other places and divides his material into two groups :

texts containing fixed formulae and texts consisting of names and titles only. The more frequent formulae are: ir nfr, ir nfr (cfr our number 68399), $i.mḥ$ $ḥt.f$, $ḥbsw$ $3ty.f$ (cfr our number 73477), and ir $p3$ nty $iw.f$. Some texts contain vows and demand special actions of the gods, or consist of the beginnings of letters. The texts intend to establish the name of the writer in the holy place where the Holy Bark of Amon rested one night every year, during the Festival of the Valley (cfr our number 71389). One text may contain evidence for a *sed*-festival in the 32nd year of Ramses III (the author was uncertain whether indeed it was this king or Ramses II; cfr p. 41 f. and 37).

Most pilgrims appear to have been middle-class people. On account of the palaeography and orthography of the texts their visits are to be dated to the second half of the XXth Dynasty. In a special chapter the author discusses the popular cult of Hathor at Deir el-Bahri, its history and its importance, which he connects with the growth of a strong personal piety at the end of the New Kingdom.

The catalogue (p. 54-158) gives of each text the technical data and a hieroglyphic transcription with some textual notes and remarks on the persons mentioned, but no translation. There follow indexes of proper names and titles.

The next part (171-266) consists of a list of many hieratic signs in the various forms found in the graffiti, arranged according to Gardiner's sign-list, followed by the signs for groups and ligatures (247-266).

The plates contain of every text a photograph and, on the opposite page, a facsimile.

MARTHELOT, Jacques, see our number 74663.

74476 MARTIN, Geoffrey T., Excavations in the Sacred Animal Necropolis at North Saqqâra, 1972-3: Preliminary Report, *JEA* 60 (1974), 15-29, with 7 plans (1 folding), 4 sections, 1 fig. and 6 pl.

During the first part of the season Professors Smith and Pierce prepared a preliminary transcription of 168 Demotic documents and 4 hieratic fragments, while the late Professor Barns recopied and collated Demotic and Greek material from the Baboon galleries.

The archaeological work in sectors 7 and 4 consisted of four tasks, recording a large O.K. mastaba (No. 3050), excavating certain other tombs, investigating a small group of buildings due west of the main temple complex and tracing the approach road and ramp leading from the Serapeum-Abûsîr road to the temple terrace. Fifty seven Demotic documents were found including several letters and seven Greek papyri. Coptic mud-brick tombs were also uncovered and streets of 'Archaic' mastabas located. *E. Uphill*

74477 MARTIN, Geoffrey Thorndike, The Royal Tomb at El-'Amarna. The Rock Tombs of El-'Amarna, Part VII. I. The Objects, London, Egypt Exploration Society, 1974 (24.8 × 31.1 cm; XX + 123 p., 2 plans, 7 fig., 63 pl. [2 folding] containing a map, 4 plans, drawings and numerous ill.) = Archaeological Survey of Egypt. Edited by T.G.H. James, Thirty-Fifth Memoir; rev. *BiOr* 32 (1975), 362-364 (William H. Peck); *CdE* LI, No. 101 (1976), 112-114 (Pierre Gilbert); *JARCE* 12 (1975), 115-116 (Earl L. Ertman).

The volume continues the edition of the Rock Tombs of El Amarna by N. de G. Davies, the sixth volume of which has appeared in 1908. The present volume discusses the objects found in the royal tomb; publication of its reliefs is intended to follow.

After an introduction describing the site of the tomb the author first discusses earlier publications and unpublished material, particularly the mss. of Pendlebury which he was able to consult. He then deals with the date of the discovery, and the expeditions of Bouriant, Pendlebury (1931-32 and 1935) and the Service des Antiquités, as well as illegal digs. A very brief description of the tomb follows.

The main part of the volume consists of the catalogue of the objects, all together 483 numbers, which are certainly or in some instances possibly found in the tomb. They are: the two sarcophagi of Akhnaton and Meketaton with their lids, broken into numerous small fragments; the canopic chests; some human remains; 215 shawabtis (preceded by a general discussion), of 11 of which the present whereabouts are unknown; ostraca, jar inscriptions and sealings; jewellery and scarabs; objects in faience, in alabaster, in limestone (among which a square stela) and other stones; metal objects; wood and other organic materials; gypsum plaster reliefs; and some miscellaneous fragments.

Each object is carefully described, with measures, museum numbers, etc. added. Inscriptions are reproduced, some small objects are represented in drawings.

Summary and conclusions on p. 104-106, stating, i.a., that all objects in the tomb were systematically broken up into small fragments, and that both Meketaton and Akhnaton have been buried in this tomb.

There follow concordances of the catalogue numbers and museum numbers (p. 107-110), as well as the numbers of Newberry's *Funerary Statuettes and Sarcophagi* (Cat. gén.) and those assigned by Pendlebury to his finds in the Royal Wâdi. Bibliography on p. 114-118, indexes 119-123. The plates contain i.a. 4 sketch-plans of the wâdi and the tomb by J.H.S. Waddington, reconstruction drawings of the sarcophagus of Akhnaton, and photographs of many of the more important objects.

74478 MARTIN, Geoffrey T. and W.V. DAVIES, Current Research for Higher Degrees in Egyptology, Coptic. and Related Studies in the United Kingdom, *JEA* 60 (1974), 261-263.

List of doctoral and other dissertations currently in preparation in universities in Great Britain.

MARTIN, Geoffrey T., see also our umber 74270.

74479 MARTIN, K., 𓊪𓏏, *Studia Aegyptiaca I*, 287-295.

The royal epithet *dỉ ʿnḫ* is ambivalent and means both "given life" (by a god) and "giving life" (i.e., distributing this gift as a mediator between god and man). *Dieter Mueller*

el-MASRY, A.A., see our number 74634.

MASSER, I., see our number 74045.

74480 MATSON, F.R., Technological Studies of Egyptian Pottery — Modern and Ancient, *Recent Advances in Science and Technology of Materials*, 129-139, with 2 ill. and 2 tables.

Study of clays from various Egyptian sites shows that there are significant differences in the physical properties of some of them, a conclusion which may be useful in studying ancient pottery.

74481 MEEKS, Dimitri, Les fêtes Amesysia : essai d'étymologie, *CdE* XLIX, No. 98 (1974), 380-383.

En complément de l'article de Danielle Bonneau consacré aux fêtes Amesysia de l'Égypte gréco-romaine (*CdE* XLIX, No 98 [1974], 366-379) l'auteur propose de reconnaître sous la transcription grecque le nom égyptien de la fête *hrw mswt 'Ist*, "jour de la naissance d'Isis", convenant parfaitement à ce qu'on en sait. *Ph. Derchain*

74482 MEEKS, Dimitri, Notes de lexicographie (§1), *RdE* 26 (1974), 52-65.

Le mot *ꜣb(w)t* (*Wb* I,7,8) signifie en réalité "domesticité, maisonnée" et non "famille" au sens étroit du mot et est à rapprocher étymologiquement des mots *ꜣb*, «marquer au fer» et *ꜣbt*, "fer à marquer". Sous l'Ancien Empire, le mot semble couvrir un statut juridique défini, tandis que plus tard il ne paraît plus être qu'un mot du langage choisi des autobiographies privées d'un sens beaucoup plus vague. *Ph. Derchain*

74483 MEGALLY, Mounir, A propos de l'organisation administrative des ouvriers à la XVIIIe dynastie, *Studia Aegyptiaca I*, 297-311.

After discussing five ostraca from the Theban necropolis dating from the XVIIIth Dynasty the author concludes that various teams of workers were divided into two similar parts, parallel from the point of view of the administration and performing the same kind of work.

74484 MEGALLY, Mounir, A propos du papyrus CGC 58070 (Papyrus Boulaq XI), *BIFAO* 74 (1974), 161-169, with 2 pl.

Some remarks on account of Pap. Cairo Cat. Gén. 58070. 1. The papyrus is incomplete, the beginning being lost, the continuation being Pap. Cairo 58081; 2. The text once more attests the dual administration of the New Kingdom, recto and verso having been written simultaneously; 3. The text is not a "journal".
The author adds some corrections to Peet's transcription in Mélanges Maspero I, 185-199.
For the publication of CGC 58081, see now *BIFAO* 75 (1975), 165-181.

74485 MEGALLY, Mounir, Les textes de comptabilité, *Textes et langages III*, 33-39.

After a survey of what has been published of and concerning account texts, papyri and ostraca, the author gives a survey of this kind of documents and their various types, sketching the main development from the analytic style of the Old Kingdom to more synthesis in the New Kingdom. He points out the importance of the documents for the economic as well as for the political history, and mentions some detail problems, such as that of weights and measures and the development of hieratic writing in these texts.

MEKHITARIAN, Arpag, see our number 74093.

74486 MELLINK, Machteld J. und Jan FILIP, Frühe Stufen der Kunst, Berlin, Propyläen Verlag, 1974 (19.5 × 27.5 cm; 172 p., 53 fig., 416 pl., 58 colour pl.) = Propyläen Kunstgeschichte, 13.

Two chapters of this work on early art deal with Egypt; one by Machteld Mellink presents a general introduction (p. 67-92), and one in the part called "Documentation", written by Helene J. Kantor (227-256) contains first a historical survey of the art of the Neolithic and Archaic Periods in Egypt, followed by a description of the pertinent plates (pl. 188-225 and colour pl. 31-33) and fig. (16-28). Among the objects depicted and described are statuettes, vessels, palettes, etc., some well known (e.g., the Gebel el-Arak knife or the mace of King Scorpion), others rarely represented.

From the next chapter, on African early art, written by Günter Smolla, we mention pl. 242-245 (described on p. 266-267), representing examples of Nubian rock art.

74487 MELTZER, E.S., Adjective and adjective-verb in Egyptian, *Language Sciences*, Bloomington, Indiana No. 33 (December 1974), 18.

In connection with an article of Hodge (our number 74325) the author raises the problem of the relation between adjectives and adjective verbs. There is no need to conceive the former as participles of the latter.

74488 MELTZER, Edmund S., Egyptian Parallels for an Incident in Hesiod's *Theogony* and an Episode in the Kumarbi Myth, *JNES* 33 (1974), 154-157.

For some time it has been known that the account of the early generations of gods in Hesiod goes back to a Hurrian original, and was passed to the Greeks by Phoenicians. Further M.C. Astour would show many Sumerian and Babylonian motifs as well as W. Semitic borrowings in the Kumarbi myth itself, while P. Walcot has indicated both Babylonian and Egyptian sources, particularly from the sarcophagus chamber of the cenotaph of Sety I, later wisdom books, *Amenemope* and *Onkhsheshonqy* and the *Tale of Two Brothers*. Here the writer discusses another possible source for the story of the emasculating of Ouranos by Kronos at the instigation of Gaia, i.e. Spell 17 of the *Book of the Dead*. E. Uphill

74489 MELTZER, Edmund S., A Funerary Cone by Merimose, Viceroy of Kush, *Newsletter SSEA* 5, No. 2 (December 1974), 9-12, with 1 pl.

Publication of a copy of a funerary cone from the author's collection belonging to the Viceroy of Kush Merimose (Davies-Macadam No. 170), with some remarks as to the Viceroy's family relations.

74490 MELTZER, Edmund S., A Suggestion on the Behavior of the s$\underline{d}$m.in.f Form, *Newsletter ARCE* No. 88 (Winter 1974), 41.

Abstract of a paper.

The author proposes to derive the formative *in* in the s$\underline{d}$m.in.f form the particle, which is identical with the preposition *in*.

L.M.J. Zonhoven

74491 MELTZER, Edmund S., A 26th Dynasty Official and a 17th Century Cartographer, *Newsletter SSEA* 4, No 4 (May 1974), 2-7, with 2 fig. and 1 map.

Publication of an other funerary cone (compare our number 73486) from the same collection (= Davies-Macadam No. 444), belonging to the steward of the Divine Votaress Shoshenq from the XXVIth Dynasty (compare our number 4462).
The second section deals with a map entitled "Aegyptus et Cyrene" in the early 18th century atlas of Herman Moll, with vignettes of extremely thin pyramids.

74492 MENDELSSOHN, Kurt, The Riddle of the Pyramids, [London], Thames and Hudson, [1974] (18.5 × 24.8 cm; 224 p., 40 fig., 40 pl. [8 in colour]); rev. *The Antiquarian Journal* 55 (1975), 417-418 (I.E.S. Edwards). Pr. £ 3.50

The first two chapters of this study about the pyramids and the organization of their builders the author sketches the historical background, dealing with the first dynasties and with the Pyramid Age, with special attention for the royal tombs.
Chapter 3 ("The Unsolved Problems") discusses the major pyramids and some problems concerning their building which have not yet been solved. He offers a simple explanation for the question why the Egyptians came to the gradients of the Red and the Bent Pyramid (3:1) and that of the Great Pyramids (4:1). He doubts whether the pharaohs were ever buried in these tombs, connecting the point with the problem of the multiple tombs. The main problem, however, is why the enormous pyramids of the IVth Dynasty were erected.
In chapter 4, on the Meidum Pyramid and its collapse during the third stage of its construction, the author repeats his thesis set forth in earlier articles (see our numbers 71402 and 73489), illustrating his argument by a number of minor observations concerning the present state of the building. Chapter 5 deals with the Bent Pyramid at Dashûr, where the author finds the confirmation of this thesis, arguing that its shape was due to the wish to avoid a similar catastrophe as at Meidum. This means, that the construction of the later pyramid was well advanced while the earlier one was not yet completed. There follows a description of the devices used in later pyramids in order to prevent the catastrophe at Meidum. The author also sketches the religious development during the IVth Dynasty which may have caused the end of a period of pyramid building on a large scale.
Chapter 6 argues that the pyramid building in the IVth Dynasty was a continuous operation, the construction periods overlapping each other (see our number 73490). It was the large standing

labour force which was required that was in itself the main reason for the buildings, not the wish to provide an eternal tomb for the pharaohs. The organization of the building force was the preponderant factor in the creation of the civil service, which by its increasing hold over the population welded it into a state. From this conception the author draws conclusions as regards the history of the IVth Dynasty, even suggesting a competition between the priesthoods of Re and Ptah.

Chapter 7 is devoted to the Mexican pyramids, where the author suggests to find a similar influence on state building. The last chapter contains a summary and an appeal to the modern world. In an appendix some remarks about "pyramidiots" and suchlike cranks.

A select bibliography on p. 213-215; index p. 219-224.

For an extensive discussion, see Jean-Philippe Lauer, A propos du prétendu désastre de la pyramide de Meïdoum, *CdE* LI, No. 101 (1976), 72-89.

There has also appeared a German version: Bergisch Gladbach, Gustav Lübbe Verlag, 1974; pr. DM 58; rev. *Asien-Afrika-Lateinamerika* 3 (1975), 360-362 (Steffen Wenig).

74493 MENU, Bernadette, La bibliographie des textes juridiques, *Textes et langages III*, 293-300.

After explaining the necessity to draw up a complete bibliography of juridical texts the author discusses the extant bibliographies, which partly have appeared in juridical periodicals. A second section is devoted to the demands to be made on juridical bibliographical records.

74494 MENU, Bernadette, Une stèle démotique inédite, *RdE* 26 (1974), 68-72, with 1 pl.

Publication d'une petite stèle démotique provenant de Delîngat dans le Delta occidental, portant une inscription datable de la fin de l'époque ptolémaïque ou plutôt du début de l'occupation romaine, dans laquelle sont nommés les cinq dédicants représentés dans le cintre.

L'auteur analyse à l'occasion le formulaire habituel des stèles funéraires démotiques où elle reconnaît six types principaux. Elle fournit de la stèle une photographie, une transcription hiéroglyphique, une traduction et un bref commentaire textuel.

Ph. Derchain

74495 MENU, Bernadette et Ibram HARARI, La notion de propriété privée dans l'Ancien Empire Égyptien, *CRIPEL* 2 (1974), 125-154.

The authors first describe the juridical aspect of the Old Kingdom civilisation as dualistic, being a combination of the continuation of tribal customs and the new centralized administrative organization.
Within this context the authors study three inscriptions concerning benefices and private landed properties from the tomb of Meten, each with translation and comments. There follow sections on the methods of acquisition and devolution of landed properties. Various ways to dispose of properties are discussed, which apply only to movables and those immovables which are of small value.
The authors conclude that landed property in this period always came from the king. It could be granted by him to his principal servants so that they were able to participate in the government, but only for their lifetime. Actual private property of land only existed in the form of funerary domains.

74496 MERRILLEES, R.S., Some Notes on Tell el-Yahudiya Ware, *Levant*, London 6 (1974), 193-195.

Critical remarks to our number 73577, with some additions.

74497 MERRILLEES, R.S., Trade and Transcendence in Bronze Age Levant, Göteborg, Studies in Mediterranean Archaeology, 1974 (22.7 × 30.5 cm; [IV +] 81 p , 2 maps, 1 plan, 5 fig., 55 ill.) = Studies in Mediterranean Archaeology, 39; rev. *AJA* 80 (1976), 309-310 (Gerald Cadogan). Pr. Sw. Kr. 90

The first of the three studies here assembled deals with Cypriote relations with the Bronze Age Aegean.
The second chapter is entitled "Ancient Egypt's Silent Majority" and contains discussion of the contents of an ordinary middle class burial form the first half of the 15th century B.C., namely Sidmant Tomb 254, discovered by Petrie. The contents, a coffin with four mummies, two females, a male and a child, and five baskets filled with various objects, and three jars outside the coffin, are dealt with in detail. All objects, now in University Museum, Philadelphia, are depicted in photograph.
Three themes are particularly set forth : the (partly foreign) origin and the function in daily life of the objects; the overlapping of customs between the sexes (kohl tubes and kohl pots used by both); the conceptional primacy of shape over material (faience copies of various types of pots and even a casket). Discussing the base-ring I juglets the author repeats his hypothesis that these juglets, so far as Cypriote, came to Egypt filled with opium, their form resembling that of the seed head of the opium poppy. In Egypt they may have contained liquids, though these in a magical way may have been thought to have the same results as the substance the jugs were initially designed to hold.

Chapter III is devoted to the pottery and a few other objects from a Middle Cypriote III tomb group at Arpera (Mosphilos), not far from Larnaca (Cyprus). Among the vessels there occur three instances of wheel-made El-Lisht Ware juglets (p. 49-52). This ware, the typological antecedent to the Tell el-Yahûdîya Ware, is extensively discussed, with a list of sites where it has been found, in Egypt, Syria-Palestine and on Cyprus. The ware belongs to the period from the XIIIth Dynasty to half way through the Hyksos period.

74498 de MEULENAERE, Herman, Le grand-prêtre memphite Séhétepibrê-ankh, *Festschrift Ägyptisches Museum Berlin*, 181-184, with 3 ill. on 2 pl.

While the name Sehetepibre is to be struck from the list of high-priests of Ptah, the author publishes two new documents of another high-priest called Sehetepibre-ankh, proving that he is not to be identified with Sehetepibre-ankh-nedjem of statue Louvre A 47. The monuments here published are: part of the socle of a statue in the Brooklyn Museum (No. 16.580.87) and an offering table of the same collection (No. 37.1498 E).
The author also proposes to interpret the title ⌘ as *ḥmww wr sḫm*, "the craftsman of the Very Mighty".

74499 de MEULENAERE, Herman, La statue d'un chef de chanteurs d'époque saïte, *Metropolitan Museum Journal*, New York 8 (1973), 1974, 27-32, with 4 ill. and an English summary on p. 32.

Publication of the texts on the back pillar and the base of a damaged kneeling statue in the Metropolitan Museum of Art (No. 24.2.2), dated on account of iconographic criteria to the reign of Psammetichus I. The text states the person represented to be the chief of the singers of the North and of Amenemope, Amenemope-em-hat.
For a discussion of the statue itself, see Russmann (our number 74625).

74500 de MEULENAERE, Herman et Bernard V. BOTHMER, Une statue thébaine de la fin de l'époque ptolémaïque, *ZÄS* 101 (1974), 109-113, with 3 pl.

Publication d'une statuette acéphale, en calcaire, au Musée de Brooklyn, inv. No 36.834. Le propriétaire, père divin et prophète d'Amon à Karnak (etc.), s'appelle Ounnefer. L'inscription commence par "O (*hy*) Osiris" N.N. et souhaite pour lui "l'eau fraîche de la main d'Amenemopé tous les dix jours"; comparer notre No 72270, 299-301. Les auteurs offrent une analyse stylistique de cette pièce et de statues contemporaines.

M. Heerma van Voss

74501 MEYER, Klaus-Heinrich, Kanon, Komposition und "Metrik" der Narmerpalette, *SAK* 1 (1974), 247-265, with 6 fig.

The author seeks for a relatively simple explanation for the system of proportions and composition in Egyptian art, since it already occurs on the palette of Narmer.
Proceeding from Iversen's observations concerning the canon for the human figure (see our numbers 3997 and 71293), which he applies with small corrections to the palette while stressing the usual Egyptian inaccuracy, he argues that the proportions of its larger royal figure are in accordance with the canon of the Old Kingdom. Moreover, the same proportions recur in the composition of the scene as a whole, which can be covered by a grid the unit of which is 1 fathom = 4 cubits = 18 fists.
At the end Meyer applies this construction grid on the relief of the Mnevis-stela in Hannover (Kestner-Museum No. 1925.189).

MEYERS, P., see our number 74512.

74502 MICHAŁOWSKI, Kazimierz, Ausgrabungen in Faras, *in*: *Festschrift des 125jährigen Bestehens der sächsischen Akademie der Wissenschaften zu Leipzig*, Berlin, Akademie Verlag, 1974, 87-99, with 16 pl. including 4 plans.

Survey of the results of the Polish excavations at Faras in which the author not only deals at length with the cathedral and Christian Nubia but also mentions the palace of the X-group.

74503 MICHAŁOWSKI, Kazimierz, Faras. Die Wandbilder in den Sammlungen des Nationalmuseums zu Warschau. Die Inschriften bearbeitete Stefan Jakobielski, Warszawa, Wydawnictwo Artystyczno-Graficzne — Dresden, VEB Verlag der Kunst, [1974] (23.9 × 31.3 cm; 344 p., 2 maps, 2 plans, 18 fig., 63 ill., 40 colour ill.).

This is a translation of the original Polish edition (not seen). The volume contains a complete study of all 67 wall paintings from the church of Faras at present preserved in the National Museum at Warsaw, preceded by a general discussion in which the author deals with: the historical background, the development of wall painting at Faras, problems of iconography and identification of the figures represented, and the discovery and conservation of the wall paintings.
The catalogue describes each single piece, which is represented by splendid photographs in colour and black-and-white. Technical data such as Inventory and Museum numbers, exact provenance, and measures are mentioned.

The third part, by Jakobielski, is devoted to the epigraphic material from Faras. 57 Coptic and Greek inscriptions are given in facsimile, transcription and translation, while short comments are added. The 30 legenda to the paintings are divided into four chronologically arranged groups, followed by 4 dedications and 23 graffiti.

Bibliography on p. 324-331. A chronological table of the bishops of Faras on p. 332-334. Indexes on p. 335-341.

74504 MICHAŁOWSKI, Kazimierz, Od Edfu do Faras. Polskie odkrycia archeologii śródziemnomorskiej, Warszawa, Wydawnictwa Artystyczne i Filmowe, 1974 (11.5 × 16 cm; 269 p., 7 colour pl., 101 fig., 1 map). Series: Archeologia.   Pr. 30 zł

"From Edfu to Faras. Polish discoveries of the Mediterranean Archaeology".

The popular account of the excavations directed by the author on several sites of the Mediterranean region, including chapters on Edfu, Mirmeki (Crimea), Tell Atrib, Nubia, Palmyra (Syria), Alexandria, Deir el-Bahari, Faras, Dongola, Nea Paphos (Cyprus), supplemented by the chapters on the activity of the Polish Centre of Mediterranean Archaeology in Cairo, and the author's participation in the Abu Simbel project. The bibliography on the subjects is included, also the lists of members of the particular expeditions.   *J. Lipińska*

74505 MICHAŁOWSKI, Kazimierz, La publication des textes égyptiens des musées de Pologne, *Textes et langages III*, 219-224.

The author, after mentioning the oldest publication of an Egyptian papyrus in Poland (the funerary Pap. Sękowski, in 1827), lists the editions of papyri and inscriptions from the National Museum at Warsaw and papyri from the National Museum at Cracov (section Czartoryski). At the end a brief mention of Coptic texts in Warsaw.

74506 MICHAŁOWSKI, Kazimierz, Tebi. Zdjęcia Andrzej Dziewanowski, Warszawa, Wydawnieto Arkady, 1974 (20.5 × 28 cm; 26 p., 2 maps, 5 plans, 86 pl., a loose p. with a second index to the pl.).

This fourth volume of the series (cfr our numbers 70388, 72490 and 72491) dealing with ancient Egypt is devoted to the West Bank of Thebes, the temples and the tombs. As in the preceding volumes most views are the usual ones, but some others are taken from less usual corners.

There are also editions in other languages, e.g. a Russian edition Фивы (Варшава, 1973; pr. 2 руб. 50 коп.) and a German one, Wien-München, Verlag Anton Schroll & Co., 1974.

74507 MILLET, Nicholas B., Egyptian Department, *Annual Report. Royal Ontario Museum*, Toronto 24 (1973-1974), 8-9, with 1 ill.

Report of the activities of the Royal Ontario Museum at Toronto in 1973-1974. The author mentions one new acquisition, namely an incomplete faience inlay figure of a pharaoh of the 4th century B.C. (see ill.).

74508 MILLET, N. B., A Meroitic Number-Word, *Actes premier congrès de linguistique sémitique*, 393-398.

The author lists a number of occurrences of Meroitic *tbê* and argues that it is a noun meaning "two". Less certain, but possible, is the translation of *wi* as "one".

MILLS, A. J., see our number 74443.

74509 MINAULT, Anne - Florence THILL, Tombes du Nouvel-Empire à Saï (SA.C.5), *CRIPEL* 2 (1974), 75-102, with 3 fig., 2 plans and 21 ill.

Die bedeutende ägyptische Nekropole liegt im Süden des Forts; eine Beschreibung der Gräber und ihres Inventars wird gegeben. Auf Skarabäen und Plaketten sind an Namen belegt: Thutmosis III., ein Antef, Ramses III. und der Königssohn von Kusch Ramses-Nacht unter Ramses IX. Auf den Uschebtis finden sich ein Kiky und ein Neby. Das Ausgrabungsmaterial kann mit dem von Soleb und Aniba verglichen werden.
Einige kleine Gefäße der X-Gruppen-Keramik wurden gefunden. *Inge Hofmann*

74510 MINKOVSKAYA, E. Ye., Вог Мандулис, *ВДИ* 4 (130), 1974, 111-124, with an English summary on p. 130.

"The God Mandulis".
The author discusses on account of inscriptions in various Nubian temples and Greek hymns in the Kalabsha temple the origin of the god Mandulis, the nature of his cult, its relationship with the cults of other gods, and its ethnic affinities. The main conclusions are that it was a solar deity who became egyptianized to a considerable degree, but originally may have been a god of the Medjay-Blemmyes.

74511 MIOSI, F. Terry, A Possible Reference to the Non-Calendar Week, *ZÄS* 101 (1974), 150-152.

The author's conclusion is that *sw 10* is the technical term for the fixed calendar week while *hrw 10* may refer to the less specific non-calendar week. *M. Heerma van Voss*

74512 MISHARA, J. and P. MEYERS, Ancient Egyptian Silver: A Review, *Recent Advances in Science and Technology of Materials*, 29-45, with 4 tables.

Critical survey of the literature concerning Egyptian silver. After having made remarks on the occurrence and methods of production of silver in Antiquity the authors deal with the occurrence in Pharaonic times, mentioning also philological problems. They i.a. argue that *nbw ḥḏ* means "white gold", not "white metal", as Forbes suggested. Discussing the analytical data at present available they state that objects with a small gold concentration are probably of foreign origin or made in Egypt of remelted materials, while those with a gold content above 3% may have been made of local Egyptian silver. At the end four methods capable of providing more information are listed.

MOHAMMED, Ferial M., see our number 74531.

74513 MOKHTAR, Gamal, Registration of the Hieroglyphic Texts. The Technique adopted by Cairo Centre of Documentation, *Textes et langages III*, 279-283.

The article describes the activities of the C.E.D.A.E. and the process of documentation applied to the temples in Nubia and, more recently, to buildings at Thebes. It also lists the main results and the publications of the Centre.

MOKHTAR, Gamal, see also under MOUKHTAR.

74514 van MOORSEL, Paul, Nubian Studies in Preparation, *Orientalia* 43 (1974), 228-236.

List of Nubian studies which were in print or in preparation on 1.XII.1973, followed by a list of names and addresses of the authors.

74515 van MOORSEL, P., Zur Diskussion: Was ist "Nubologie"?, *MNL* No 14 (Février 1974), 56.

Da der Begriff "Nubologie" auf der Konferenz in Warschau nicht ausdiskutiert wurde, wird er an dieser Stelle zur Diskussion gestellt; Verf. schlägt vor, einstweilen die "Nubologie" als jenen Teil der Wissenschaft zu betrachten, der sich mit der Vorgeschichte und Geschichte aller Perioden des Landes, das wir heute Nubien nennen, befaßt. *Inge Hofmann*

74516 MOSS, Rosalind, Topographical Bibliography, *Textes et langages III*, 285-288.

The author briefly relates the history of the *Topographical Bibliography*, explaining the working methods of Miss Porter and those of herself, later assisted by Mrs. Burney. She lists the valuable records available at the Griffith Institute at Oxford, and mentions the plans for future publications.

MOSS, Rosalind B., see also our number 74583.

MOUKHTAR, Gamal Eddine, see our numbers 74259 and 74513.

MOUSSA, Ahmed M., see our number 74017.

74517 MÜLLER, Christa, Wissenschaftsgeschichte und Selbstverständnis. Zwei Beiträge aus England, *GM* Heft 12 (1974), 51-54.

A summary of papers by T. E. Peet and S. R. K. Glanville on the position of Egyptology. *Dieter Mueller*

MÜLLER, Christa, see also our number 74342.

74518 MÜLLER, Hans Wolfgang, Staatliche Sammlung Ägyptischer Kunst, *Münchner Jahrbuch der Bildenden Kunst*, München Dritte Folge 25 (1974), 215-223, with 18 ill.

Among the recent acquisitions of the Egyptian collection at Munich here described we mention: a large Old Kingdom relief from the tomb of Ni-ankh-nesut at Saqqâra (ÄS 5970) with slaughtering scenes; vessels from the Middle Kingdom; a wooden relief figure, covered with gold leaf, of Queen Tiye (ÄS 5873); a fragment of an inscription from the tomb of vizier Bakenrenef in Saqqâra (ÄS 5897). All these pieces are now described in the second edition of the catalogue: Staatliche Sammlung Ägyptischer Kunst, München, 1976.

74519 MÜLLER, Ingeborg, Die Ausgestaltung der Kultkammern in den Gräbern des Alten Reiches in Giza und Saqqara, *Forschungen und Berichte* 16 (1974), 79-96, with 7 tables.

On the evidence from 40 tombs from the late IVth to the early VIth Dynasties the author designs a scheme of the place of motifs in non-funerary scenes on the walls. Although preference for the East wall in a few instances may be due to the conception of the East as the present world against the West as the Netherworld, the division of the scenes in 23 tombs is mainly a reflection of the geographical differences between the Delta (marshes and pastures) and the Nile valley (agriculture); the former scenes are found on the N. wall, the latter at the S. side. In other tombs, however, the order of the seasons and the work on the land determined the place of the scenes.

74520 MÜLLER, Ingeborg, Die Eingeweidekrüge des Berliner Ägyptischen Museums, *Festschrift Ägyptisches Museum Berlin*, 185-193.

Publication of 51 canopic vessels with inscriptions and one lid of a vessel, preserved in the Berlin collection. The author arranged them according to the typology proposed by Sethe (Zur Geschichte der Einbalsamierung bei den Ägyptern und einiger

damit verbundener Bräuche, Sitzungsberichte Pr. Akad. der Wiss., Phil.-hist. Kl. 1934, 211-239 and 1*-16*). She offers the technical data and a facsimile of the more important parts of the texts, with remarks on the names.
For the study of Sethe, see now the reprint "Leipziger und Berliner Akademieschriften (1902-1934), Leipzig, Zentralantiquariat der Deutschen Demokratischen Republik, 1976, 587-615.

74521 MÜLLER, Wolfgang, Vorwort, *Festschrift Ägyptisches Museum Berlin*, 9.

74522 MÜLLER-KARPE, Hermann, Geschichte der Steinzeit, München, Verlag C.H. Beck, [1974] (14.2 × 22.3 cm; 393 p., 33 pl. with fig. [= p. 347-379]). Pr. DM 29.50

This is a summary of the author's two volumes "Handbuch der Vorgeschichte" (our numbers 66445 and 68423), without the scientific documentation and bibliographical references.
The study is divided into six chapters, each dealing with a special subject in various areas of Europe, Africa and Asia, and each divided into two parts, one for the Palaeolithic Age and one for the Neolithic Age. The subjects of the chapters are: historical contacts and the formation of groups; techniques and economy; settlement; social relations; cult and religion.
In several sections, particularly in the parts on the Neolithic Age, passages are devoted to Egypt's pre- and protohistory, while some sections are entirely dealing with Egypt; they are: Egyptian sculpture (p. 202-203); reliefs (213-217); writing (236-241); offerings and cult-places (282-288); representations of animals (316-321).
In the indexes (381-393) there occur several words referring to Egypt (e.g. Badari, Narmer, Wadi Hammamat, etc.), but no general lemma "Ägypten".

74523 MÜLLER-KARPE, Hermann, Handbuch der Vorgeschichte. Dritter Band. Kupferzeit. Erster Teilband: Text. Zweiter Teilband: Regesten. Dritter Teilband: Tafeln, München, C.H. Beck'sche Verlagsbuchhandlung, 1974 (20.5 × 28.5 cm; [Band 1:] XIV + 770 p.; [Band 2:] p. 771-1125, with 8 fig. and 10 maps; [Band 3:] VI + 1 p., 746 pl. containing plans, fig. and ill.).
Pr. DM 152 + 92 + 156

Sequel to our number 68423.
By "Copper Age" the author understands the period from the 27th to the 17th century B.C., for Egypt the period from the Old to the beginning of the New Kingdom. In this study on the archaeology and civilizations of a large number of regions in Europe, Asia and N. Africa during the period Egypt is mentioned

in every chapter, while a relatively large number of sections are even specially devoted to that country.

The text volume consists of 9 chapters. After an introduction about the study of the Copper Age in general there follow two chapters on literary sources (Egypt : p. 15-35) and archaeological sources (Egypt : 68-89). Chapter 4 to 9 are each devoted to a special aspect. Entire sections on ancient Egypt discuss: settlement (387-390); trades and classes (449-453); state and ruler (458-462); architecture (495-512); statuary (525-541); reliefs (566-578); painting and drawing (595-600); temples and gods (605-620); funerary cult (662-690); and animal and human representations (744-746 and 753-756).

Other chapters do not contain special sections on Egypt (e.g. ch. 5 : economy; ch. 6A : the family), but everywhere remarks to the Egyptian civilization are made.

The second volume begins with synoptic tables (774-777), followed by a lexicon to archaeological sites. For Egypt (781-818) forty-two sites are listed in an alphabetical order, from Abûsîr to el-Tôd, with descriptions mainly of tombs from the Old and Middle Kingdoms with their contents, but also of a few temples.

To these two volumes belong the innumerable small ill. and fig. on the 746 plates of the third volume : those for Egypt on pl. 1-167, a few to Nubia, mainly 'Aniba and Kerma, on pl. 736-744. The plates bear small photographs, plans, sections of buildings, drawings of reliefs, paintings, furniture, vessels, etc.

All three together these volumes give a valuable survey of Egyptian archaeology and civilization within the frame of the history of the Copper Age in general.

74524 MUHLY, J. D. and T. A. WERTIME, Evidence for the Sources and Use of Tin during the Bronze Age of the Near East : a reply to J.E. Dayton, *World Archaeology*, Henley-on-Thames 5 (1973-1974), 111-122.

The names in Sumerian, Akkadian, Hittite and Egyptian of metals which played an important role in the Ancient Near East are given in a table on p. 116. *L.M.J. Zonhoven*

MUHLY, James D., see also our number 74468.

74525 MUNRO, Peter, Bemerkungen zur Gestaltwandel und zum Ursprung der Horus-Kinder, *Festschrift Ägyptisches Museum Berlin*, 195-204.

The author studies the change of the figures of the four children of Horus in the course of Egyptian history, as well as their origin. After summarizing our knowledge about the dieties he argues that they originally have been represented in human form

(Imseti as a female), in the Middle Kingdom also as animals, but only during the New Kingdom they were connected each with a particular animal. Their forms of falcon and jackal they may have derived from the bȝw of P and Nḫn. In analogy to the šmsw-Ḥr, followers of the living Horus, i.e., the king, the msw-Ḥr may have originally been royal children playing a special role in some ceremonies. The names Duamutef and Kebehsenuf may point to the actual family of the pharaoh.

MUNRO, Peter, see also our number 74071.

MUSCARELLA, Oscar White, see our number 74021.

74526 Museo Egizio. Atti del centocinquantenario 1824-1974, Torino, G. Giappichelli Editore, [1974] (15.7 × 22.7 cm; 31 p., 2 pl.).
Pr. Lire 1500

The booklet, published at the occasion of the 150th anniversary of the Egyptian Museum at Turin, contains a survey of the activities during the celebration.
The first chapter, after the introduction, presents a report of the official ceremony, including the text of Silvio Curto's lecture concerning the museum's activities during the period (p. 9-29). A second chapter contains very brief summaries of the lectures held during the conference 6-7 October, all dealing with various aspects of the museum and its international relations. The lectures were i.a. by Riad, Mme Desroches-Noblecourt, Edwards and Curto. A last chapter gives a survey of an exhibition 6-18 October, at which i.a. publications, objects from the beginning of the collection, and recently restored objects were shown.
Pl. 2 represents the medal of the 150th anniversary.

74527 NAGEL, Peter, Diktion der römischen Kommandosprache in den Praecepta des Pachomius, ZÄS 101 (1974), 114-120.

Verfasser erörtert einen Block von stereotypen Verbotssätzen. In ihnen hat Pachom, der Soldat gewesen war, ein Element der lateinischen Militärdiktion koptisch wiedergegeben.
M. Heerma van Voss

74528 NAGEL, Peter, Die Septuaginta-Zitate in der koptisch-gnostischen "Exegese über die Seele" (Nag Hammadi Codex II), *Archiv für Papyrusforschung und verwandte Gebiete*, Leipzig 22-23 (1974), 249-269.

Comparing a number of quotations from the Old Testament occurring in the "Exegesis about the Soul" in Nag' Hammadi Codex II with the versions in Sahidic and Akhmimic translations of the Septuaginta the author reaches the conclusion that the quotations have been translated directly from the Greek text of the Exegesis, independently from the Coptic LXX-versions. They provide valuable material for the study of the early Coptic translation practice.

74529 NAGY, István, Archaizáló tendenciák a későkori Saisban, *Idö történelem*, 185-193.

"Archaisierende Tendenzen im spätzeitlichen Sais".
Das Archaisieren zeigt sich in der Kunst, in der Restaurierung der Denkmäler, in der Titulatur. Züge der Archaisierung in der Religion versucht Verfasser in der Gestalt der Neith und dem mit ihr zusammenhängenden Kult der Biene darzustellen.

V. Wessetzky

74530 NAGY, I., Du rôle de l'abeille dans les cultes de basse époque, *Studia Aegyptiaca I*, 313-322, with 1 fig.

The author studies a scene of a man kneeling in front of eight jars and two rows of together ten bees from the tomb of Pabasa (Theban Tomb No. 279; cfr Porter-Moss I², 2, 358, C (*c*) II). Referring to the *Ḥwt bỉt* mentioned in XXVIth Dynasty texts, probably a building within the enclosure wall of the Neith temple at Sais, he argues that the bee was venerated in that period. Pabasa, who came from a family from Sais, depicted here a veneration scene. The author has also collected several, mostly obscure references to the religious roles of honey and bees.

74531 NAKHLA, Shawki M. and Ferial M. MOHAMMED, Cairo Natural Radiocarbon Measurements I, *Radiocarbon*, New Haven, Connecticut 16 (1974), 1-5.

Short description of the methods applied to samples in the Centre of Research and Conservation of Antiquities, Cairo, and of the results of 20 measurements. No evaluation of the differences between the results of the measurements and the generally accepted archaeological dates of the samples.

74532 The Nature and Making of Papyrus, Barkston Ash, Yorkshire, The Elmete Press, 1973 (15 × 22.8 cm; XVI + 70 p., 9 pages of hand-made paper with fig., 1 map, 4 fig., 1 sample of genuine papyrus, fig. on endpapers).

This is a bibliophile edition devoted to the papyrus and its use as writing material. The foreword is by Hassan Ragab, president of the Papyrus Institute of Egypt, and the various chapters, based on material provided by several scholars and assembled by Norman Λ. Lunn, are composed by the director of the Elmete Press, Ian O'Casey. They deal with the plant, rolls and codices, scribes and papyri, ancient and modern techniques of making papyrus sheets, a practical method of sheet-making, and the future of the papyrus. Although addressed to the general public the handsome book contains some valuable information. No notes or bibliographical references.

von NEITZSCHITZ, George Chr., see our number 74781.

NETZER, E., see our number 74544.

NEWTON, Derek, see our number 74187.

74533 NIBBI, Alessandra, Further remarks on w3d wr, Sea Peoples and Keftiu, *GM* Heft 10 (1974), 35-40.

A reply to Sledzianowski's review of our number 72524, asserting that w3d wr denotes the Nile Delta, not the sea.
Dieter Mueller

74534 NIBBI, Alessandra, The Identification of the "Sea Peoples", *in*: *Bronze Age Migrations in the Aegean*. Archaeological and Linguistic Problems in Greek Prehistory. Proceedings of the First International Colloquium on Aegean Prehistory, Sheffield, Organized by the British Association for Mycenean Studies and the Departments of Greek and Ancient History of the University of Sheffield. Edited by R.A. Crossland and Ann Birchall, [Park Ridge, New Jersey], Noyes Press, [1974], 203-207.

In her paper the author states that the Egyptian sources do not suggest the movements of the Sea Peoples to be a migration, and that the attackers of Egypt were actually Asiatics. In the discussion (p. 205-207) R.D. Barnett and M.S. Drower refuted the arguments of the speaker.

NICOLA, G.L., see our number 74617.

NIERMEYER, Oscar, see our number 74054.

NOLTE, Birgit, see our number 74632.

74535 NOTTER, Viktor, Biblischer Schöpfungsbericht und ägyptische Schöpfungsmythen, Stuttgart, KBW Verlag, [1974] (13.6 × 20.8 cm; 191 p., 5 fig.) = Stuttgarter Bibelstudien, 68; rev. *ZAW* 86 (1974), 382 ([G. Fohrer]). Pr. DM 18

The author of this book, which is introduced by Hellmut Brunner and Herbert Haag, is a missionary on Taiwan. He deals with the various verses of Gen. 1 and 2, each separately, attempting to indicate throughout parallel conceptions occurring in Egyptian religious texts from various periods. As reference material he quotes mostly recent publications, articles and books as well as text editions.

What he attempts to prove is that the Jewish author of Genesis derived his material from Egypt, though certainly he used only that part of Egyptian conceptions which was in accordance with his own, which principally differ from those of ancient Egypt.

74536 NOTTON, J.H.F., Ancient Egyptian Gold Refining. A Reproduction of Early Techniques, *Gold Bulletin*, Johannesburg 7 (1974), 50-56, with 1 map and 6 colour ill.

The author has simulated the technique of smelting gold ore concentrates as described by Diodorus Siculus. Sealing up portions of gold alloy with salt in a sillimanite pot and heating the pot at 800° C the gold content appeared after five days to be raised to over 93 per cent.

74537 NUR EL-DIN, Mohamed Abd el-Halim Ahmed, The Demotic Ostraca in the National Museum of Antiquities at Leiden. Proefschrift ter verkrijging van de graad van doctor in de letteren aan de Rijksuniversiteit te Leiden, Leiden, E.J. Brill. 1974 (24 × 31 cm; XIV + 680 p., including 100 p. of facsimiles, 32 pl.) = Collections of National Museum of Antiquities at Leiden, 1.

This thesis for obtaining the doctor's degree in Arts at the Leiden University (May 29, 1974) contains the publication of all 590 Demotic ostraca preserved in the Museum of Antiquities, Leiden.

After a short introduction concerning museum numbers, provenance, earlier publications, etc., there follows (p. 7-374) the study of the texts themselves. They are divided into 8 categories: taxes (nos 1-51), various payments (52-62), texts concerning land (63-82), reminders and accounts (83-277), legal and literary texts (278-364), lists of records or personal names (365-408), miscellaneous texts (409-426) and unidentified or unclear texts and fragments (427-590). Each chapter is briefly introduced and mostly subdivided into several sections.

For every text are given: technical data, transliteration, translation with (mainly textual) notes, while pages 581-680 bear facsimiles of almost all of them. Only in a few instances a very brief comment as regards the text as a whole follows the notes. The plates bear photographs of a limited number of ostraca illustrating so far as possible all categories.

The 15 indexes (p. 375-578) constitute an important part of the publication, since the sections a-m present vocabulary, titles and professions, months and seasons, etc., numerals and various kinds of names, all in facsimile, with a translation and a transliteration. Moreover, Ptolemaic and Roman writings are given in different columns. Further indexes contain lists of dates of the texts and inventory numbers.

74538 OCHSENSCHLAGER, Edward L., Unbaked Pottery at el-Hiba, *AJA* 78 (1974), 173.

Short summary of a paper about the use of unbaked and partially baked pottery.

O'CONNOR, David, see our number 74391.

74539 O'FAHEY, R.S. and J.L. SPAULDING, Kingdoms of the Sudan, London, Methuen and Co., 1974 (11 × 17 cm; IX + 235 p., 3 maps, 1 fig.) = Studies in African History, 9.

Aus zwei Dissertationen entstanden, bietet das vorliegende Werk eine Geschichte des Reiches Sinnār mit einem Rückblick auf die Zeit seit 1300 n.Chr. und von Dār Fūr seit der Daju-Dynastie.
Inge Hofmann

74540 OGDEN, J.M., An Additional Note on 'Cylindrical Amulet Cases', *JEA* 60 (1974), 258-259.

This short note draws attention to Brigitte Quillard's article (*Karthago* 16 [1973], 5-32] on amulet cases from Carthage, Spain and the W. Mediterranean, many of which are clearly in Egyptian form and feature Egyptian deities. *E. Uphill*

74541 OGILVIE, R.E., R.M. FISHER and W.J. YOUNG, Scanning and High Voltage Electron Microscopy of Ancient Egyptian Glass, *Recent Advances in Science and Technology of Materials*, 71-84, with 17 ill.

Investigation of samples of Egyptian and Roman glass in order to observe microstructural features related to early glass making technology.

74542 OREN, Eliezer D., An ancient city of the Negev, *Illustrated London News*, London 262, No. 6910 (march 1974), 69-72, with 7 ill.

In this survey of the excavations at Tell esh-Shariʿa midway between Gaza and Beersheba, which is probably the O.T. town Ziklag, the author i.a. mentions the find of 11 bowls and ostraca with Egyptian hieratic texts from the New Kingdom dealing with taxes paid to the local temple or fortress.

74543 OREN, Eliezer, Bir el-ʿAbd (Sinaï Nord), *Revue Biblique*, Paris 81 (1974), 87-89.

Communication about the excavations near Bir el-ʿAbd in 1973, where a military station along the road from Egypt to Canaan has been discovered.
Compare our number 73540.

74544 OREN, E.D. and E. NETZER, Tel Sera' (Tell esh-Shari'a), *Israel Exploration Journal*, Jerusalem 24 (1974), 264-266, with 6 ill. on a pl.

The third season of excavations at Tel Sera' brought to light several objects of Egyptian origin; a structure of the LBA II is suggested to have been the fortified residence of the local governor, possibly an Egyptian.

74545 ORLANDI, Titus, Constantini episcopi urbis Siout encomia in Athanasium duo. Edidit, Louvain, Secrétariat du Corpus SCO, 1974 (16.5 × 25 cm; XII + 52 p., 2 pl.) = Corpus scriptorum christianorum orientalium, vol. 349 = Scriptores coptici, tomus 37.

Edition of two Sahidic encomia of Athanasius composed by bishop Constantin of Asyût, the main Ms. of which is Pierpont Morgan Library, Cod. M. 579. The introduction (in Italian) describes this Ms. and lists the fragments of another Ms., originally in the White Monastery and now dispersed among several collections.

For the translation and comments, see our following number.

74546 ORLANDI, Titus, Constantini episcopi urbis Siout encomia in Athanasium duo. Interpretatus est, Louvain, Secrétariat du Corpus SCO, 1974 (16.5 × 25 cm; XX + 29 p.) = Corpus scriptorum christianorum orientalium, vol. 350 = Scriptores coptici, tomus 38.

Latin translation of the encomia edited in our preceding number. In the introduction (in Italian) Orlandi deals briefly with life and works of their author, their literary aspects, and their historical background and contents.

74547 ORLANDI, Tito, Koptische Papyri theologischen Inhalts. Herausgegeben und in das Italienische übersetzt/Papiri copti di contenuto teologico. Edizione e traduzione in italiano, Wien, In Kommission bei Verlag Brüder Hollinek, 1974 (16.5 × 23.5 cm; VI + 221 p, 33 folding pl.) = Mitteilungen aus der Papyrussammlung der österreichischen Nationalbibliothek (Papyrus Erzherzog Rainer). Neue Serie, IX. Folge. At head of title : Österreichische Nationalbibliothek; rev. *Aegyptus* 55 (1975), 329-330 (Sergio Pernigotti); *BiOr* 33 (1976), 185-186 (K.H. Kuhn); *Orientalia* 44 (1975), 135-136 (H. Quecke).

The introduction, like the rest of the study in Italian, deals with the Coptic manuscripts in the Österreichische Nationalbibliothek in general and with the provenance of the fragments here published, which formerly belonged to the collection of the archduke Rainer. Orlandi argues from letters from the 19th century and introductions to earlier publications that they, or at least the majority of them, came from the White Monastery. The publication consists of a large number of fragments, together 31 in total, some of which contain parts of more than one text. They comprise books of the Bible, works of the Fathers of the Church (i.a. of Cyrillus of Jerusalem and Johannes Chrysostomus), a synaxary, martyrdoms, homilies, etc. Each text is represented by a photograph on the plates and is given in printed characters, with notes, translation, introduction and remarks on the writing. Indexes p. 197-208; bibliography p. 209-218.

74548 ORLANDI, Tito, Notizie su parte di un codice papiraceo copto neotestamentario dell'Università statale di Milano, *Akten des XIII. Internationalen Papyrologenkongresses*, 321-324.

Notes on parts of a Coptic papyrus codex recently acquired by the University of Milan, written in the Middle-Egyptian dialect and containing portions of the Epistles of St. Paul.
Compare our following number.

74549 ORLANDI, Tito, Papiri della Università degli Studi di Milano (P. Mil. Copti). Volume quinto. Lettere di San Paolo in copto-ossirinchita. Edizione, commento e indici. Contributo linguistico di Hans Quecke, Milano, Istituto Editoriale Cisalpino — La Goliardica, 1974 (21.5 × 29.7 cm; 146 p., 16 pl.); at head of title: Istituto di papirologia dell' Università degli Studi di Milano; rev. *Aegyptus* 55 (1975), 331-333 (Sergio Pernigotti).
Pr. Lire 15.000

Publication of a fragmentary papyrus codex containing the translation of the Epistles of St.-Paul in the dialect of Oxyrhynchus. The ms. probably dates from the 4th or 5th century A.D.
After a description of the codex and its palaeography the Coptic text is presented, with textual notes. There follows an extensive discussion (in German) of its dialect, by Hans Quecke (p. 87-108). The editor himself then deals with the characteristics of the version. On p. 125-146 indexes to names and to Coptic words.

74550 ORLANDI, Tito, Les papyrus coptes du Musée Égyptien de Turin, *Le Muséon*, Louvain 87 (1974), 115-127.

After describing the history of the collection of Coptic manuscripts in the Egyptian Museum at Turin the author lists 17 codices, each with a short description of its contents.

74551 OSING, Jürgen, Isis und Osiris, *MDAIK* 30 (1974), 91-113.

The original form of the name of the Egyptian goddess Isis is ꜣst = *ꜣūsit; it has no connection with the word for "throne", but is derived from the root wꜣs and may be a *nomen agentis* or an adjective ("the dominant one"). The name of Osiris was ꜣst irt = *ꜣūsit jurut, a feminine form of the pattern sḫm-iri, and may have denoted one of the royal insignia with the same transition from fem. to masc. as in Bq.s > 'Bqs.

Dieter Mueller

74552 OSING, Jürgen, Die neuägyptische Partikel 𓇋𓈖𓏌𓏥 "wenn; ob", *SAK* 1 (1974), 267-273.

From the Coptic vocalisation it appears that the interrogative particle in did not bear full stress (*jăn > *'ăn). The author adduces arguments against Černy's suggestion (cfr *JEA* 27, 1941, 106-112) that the origin of inn is in wn. He argues that inn is merely a variant writing for in (> B ᴀɴ, S ᴇɴ, influenced by the writing of the independent pronoun of 1. ps. plur.

74553 OTTO, Eberhard, Archäologische Arbeiten in Nubien, *Antike Welt*, Küsnacht-Zürich 5, Heft 3 (1974), 31-40, with 8 ill. and 3 fig.

Nach einem kurzen Überblick über die Bedeutung des nubischen Raumes und seiner Geschichte werden die Unternehmungen geschildert, die zur Rettung der nubischen Denkmäler durchgeführt wurden, so vor allem in Abu Simbel und Kalabsha.

Inge Hofmann

74554 OTTO, Eberhard, Der Begriff der "Maat" in Altägypten, [in: Oskar Köhler, Versuch einer "Historischen Anthropologie"], *Saeculum*, Freiburg/München 25 (1974), 230-231.

Brief remarks about the concept "Maat" and about guilt and sin in ancient Egypt.

74555 O[TTO], E[berhard], Egyptian Religion, *Encyclopaedia Britannica*. Vol. 6, 503-509, with 2 ill.

After having dealt with nature and significance and with the sources of the Egyptian religion, the author turns to the religious beliefs and the forms of the religion. At the end a short section on Egyptian religion in the Graeco-Roman world. Two tables containing lists of major and minor gods are added.
For other references to the Egyptian religion and cosmogony see the above edition. Micropaedia. Vol. III.

L.M.J. Zonhoven

74556 OTTO, Eberhard, Erhaltung der bestehenden Ordnung als Grundzug ägyptischer Herrschaftsauffassung, [in: Oskar Köhler, Versuch einer "Historischen Anthropologie"], *Saeculum*, Freiburg/München 25 (1974), 185-186.

The author sketches the peaceful character of the Egyptian civilization, even in the time of the Empire.

OTTO, Eberhard, see also our numbers 74070 and 74445.

74557 PADRO I PARCERISA, Josep, A propósito des escarabeo de la Solivella (Alcalá de Xivert, Castellón), y de otras piezas egipcias de la zona del Bajo Ebro, *Cuadernos de Prehistoria y Arqueología Castellonense*, Castellón de la Plana 1 (1974), 71-78, with 3 fig.

Der hier behandelte Skarabäus aus weißlichem Pastenmaterial mit Resten grüner Tönung wurde in Grab 6, einer Brandbestattung, der Nekropole van La Solivella gefunden, die der Ausgräber in das 3. Viertel des 5.Jhds. v.Chr. datiert hat. Die Unterseite füllt das Bild eines liegenden Löwen, in seinen Pranken erkennt man eine Feder (oder *ḥs*-Gefäß?), über dem Rücken die Sonnenscheibe. Verf. sieht darin eine Schreibung des Rê-Namens. An der Herkunft des Skarabäus aus Naukratis gibt es für Verf. keinen Zweifel; damit aber auch an einer Datierung ins 6.Jhd. v.Chr., was für Verf. eine Höherdatierung des Gräberfeldes impliziert.

Es folgen zusätzliche Bemerkungen zu dem Cowroid aus Tossal del Moro bei Pinyeres, der für Verf. den abgekürzten Horusnamen Psammetichs II. enthält und damit angeblich wieder einen Hinweis auf eine Höherdatierung auch dieses genannten Platzes mindestens in das 6.Jh.

Schließlich wird die Zeichnung eines Skarabäus der ehem. Slg. Mestre i Noé bekannt gemacht, der in der Nähe von Tortosa gefunden worden sein soll. Das Dekormotiv seiner Unterseite, ein menschliches Wesen mit Krokodils(?)kopf auf *nb*-Korb, davor Skarabäus und Kobra, erinnert an Skarabäen der Hyksoszeit; für Verf. handelt es sich hier um eine ägyptische Imitation der Saitenzeit. *Ingrid Gamer-Wallert*

74558 PADRÓ PARCERISA, J., Los escarabeos de Empórion, *in*: *Miscelánea Arqueológica*. XXV Aniversario de los Cursos Internationales de Prehistoria y Arqueología en Ampurias (1947-1971). Tomo II, Barcelona, Diputación Provincial de Barcelona. Instituto de Prehistoria y Arqueología, 1974, 113-125, with 3 ill.

Zwölf "aus Ampurias" stammende Skarabäen werden publiziert; allerdings ist nur zu zweien Näheres über ihre Auffindung bekannt.

Nr. 1, ein Herzskarabäus mit glatter Unterseite, wurde im Kunsthandel erworben; Verf. datiert ihn in das 10.-6.Jh.v.Chr. Nr. 2 (aus Diaspro), Nr. 3 (aus grünem Stein), Nr. 4 (aus Diaspro), Nr. 5 (aus Onyx), Nr. 6 (aus Karneol), Nr. 9 (aus Karneol) und Nr. 11 (aus Karneol) stellen für Verf. sardische bzw. etruskische Arbeiten dar, am ehesten des 4.Jhs.v.Chr. Auch für Nr. 8 aus grünlichem Pastenmaterial des 5.-3.Jhs.(?) möchte Verf. eine westliche Werkstatt annehmen.

Nr. 7, aus Pastenmaterial, mit gejagter Antilope auf der Unterseite, entstammt (für Verf.) einer ägyptischen Werkstatt des 7.-6.Jhs., ebenso Nr. 10 aus dunkler Paste.

Nr. 12, aus weißlicher Fayence, wurde 1955 in einer Brandbestattung des Friedhofs der Muralla N.E. gefunden, die der Ausgräber um 500 v.Chr. datiert. Die Unterseite füllen, auf *nb*-Korb, ein Flügelgreif und eine diesem zugewandte männliche Figur, beide stehend. Verf. sieht in diesem Skarabäus eine naukrateische Arbeit des 7.-6.Jhs. *Ingrid Gamer-Wallert*

74559 PADRÓ PARCERISA, J., Una estatua en Barcelona en el siglo XVII, *Ampurias*, Barcelona 35 (1973), 175-202, with 5 ill. and 3 fig.

Die ägyptische Hockerfigur, der dieser Aufsatz gewidmet ist, wurde bereits 1666 von A. Kircher publiziert. Damals befand sie sich in Barcelona, wo sie "inter rudera" gefunden worden sein soll. Für Verf. dürfte sie nicht allzu lange davor auf die Halbinsel gelangt sein. Verf. verfolgt ihr weiteres Schicksal bis zu ihrer Eingliederung in das Gabinete de Historia Natural von Madrid und schließlich in das Museo Arqueológico Nacional von Madrid (Nr. 2014) im Jahre 1868.

Der 2. Teil der Untersuchung gilt der Beschreibung der Figur und der Vorlage ihrer Inschriften, die den Dargestellten als einen Harsomtusemhe ausweisen, der offensichtlich während der Regierung Psammetichs I. hohe profane wie priesterliche Ämter innehatte. Eine zweite Statue dieses Mannes ist bekannt; sie stammt allem Anschein nach aus dem Ptahtempel von Memphis. Von dort möchte Verf. auch die Madrider Figur ursprünglich kommen lassen.

Der Aufsatz ist auch erschienen in den Monografías del Instituto de Prehistoria y Arqueología de la Diputación Provincial de Barcelona, Abh. 42.

Man vergleiche unsere Nummer 74214. *Ingrid Gamer-Wallert*

74560 PANIĆ, M., Двадесет девети међународни конгрес оријенталиста, Париз, 16-22 јула 1973, *Историјски гласник*, Београд 2 (1973), [1974], 164-166.

"Twenty-ninth International Congress of Orientalists, Paris, 16-22 July 1973".

A partial summary of work in the Egyptological "Subsection b" of the Congress at Paris. *S. P. Tutundžić*

74561 PANIĆ, Miroslava, Четири 'канопе' у Градском музеју у Вараждину, *Зборник Филозозског факултета*, Београд 12,1 (1974), 15-24, with 5 ill. on 5 pl. and an English summary on p. 25.

"Four 'Canopic' Jars in the City Museum in Varaždin".
In publishing these alabaster canopic jars, the author points out that the part of the text referring directly to the deceased: *Wsir ktn W3ḥ-ìb-Rʿ mry Ptḥ* contains either his name or the title "Osiris charioteer (of) *W3ḥ-ìb-Rʿ* [Psamtik]"... According to the contents and the orthography of their entire texts, the jars belong to the period from the 26th Dynasty onward.

S.P. Tutundžić

PARÁSSOGLOU, George M., see our number 74762.

74562 PARKER, R.A., Ancient Egyptian Astronomy, *in*: *The Place of Astronomy in the Ancient World*. A Joint Symposium of The Royal Society and the British Academy organized by D.G. Kendall, S. Piggott, D.G. King-Hele and I.E.S. Edwards. Edited by F.R. Hodson, London, Published for the British Academy by Oxford University Press, 1974 (= Philosophical Transactions of the Royal Society London A vol. 276, No. 1257), 51-65, with 3 fig., 2 tables and 4 pl.

In the introduction to this survey of Egyptian astronomy the author stresses its relatively small importance for the Egyptian civilization until the Ptolemaic Period. He further discusses the major subjects of Egyptian astronomy: early calendars; the diagonal star clocks (depicted on Middle Kingdom coffin lids) and their mechanism; the decanal hours; the so-called cosmology of Sethi I and Ramses IV; the later star clocks preserved in the ceiling adornment of some Ramesside royal tombs; the astronomical ceiling in the tomb of Senmut; the planets, the northern constellation (including the Big Dipper) and the zodiacs (a Babylonian import), etc. The last section is devoted to late Demotic astronomical papyri.

74563 PARKER, Richard A., The Orthography of Article Plus Prothetic *r* in Demotic, *JNES* 33 (1974), 371-376, with 2 tables.

The author refutes the commonly held ruling that when the participle *r-wnw* or a relative form with prothetic *r* is preceded by an article, a demonstrative, or a copula, the prothetic *r* is not written, and suggests that this is only partly true, mainly in cases of theophoric personal names. Using evidence from Pap. Rylands 9, differentiation in writing article, demonstrative and copula can be shown, and tables are accordingly included. A much later papyrus entitled Mythus also provides additional proof of this differentiation, and a possible explanation is given for the combination of prothetic r with a definite article. E. Uphill

74564 PARLASCA, Klaus, Falkenstelen aus Edfu. Bemerkungen zu einer Gruppe zerstörter Reliefs des Berliner Museums, *Festschrift Ägyptisches Museum Berlin*, 483-487, with 7 pl.

The author publishes the available data on a group of 13 falcon stelae from Edfu formerly in the Ägyptisches Museum, Berlin (Inv. Nos. 22469-22481) but lost during the last war. He adduces as material for comparison a number of stelae from other collections as well as some from Berlin itself in order to illustrate the descriptions of the lost pieces.

74565 PARLEBAS, Jacques, L'origine égyptienne de l'appellation "Hermès Trismégiste", *GM* Heft 13 (1974), 25-28.

The author quotes four examples of the epithet *'3 '3 wr nb Ḥmnw* (and var.) from Edfou dated to the reigns of Ptolemy V, Ptolemy VII, and Ptolemy XI. Originally translated into Greek as *megistos kai megistos theos megas Hermes*, they were condensed into *Hermes Trismegistos* when the old designation of the local god of Hermopolis was no longer in use.

Dieter Mueller

74566 P[ARROT], A[ndré], Jacques Vandier (1904-1973), *Syria*, Paris 51 (1974), 202-221, with portrait.

Obituary article. Compare our number 73828.

74567 PATTIE, T.S. and E.G. TURNER, The Written Word on Papyrus. An Exhibition Held in the British Museum. 30 July - 27 October 1974, London, Published for the British Library Board by British Museum Publications Limited, 1974 (18.5 × 25 cm; 48 p., 1 map, frontispiece, 21 ill.).

Catalogue of an exhibition held in the British Museum and devoted to writing on papyrus.
Chapter 1 briefly deals with papyrus as writing material. Chapter 2 mentions five examples, among which a Demotic text from el-Hîba (Pap. 10838). Chapter 3 is devoted to Egyptian papyri, describing an example from the Abusîr archive (Pap. 10735), the *Book of the Dead* of queen Nodjmet and Herihor (Pap. 10541), a cancelled Demotic marriage settlement (Pap. 10606), a carbonized papyrus from Tanis (Pap. 10837) and fragments with Meroitic texts from Qasr Ibrîm (Pap. 10816). Chapter 5 deals with the scribe's tools and types of books, among which an example of Coptic binding. The other chapters are entirely devoted to Greek and Latin texts. All items are briefly described and some represented by photographs.

74568 PAWLICKI, Franciszek, Egipskie sistra, *Rocznik Muzeum Narodowego w Warszawie*, Warszawa 18 (1974), 7-21, with 3 fig. and 4 ill., and summaries in Russian and English on p. 20-21.
"Les sistres égyptiens".
L'auteur décrit trois sistres du type en naos et un du type en arc du Musée National de Varsovie. Tous les trois sistres en naos sont en faïence et remontent à la Basse Époque.
A. Szczudlowska

PELTENBURG, E. J., see our number 74383.

74569 PERC, Bernarda, Spomeniki starega Egipta. Razstava v Arkadah, Ljubljana, [Narodni muzej v Ljubljani], 1974 (20.8 × 20.9 cm; 40 p., 23 [unnumbered] fig., 1 map, 2 + 80 ill. [a frontispiece], colour ill. on cover and coverback; English summary on p. 39). At head of title : Društvo muzealcev Slovenije in Narodni muzej v Ljubljani.
"Monuments of Ancient Egypt. The Exhibition in Arkadah". After a foreword and an outline on ancient Egypt follows the catalogue of 50 monuments from museums in Egypt (ill. 1-50), most of them being included in the exhibitions "5000 Years of Egyptian Art". A note about the modular composition in architecture is given by T. Kurent. Published on the occasion of the exhibition of Dynastic, Graeco-Roman and Coptic monuments from Yugoslavian, mainly Slovenian, museums (ill. 51-80). For objects from the territory of Illyricum, cfr our No. 68459. *S. P. Tutundžić*

74570 PERNIGOTTI, Sergio, Ricerche su personaggi egiziani di epoca etiopica e saitica, *Aegyptus* 54 (1974), 141-156, with 12 ill. on 6 pl. and 3 fig.
I. La statuette du Caire J.E. 37885 (cachette de Karnak 536), en grès rouge, dédiée par le prêtre thébain de Montou Ankh-pa-khred, représente le père de celui-ci *Ḥrj*, dont le "beau nom" est *Ḥr-sȝ-'Ist*. Agenouillé, ce personnage barbu tient une image d'Osiris debout. Malgré l'absence de pilier dorsal, on peut attribuer le morceau à la XXVᵉ dynastie finissante. Les inscriptions sur la large base évoquent 5 générations de personnages dont les noms font intervenir le dieu Horus.
II. La petite statue de schiste J.E. 36674 (Karnak 23) figure agenouillé le *ḥm-wn*, portier du ciel *Ns-pȝ-sf(j)*. Ce dernier porte un Osiris assis. La pièce pourrait être datée du XXVIᵉ dynastie, entre la fin du VIIᵉ siècle et le début du VIᵉ.
III. La statue-bloc J.E. 15.12.24.1, en granit gris, aux pieds apparents, provient de Karnak et représente le Père divin *'Irt-Ḥr-r-w*. Elle prolonge d'une génération la descendance d'une

famille sacerdotale thébaine, contemporaine de la XXVIe dynastie. La génération précédente avait déjà pu être datée de la deuxième partie du règne de Psamétik Ier. *J. Custers*

74571 PERROT, J., Suse, *Iran*, London 12 (1974), 217-218, with 4 pl.

Short notice about the excavations on the tepe of Apadama mentioning the discovery of the statue of Darius (see our number 72794). For very fine photographs, see pl. 6 and 7.

74572 PETERSON, B., A Note of the Wisdom of Amenemope 3,9–4,10, *Studia Aegyptiaca I*, 323-328.

Publication of the fragmentary O. Cairo 1840, after a copy of Černý. It contains a few words of the Instruction of Amenemope (from 3,9 to 4,10), and the copy may date from the XXIst or the XXIInd Dynasty.

The text, in Černý's transcription, is accompanied by notes of the author.

74573 PETERSON, Bengt, Ramesside Mannerism, *Medelhavsmuseet Bulletin*, Stockholm 9 (1974), 5-12, with 3 fig.

The tombs of the New Kingdom cemetery at Memphis are largely destroyed, their reliefs and paintings being scattered all over the world. The author studies three relief fragments very probably originating from this necropolis, now preserved in the Medelhavsmuseet (MM 10025, NME 26 and NME 41), all three showing the mannerism of the Ramesside Period, and discusses the decline of art in that time.

74574 PETERSON, B. and Marie-Louise WINDBLADH, A Selection of Some Recent Acquisitions, *Medelhavsmuseet Bulletin*, Stockholm 9 (1974), 66-73, with 16 ill.

Among the recent acquisitions here mentioned are the upper part of a wooden cover to be placed upon a mummy (MME 1971.5) and the upper part of the lid of an anthropoid coffin (MME 1971.4), both from the Late Period, an XVIIIth Dynasty pottery vase inscribed with the name of "the Lady of the House M'ỉ3 (MME 1974.46), and another vase of uncertain date.

74575 PETROVSKY, N.S., Употребление египетского предлога *m* в непредикативных словосочетаниях, *in* : *Основные проблемы африканистики. Этнография. история. филология*. К 70-летию члена-корреспондента АН СССР Д. А. Ольдерогге, Moscow, Издательство « Наука », 1973, 339-347.

"The Use of the Egyptian Preposition *m* in Non-Predicative Word-Combinations".

After dwelling on some general characteristics of the preposition *m* and its cognates in the hamito-semitic stratum, the author establishes five subclasses where $m+$ adjunct occurs after another word in a non-predicative function with examples (no sources quoted): (1) as a verbal complement: '(to go) m niw.t, out of town'; (2) as a noun modifier: '(a pyramid) m inr in stone'; (3) similarly, modifying an adjective: '3 m s3w, 'great in weight'; (4) following a cardinal number: w' im=n, 'one of us'; (5) after an ordinal number: tpy m smnḫ, 'the first one in embellishing'. A few remarks on other syntactic usages conclude the article. *J.F. Borghouts*

74576 PIANKOFF, Alexandre, The Wandering of the Soul. Texts Translated with Commentary. Completed and Prepared for Publication by Helen Jacquet-Gordon, Princeton, N.J., Princeton University Press, [1974] (23 × 31.5 cm; XVIII + 124 p., 48 pl. [1 folding]) = Egyptian Religious Texts and Representations, 6 = Bollingen Series 40; rev. *AJA* 79 (1975), 154-155 (Hans Goedicke); *Archaeological News* 3 (1974), 83-84 (William Kelly Simpson); *BiOr* 33 (1976), 166-171 (Jean-Claude Goyon); *JARCE* 12 (1975), 110 (David Lorton); *JEA* 61 (1975), 294 (J. Gwyn Griffiths); *Times Literary Supplement*, October 18, 1974, 1170 ([T.G.H. James]). Pr. $ 25

This last volume of the series is edited from a manuscript of the author (deceased in 1966) by Mme Jacquet, who added i.a. a general introduction and rearranged part III.
Part I (p. 1-37) is devoted to the *Book of Two Ways*. First an introduction explaining the meaning of the text, illustrated by several quotations from the *CT*, and then a translation of *CT* Spells 1029-1130, followed by some other spells (91-96, 576 and 914). The translations are mainly after Cairo Coffin 28083 and Berlin Coffin 14385. The author could not yet consult the translation by Lesko (our number 72429).
Part II (39-114), on the *Querets* or *Caverns*, first deals with the two versions of the text and the sources for them. Then the composition of the book is studied, which consists of four elements: representations of the deceased (with accompanying texts), introductory texts specifying numbers and names of the caverns, representations of the gods inhabiting the caverns, and offering texts pertaining to each group of gods. There follow descriptions of the vignettes and translations of the texts as found in each of the ten mss. known. Five of them, Pap. Cairo 24742, Brit.Mus. 10.478, Hermitage 1113, Metrop.Mus. 35.5.19 and Brit.Mus. 10.010, are represented in splendid photographs on the plates.
Part III (115-124) discusses the Egyptian game of draughts, particularly the *senet*-game, which was played in the Netherworld between the soul and an anonymous inimical opponent, the stake being the future life of the soul. A text concerning the 30-square

game, Cairo Pap. JE 58037, is here translated (see pls 43-45). In an appendix, by Siadhal Sweeney, several references to examples from folklore and legend in various parts of the world, in which a game for one's soul is played.

74577 PILLOT, Christine, La publication des textes égyptiens du British Museum, *Textes et langages III*, 123-130.

Annotated bibliography of the editions of various kinds of texts in the British Museum, from the *Hieroglyphs Collected by the Egyptian Society* by Thomas Young (1823), through the publications of Birch, Budge and others down to the most recent ones such as the *Abu Sir Papyri* (our number 68486) and the *Wooden Model Boats* (our number 72257).

74578 PINCHERLE, Mario, La rampa, la slitta e i famosi "legni corti" per il sollevamento dei monoliti della piramida di Cheope, *Atti della Accademia Nazionale dei Lincei*. Anno CCCLXX. Serie Ottava. Rendiconti. Classe di Scienzi morali, storiche e filologiche, Roma 28 (1973), 1974, 357-375, with 1 fig., 5 ill. and 1 folding pl.

Reply to our number 72461.
The author modifies his theory concerning the way in which the monoliths of the Cheops Pyramid have been lifted (see our number 69480). He first lists the objections raised by his critics and then 57 questions and their answers.

PIOTROVSKY, B., see our number 74181.

74579 PLEIDELL, Orsolya, Statikus és dinamikus világkép az ókori Egyiptomból, *Idö és történelem*, 195-203.

"Statisches und dynamisches Weltbild im Alten Ägypten".
Das Wesentliche im Göttersystem der Achtheit ist die Unveränderlichkeit. Im heliopolitanischen System tritt schon auf göttlicher Ebene die menschliche Sphäre auf. Osiris ist ein Mensch, aber auch die Vegetation die sterben muss um Leben spenden zu können. Gegenüber dem zentrischen, heliopolitanischen System stellt das Königtum als Hauptgestalt den dynamischen Ptah. *V. Wessetzky*

74580 PLUMLEY, J. Martin, and W. Y. ADAMS, Qaṣr Ibrîm, 1972, *JEA* 60 (1974), 212-238, with 12 pl., 4 plans and 1 fig.

The season lasted from Oct. 9th to Dec. 4th, and excavations were mainly carried out in a single area to the S. and S.W. of the cathedral. This very detailed report lists all finds under three main headings: 1. Further work in the Cathedral and Church 2; 2. The X-Group remains; 3. The Temple-Church. The E. end of Church 2 was found to date to the 9th cent. A.D. and overlies

the wall of an earlier Christian building, which itself overlies X-Group structures. Some large well built stone houses, X4-X7, mainly date to the post-Meroitic period. They represent a standard plan 8-10 m square, with from five to eight rooms entered from a single door and with deep substructures used as storage cellars. Large quantities of pottery were recovered as well as texts on papyrus. The Temple-Church yielded inscriptions of the New Kingdom, i.e. from Amenophis I to Ramesses IV, and has mud brick walls over earlier ones of sandstone. A temple of Taharqa stood here with a fresco unique to Nubia, as well as a very unusual pylon-shaped altar. Among the finds was the largest existing corpus of Nubian textile materials yet found, a fine bronze drinking vessel with leopard handle, and many scrolls.
E. Uphill

PLUMLEY, J. Martin, see also our number 74270.

74581 POETHKE, Günter, Über die Einrichtung einer Kerblochkarten-Kartei in der Papyrus-Sammlung, *Forschungen und Berichte* 16 (1974), 119-122, with 1 fig.

Description of the system of cataloguing the contents of the Papyrus-Sammlung at Berlin on punch-cards.

74582 POLAČEK, Adalbert, Lehre der Antike. Randglossen zu Ptahhoteps Anstandsregeln, *Akten des XIII. Internationalen Papyrologenkongresses*, 339-348.

After an introduction about the Instruction of Ptahhotep (called by the author "Anstandsregeln", "rules of good manners") Polaček sets forth his views on the social organization up to the New Kingdom as appearing from this piece of wisdom literature.

POOLE, Derek, see our number 74187.

74583 PORTER†, Bertha and Rosalind B. MOSS, Assisted by Ethel W. BURNEY, Topographical Bibliography of Ancient Egyptian Hieroglyphic Texts, Reliefs, and Paintings. III. Memphis. Part I. Abû Rawâsh to Abûsîr. Second Edition Revised and Augmented by Jaromír Málek, Oxford. At the Clarendon Press, 1974 (18.5 × 27.2 cm; XXX + 392 p., 1 map and 40 plans on unnumbered p.); rev. *BiOr* 33 (1976), 21-24 (Henry G. Fischer); *JEA* 62 (1976), 197-198 (C.H.S. Spaull). Pr. cloth £ 12.50

This is part one of the third volume in the second edition, the first edition having been published in 1931. Apart from being revised it has been augmented to such an extent that the first part of the volume now has 392 pages, while the entire volume III originally contained 254 pages. As Málek explains in the introduction, this is mainly due to the large number of objects discovered or published since 1931, but another reason is the wider scope of references. See, e.g., the extensive bibliography to the statues of Menkaure (p. 27-31), as compared with the few references on p. 7-8 of the first edition.

Completely new are the four appendices (355-365), presenting a classification of selected scenes from Old Kingdom private tombs, a classification of selected texts, a list of pyramids with their various numbers, and a list of numbered Gîza tombs and shafts. In order to appreciate the measure of augmentation one may compare the pages devoted to the Gîza necropolis: in the first edition p. 9-69, in the present p. 47-297. The area from Gîza to Abûsîr was originally covered by half a page (69-70), while it now takes up almost $2^1/_2$ pages (312-314), in quite a different arrangement. That the "royal mastabas" of Nebka and Kha'ba from the first edition have now become "pyramids", while the royal names are given with hesitation, reflects the advances of scientific research in the last forty years.

As in the preceding volumes of the second edition the plans are all re-drawn and assembled in a special part at the end of the text (between p. 366 and 367).

The indexes too have been augmented, not only by inclusion of the new material, but also by listing besides royal and private names the names of divinities, objects in the museums (with their museum number), and names of selected objects: various types of statuary, architectural elements, and special and less common categories of objects such as articles of furniture, seals, slab-stelae, etc.

74584 POSENER, Georges, La littérature égyptienne, *Textes et langages III*, 1-5.

Proceeding from the publication of the *Story of Two Brothers* by E. de Rougé in 1852 the author presents a short survey of the study of Egyptian literature mentioning scholars such as Chabas, Erman, Golenischeff and Gardiner who all published important texts. He also enumerates the various genres, stressing the Egyptian preference for didactic and narrative writings, and expresses his expectation that still unknown pieces of literature can be discovered. Modern editions of the texts are still necessary.

74585 POSENER, J., *Mwkd* — V, *GM* Heft 11 (1974), 39.

The author cites further occurrences of the toponym *mwqd* "Red Sea" (see our No. 74241). *Dieter Mueller*

74586 POSENER, Georges, Philologie et archéologie égyptiennes, *Annuaire du Collège de France*, Paris 74 (1973-1974), 397-405.

Sequel to our number 73572.

Working destructive magic by means of images of an enemy ('rites d'envoûtement') is well attested by sherds of pottery vases, broken by intent, inscribed with curses against certain classes of enemies ('Ächtungstexte'). They have often been associated with a ceremony known as the 'breaking of the red pots', found as early as *PT* §249, but also in private tombs and once even in a temple scene. While the enactment of the rite and its material may vary, the characteristic red colour remains. However, this rite seems to be a specific interpretation of a more widely attested practice of intentionally breaking pottery vessels at different occasions, for which a consistent explanation is still lacking. The find of magical objects in the desert depot near the Mirgissa fortress (see our number 64525) shows the complexity of the rite and also that it is a mere variety of a similar practice with an enemy figurine, mostly in clay. This substitute is identified with the ultimate object of the magical rite by careful mention of the name (and the filiation). However, the destructory forces do not start working immediately but only if the object perpetrates certain criminal acts, expressedly stipulated in the formulae. Only in the case of dangerous dead persons and similar this 'safety catch' is absent.

The ultimate purpose of these rites is the safeguarding of the king of Egypt. They were enacted in several temples. They are especially directed against Seth and Apopis, the protagonists of disorder and chaos on the mythical plan. But in fact, actual political purposes were served. In this way the mythical role of Pharaoh can be translated into the political role of the Pharaoh; their mutual relationship is overtly expressed in ritual texts like the *pap. Bremner-Rhind*. Also private persons could benefit from these protective rites.

Pursued in the next year's issue. *J.F. Borghouts*

74587 POSENER-KRIÉGER, Paule, Les barques du temple funéraire de Neferirkareʽ, *Festschrift Ägyptisches Museum Berlin*, 205-209, with 1 ill. on a pl. and 2 fig.

The author discusses a small fragment of the Abûsîr papyri (Berlin P 15727), published on pl. 87 of the main text publication (our number 68486), which mentions the barks $w3$ and bit. The hitherto unknown words occur various times in these texts and indicate small ships used for transport between the solar and the funerary temples of Neferirkare. They may have been shaped like the boat-shaped baskets represented in the same offering scenes.

74588 POULSEN, Vagn, Ny Carlsberg Glyptothek. A Guide to the Collections. Revised by Flemming Johansen. 17th revised edition, Copenhagen, 1974 (14 × 22 cm; 113 p., numerous ill.)

Ancient Egypt on p. 7-15, with 7 ill. See our no. 73576.

There is also a German version: *Ny Carlsberg Glyptothek*. Führer durch die Sammlungen. 3. Ausgabe.   *Torben Holm-Rasmussen*

74589 PRAG, Kay, The Intermediate Early Bronze - Middle Bronze Age: An Interpretation of the Evidence from Transjordan, Syria and Lebanon, *Levant*, London 6 (1974), 69-116, with 2 maps, 1 table and 7 fig. containing drawings.

After defending the use of the term "Intermediate Bronze - Middle Bronze Age" (EM.MB) for the period between c. 2350 and 1900 B.C. the author extensively discusses the history and the evidence for the civilization of the period. In the conclusions a special section (p. 103-104) is devoted to the relations with Egypt.

74590 PRAG, Kay, A Tell el-Yahudiyeh Fish Vase: An Additional Note, *Levant*, London 6 (1974), 192.

Addition to our number 73577. See also our number 74496.

74591 PRIESE, Karl-Heinz, '*rm* und '*ȝm*, das Land Irame. Ein Beitrag zur Topographie des Sudan im Altertum, *Altorientalische Forschungen*, Berlin 1 (1974), 7-41, with 1 map.

Durch eine Reihe von meroitischen Inschriften in Kawa, die fünfmal die Herkunft des Verfassers als *Arme* angeben, muß geschlossen werden, daß dieses nicht allzuweit entfernt von Kawa gelegen haben kann. Für das Neue Reich kann '*rm* im obernubischen Raum lokalisiert werden, doch kann es auch für ganz Kusch stehen, so wie in der Ptolemäerzeit '*rm* für "Äthiopien" gebraucht werden kann. Im Alten und Mittleren Reich ist als Lokalität '*ȝm* gegeben, was nach den Regeln des "älteren Umschriftsystems" als '*rm* oder '*lm* zu lesen ist. Verf. schließt sich der Ansicht von Edel an, daß '*ȝm* im Gebiet von Kerma zu suchen sei und erwägt, ob sich der Name von /ir(a)me/ erhalten hat in dem modernen Ortsnamen *Kermā(n)* als eines nubischen *ka-érmā-n "Haus von *Ermā*" = /Ir(a)me/.

Inge Hofmann

74592 PRIESE, Karl-Heinz, Die Statue des napatanischen Königs Aramatelqo (Amtelqa), Berlin, Ägyptisches Museum Inv.-Nr. 2249, *Festschrift Ägyptisches Museum Berlin*, 211-232, with 17 fig. and 3 pl.

Es handelt sich um die Statue des Königs Amtalqa (568-555 v.Chr.), vom Verfasser Aramatelqo gelesen, die 1844 von Lepsius in Alt-Merowe gefunden und nach Berlin gebracht wurde. Möglicherweise ist sie mit der identisch, die von Waddington und Hanbury 1820 vom Jebel Barkal über den Fluß nach Merowe gebracht worden war. Da die Statue Bln. 2249 zu den

nicht häufigen vollplastischen Darstellungen von Königen im "langen Mantel" zählt, hat Verf. einige Überlegungen zu dem Statuentyp und seiner Bedeutung, die er in Ägypten und noch im Reich von Napata gehabt haben könnte, angestellt. Es fällt auf, daß viele dieser Statuen im "Sedfestgewand" in Nubien gefunden wurden (was aber nur dann zutrifft, wenn auch die nicht ganz sicheren Beispiele mit herangezogen werden). Verf. faßt das Sedfestgewand als Gottesgewand auf, das der "Gottkönig" seit der 1. Dynastie mit den Göttern teilt und von daher auch auf Osiris übergehen konnte. Daß sich der napatanische Herrscher als "geliebt von Amon-Reharachte" bezeichnet, läßt sich dadurch erklären, daß in der Statue der König als "Gottkönig" dargestellt ist. Als solcher ist er der Sohn des Horus, der seit der 4. Dynastie als Reharachte verstanden wurde. Es folgt eine Begründung der neuen Namenslesung Hrw-mʒ-tj-rw-q, welches meroitisch Ar-mte-l-qo lauten würde und vom Verf. gedeutet wird als "Welcher Sohn/Erbe/jüngere Erscheinungsform o.ä. des Horus, der Edle (ist)".
Inge Hofmann

74593 PUSCH, Edgar, Register der ägyptischen Wörter zu Junker Giza I-XII, *ZÄS* 101 (1974), 13-35.

Ergänzung zu den in unserer Nummer 4022 gegebenen drei Gesamtverzeichnissen. Im ersten Abschnitt stellte Verfasser die Wörte zusammen. Der zweite enthält die *Bemerkungen zu Schrift und Sprache*. Pusch hat auch die in Gîza XII bereits aufgenommenen Indices der Titel und Personennamen überprüft; Nachtrag auf S. 31. *M. Heerma van Voss*

74594 QUAEGEBEUR, Jan, A propos de Teilouteilou, nom magique, et de Têroutêrou, nom de femme, *Enchoria* 4 (1974), 19-29.

The name of the demon *teilouteilou* attested in a Greek love charm (SB I, 4947) is probably the Fayyoumic form of the proper name *têroutêrou* (Dem. $dr.w$-$dr.w$) known from several Greek and Demotic documents. Its etymology (whether $drdr$ "stranger" *Wb.* V, 604?) remains problematical.
Dieter Mueller

74595 QUAEGEBEUR, Jan, Inventaire des stèles funéraires memphites d'époque ptolémaïque, *CdE* XLIX, No 97 (1974), 59-79.

Le présent inventaire tend à compléter celui qu'a dressé P. Munro, *Untersuchungen zu den spät-ägyptischen Totenstelen* (= notre No 73523) en ajoutant aux seules stèles privées celles des Apis, des vaches-mères, les stèles votives et commémoratives du Sérapéum, le décret de Memphis et les stèles magiques. L'inventaire passe ainsi de 28 à 40 numéros. Un index des noms propres dans lequel les personnages sont identifiés complète l'article. *Ph. Derchain*

74596 QUAEGEBEUR, Jan, Prêtres et cultes thébains à la lumière de documents égyptiens et grecs, *BSFE* 70-71 (Juin et Octobre 1974), 37-55, with 2 ill. and 2 fig.

After an introduction the author first pays attention to two families of priests at Thebes, one of first prophets of Amon, among which Osoroeris and Spotous, from the first half of the 3rd century B.C., and another, of prophets of Min-Amon, with the same names but of the second half of the 2nd century B.C. He then deals with the temples of the Greek period and their Greek names, first those at Karnak, e.g. the Demetrion, also called Papoerieion = the Temple of Opet, and then those on the West Bank, particularly those at Deir el-Bahari and Deir el-Medîna (among which a sanctuary of Arsenuphis), and the temple of Thoth at Qasr el-Agûz, in which the god is called i.a. Teephibis, that is *dje(d)-he(r)-p-heb* (compare our number 74834).

74597 QUAEGEBEUR, Jan, The Study of Egyptian Proper Names in Greek Transcription. Problems and Perspectives, *Onoma*, Leuven 18 (1974), 403-420.

The author describes the problems associated with the study of Egyptian proper names in Greek transcription, and draws attention to the significance of such names for Egyptological studies in three main areas : the information they yield about the names of Egyptian deities and their popularity; the vocalization of ancient Egyptian five centuries before the use of Coptic; and the light they shed on the Egyptian dialects. *Dieter Mueller*

74598 QUECKE, H., Ein altes bohairisches Fragment des Jakobusbriefes (P. Heid. Kopt. 452), *Orientalia* 43 (1974), 382-392, with 1 pl.

Publication of a fragmentary Bohairic parchment manuscript containing parts of the *Epistle of St. James* (Pap. Heidelberg Kopt. 452), which is of particular importance since it is in early Bohairic and appears to belong to a translation different from the later one. The author deals extensively with outer appearance and writing of the ms. and presents a transcription with some notes.

74599 QUECKE, H., Ein neues Fragment der Pachombriefe in koptischer Sprache, *Orientalia* 43 (1974), 66-82, with 1 pl.

Publication of a fragmentary papyrus codex containing parts of the Coptic version of Apa Pakhom's letters (Nos 11b, 10, 11a, 5, 9a and b, in this order) and preserved in the Chester Beatty Library in Dublin (No. 54). The author discusses the letters of Pakhom and the relations between the Greek and Latin translations and the Coptic text. He presents a transcription of the ms. here discussed with some notes.

74600 QUECKE, Hans, Die Schreibung des ⲟⲩ in koptischen Handschriften, *Archiv für Papyrusforschung und verwandte Gebiete*, Leipzig 22-23 (1974), 275-284.

There have not been fixed rules in Coptic for writing the combination of signs ⲟⲩ. The writing ⲟ above ⲩ is more frequent than the reverse, but it is not always placed exactly above the ⲩ. They may also be combined to a ligature.

QUECKE, Hans, see also our number 74549.

74601 RADWAN, Ali, Ein Relief der Nachamarnazeit, *Orientalia* 43 (1974), 393-397, with 1 pl. and 1 fig.

Le beau relief en creux Caire 12.2.25.8, en calcaire, datable de la fin de la XVIIIe dynastie mais de provenance inconnue, montre une scène assez bien conservée. Il constituait apparemment la moitié gauche d'un linteau et représente le dieu Sobek-Rê assis crocodilocéphale, coiffé de l'*atef*. Un souverain lui offre des fleurs; il est suivi d'un petit personnage en adoration. D'après le style il s'agit d'un roi amarnien, mais le cartouche actuel est d'Horemheb : l'auteur croit y reconnaître Toutankhamon. La pièce aurait pour provenance un temple de Sobek-Rê plutôt que la tombe du fonctionnaire représenté. Le dieu est désigné par le toponyme *w(t)-Ḥr* : peut-être celui du nome létopolitain. La figure du personnage, flabellifère, "loué du roi" et décoré, aurait été ajoutée lors du changement de cartouche royal. Son nom ..-*nḥḥ* semble désigner le militaire *Pr-ʿꜣ-nḥḥ* connu par une stèle d'Abousir (Berlin 14820). L'adaptation sous Horemheb ne serait pas intervenue au profit du roi seul, mais également à celui du fonctionnaire. *J. Custers*

74602 RADWAN, Ali, Der Trauergestus als Datierungsmittel, *MDAIK* 30 (1974), 115-129, with 21 fig. and 1 pl.

The main gestures of mourning (supporting the chin with one hand and/or touching the mouth) appear for the first time in the post-Amarna Period, and are also attested in tombs from the time of Horemhab. Their imitation in several tombs from the second half of the XIXth Dyn. lacks expressiveness, and may therefore serve as a criterium for dating such scenes.
Dieter Mueller

74603 RAEPSAET-CHARLIER, Marie-Thérèse, La XXVIIIe Session de la Société Internationale Fernand De Visscher pour l'histoire des droits de l'antiquité. Athènes, 12-15 septembre 1973, *Revue internationale des droits de l'antiquité*, Bruxelles 3ᵉ série, 21 (1974), 345-367.

Pour une paraphrase de la communication d'Aristide Théodoridès, "La Procédure civile dans l'Égypte pharaonique", voir p. 363-364.

74604 RAINEY, A. F., El-'Amârna Notes, *Ugarit-Forschungen*, Kevelaer/Neukirchen-Vluyn 6 (1974), 295-312.

Notes to a large number of details of the Amarna Letters intended to be additions and corrections to our numbers 70447.

74605 RATIÉ, S., La collection égyptienne du Musée d'Annecy, *Revue Savoisienne*, Annecy 114 (1974), 44-63, with 12 pl.

This description of the Egyptian and Egyptianizing objects in the museum at Annecy begins with the history of the collection, mentioning i.a. the role of Prisse d'Avennes and the most important object, viz. a shawabti of the general Potasimto, found at Annecy itself in 1835 (see pl. I).
The catalogue is divided into four chapters: objects from the tombs (among which items of linen mummy wrappings, two mummy masks, the lid of a canopic vessel, and six shawabtis); fragments of monuments (i.a. part of an obelisk from el-Qantara and the base of a statue of Ramses II from Abydos); objects from private houses, i.a. bronze statuettes, scarabs and scaraboids; and some Egyptianizing objects and casts.

74606 RAY, J.D., Pharaoh Nechepso, *JEA* 60 (1974), 255-256.

This co-author of a famous astrological work is identified with a king Nekauba, i.e. 'Necho the Ram', possibly the first Necho of Sais dated by Kitchen c. 688-672 B.C.   *E. Uphill*

74607 el-RAYAH, Mubarak B., The Problems of Kerma Culture of Ancien Sudan. Re-considered in the Light of Ancient Sudan Civilization as a Continuous Process, *Ethnographisch-archäologische Zeitschrift*, Berlin 15 (1974), 287-304.

Der Artikel ist die Kurzfassung einer Promotion aus der Humboldt-Universität zu Berlin. Es wird Stellung bezogen gegen die Auffassung von Reisner, wonach der ägyptische Anteil an der Kerma-Kultur überbetont wurde. Die Eigenständigkeit der Kerma-Kultur wird herausgestellt (Kleinkunst, Keramik, Begräbnissitten, Faience-Industrie) und eine Erklärung für das Vorkommen ägyptischer Objekte geboten. Es wird versucht, die Geschichte des Königreiches Kerma sowie seine Ausdehnung darzulegen; die Gesellschaftsstruktur ("the ruling class, the ruled citizens and slaves") wird aus den Begräbnissitten erschlossen, der Wohlstand der Kerma-Gesellschaft weitgehend auf Handelsbeziehungen zurückgeführt. In einem 10. Abschnitt werden die kulturellen Zwischenbeziehungen zwischen der C-Gruppe und der Kerma-Kultur dargelegt und die Gemeinsamkeiten herausgearbeitet. Es wird versucht nachzuweisen, daß sich die Kerma-Kultur ihre Eigenständigkeit auch während des Neuen Reiches unter ägyptischer Herrschaft erhalten konnte und während der Napata-Meroe-Epoche wieder zum Tragen kam. Kerma-Traditionen sollen sich bis ins Mittelalter erhalten haben. Menschenopfer bei den Mangbetu und Azande sowie die sudanische Sitte, den Toten auf einem Bett zum Grab zu tragen, werden als Beispiele für das Weiterleben der Kerma-Kultur bis in die heutige Zeit gewertet. Abschließend wird darauf verwiesen, daß die einheimische Kultur in der meroitischen Kultur ihren Höhepunkt fand. *Inge Hofmann*

74608 REGÖLY-MÉREI†, G., Surgery in Ancient Egypt, *Acta Chirurgica Academiae Scientiarum Hungaricae*, Budapest 15 (1974), 415-425, with 6 ill.

Survey of our knowledge of surgery in Ancient Egypt.

74609 REYMOND, E.A.E., Fragment of a Temple Account Roll. P. Fitzhugh D.3 + D.4 (23.5 × 20.5 cm), *JEA* 60 (1974), 189-199, with 2 pl.

This papyrus is in a private collection in Monterey, California, and of unknown provenance. Both sides have accounts in Demotic hands of different dates, on palaeographical evidence dating to the period between the Persian Era and the end of the Thirtieth Dynasty, and to the time of Ptolemy II. The Meidum temple is mentioned in the text which is concerned with the allotment of priestly shares. The second account records corn taxes. Transliteration, translation and very detailed notes are given. *E. Uphill*

74610 RIEDERER, Josef, Die Erhaltung ägyptischer Baudenkmäler, *Maltechnik-Restauro* 1/80 (1974), 43-52, with 10 ill. and a summary in English (p. 51-52).

The author recommends techniques for the preservation of various kinds of stone, including bricks, in Egyptian monuments, i.a. techniques of desalinization, and for the cleaning of reliefs.

74611 RIEDERER, J., Recently Identified Egyptian Pigments, *Archaeometry*, Oxford 16 (1974), 102-109, with 2 tables.

Modern scientific methods have resulted in the discovery of three hitherto unknown pigments on objects in the collection at Munich. They are: huntite (white) on bowls of the C-culture and a New Kingdom canopic jar, cobalt (blue) on two vessels

from the Amarna Period, and atacamite (green) on reliefs of the XIth Dynasty.
For huntite, see also the article by Barbieri, Calderoni, Cortesi and Fornaseri on p. 211-220 of the same journal.

74612 RISING, Gerald R., The Egyptian Use of Unit Fractions for Equitable Distribution, *Historia Mathematica*, Toronto 1 (1974), 93-94.

The author suggests a correction of the note in Gillings' "Mathematics in the Time of the Pharaohs" (our number 72249), p. 105. In his Response (p. 94) Gillings agrees with the suggestion.

74613 [ROCCATI, Alessandro], Centocinquantenario del Museo Egizio di Torino. Mostra dei restauri 1974, [Torino], Edizioni d'arte Fratelli Pozzo, [1974] (16.5 × 20 cm; 7 [unnumbered] p., fig. on cover).

On occasion of the onehundredfiftieth anniversary of the Egyptian Museum at Turin an exhibition is held of objects restored during the last five years. In this catalogue for the general public they are briefly described, divided into 10 categories, while technical notes are added. The objects are e.g. a naos of Sethi I from Heliopolis, a Ptolemaic *Book of the Dead*, ostraca, vessels, sarcophagi, reliefs, wooden statues, and the temple of Ellesîya.

74614 ROCCATI, Alessandro, L'Egittologia in Italia, *GM* Heft 11 (1974), 11-15.

A concise description of the present position of Egyptological studies in Italy. *Dieter Mueller*

74615 ROCCATI, Alessandro, Invito a Deir el Medina, *Bolletino della Società piemontese di belle arti*, Torino NS 25-26 (1971-1972), [1974], 5-12, with 1 fig. and 4 pl.

After a survey of our knowledge concerning the settlement of necropolis workmen at Thebes the author deals with some objects reconstructed from fragments, one of which preserved in the Turin Museum and the other discovered elsewhere. Some have already been mentioned in our number 72710, e.g. numbers CGT 50222, 50144 and 50067. A recent discovery is that Bruyère, *Mert Seger* II, pl. X, No. 23 joins CGT 50105.
Roccati also mentions the recent acquisition of a fragmentary relief with three less well known names from the settlement.

74616 ROCCATI, Alessandro, Il Museo Egizio di Torino. Prima edizione, [Roma], Istituto poligrafico dello stato. Libreria dello stato, [1974] (13 × 18.6 cm; 95 p., 96 ill. [on p. 41-87], 1 folding map, plans on endpapers, town plan on cover). At head of title:

Ministerio della publica istruzione. Direzione generale della antichità e belle arte. Itinerari dei musei, gallerie e monumenti d'Italia, N. 7. Pr. Lire 1.500

This is the official guide to the Egyptian collections of the Turin Museum. After a preface by Silvio Curto and an introduction about Egyptian history in general there follows a room by room description of the collection as it is exhibited. First come two sections on the ground-floor, one dealing with the two rooms containing the larger pieces of statuary, and one devoted to the Nubian room. The rest of the collection is to be found on the first floor, spread over eight rooms, each of which concentrated upon a subject such as sculpture, funerary equipment, textiles, writing, religion, etc. In three annexes to room III the contents of a Vth Dynasty tomb, the chapel of Maia and the tomb of Khaʿ (both XVIIIth Dynasty and from Deir el-Medîna) are exhibited.
The 96 illustrations represent the most significant objects in the same order.

74617 ROCCATI, A., [Scavi nel Museo di Torino]. II. Una tomba dimenticata di Asiut, *Oriens Antiquus* 13 (1974), 41-52.

Publication of some inscribed fragments in the Egyptian Museum of Torino. They were apparently cut from the walls of a tomb of the early 12th Dyn. at Assiut during Schiaparelli's excavations in that region in 1905/06. The texts form part of a biographical inscription of some interest; they are studied in detail, and special attention is paid to the color of the hieroglyphs. A note by G.L. Nicola on the preservation of the fragments concludes the article. *Dieter Mueller*

74618 ROCCATI, A., I testi dei sarcofagi di Eracleopoli, *Oriens Antiquus* 13 (1974), 161-197, with 7 fig. (2 folding) and 1 pl.

In 1968, a Spanish mission excavating at Herakleopolis discovered a series of tombs predating the beginning of the Middle Kingdom. The walls of two of these tombs, that of *Nfr-ìrìwt* (labelled H$_1$H) and that of *Z3-kt* (labelled H$_2$H) preserve fragmentary copies of spells from the *Coffin Texts*, whose arrangement shows that they go back to one single papyrus manuscript. The author transcribes the titles of these spells and identifies them as far as possible with the texts published by de Buck.
Their arrangement shows a close affinity to that found on coffins from Bersheh. An appendix lists the spell sequences of the *CT* copies used for de Buck's edition of the *Coffin Texts*.
Dieter Mueller

ROCCATI, Alessandro, see also our number 74139.

ROCCHETTA, Aquilante, see our number 74780.

74619 RÖLLIG, Wolfgang, Politische Heiraten im Alten Orient, *Saeculum*, Freiburg/München 25 (1974), 11-23.

Bei der Darstellung internationaler Heiraten von Sumer bis Semiramis, die meist der Versöhnung und dem Ausgleich zwischen großen Staaten und Kleinfürstentümern dienten, werden auch die ausländischen Prinzessinnen erwähnt, die an den ägyptischen Hof von Amenophis III. bis Ramses II. kamen, ebenso der mißglückte Versuch der Anches-en-Amun, einen Hethiterprinzen nach Ägypten zu holen.   *H. Brunner*

74620 ROMER, John, with an Appendix by Charles Cornell van SICLEN, III, Tuthmosis I and the Bibân El-Molûk: Some Problems of Attribution, *JEA* 60 (1974), 119-133, with 4 fig.

The writer comments on the apparent insignificance of the tomb KV 38 attributed to Tuthmosis I, and also notes the anomaly of the impressive sarcophagus found in it being made by order of Tuthmosis III for his grandfather. Five finely cut quartzite blocks on the floor also suggest a reburial by the later king, as these are similar to some in KV 34 (Tuthmosis III), while an uninscribed foundation deposit may be discounted as dating evidence. Instead the immense KV 20, the longest and deepest of the royal tombs, is suggested as this king's original tomb, and it is also suggested that the burial chamber may have been added to the much larger Gallery III which was itself the first intended burial chamber.

The appendix, on p. 129-133, gives the readings of some groups of hieratic signs upon certain blocks in the tomb of Amenophis II (KV 35). The palaeography is that of the end of the Twentieth Dynasty and the year 13 mentioned is possibly of the Tanite king Smendes, when the tomb seems to have been inspected and sealed.   *E. Uphill*

74621 ROSENVASSER, A., Concerning the Development of Egyptological Studies in Argentinia and Latin America, *GM* Heft 10 (1974), 7-10.

A brief report about the past achievements and the present situation of Egyptological studies at Argentinian universities. Despite the efforts of the scholars involved, the constant threat of government intervention in university affairs makes the prospects for the future rather gloomy.   *Dieter Mueller*

74622 RÜBSAM, Winfried J.R., Götter und Kulte in Faijum während der griechisch-römisch-byzantinischen Zeit, Bonn, in Kommission bei Rudolf Habelt Verlag GmbH, 1974 (14.8 × 21 cm; XX + 267 p.); rev. *Aegyptus* 55 (1975), 305-306 (Sergio Daris).
Pr. DM 32

Although the period dealt with is outside the scope of the *AEB* and the texts on which the study is based are almost exclusively written in Greek (for the few Demotic texts, see the index, p. 246), the thesis is of importance to Egyptologists since it discusses the later development of the Egyptian divinities and cults.

After a chapter on religion and cults in general in the periods studied, the second chapter is devoted to the two nome gods of the Faiyûm, Arsinoe II and Sukhos. Then follows a catalogue of the evidence concerning deities and cults in the region, arranged after the places with which they are connected: first the metropolis Crocodilopolis-Arsinoe, and then the other places in an alphabetical order. For each of them the author separates evidence for indigenous gods from that for the cult of the rulers and of Greek and Roman cults. From the Egyptian deities we mention, apart from Sukhos: Ammon, Bubastis (Bastet), Horus, Isis and Osiris, Min, Thoeris, Thot, and special forms of Sobk such as Petesukhos and Sobknebtynis. Also sacred animals, the falcon, the ibis and Butapheion (a bull). Outside the metropolis the same dieties occur, but also others, e.g. Ptah at Alexandrou Nesos or Anubis, Apis and Imhotep at Karanis. Some gods not exactly localizable are listed in the last chapter. Of the four indexes we mention that to the names of the gods (p. 232-243).

74623 RUPP, Alfred, Allgemeine religionsgeschichtliche Erwägungen zur Personvorstellung im Hinblick auf ägyptische Jenseitstexte des Neuen Reiches, *ZÄS* 101 (1974), 35-49.

The author tries to analyse the Egyptian concept of personality by studying the description of gods and demons in Egyptian Guides to the Hereafter. He seems to find its essence in the tendency to personify individual aspects whose dynamic interaction defines the personality of the described, and stresses the necessity of studying concepts such as *ba*, *ka*, etc., in relation to the personality as a whole.   *Dieter Mueller*

74624 RUSSMANN, Edna R., The Representation of the King in the XXVth Dynasty, Bruxelles-Brooklyn, Published jointly by the Fondation Égyptologique Reine Élisabeth and The Brooklyn Museum, 1974 (22 × 28 cm; 74 p., 26 ill. on 10 pl.) = Monographies Reine Élisabeth, 3.   Pr. $ 13

The study deals with the style and iconography of the representations of the XXVth Dynasty rulers.
Chapter I is devoted to the representations, particularly the statuary, and the style. The type seems to have been set by Shabako's bronze kneeling figure in Athens (National Museum ANE 632). On account of other works the Brooklyn schist head (No. 64.74) is ascribed to this king. From this time

onwards most heads show a thickening at the sides of the nose, the "Kushite fold". Probably Cairo Cat. gén. 1291 is to be ascribed to Shebitku, of whom no certain statues are known. Those of Taharqa possess a refinement in balance with the vigour of expression characterizing the best of Shabako's work. To Taharqa may be ascribed the heads in Florence (No. 7655) and in Copenhagen (Ny Carlsberg Glypt. 1538). His statues in Nubia (Gebel Barkal, Kawa) are probably local products. From Tanwetamani only very little has been preserved. At the end the author discusses the influence of Old and Middle Kingdom models on Kushite art as well as that of the standard Egyptian representations of Nubians.

Chapter II deals with the costume. Basically it is the orthodox Egyptian royal ornate, but the Kushite kings favoured an abundance of armlets and bracelets. The author discusses the amulets in the form of a ram's head, the closely fitting skull-cap which replaces both the Blue and the White Crown, the headdress with four tall plumes, and the double uraeus. In several instances the history of the item is amply set forth.

There follow two appendices, containing a full catalogue of the royal representations in stone and faience (I) and in metal (II), arranged in chronological order. Each object is mentioned with all technical data. The first group consists of 23 identified, 1 doubtful, 9 unidentified and 3 uncertain pieces, followed by 2 wrongly ascribed works; the second of 4 identified, 29 unidentified and 5 uncertain ones, also followed by 2 wrongly ascribed works. The author i.a. explains why she thinks that these 4 objects do not belong to the Kushite Period, and on p. 45 why the head of Shabako (Cairo Cat. gén. 42010) is an usurped work from the XVIIIth Dynasty.

74625 RUSSMANN, Edna R., The Statue of Amenemope-em-hat, *Metropolitan Museum Journal*, New York 8 (1973), 1974, 33-46, with 8 ill.

The kneeling figure the texts of which are published by de Meulenaere (see our number 74499) is here studied as an important piece of sculpture. It is made of dark green schist, and although headless and badly damaged clearly of high quality. The author deals with the Hathor head which the person is holding in front of his knees, and pays particular attention to the way in which the calf muscle is represented, a characteristic detail of northern rather than southern sculpture of the period, as several parallels may prove.

In an addendum the author mentions an Old Kingdom instance of a similar representation of the calf muscle, which may suggest that it was another instance of archaism in the Saite Period.

74626 SAÂD†, Ramadan, The Stelae of Zernikh. Recent Documentation and Information, *MDAIK* 30 (1974), 215-220, with 2 plans and 3 pl.

A report on the condition of the three stelae of Amenhotep IV at Zernikh (*Urk*. IV, 1963-1964) with a republication of their texts and decorations. They were subsequently dismantled and are now in the garden of the Inspectorate of Antiquities at Luxor. *Dieter Mueller*

74627 SADEK, A.F., Graffiti de la montagne thébaine. IV, 4. Transcriptions et indices, Le Caire, Centre de documentation et d'études sur l'ancienne Égypte, 1973 (21 × 27 cm; portefolio containing 36 loose p. [numbered 185-220]). At head of title: Collection scientifique.

Sequel to our number 73626.
Not seen.

74628 SADEK, A.F., Graffiti de la montagne thébaine. IV, 5. Transcriptions et indices, Le Caire, Centre de documentation et d'études sur l'ancienne Égypte, 1974 (21 × 27 cm; portefolio containing 20 loose p. [numbered 221-240]). At head of title: Collection scientifique.

Sequel to our preceding number.
Transcriptions of graff. 3662-3838 so far as consisting of Coptic and hieroglyphic texts. The drawings are only mentioned with their numbers.
Indexes on p. 234-240.

74629 SADEK, A.F. et M. SHIMY, Graffiti de la montagne thébaine. III, 6. Fac-similés, Le Caire, Centre de documentation et d'études sur l'ancienne Égypte, 1974 (21 × 27 cm; portefolio containing 3 loose p. and 34 loose pl. [numbered 259-292]); at head of title: Collection scientifique.

Sequel to our number 73629.
This volume contains the facsimiles collected during the campaign of 1973, numbered 3580-3834.

SADEK, A.F., see also our number 74727.

74630 SÄVE-SÖDERBERGH, Torgny, Über die Ägyptologie in Schweden, *GM* Heft 10 (1974), 11-12.

A brief report about the organization of Egyptological studies in Sweden. *Dieter Mueller*

74631 SAFFIRIO, Luigi, Le origini dell' agricoltura: l'ipotesi nilotica, *Archivio per l'Antropologia e la Etnologia*, Firenze 104 (1974), 245-260.

Substantial archaeological evidence for the existence of a proto-agricultural phase in the late Pleistocene Age from Upper Egypt and Nubia suggests that the Nile Valley may be among the centers from which agriculture originated. *Dieter Mueller*

SAID, Rushdi, see our number 74798.

74632 von SALDERN, Axel – Birgit NOLTE – Peter LA BAUME – Thea Elisabeth HAEVERNICK, Gläser der Antike. Sammlung Erwin Oppenländer, Mainz am Rhein, Verlag Philipp von Zabern, [1974] (21.7 × 26 cm; 260 p., frontispiece [portrait], 257 ill. [67 in colours]); rev. *AJA* 80 (1976), 319-320 (Elsbeth B. Dusenberg).

This publication of what may be the most important private collection of ancient glass begins, after a foreword and introductory remarks, with a chapter on pre-Roman glass made in sand-core technique by Birgit Nolte. She is also responsible for the first part of the catalogue devoted to the objects from ancient Egypt, comprising 100 items and divided into two groups: vessels (27 items) and inlays, jewellery and amulets. Among the major pieces we mention: an amphoriskos from the time of Amenophis III-IV (No. 2), a fish vessel of the same time (No. 3), two lentoid flasks (Nos. 4 and 5), a bronze ibis with a glass body from the Ptolemaic Period (No. 73), etc. Each object is carefully described, with indication of its date, provenance and measurements, and bibliographical references. The major pieces are represented in photograph, several in colour.

74633 SALEH, Abdel-Aziz, Excavations Around Mycerinus Pyramid Complex, *MDAIK* 30 (1974), 131-154, with 2 plans (1 folding) and 16 pl.

A report about the excavations carried out in 1971/72 by the University of Cairo in the Giza necropolis near the Mycerinus Pyramid. The discoveries include a small industrial settlement south of the causeway, several tombs which yielded some statues and an interesting stela from the time of Mycerinus, and some enigmatic structures whose purpose has not yet been determined. *Dieter Mueller*

74634 SALEH, S.A., Z. ISKANDER, A.A. el-MASRY and F.M. HELMI, Some Ancient Egyptian Pigments, *Recent Advances in Science and Technology of Materials*, 141-155, with 5 ill., 6 fig. and 2 tables.

Report of the analysis of a collection of pigments discovered in 1958 in a chest in the courtyard of the tomb of Kheruef (see the ill.).

SALEH, S.A., see also our number 74182.

SALLAM, H.A., see our number 74182.

SANGUIN, Georges, see our number 74094.

74635 SATZINGER, H., Zu den Men-cheper-rē'-Skarabäen, *Studia Aegyptiaca I*, 329-337, with 3 fig.

Egyptian scarabs owe their popularity to their function and their shape : as seals which close and protect, they were ideally suited for use as amulets; beetle-shaped, they were reminiscent of the eternal rejuvenation expressed by the word *ḫpr*.
Three scarabs bearing the name *Mn-ḫpr-r'* combined with *Mn-m3't-r'* and *Stp.n R'* (Vienna Inv. No. 6070, 5652, and 2041) are published in conclusion. *Dieter Mueller*

SAUNERON, Nadine, see our number 74780.

74636 SAUNERON, Serge, La bibliographie des temples de l'époque ptolémaïque et romaine, *Textes et langages III*, 289-291.

The author discusses the problems concerning the study of inscriptions and reliefs on walls of the Graeco-Roman temples. He mentions that Mme Sauneron's *Répertoire* (our number 4838) will be followed by a second volume.

74637 SAUNERON, Serge, Liste des signes et liste des valeurs en Ptolémaïque, *GM* Heft 14 (1974), 21-29.

A report about the improved version of the sign-list of the IFAO, and about a project to publish a manual of Ptolemaic signs. *Dieter Mueller*

74638 SAUNERON, Serge, Le temple d'Esna, *Textes et langages III*, 249-257.

The author briefly discusses early studies of the temple since the *Description de l'Égypte*, mentioning the work of Champollion, Lepsius, Brugsch and Daressy, as well as his own publications of the texts. After pointing out some complementary studies, e.g. that on religious festivals (our number 62514) and an index in preparation, he makes some remarks on the studies of hermitages and monasteries in the area of Esna.

74639 SAUNERON, Serge, Les travaux de l'Institut français d'Archéologie orientale en 1973-1974, *BIFAO* 74 (1974), 183-233, with 22 pl. and 3 folded tables.

Sequel to our number 73640.
The author successively deals with the activities of the Institute, from Aswân to Tanis and the Oasis of Bahrîya, particularly

those at 'Adaïma (hermitages near Esna), Karnak (cfr our number 74354), Deir el-Medîna (with tables listing the work on the various tombs, accompanied by references to earlier publications), the White Monastery of Sohag, etc. He also discusses the publications of the Institute and its members, and their present studies.

74640 SAUNERON, Serge, Travaux de l'Institut français d'Archéologie orientale, 1969-1974, [Le Caire, Institut français d'Archéologie orientale, 1974] (20.3 × 27.5; XII + 247 p., 100 pl.).

Reprint of our numbers 71500, 71501, 72628, 73640 and 74639, preceded by an introduction in which the author presents a general survey of the activities of the French Institute. Added are corrigenda (p. 207) and extensive indexes (209-238), as well as a list of the members of the IFAO, and the studies published between 1969 and July 1974.

74641 SAUNERON, Serge, Villes et légendes d'Égypte, [Le Caire], Institut français d'Archéologie orientale du Caire, [1974] (20.4 × 27.5 cm; VIII + 208 p., 10 pl., 4 maps, 12 fig. (one folded]).

The first 126 pages of this book contain a reprint of our numbers 64428, 66522, 67491, 68531, 69545, 71502-71504, preceded by a preface.

There follow ten more studies of the same type (§XXXVI-XLV = p. 127-192), here published for the first time. They deal with i.a. the following subjects: The 7000 years of Amon at Xoïs (XXXVI); the village of ϭⲓⲙⲓϭⲧⲟⲩⲉ, not to be identified with Somosṭa (XXXVII); some monuments found at the site of the "Station Ramses", that is, Tell el-Maskhûta (XXXIX); the first description of the ruins of Bir Abu Darag by Edward Brown in 1674 (XLIV); Bolqîna, a village in the centre of the Delta described by Edward Brown (XLV). The longest note is devoted to the hills of Alexandria (XLIII; p. 158-186).

Indexes to the entire volume on p. 195-205; some additions and corrections to the sections published before on p. 193-194.

SAUNERON, Serge, see also our numbers 74100 and 74780.

SAVAGE, Howard, see our number 74443.

74642 el SAYED, Ramadan, A propos des Spells 407 et 408 des Textes des Sarcophages, *RdE* 26 (1974), 73-82.

L'auteur traduit et commente les formules 407 et 408 des *CT* contenant les sept paroles de Méhyt Ouret (Méthyer), qui décrivent, selon ses analyses, un processus de création du monde. Les paroles *ṯsw* seront plus tard hypostasiées et deviendront les *dȝjsw* connus comme compagnons de Thoth et comme guides

des morts. Pour cette dernière explication, cf. Sauneron, Esna 5,270 = notre No. 62514.   *Ph. Derchain*

74643 el-SAYED, Ramadan, Quelques éclairissements sur l'histoire de la XXVIe Dynastie, d'après la statue du Caire CG 658, *BIFAO* 74 (1974), 29-44, with 2 pl.

The author describes the fragmentary naophorous statue Cairo CG 658 (see Borchardt, *Statuen und Statuetten* III, 5-7) and offers an annotated translation of the inscriptions. Its owner, Neferibre-nefer, was an important official under Necho II, Psammetichus II and Apries, i.a. supervising restorations in the temple of Neith at Sais for Psammetichus. He was buried at Saqqâra, but the statue comes from Sais.

74644 el SAYED, Ramadan, Les rôles attribués à la déesse Neith dans certains des Textes des Cercueils, *Orientalia* 43 (1974), 275-294.

L'auteur traduit une vingtaine de Spells qu'il accompagne de commentaires, puis dégage ses conclusions. Neith est attestée dans les *Textes des Cercueils* de sept localités, surtout d'Hermopolis. Certains autres Spells sont originaires d'Abydos; le 132 évoque les lieux de pélerinage. Neith est dite résider à Memphis ou à Saïs. Elle y apparaît déjà avec toute sa personnalité complexe. Avant tout protectrice du défunt, elle donne le souffle et pourvoit aux vêtements et aux nourritures. De nature aquatique et mère de Sobek, elle est aussi divinité céleste et participe à la genèse du monde (Voir notre No 74642). Elle intervient dans le conflit d'Horus et de Seth. On la trouve associée aux dieux primordiaux, à Hathor et aux déesses dangereuses; elle prend des aspects de poisson latès ou de serpent, voire d'uraeus. Le mort peut s'identifier à elle ou se dire sa "caille". On pourrait déjà reconnaître comme attestée ici la tradition saïte sur les Sept Paroles de la création.

J. Custers

74645 SAYRE, E. V. and R. W. SMITH, Analytical Studies of Ancient Egyptian Glass, *Recent Advances in Science and Technology of Materials*, 47-70, with 6 fig., 6 ill. and 1 table.

Report of an analysis of some sixty specimens of glass ranging in date from the New Kingdom to the Early Islamic Period. The authors established the various materials and their ratios, stating a clear difference between the glass from the New Kingdom and early first millennium B.C. and that of the subsequent period; the first group shows a high magnesia and potash formulation, the latter a low.

SAYRE, Edward V., see also our number 74738.

74646 SAYYID, ʿAbd al-Munʿim ʿAbd al-Ḥalim, موقع لتحديد محاولة
بونت, *Archaeological and Historical Studies*, Alexandria 5 (1974), Arabic section 5-34, with 3 pl. containing 8 ill., 1 fig. and 2 maps.
"An Attempt to Locate Punt".
After having discussed former opinions of the location of Punt, the author argues, basing himself on evidence of the occurrence of certain trees, herbs, and the baboon, that the *ḫtyw ʿntỉw nw Pwnt* were situated in the North-Eastern part of the Republic of Somalia.

74647 SCHÄFER, Gerd, 'König der Könige' — 'Lied der Lieder'. Studien zum Paranomastischen Intensitätsgenitiv, Heidelberg, Carl Winter-Universitätsverlag, 1974 (17 × 24.5 cm; 182 p.) = Abhandlungen der Heidelberger Akademie der Wissenschaften. Philosophisch-historische Klasse, Jahrgang 1973, 2. Abhandlung.

The author studies phrases of the type "song of songs", "king of kings" in various languages and discusses in his conclusions the construction in general, which he calls "paranomastic intensive genitive".
The first chapter (p. 15-23) deals with Ancient Egypt. The author lists evidence for a number of expressions such as *nswt nsywt* and *ḥḳȝ ḥḳȝw* (both used for kings and gods), *nb nbw*, *nṯr nṯrw*, *Ḥr Ḥrw*, *ỉt ỉtw*, etc. (only for gods) and *wr wrw*, *ḥrp ḥrpw* (for officials). The construction occurs rarely during the Middle Kingdom, more frequently during the New Kingdom, always in epitheta ornantia, and afterwards only for Ptolemy XIII, who probably derived it from the Persian tradition.

74648 SCHÄFER, Heinrich, Principles of Egyptian Art. Edited, with an Epilogue, by Emma Brunner-Traut. Translated and Edited, with an Introduction, by John Baines, Oxford, Clarendon Press, 1974 (15.6 × 23.6 cm; XXVIII + 470 p., 109 ill. on 70 pl., 331 fig.); rev. *JEA* 61 (1975), 307-308 (E.P. Uphill).

English translation of our number 63452, with a preface by E.H. Gombrich and an introduction by the translator (p. XI-XIX).

74649 SCHENKE, Hans-Martin, Zur Faksimile-Ausgabe der Nag-Hammadi-Schriften. Nag-Hammadi-Codex VI, *OLZ* 69 (1974), 229-243.

Review article of our number 72214, with translations of several passages.

74650 SCHENKEL, Wolfgang, Amun-Re. Eine Sondierung zu Struktur und Genese altägyptischer synkretistischer Götter, *SAK* 1 (1974), 275-288.

The author first discusses in general the problem of gods whose names consist of two names connected by a hyphen, like Amon-Re. One can either study their unity and its features or the function of each of the composing parts, the first approach leading to syncretism as the product of a development, the second to syncretism as a process.

The second part of the article deals with the latter approach as regards Amon-Re: the origin of the combination in the XIth Dynasty and its historical background. It appears that names, attributes and representations of Amon-Re and Amon are interchangeable, but not the names Amon-Re and Re. Hence Amon-Re is the dogmatic name of Amon. In the XIth Dynasty (temple of Mentuhotep at Deir el-Bahri) he still merely occurs as god of the king, in the chapel of Sesostris already as king of the gods.

In an appendix the author makes remarks on the concept "syncretism" in general.

74651 SCHENKEL, Wolfgang, Die Einführung der künstlichen Felderbewässerung im Alten Ägypten. Zusammenfassung der vorläufigen Ergebnisse einer vorbereiteten dokumentierten Darstellung, *GM* Heft 11 (1974), 41-46.

A preliminary report about an investigation of ancient Egyptian irrigation techniques. Regular irrigation is apparently first attested in the First Intermediate Period (basin irrigation); the New Kingdom saw the introduction of canal irrigation. Irrigation is apparently not at all involved in the emergence of Egyptian civilization at the beginning of the Third Millennium B.C.

Dieter Mueller

74652 SCHENKEL, Wolfgang, Gesichtspunkte für die Neugestaltung der Hieroglyphenliste, *GM* Heft 14 (1974), 31-45.

An outline of desirable characteristics of a revised list of hieroglyphic signs. Critical comments made after this paper was read during a colloquium held near Basel are summarized by Erik Hornung (see our number 74344). *Dieter Mueller*

74653 SCHENKEL, Wolfgang, Mit welchen Zielen man die altägyptische Sprache erforschen sollte, *GM* Heft 13 (1974), 41-57.

The author stresses the necessity of a historical study of the Egyptian language because of its significance in the framework of modern linguistics. *Dieter Mueller*

SCHENKEL, Wolfgang, see also our number 74342.

74654 SCHER, T., Peteese in Elephantine, *Studia Aegyptiaca I*, 339-344.

The name Petisi (Peteese) occurs in the Aramaic Elephantine Papyrus No. 53 (cfr Grelot, our number 72276), together with other Egyptian-sounding and Jewish names. Although bearing a theophorous name, the owner was a Jew. The author quotes other instances of Jews bearing Egyptian names.

SCHILD, Romuald, see our number 74798.

SCHIMMEL, Norbert, see our number 74021.

74655 SCHNEIDER, Hans D., Maya l'amateur de statues. A propos de trois statues fameuses du Musée de Leyde et d'une sépulture oubliée à Saqqarah, *BSFE* No 69 (Mars 1974), 20-48, with 4 ill., 2 plans, and 1 fig.

The article about the Overseer of the Treasury Maya, three of whose statues are at present preserved in the Leiden Museum, has been written before the beginning of the Anglo-Dutch excavations at Saqqâra South, one of the aims of which is the re-discovery of Maya's tomb. The author subsequently discusses what is known about the New Kingdom cemeteries at Saqqâra; Memphite sculpture of the late XVIIIth Dynasty in general and the statues of Maya and his wife Merit in particular; the site of Maya's tomb as indicated by Lepsius; Maya's family and colleagues; the question whether he is identical with the fan-bearer on the right hand of the king May from el-Amarna, for which Schneider adduces arguments; Maya's career under Tutankhamon, Eye and Horemheb.
Compare our number 74287.

74656 SCHOTT, Erika, Admonitions 9, 3, *GM* Heft 13 (1974), 29-30.

The author proposes the emendation *iw.f ḥr* (*ḏd*) *hꜣ ir.k swt r mk ḫꜥw.f* "who says, 'then perish' to save his own skin".

Dieter Mueller

74657 SCHOTT, Erika, Das Goldhaus unter König Pepi II, *GM* Heft 9 (1974), 33-38, with 2 fig.

A re-examination of the Old Kingdom fragment Cairo CG 1747 commemorating the dedication of a golden statue of King Pepi II. The ceremony of "Opening its Mouth" took place in the Gold House of a temple whose name should probably be read *ḥwt-wr-Nfr[-kꜣ-]Rꜥ*. The author discusses the role of the goddess *Mnt*, and the connection of the Gold House and the Opening of the Mouth with the traditions of Lower Egypt.

Dieter Mueller

74658 SCHÜSSLER, Karlheinz, Die koptische Überlieferung des Alten und Neuen Testaments, *Enchoria* 4 (1974), 31-60, with 9 pl.

First instalment of a survey of Coptic biblical manuscripts. It lists 26 fragmentary Sahidic and Fayyoumic versions of the Catholic Letters, of which seven are published in this article. To be continued. *Dieter Mueller*

74659 SCHULMAN, Alan R., A Rare Representation of Tutu from Tel el-Fada (Sinai), *Museum Haaretz Yearbook*, Tel-Aviv 15/16 (1972/73), 69-76, with 7 ill. on 3 pl.

Publication of a bronze statuette found at Tel el-Fada (NW Sinai) and datable to the 2nd to 3rd century A.D. It represents the pantheistic deity Tutu (Tithoes) as an animal, the principal element of which is a lion, with two uraei on the head and the body and the head of a ram emanating out of the back of its mane.

The author refers to our number 60617 and quotes other representations of Tutu.

74660 SCIEGIENNY-DUDA, Jadwiga, A propos d'une étude sur Apedemak, *MNL* No 15 (Octobre 1974), 7-9.

Nach dem vorliegenden ikonographischen und epigraphischen Material kommt Apedemak zuerst im 3. vorchristlichen Jahrhundert in Musawwarat es Sufra vor. Ein zweites wichtiges Zentrum des Kultes des Löwengottes bestand in Naqa. Apedemak erscheint in der meroitischen Theologie unter mehreren Aspekten: ausgerüstet mit Pfeilen, Bogen, Gefangenen, ist er ein Kriegsgott oder ein Gott der Jagd; mit Blumen, Durrabüscheln, Lebenszeichen erscheint er als Gott des Lebens und der Fruchtbarkeit. Gleichermaßen beinhaltet er solare Elemente. Er wird verbunden mit Isis sowie einer meroitischen Göttin, der sogenannten "Negergöttin". Ihm scheint der Elefant geweiht gewesen zu sein. Apedemak wird löwenköpfig, gelegentlich auch ganz zoomorph dargestellt.

Für Apedemak, sehe jetzt auch: L.V. Žabkar, Apedemak. Lion God of Meroe, Warminster, Aris & Phillips Ltd., 1975.
Inge Hofmann

74661 SCIEGIENNY-DUDA, Jadwiga, Apedemak, dieu lion méroïtique, *Annuaire. École Pratique des Hautes Études*. V^e section — sciences religieuses, Paris 82 (1973-1974), fasc. 2, 97.

Abstract of a thesis. Compare our preceding number.

74662 SCIEGIENNY-DUDA, Jadwiga, La symbolique de la grenouille à Meroe, *MNL* No 15 (Octobre 1974), 2-6.

Ein häufig verwendetes Motiv auf meroitischer Keramik ist der Frosch, der entweder allein oder mit anderen dekorativen Elementen (Lotos-blumen, Lebenszeichen) dargestellt wird. Besonders oft kommt er auf einem Gefäßtyp vor, der sicher als Wasserbehälter benutzt wurde und im Grab neben dem Kopf des Toten stand. Die Beziehung Wasser und Frosch liegt auf der Hand. Dafür sprechen auch die beiden Froschskulpturen, die das Wasserreservoir von Basa bewachten. Wie in Ägypten, so scheint auch in der meroïtischen religiösen Vorstellung der Frosch in der Wiedergeburt und Auferstehung eine Rolle gespielt zu haben, ohne daß wir bisher sagen könnten, welcher meroitischen Gottheit der Frosch zugesprochen werden könnte.

Inge Hofmann

74663 SÉE, Geneviève, Grandes villes de l'Égypte antique. Préface de Jean Leclant. Avec la collaboration de Jean-Pierre Baux et les photographies de Jacques Marthelot, [Paris], Éditions Serg, [1974] (18 × 23 cm; 385 p., numerous maps, plans, fig. and ill., 1 folding map, map on endpapers).

Sequel to our number 73662.

Like its predecessor, this volume is particularly impressive because of its abundant illustration, several of its photographs not being published elsewhere. Although mainly dealing with architecture the illustration covers the entire Egyptian civilization in all its aspects.

The first two chapters are devoted to religious and domestic architecture, the former particularly during the first reigns of the XVIIIth Dynasty. Then follows a chapter on Deir el-Medîna, the village, its houses and its tombs, and one on Abydos in the early XVIIIth Dynasty. Two long chapters deal with both banks of Thebes during the entire Dynasty and with el-ʿAmarna, city, palaces, private houses and necropolis. A short chapter "The Return to Thebes", on Tutankhamon, is followed by one on Thebes at the end of the XVIIIth Dynasty and a very short one (2 pages of text) on Memphis.

The discussion of the Ramesside Period begins with Abydos (the temples of Sethi I and Ramses II), then Thebes (mortuary temples and Karnak), Nubia (mainly Abu Simbel), Tanis and Wâdi Hammamât (with the list of architects in translation).

The last chapter is on the Valley of the Kings, and is followed by a short homage of the author to the Egyptian builders.

On p. 355-366 a synoptic table, like in the preceding volume entitled :"Une architecture et un urbanisme pour les morts, les vivants et les dieux", actually serving as table of contents.

Indexes to plans and ill. on p. 367-383 (containing also some notes), no general index.

SEEBER, Christine, see our number 74348.

74664 SEELE†, Keith C., University of Chicago Oriental Institute Nubian Expedition: Excavations between Abu Simbel and the Sudan Border, Preliminary Report, *JNES* 33 (1974), 1-43, with 31 ill. and 1 folding map.

The O.I.C. Nubian expedition concession comprised the area on both sides of the Nile from Abu Simbel to the Sudan border. The very long report covers the seasons 1962-4, and the purpose of the work was to further explore and excavate the area worked by the late Prof. W.B. Emery. Excavation commenced with Area A, between Shafiq Farid's Tumuli 35 and 36, where X-group graves were found; although mostly plundered these yielded plenty of unbroken pottery. 56 rectangular structures 4 mud bricks high were found, 14 with a mud brick podium in front, on some of which stone offering tables were placed. Two further rows appeared, all with doors facing an individual tumulus, possibly indicating some kind of mortuary cult for persons buried elsewhere in Cemetery 220. Small Christian cemeteries were also found and remains of 24 mud brick Meroitic pyramids. In all 700 graves were excavated. An important New Kingdom cemetery was also discovered nearly 2 kilometers long. 330 graves were excavated in cemetery 221 (Meroitic) and a proportion of blond individuals of Caucasoid type found. Important dating details re C-Group pottery are also included. Perhaps the most exciting discovery of all was the A-Group jeweller's tomb with a necklace of approximately 60 gold beads and a gold fly pendant, as well as a stock of 5,528 finished or incomplete ornaments. Other First Dynasty period tombs included a limestone object covered with Nilotic boats and a niched facade building, probably used as a huge cylinder seal. *E. Uphill*

SEGUEZZI, Santo, see our number 74781.

74665 SEIBERT, Peter, Kolloquium über Grundsatzfragen der Ägyptologie am 17./18. Februar 1973 in Göttingen, *GM* Heft 9 (1974), 49-50.

A brief report about a colloquium on Egyptology as a discipline. See also Horn (our No. 74341). *Dieter Mueller*

74666 SEIDL, Erwin, Griechisches Recht in demotischen Urkunden, *Akten des XIII. Internationalen Papyrologenkongresses*, 381-388.

The author studies the influence of Greek law, as well that of the Greeks living among the native Egyptians as that of royal law, upon the Demotic documents, listing a number of allegedly Greek concepts in contracts, lawsuits, public law, etc. In several instances the Greek origin is not beyond doubt.

74667 SEIDL, Erwin, Nachgiebiges oder zwingendes Erbrecht in Ägypten, *Studia et documenta historiae et iuris*, Roma 40 (1974), 99-110.

In the "Codex of Hermopolis" it was stipulated that a father was obliged to let inherit his eldest son a double portion of the inheritance, while he also received the portions of the sons who had deceased before the father. In actual practice these rules appear not to have been followed, as the author demonstrates from a large number of texts. He concludes that the testator was free in theory to divide his possessions as he wanted, but that in many instances a man had promised in a marriage deed that the first born son of his wife would be his "eldest son", and thus inherit a double portion. That situation was presupposed in the codex.

74668 SEIDL, Erwin, Die Verjährung als sozialer Behelf im Rechtsbuch von Hermopolis, *Zeitschrift der Savigny-Stiftung für Rechtsgeschichte. Romanistische Abteilung*, Weimar 91 (1974), 360-363.

From Codex Hermopolis IX, 13-14 it appears : in case one is due to pay alimentation but the payment is claimed for the first time in the fourth year and the debtor declares to be unable to pay the preceding year payments, then these three payments are superannuated and only the fourth instalment has to be paid.

74669 SEIDL, Erwin, Die Verwendung des Eides im Prozeß nach den demotischen Quellen, *Zeitschrift der Savigny-Stiftung für Rechtsgeschichte. Romanistische Abteilung*, Weimar 91 (1974), 41-53.

The author, dealing with the function of the oath in a process, gives a new transliteration and translation of Pap. Cairo 50144 and 50145, from which he concludes that here an oath was taken by agreement of the parties themselves, without interference of the court. The sources demonstrate that one preferred damage above perjury. Therefore, as Seidl argues from several paragraphs of the Codex of Hermoplis, an oath was required also where other evidence was more likely. At the end Seidl discusses the relations between the oath and written documents, actual possession, and witnesses of a deed.

74670 SEIDL, Erwin und Dietrich WILDUNG, Uschebtikauf und Geldbezahlungsurkunde, *SAK* 1 (1974), 289-294.

Apart from representing the owner himself the shawabtis are also figures of his servants, and this conception leads during the Third Intermediate Period to a juridical consequence : the shawabtis should be acquired in a legal way. The proof is to be found in the Decree of Neskhons (Tabl. Rogers and

McCullum), and particularly in Pap. Brit. Mus. 10800 (see our number 71173). Like the Early Demotic "money-payment documents" the latter does not mention the price, while it uses a formula roughly similar to that of later times ("received ... to my satisfaction"). The Pap. Brit. Mus. 10800 hence represents an early stage in the development.

74671 SEITZ, S., Kulturelle Aspekte der beabsichtigten Kopfumformung, *Homo*, Göttingen 25 (1974), 231-252, with 6 fig.

The article deals with intentional deformation of skulls, ascribing the custom to the wish to rise above the social and ethnic group. In this connection the author also discusses the heads of Akhnaton's daughters, quoting Gerhardt (our number 67212) and stating that this was no instance of that custom.

SESTON, William, see our number 74157.

74672 SHARMAN, J.C., Meroitic: its Ancestors and Descendants — some Relationships, *Azania*, Nairobi 9 (1974), 207-218.

Ohne Beachtung der bisherigen Ergebnisse der meroitistischen Forschung kommt Verfasser durch Vergleich meroitischer Syntagmata mit ähnlich aussehenden aus der Kanuri-Sprache zu dem bisher häufig postulierten (vgl. unsere Nummer 73728), aber auf diese Weise kaum zu verifizierenden Ergebnis, daß das Meroitische der East Saharan group zuzuordnen sei (so soll z.B. das suffigierte *-te* einer Determination entsprechen, *-li* wird als Lokativ angenommen usw.). Als weitere Hypothese wird dargelegt, daß das Ostsaharanische ein Zweig der sumerischen Sprachgruppe sei. "Even if both hypotheses can be shown to be wrong, the general shock and shake-up entailed in making the refutations should at least produce some fall-out of accumulated dust: or even some centrifugal spin-off" (p. 218).
Inge Hofmann

SHIMY, M., see our number 74629.

74673 SHINNIE, P.L., Bryan George Haycock, 1937-1973, *MNL* No. 14 (Février 1974), 2-3.

Obituary notice. Compare our number 74844.

74674 SHINNIE, P.L., Polish Excavations at Kadero, *Nyame Akuma*, Calgary 5 (October 1974), 30-32.

Der Hauptzweck der Grabungssaison 1973/74 war die Weiterführung der Arbeiten im Südteil der Siedlung und auf dem Friedhof. Die Artefakten der Siedlung gehören typologisch zum Khartumer Neolithikum (Shaheinab), doch deutet das völlige Fehlen von Keramik mit Wavy-line-Mustern darauf, daß Kadero später als Shaheinab anzusetzen ist. Kadero Site No. 1 scheint zeitgleich mit der A-Kultur in Unternubien zu sein.

Inge Hofmann

74675 SHINNIE, P. L., Sudan, *Nyame Akuma*, Calgary 4 (April 1974), 26-27, with 1 fig.

Bericht über die Ausgrabungen in Kadero, dessen Material später sein dürfte als das von esh Shaheinab und in Meroe, wo drei weitere Schmelzöfen (vgl. unsere Nummer 70501) gefunden wurden. Diese scheinen aus dem 7. nachchristlichen Jahrhundert oder noch später zu stammen. Die Grabhügel von Sururab scheinen der nachmeroitischen Zeit anzugehören, doch muß eine weitere Materialuntersuchung abgewartet werden. Über die Ausgrabungen von Alt-Dongola, Sai, Sadenga und Tabo liegen keine Informationen vor. *Inge Hofmann*

74676 SHISHA-HALEVY, Ariel, Protatic ⲉϥⲥⲱⲧⲙ̄ : A Hitherto Unnoticed Coptic Tripartite Conjugation-Form and Its Diachronic Connections, *Orientalia* 43 (1974), 369-381.

The author suggests that to the Tripartite Clause, real-condition protasis-form ⲉϥϣⲁⲛⲥⲱⲧⲙ̄ there existed a collateral variant form ⲉϥⲥⲱⲧⲙ̄ (neg. ⲉϥⲧⲙ̄ⲥⲱⲧⲙ̄), which only seems to occur in post-classical non-literary texts but may be preserved from the earlier spoken language. Whether indeed it was merely a collateral form of ⲉϥϣⲁⲛⲥⲱⲧⲙ̄ is not quite clear. Its Demotic ancestor may be *i-ir.f sḏm*. The author rejects the theory of Groll in this respect (see our number 69277; compare also Logan, our number 70359), adducing several arguments, although admitting that the Demotic evidence is not quite unequivocal. At the end a few remarks on the Old and Middle Egyptian *ir*-introduced protasis. Compare our number 73679.

74677 SHORE, A. F., The Demotic Inscription on a Coin of Artaxerxes, *Numismatic Chronicle*, Oxford 14 (1974), 5-8.

The coin, from unknown provenance, is discussed by Otto Mørkholm in the preceding article, and illustrated on pl. 1. The legend, completing one on a coin in the British Museum from the same issue, runs : Artaxerxes *pr-ʿ3*, without a cartouche. Shore discusses the Demotic signs and adds remarks on the Persian Period in Egypt.

74678 SHORE, A. F., A Soldier's Archery Case from Ancient Egypt, *The British Museum Quarterly*, London 37 (1973-1974), 4-9, with 1 pl. and 2 fig.

Publication of a painted wooden box (No. 20648), $52^1/_4$ to $4^1/_4$ to 5 in., hewn out of a solid block and at present containing seven arrows. On one of the long sides a hunting scene is depicted, with what may represent a palisade fencing of the area of the hunt; on the other the same type of enclosure and the picture of a bullfight. On the small sides only remnants of pictures are visible. The box is to be dated to the XVIIth or the early XVIIIth Dynasty.

74679 van SICLEN III, Charles Cornell, A Ramesside Ostracon of Queen Isis, *JNES* 33 (1974), 150-153, with 1 fig. and 1 ill.

In 1936 a large number of ostraca probably from Deir el Medineh were added to the O.I.C. collection. One of these No. 17006 bears a female figure drawn in black ink over a red pattern in Ramesside style. The writer suggests this is a queen as she wears a uraeus, and finds a parallel with a scene in the tomb of Isis in the Valley of Queens (No. 51).

E. Uphill

van SICLEN, Charles Cornell, III, see also our number 74620.

74680 SIEFERT-CATTEPOEL, Renate, Aspekte der Menschwerdung in der altägyptischen Kultur, *Deutsches Ärzteblatt*, Lövenich 21 (23. Mai 1974), 1583-1586, with 3 ill.

The author briefly describes the conception of life and its religious background, and declares, on account of it, the occurrence of abortus provocatus by a physician in these times for highly unlikely.

74681 SILVERMAN, David P., Late Egyptian Features in Middle Kingdom Non-Literary Inscriptions, *Newsletter ARCE* No. 89 (Spring 1974), 28-30.

A short report of the author's activities in collecting material for the existence of Late Egyptian features on Middle Kingdom stelae and inscriptions from i.a. the Cairo Museum and Aswân.

L.M.J. Zonhoven

74682 SILVERMAN, David, Late Egyptian Features in Middle Kingdom Non-Literary Inscriptions. Progress Report April 1974, *Newsletter ARCE* No. 90 (Summer 1974), 4-5.

A sequel to our preceding number.
The author has been able to collect all unpublished stelae from the Middle Kingdom in the Cairo Museum and to record inscriptions from unpublished tombs ranging in date from the late Old Kingdom to the early New Kingdom.
So far he has discovered some elements of Late Egyptian Grammar (i.a. *p3*, *t3* and *n3*, circumstantial *iw*).

L.M.J. Zonhoven

74683 SIMPSON, William Kelly, A Commemorative Scarab of Amenophis III of the Irrigation Basin/Lake Series from the Levant in the Museum of Fine Arts, Boston, and Remarks on the Two Other Commemorative Scarabs, *JEA* 60 (1974), 140-141, with 2 pl.

In the monograph by C. Blankenberg-van Delden (our number 69074) ten of these lake scarabs are listed. Boston acquired its first example, MFA No. 1972.873 in 1972. A detailed description is given, and also of a marriage scarab on loan to the museum and one of Amenophis IV with his titulary and that of queen Nefertiti.　　　　　　　　　　　　　*E. Uphill*

74684 SIMPSON, William Kelly, The Middle Kingdom in Egypt : Some Recent Acquisitions, *Boston Museum Bulletin*, Boston 72, No. 368 (1974), 100-116, with 14 ill. and 2 fig.

Discussion of some recent acquisitions of the Museum of Fine Arts, Boston.
1. a black granite group of the nomarch Ukhhotpe from Meir with his two wives and his daughter (No. 1973.187), acquired by exchange from the Walters Art Gallery, Baltimore; it is compared with a similar group of the same persons in the Cairo Museum (Cat. gén. 459); 2. a small alabaster seated statue of an unknown official, from Asyût (No. 1971.20), in the provincial style of the First Intermediate Period; 3. a fragment of a relief with two offering bearers from the chapel of Queen Nofru at Deir el-Bahri (No. 1973.147); 4. part of a limestone lintel of Si-Hathor-Nehy (No. 1972.17), the right half of which is in Cairo; it may also be an archaizing work from the XXVth Dynasty (see our number 72667); 5. a fragmentary sunk relief from the shrine of tomb no 3 at Deir el-Bersheh (No. 1972.984); 6. a miniature alabaster offering table from Meir (No. 138.1973); 7. the head of a quartzite statuette (No. 1970.441), from the XIIth Dynasty or from the Late First Intermediate Period (see our number 72663); 8. a limestone bas-relief of the overseer of the fields Ankhu (No. 1971.403), with a biographical inscription (see our number 72673 and Goedicke, *GM* Heft 17 [1975], 27-30); 9. the stela of police officer Ameny and his family (No. 1970.630), probably from Abydos (cfr our number 72663).

74685 SIMPSON, William Kelly, Polygamy in Egypt in the Middle Kingdom?, *JEA* 60 (1974), 100-105.

Although the evidence is very equivocal a number of Middle Kingdom cases of plurality of wives seem to be attested, but the documentation cited may indicate that the officials may have simply been widowed or divorced and remarried. The cases cited are Mery-'aa of Hagarseh, c. Ninth Dynasty; Intef son of Ka;

'Ab-kau, Eleventh Dynasty; the well-known Ḥepdjefa of Siut; Intef son of Sit-Amun, year 25 Sesostris I; Imsu, year 33 ibid.; Ameny son of Kebu, Twelfth Dynasty; the famous Khnumhotpe son of Neheri; Ukhhotpe, reign of Sesotris II or III; Ameny; Iri; Ḥa-'ankhef of Edfu and Nui of Dendera. Two cases of polyandry seem very dubious.   *E. Uphill*

74686 SIMPSON, William Kelly, A Portrait of Mariette by Théodule Devéria, *BIFAO* 74 (1974), 149-150, with 1 pl.

Publication of a portrait of Mariette in pencil with colours by Devéria, dated in 1859 and at present in the Museum of Fine Arts, Boston.

74687 SIMPSON, William Kelly, The Publication of Texts in Museums: Boston, Museum of Fine Arts, *Textes et langages III*, 203-207.

The author describes the origin of the inscriptional material in the Department of Egyptian Art of the museum, which is mainly derived from excavations. Hence no systematic catalogue exists, the objects being published in the excavation reports of the expeditions to Gîza, Nag' el-Deir, Deir el-Bersha, and the Nubian campaigns at the Second Cataract Forts, at Kerma, and Gebel Barkal and its surroundings. At the end a list of recent publications on inscriptional material in periodicals.

74688 SIMPSON, William Kelly, The Terrace of the Great God at Abydos: The Offering Chapels of Dynasties 12 and 13, New Haven and Philadelphia, The Peabody Museum of Natural History of Yale University — The University Museum of the University of Pennsylvania, 1974 (26.5 × 33.7 cm; VIII + 30 p., 1 plan, 1 diagram, 84 pl.) = Publications of the Pennsylvania-Yale Expedition to Egypt, 5; rev. *AJA* 78 (1974), 433-434 (John D. Cooney); *JEA* 61 (1975), 283-284 (C.H.S. Spaull).

The study intends to bring into some sort of order the widely dispersed elements of the private offering chapels (stelae, offering tables and statuary) from the N. necropolis of Abydos. The material mainly consists of objects dispersed by dealers (particularly d'Athanasi and Anastasi) among European museums and those found by Mariette, now in Cairo.
Since several individuals appear to be represented by more than one stela and a statuette and/or offering table it is clear that these elements belonged to a chapel. Most of the chapels date from the period between the reigns of Sesostris I and Amenemhat III. The main function of the chapel seems to have been that of an ex-voto by which the owner seeks for himself and his family association with the celebration of the Abydos festivals, though

they may also have served as funerary chapels. The study of the material leads the author to pose several questions, as, for example, whether the chapels were cenotaphs or not; whether the owners belonged to special classes or professions; where they did live; what the exact position of the "staircase (terrace) of the Great God" (rwḏw n nṯr ʿ3) was after which the region was called. To most of the problems there is at present no answer. Two chapters are devoted to the study of the sources and the site of the terrace. In the first one Simpson discusses the auction catalogues of d'Athanasi and Anastasi; in the second he i.a. quotes a letter of Gabet to Mariette concerning the excavations in the area. He concludes to a variety of architectural settings for the stelae. Study of the inscriptions sheds light on the terrace itself and the buildings (mʿḥʿt), while the various wʿrt terms mentioned appear to indicate this area, all referring to the offerings with which the chapels were provided.

On p. 13-16 the ANOC-list (Abydos North Offering Chapels) is studied in general, that is, the list of chapels of which more than one element is known. The author stresses the possibilities of mistakes, due i.a. to faulty information or lack of information about the provenance of the stelae, and the probability that the list can be enlarged.

The list itself (p. 17-29) contains 78 groups, each member being briefly described. Comments on p. 22-24, indexes to the present places of preservation on p. 24-26, a list of dated and datable stelae on p. 26-29, of the principal persons and their titles on p. 30. On the plates representations of 195 different elements in photograph.

SIMPSON, William Kelly, see also our number 74172.

74689 SLEDZIANOWSKI, Bernd, Ägyptologie zwischen Positivismus und Nationalismus, *GM* Heft 12 (1974), 43-50.

Kurt Sethe is characterized as a protagonist of German chauvinism and capitalist exploitation. *Dieter Mueller*

SLEDZIANOWSKI, Bernd, see also our number 74342.

74690 ŚLIWA, Joachim, Ägyptische Fayence-Kacheln mit Darstellungen von Fremdvölker, *Festschrift Ägyptisches Museum Berlin*, 233-238, with 2 pl. and 3 fig.

After a short general survey of the fayence tiles from the New Kingdom the author publishes the 11 tiles preserved in the Ägyptisches Museum, Berlin (inv. nos. 7944-8; 7950-1; 15729; 17019 and 17277-8). The first seven come from the palace of Ramses III at Tell el-Yahûdiya, the others from that of Medînet Habu. The author offers of each a short description with mention of the technical data and bibliography, and either a drawing or a photograph.

74691 ŚLIWA, Joachim, Łukasz Dobrzański jako jeden z prekursorów polskich zainteresowań starożytnym Egiptem, *Meander*, Warszawa 29 (1974), 91-96, with a portrait.

"Lukasz Dobrański as a Precursor of Polish Interest in Ancient Egypt".
Dobrzański, a Polish amateur-egyptologist, stayed in Egypt during the last years of the 19th century. He was a pioneer of photography in his country and took an enormous number of photographs there. Unfortunately, his valuable collection was destroyed during the last war. He also excavated at Koptos and brought back at least one object, an alabaster vessel at present in Vienna.

74692 ŚLIWA, Joachim, Inwazja "ludów morskich" na Egipt w drugiej połowie II tys. p.n.e., *Zeszyty Naukowe Uniwersytetu Jagiellońskiego* Nr. 369, *Prace Archeologiczne*, Zeszyt 19, Krakow (1974), 7-26, with 8 ill.

"The Invasion of Egypt by the 'Sea Peoples' in the Late Second Millennium B.C.".
The article deals with the invasion of Egypt and other parts of the Mediterranean region by the Sea Peoples. It discusses the various peoples separately and gives a review of recent attempts at identifying them.

74693 ŚLIWA, Joachim, Some Remarks Concerning Victorious Ruler Representations in Egyptian Art, *Forschungen und Berichte* 16 (1974), 97-117, with 20 ill.

The author discusses five types of representations of the ruler's triumph over his enemies, namely: the king smiting defeated enemies, triumphing over them as a sphinx, supervising the counting of prisoners and dead enemies, captured enemies are conducted by a commander into the presence of the ruler or by the latter to the gods, and the ruler riding in a war chariot. These representations were intended to glorify the king and to show the divine character of his authority. See our following number.

73694 ŚLIWA, Joachim, Zagadnienie przedstawień zwycięskiego władcy w sztuce egipskiej, *Zeszyty Naukowe Uniwersytetu Jagiellońskiego* Nr. 330, *Prace Archeologiczne*, Zeszyt 16, Krakow (1973), 7-22, with 10 pl.

"The Problem of the Representations of the Victorious Ruler in the Egyptian Art".

The representations of Pharaoh's triumph over his enemies may be divided into five main groups: 1. the king smiting his defeated enemies; 2. the king as a sphinx triumphing over his enemies; 3. the king supervising the counting of prisoners and dead enemies; 4. scenes of conducting captured enemies, either by a commander to the pharaoh or by him to the gods; 5. the king riding on a war chariot. The representations date from various periods, nrs 1 and 2 assuming the rank of symbols, while the other remain narrative and decorative. During the XVIIIth-XXth Dynasties they usually form part of large battle scenes. The author investigates each of the five groups separately, discussing its development and characteristics and attempting to determine its popularity. Compare our preceding number.

74695 SMITH, H.S., The Archives of the Sacred Animal Necropolis at North Saqqâra. A Progress Report, *JEA* 60 (1974), 256-258.

A summary of all the textual and inscriptional material found since the inception of the E.E.S. excavations in 1964, and covering hieratic and demotic papyri, Aramaic, Greek and Arabic fragments, stelae and wall inscriptions, hieroglyphic and Carian, Coptic and Latin inscriptions and numerous ostraca.

E. Uphill

74696 SMITH, H.S., Raymond O. Faulkner. An Appreciation, *JEA* 60 (1974), 5-7, with portrait = frontispiece.

Salutation to Raymond O. Faulkner at the occasion of his eightieth birthday. For his bibliography see our number 74707.

74697 SMITH, H.S., La mère d'Apis: Fouilles récentes de l'Egypt Exploration Society à Saqqara-Nord, *BSFE* No 70-71 (Juin et Octobre 1974), 11-27, with 4 ill.

Survey of the aims and results of the excavations at Saqqâra North by the EES. The author deals with the site, the underground galleries and their contents of mummified animals, the history of the area during the Late Period, the deposits of bronzes and wooden statuettes, the toponomy and cults, and the social life as reflected by the texts recently found. In his conclusion he stresses the importance of the discoveries for the knowledge of social and economic life before the Ptolemaic Period.

74698 SMITH, H.S., A Visit to Ancient Egypt. Life at Memphis & Saqqara (c. 500-30 BC), Warminster, Aris & Phillips Limited, [1974] (17.3 × 24.9 cm; [VI +] 92 p., frontispiece, 8 pl., 9 plans, 1 section, 2 fig.); rev. *BiOr* 33 (1976), 181-182 (Janet H. Johnson). Pr. £ 1.95

This book contains three lectures. The first, the author's inaugural lecture (University College London, 6th March 1973), is entitled "Memphis Under the Last Pharaohs". After an introduction concerning the history of the chair of Egyptology at University College the first section presents a survey of the XXVIIIth-XXXth Dynasties, the last sixty years of independence before Alexander. Section 2 deals with Memphis through the ages, particularly in the Late Period, sketching its plan and life in its streets. Section 3 describes daily life in the necropolis, illustrated by quotations from texts, mostly letters, found during the recent excavations at Saqqâra North.

Part II is a lecture called "The Sacred Animal Necropolis at North Saqqara", and presents a comprehensive survey of the results of Emery's excavations: the ibis catacombs, the temple terrace, the baboon galleries and those of the mothers of Apis, the Carian stelae — which are here reused and came from a Carian cemetery at Memphis — and the falcon galleries with their cache of temple furniture. A long section is devoted to the deposits found around the enclosure wall of the temple terrace. Smith explains them partly as caches for statues no longer used, partly as foundation deposits, and partly as deposits of material offered at the shrines of the temple terrace. After a few words on the area S. of this terrace the lecture ends with a discussion of some papyri and dream ostraca, and of the historical interest of the discoveries.

Part III, "Two Athenians at the Funeral of a Mother of Apis", is a short story about the visit of two Athenians to Memphis and the cemetery of the sacred animals in the year 5 of Alexander the Great, the major event being their report of the burial of Taese, Mother of Apis. Although imaginary the story contains a wealth of reliable information about the period.

SMITH, Harry S., see also our numbers 74003 and 74270.

74699 SMITH, Mark J., A Coptic Ostracon from Luxor, *Enchoria* 4 (1974), 61-66, with 1 pl.

Publication of a Coptic ostracon purchased by Dr. Ch. Nims in Luxor. It contains a letter referring to a barbarian invasion and resembles similar documents from the late 6th and early 7th century.   *Dieter Mueller*

SMITH, R.W., see our number 74645.

SMOLLA, Günter, see our number 74486.

74700 Sonderforschungsbereich 13. Orientalistik. Universität Göttingen. Arbeitsbericht 1974, Göttingen, [no publisher], 1974 (21 × 29 cm; 345 p., numerous ill. and fig.).

Von besonderer Bedeutung für Ägyptologen ist der Bericht von dem Teilprojekt D : "Sammlung und Auswertung altägyptischer religiöser Begriffe. Untersuchung synkretistischer Erscheinungen in den religiösen Texten and Darstellungen. Altägyptische Einflüsse auf das frühe Christentum" (p. 199-257).
Ausser einer Übersicht über die allgemeinen Problemen und den Stand der Forschung findet man vier spezielle Berichte :
1. D. Jankuhn : Die Erforschung des innerägyptischen Synkretismus (S. 215-225).
2. U. Köhler : Die Neubearbeitung des Kapitels 17 des ägyptischen Totenbuches (= Spruch 335 der ägyptischen Sargtexten) (226-234).
3. W. Westendorf : Altägyptische Dreieinigkeit und christliche Trinität (235-239).
4. J. Spiegel : Die Entwicklung des altägyptischen Schöpferbegriffes (239-247).
Es folgen eine Liste erschienener oder sich in Druck befindlicher Publikationen (248-255) und eine Bemerkung zum Ziel und Arbeitsprogramm und zur Stellung innerhalb des Programms des Sonderforschungsbereiches.

74701 SPALINGER, Anthony John, Aspects of the Military Documents of the Ancient Egyptians, *Dissertation Abstracts International A*, Ann Arbor, Mich. 34, No. 11 (May 1974), 7138-A.

Abstract of a doctor's thesis Yale University, 1973 (Order No. 74-11,919; 486 p.).
In this thesis the author studies the military inscriptions of the ancient Egyptians from a purely literary view-point in order to separate the various traditions. The so-called *iw.tw* form, originating from the XVIIIth Dynasty, became rigid rather soon, but lasted down at least to the Saite Period. Other literary genres served as a basis for more detailed reports. The author also separates out literary motifs, such as the Königsnovelle, the Sporting Tradition, the Oath and the "Setting", and the Literary Tradition. *L.M.J. Zonhoven*

74702 SPALINGER, Anthony, Assurbanipal and Egypt : A Source Study, *JAOS* 94 (1974), 316-328.

The author studies the Assyrian sources for the two Egyptian campaigns of Assurbanipal in order to unravel their differing traditions. Although written before the author received Kitchen's *The Third Intermediate Period* (our number 73405) his conclusions largely corroborate those of the latter (see note 15, p. 317-318). The author gives a detailed report of the events in Egypt during the Assyrian campaigns.

74703 SPALINGER, Anthony, Esarhaddon and Egypt: An Analysis of the First Invasion of Egypt, *Orientalia* 43 (1974), 295-326.

The study, like our preceding number, has been written before the author could consult Kitchen's book, although he refers to it in some notes.
The author presents a detailed analysis from Assyrian as well as from Egyptian sources of the military campaign of Esarhaddon in 671 B.C. Mainly on account of Assyrian evidence he first deals with its preparation, the conquest of Egypt and its consolidation, and the Assyrian organization of the conquered country. The fifth section is devoted to the Egyptian organization of the country, mainly on account of Yoyotte's study (our number 61770). Spalinger argues that the bureaucratic and administrative arrangements forced upon the Egyptians do not appear to have been harsh, the Assyrians wanting to destroy the power of Kush and, therefore, keeping Egypt divided in itself under native rulers and Assyrian supervisors.
The last section, on the titles Assyrian scribes gave to the rulers of Egypt and Kush and their interpretation of the differences between those two countries, confirms this conception.
In a summary (p. 324-326) the author compares Esarhaddon's policy with that of Assurbanipal, which appear to be largely identical.

74704 SPALINGER, Anthony, Some Notes on the Battle of Megiddo and Reflections on Egyptian Military Writing, *MDAIK* 30 (1974), 221-229.

Disputing Helck's interpretation of the description of the Battle of Megiddo in the annals of Thutmose III (our No. 72307) the author tries to show that the Egyptian army arrived at Megiddo on the evening of the 20th day of the first summer month, and explains the seeming difficulties with the redaction to which the royal ephemerides were subjected in the composition of the account. *Dieter Mueller*

SPALLANZANI ZIMMERMANN, Adriana, see our number 74037.

74705 SPAULDING, Jay, The Fate of Alodia, *MNL* No. 15 (Octobre 1974), 12-30.

Alodia oder 'Alwa war das südlichste der drei christlichen Königreiche in der Zeit zwischen dem Niedergang des meroitischen und dem Aufstieg des Funj-Reiches von Sinnār. Im vorliegenden Artikel wird das Schicksal Alodias nach seinem Fall untersucht und eine historische und linguistische Kontinuität zwischen Meroe und Fāzūghlī postuliert. *Inge Hofmann*

74706 SPAULDING, Jay, "Gar Mol!" — A Meroitic Survival in the Court Ritual of Sinnār?, *MNL* No. 15 (Octobre 1974), 10-11.

Verfasser versucht eine Verbindung herzustellen zwischen dem Grußwort "Gar Mol — Gott bewahre Dich" am Hof von Sinnār und dem meroitischen *qore* "König" und *ml(e/o)* "gut". Den Ausdruck "Gar Mol" läßt er aus dem Meroitischen über die Sprache des mittelalterlichen Königreiches Alodia an den Hof von Sinnār gelangen, wo er wahrscheinlich von den Hamaj verwendet wurde. *Inge Hofmann*

SPAULDING, Jay L., see also our number 74539.

74707 SPAULL, C. H. S., Bibliography of Raymond Oliver Faulkner, *JEA* 60 (1974), 8-14.

Comprises a list of works covering fifty years, 1924-73, and containing approximately 10 books and parts of same, 73 articles, editorial forewords and bibliographies, and 61 reviews.
E. Uphill

74708 SPENCER, A. J., Researches on the Topography of North Saqqâra, *Orientalia* 43 (1974), 1-11, with 1 folding map.

L'auteur a dressé un plan de Saqqâra Nord en tenant compte des plans de W. S. Smith, de Lepsius et de Firth, mais aussi des indications recueillies dans les périodiques depuis 1936 et en s'appuyant sur des observations personnelles prises sur place, par exemple à propos des deux témenos à l'W de celui de Djéser. Il a constaté quelques erreurs dans les publications. Sa liste de concordance indique, en regard du nom des propriétaires de tombes, les divers numéros donnés par les fouilleurs; en l'absence de numéro, une autre liste décrit l'emplacement relatif des tombes. La position de certains monuments ne peut être précisée sur le plan. Beaucoup de secteurs restent à fouiller.
J. Custers

74709 STAEHELIN, Elisabeth, Jacob Burckhardt und Ägypten, *ZÄS* 101 (1974), 49-62.

An analysis of Jacob Burckhardt's knowledge of ancient Egypt and his (largely positive) opinions of Egyptian art and Egyptian religion.
The second part of the article deals with his interest in obelisks and his humorous translation of the texts on the "Needle of Cleopatra" in London. *Dieter Mueller*

74710 STAEHELIN, Elisabeth, Zu den Farben der Hieroglyphen, *GM* Heft 14 (1974), 49-53.

A discussion of the colours of hieroglyphic signs and of their significance for the study of hieroglyphs and the dating and restoration of Egyptian texts. *Dieter Mueller*

STAEHELIN, Elisabeth. see also our number 74348.

74711 STARCK, Sylvia, The Victoria Museum — An Introduction, *The Gustavianum Collections*, 11-14, with 1 ill.

General description of the history of the collections in the Victoria Museum for Egyptian Antiquities, Uppsala. From 33 items in 1882 the collections increased, particularly through donations by Piehl, to over 4000 at present. Various gifts and purchases are mentioned, among which donations by the Swedish Queen Victoria after whom the museum has been named in 1895.

74712 STEINMANN, Frank, Die Schreibkentnisse der Kopten nach den Aussagen der Djeme-Urkunden, *in*: *Studia Coptica*. Herausgegeben von Peter Nagel, Berlin, Akademie-Verlag, 1974 (= Berliner Byzantinistische Arbeiten, 45), 101-110.

On account of legal documents from the Coptic village of Djeme (Medinet Habu) in the second half of the 8th century A.D. the author calculates that of a total of 616 persons appearing either in the intitulatio and completio, or as witnesses in the documents, 46% was able to write. Conclusions as to the percentage of literates in the whole of Coptic Egypt are rather hypothetical, but 40%-50% of the population being able to write may be a fair estimate.
Compare our number 71540. *L.M.J. Zonhoven*

74713 STEMBERGER, Brigitte, "Der Mann Moses" in Freuds Gesamtwerk, *Kairos*, Salzburg Neue Folge 16 (1974), 161-251.

In this extensive study about Freud's book "Der Mann Moses und die monotheïstische Religion" the author i.a. discusses the Egyptological literature Freud had read (p. 197-198) and his ideas about the influence of the Egyptian religion on that of Israel (209-213).

74714 STIEGLITZ, Robert R., The National Maritime Museum Haifa, *Archaeology* 27 (1974), 128-130, with 8 ill.

Short communication concerning the National Maritime Museum at Haifa which possesses i.a. Egyptian model boats and the figurine of a swimming girl (see ill.).

74715 STIEGLITZ, Robert R., Ugaritic *Mḫd* — the Harbor or Yabne-Yam?, *JAOS* 94 (1974), 137-138.

The Ugaritic toponym M*ḫd*/*ᵃⁱMa-ḫa-du* may be identical with *Muḫḫazu* (Amarna Tablets) and Eg. *M(i)ḫs* and refer to the harbour at Yabne-Yam.

74716 STÖRK, Lothar, "*p3 jm '3 n mw ḳd*" zum dritten?, *GM* Heft 9 (1974), 39-40.

A reply to our Number 73720. *Mw qd* is not a name, but a description of the Euphrates which can be applied to other waters flowing from N to S; in letters of the 20th Dynasty published by W. Helck, this term apparently denotes a coastal strip along the shore of the Red Sea (see our Number 67253).
Dieter Mueller

74717 STRAUß, Elisabeth-Christine, Die Nunschale. Eine Gefäßgruppe des Neuen Reiches, München-Berlin, Deutscher Kunstverlag, 1974 (17 × 24 cm; 95 p., 72 fig., 15 pl.) = Münchner Ägyptologische Studien herausgegeben von Hans Wolfgang Müller, 30; rev. *BiOr* 33 (1976), 179-180 (Barbara S. Lesko); *CdE* LI, No. 101 (1976), 114-116 (Agnes Rammant-Peters); *JARCE* 12 (1975), 109-110 (Hans Goedicke); *Welt des Orients* 8 (1975-1976), 323-324 (Emma Brunner-Traut).   Pr. DM 20

Eine Gruppe von Fayenceschalen und Fragmenten aus der Staatlichen Sammlung Ägyptischer Kunst in München werden in Katalogform vorgestellt. Die Darstellungen der Innenseiten mit einem See, Pflanzen (Lotos und Papyrus), Tieren (Tilapia und Vögeln) oder Hathorsymbolen (Sistrum oder Kuh) erlauben die Deutung dieser und ähnlicher Schalen als Trink- bzw. Libationsschalen im Grab- und Götterkult, worauf auch die wenigen bekannten Fundorte hinweisen. Die Seedarstellung und auch die Schale selbst verkörpere dabei den Gott Nun, Lotos und Tilapia deuteten auf Re, der Papyrus auf Hathor.
Als Exkurs werden die Ergebnisse der chemischen Analyse der Glasur vorgestellt. 7 Indices.   *E.M. Wolf-Brinkmann*

74718 STRICKER, B.H., De praehelleense ascese (Vervolg). Het offer [= §9-19], *OMRO* 55 (1974), 129-197.

Sequel to our number 71545.
Continuing his studies of Praehellenic asceticism the author deals with the offering. He argues (§9) that originally the custom belonged to juridical practice, the sacrifice being a substitute and the aim of the act being reconciliation. Various types of offerings are discussed. §§10 and 11 deal with offering practices, §12 with its symbolic meanings, §§13 and 14 with its place, altar and offering table. The other §§ discuss particularly Jewish offering practices, §19 the function of the priest. Here the author also deals with the Egyptian priest and his purity.

74719 STROUHAL, Eugen, Památky z antického období Egypta a Přední Asie ve sbírkách Náprstkova muzea v Praze, *Listy filologické*, Praha 97/3 (1974), 133-136, with 6 ill.

"Antiquities of Ancient Egypt and the Near East in the Collections of the Náprstek Museum at Prague".
After an outline of the development of the collections the objects from the Graeco-Roman Period, mostly from Egypt, are described, consisting i.a. of terracottas, ostraca, vessels, glass, three coffins, etc. From Nubia there are objects from the Roman town at Tâfa and the fortress of Qertassi, further the rich material from the X-Group cemeteries in Wâdi Qatna and Kalâbsha, as well as those of the region between Kalâbsha and Gerf Husein. *B. Vachala*

74720 STROUHAL, Eugen, Die Sezierung einer altägyptischen Mumie, *Anthropologie*, Brno 12 (1974), 239-241, with 2 ill.

Report on the investigation and dissection of a mummy in Detroit, Michigan, USA; cfr our number 73153.

74721 STROUHAL, Eugen, Tajemná Núbie v Náprstkově muzeu, *Lidé a země*, Praha 24/4 (1974), 178-179.

"Mysterious Nubia in the Náprstek Museum".
Announcement of an exhibition at Prague concerning the results of the Czechoslovak excavations in the years 1961-1965.
B. Vachala

74722 STROUHAL, Eugen and Luboš VYHNÁNEK, Radiographic Examination of the Mummy of Qenamūn the Seal-Bearer, *ZÄS* 100, 2 (1974), 125-129, with 6 ill. and 1 fig. on 2 pl.

Study of a mummy from the collections of the State castle of Kynžvart (Königswart) in Western Bohemia, district Cheb; see our number 74766.
Following an external description, radiographic and embalmment techniques, posthumous changes, demographic diagnosis and pathological findings are dealt with.
M. Heerma van Voss

STROUHAL, Eugen, see also our number 74072.

74723 STUCHEVSKIY, I. A., Данные Большого папируса Вильбура и других административно-хозяйственных документов о нормах палоговой Эксплуатации государственных (« Царских ») Земледельцев древнего Египта эпохи Рамессидов, *ВДИ* 1 (127), 1974, 3-21, with an English summary on p. 20-21.

"Data from the Wilbour Papyrus and other Administrative Documents Relating to the Taxes Levied on the State ("Royal") Land-Cultivators in Egypt of the Ramesside Period".

Studying the rates at which the grain tax was levied on cultivators of state (royal temple) land according to the Wilbour papyrus, the author argues that it was determined by fixing the size of the taxable portion of a piece of land. If it was very small, the tax was correspondingly small; if it amounted to a quarter of a piece of k3yt-land the tax came to 7.5% of the standard average harvest; if the entire field was taxable it came to about one-third. Since from this third of the harvest 7.5% was transferred to local temples, the state received just over 20% of the harvest.

STUCKY, Rolf, see our number 74127.

SWEENEY, Siadhal, see our number 74576.

74724 SWELIM, Nabil, Horus *Seneferka*. An Essay on the Fall of the First Dynasty, *Archaeological and Historical Studies*, Alexandria 5 (1974), 67-77, with 1 folding table and 1 pl.

Since king Ka'a had elaborate tombs in Abydos and Saqqâra it is unlikely that the Ist Dynasty ended with his reign. He may have been succeeded by Baunetjer (Turin and Saqqâra kinglists; Manetho's Bienches). The author suggests that this was Horus Seneferka, whose name occurs on a bowl found under the Step Pyramid and another one found in Tomb No. 3505 by Emery (see pl. 1). Since he failed to maintain order over the Followers of Seth his short reign ended in disorder, after which a new era started with Hetepsekhemui.

74725 SZNYCER, Maurice, Quelques remarques à propos de la formation de l'alphabet phénicien, *Semitica*, Paris 24 (1974), 5-12.

Referring to the studies of Helck (our number 72312) and Zauzich (our number 73820) concerning the Egyptian origin of the Phoenician letters, the author argues that the order of the Phoenician alphabeth and the names of the letters already existed in the 15th century B.C., as Ugaritic evidence demonstrates. Hence pictographic origin of the signs and application of the acrophonic system appear to be probable. He also suggests that part of the signs may have been derived from an earlier script, whereas others may have been created freely.

TAIEL, F.M., see our number 74182.

74726 TAIT, W.J., A Duplicate Version of the Demotic *Kufi* Text, *Acta Orientalia*, Copenhagen 36 (1974), 23-37, with 1 pl.

Publication of three small papyrus fragments from Tebtunis, probably dating from the first half of the 2nd century A.D. (property of the Egypt Exploration Society, housed in the Ashmolean Museum, Oxford). The fragments almost join up and bear a text of 20 lines which contains a version of the animal fables, *Kufi*. The author gives a photograph, a transliteration and comments, as well as an introduction in which he explains that the text is a version of col. 14, ll. 8-32 of *The Myth of the Sun-Eye* (= Pap. Leiden I 384, published by Spiegelberg in 1917).

74727 el-TANBOULI, M. A. L. et A. F. SADEK, avec la collaboration de Ch. KUENTZ, Garf Hussein. II. La cour et l'entrée du spéos, Le Caire, Centre de documentation et d'études sur l'ancienne Égypte, 1974 (21 × 27 cm; 44 loose p., 48 loose pl. with 1 folding plan, drawings and photographs [1 in colour], coloured frontispiece). At head of title: Collection scientifique.

The publication contains an archaeological description of the court and the entrance to the speos of the Ptah-temple of Ramses II at Gerf Hussein, its scenes on walls and pillars, with reproduction of the hieroglyphic texts (p. 29-38). The plates bear a plan and sections, drawings of architectural details, and photographs of the building and many details. Pl. 13 and 14 reproduce Gau's drawings and plan from 1822.

74728 TANNER, Rolf, Bemerkungen zur Sukzession der Pharaonen in der 12., 17. und 18. Dynastie, *ZÄS* 101 (1974), 121-129.

Verfasser beschäftigt sich mit der Rechtsnachfolge. Der König untersteht rechtlichen Verhaltensnormen und wird einem göttlichem Erbrecht unterworfen. Die Königsgemahlin fungiert regelmässig als Erbmittlerin.
Im zweiten Teil bespricht Tanner die Designation, d.h. die Ernennung des Thronanwärters zum Mitregenten des Königs, und die Samtherrschaft der beiden in der 12. Dynastie.
Fortsetzung in *ZÄS* 102 (1975), 50-59.   *M. Heerma van Voss*

74729 TEFNIN, Roland, A propos d'une tête royale du Musée d'Aberdeen, *CdE* XLIX, No 97 (1974), 13-24, with 7 fig.

L'auteur raccorde la tête royale de granit rouge du musée d'Aberdeen No 1426 à un torse d'ouchebti acéphale du Louvre (sans No) portant le nom d'Aménophis III, qui avait été précédemment attribuée à Aménophis II par B.V. Bothmer (voir notre No 3213). A cette occasion, il examine rapidement l'iconographie d'Aménophis II, de Thoutmosis IV et d'Aménophis III dans laquelle il tente de rétablir une certaine cohérence. Il change également l'attribution du groupe du Caire 42080 qui représente en réalité Aménophis II et non Thoutmosis IV en compagnie de la reine Tiâa.   *Ph. Derchain*

74730 THAUSING, Gertrud, Österreichische Ausgrabungen in Ägypten, *Österreichische Hochschulzeitung*, Wien 26, Nr. 16 (1.10. 1974), 3.

Preliminary report on the continued excavations by the Austrian expedition in the tomb of Ankhhor in ʿAsâsîf, spring 1974.

74731 T[HÉODORIDÈS], A[ristide] E., Egyptian Law, *Encyclopaedia Britannica*. Volume 6, 501-503.

The lemma presents a short survey of Egyptian law.
For other references to Egyptian law see the above edition. Micropaedia. Vol. III.   *L.M.J. Zonhoven*

74732 THÉODORIDÈS, Aristide, Mise en ordre chronologique des éléments de la Stèle Juridique de Karnak avec ses influences sur la procédure, *Revue internationale des droits de l'antiquité*, Bruxelles 3ᵉ série, 21 (1974), 31-74.

The author once more studies the Juridical Stela from Karnak (cfr our numbers 57489, 58577, 59584 and 62584), this time mainly in order to reconstruct the chronological sequence of the juridical actions mentioned by the text. It appears that the sections are not arranged in their chronological order; the owner, Sebeknakht, first mentions the *imyt-pr*, since this was essential to him. Théodoridès reconstructs the events as follows: a plaintiff, Sebekakht, requires from Kebsi, to whom he has lent objects to a value of 60 *deben* of gold a compensation, since Kebsi appears to be unable to render him this sum. Kebsi offers the right of succession to his office of Prince of Nekheb, and, therefore, has to prove that he is the rightful possessor of it. After it has been proved the right to the office is transferred by *imyt-pr* to Sebeknakht, who will enter the office after Kebsi's death.

74733 THÉODORIDÈS, Aristide, Les textes juridiques, *Textes et langages III*, 21-32.

After a theoretical introduction particularly concerning the religious influence on daily life the author stresses the non-primitive character of Egyptian law. The documents are written in a business-like juridical style without elements foreign to the subject. The author also argues that already during the Old Kingdom the rights of individuals were recognized.
Théodoridès next discusses the juridical vocabulary, which is poor and without rigidity; the distinction made between law and convictions; the rights of individuals and official instances; and the problem whether there have existed actual laws and how strictly they were applied.

THILL, Florence, see our number 74509.

74734 THOMPSON, John Mark, The Form and Function of Proverbs in Ancient Israel, The Hague, Mouton, 1974 (14 × 21 cm; 156 p.) = Studia Judaica, 1.

As is suitable in a study about proverbs in Israel there are many references to Egyptian Wisdom Literature. In a special section (p. 37-41) this subject is particularly discussed.

74735 THOMPSON, Thomas L., The Historicity of the Patriarchal Narratives. The Quest for the Historical Abraham, Berlin-New York, Walter de Gruyter, 1974 (16 × 23 cm; X + 392 p.) = Beiheft zur Zeitschrift für die alttestamentliche Wissenschaft, 133; rev. *BiOr* 32 (1975), 231-234 (Gerhard F. Hasel); *Welt des Orients* 8 (1975-1976), 343-346 (Siegfried Herrmann); *ZAW* 86 (1974), 264 ([G. Fohrer]).

In dieser breit angelegten archäologischen wie philologischen Untersuchung der Patriarchen-Erzählungen des Alten Testaments und der Bronze-Zeit in Palästina wird wiederholt auf ägyptische Quellen Bezug genommen. Besonders einschlägig ist das 6. Kapitel: "Egypt and the Amorite Question", in dem die ägyptischen Texte und Darstellungen vom späten AR bis zum Ende des MR neu besprochen werden mit dem Ergebnis, daß es sich bei den nach Ägypten eindringenden Asiaten nicht um Ausläufer einer großen Wanderung handelt, daß die 'ʒmw in der Ersten Zwischenzeit und dem MR vielmehr Bewohner der unmittelbar an die Ostgrenze des Niltals anstoßenden Gegenden sind. In Zeiten militärischer Stärke konnte Ägypten die Gefahr dieser Einfälle bannen, in Zeiten der Hungersnot und den Wirren aber nicht. Mit den Amoritern haben diese "Asiaten" nichts zu tun. *Hellmut Brunner*

74736 THOMSEN, Rudi, Da Ægypten var en verdensmagt. Stat og samfund under det 18. dynasti. Historiske kilder, redigeret af Rudi Thomsen, [København], Gyldendal, [1974] (15.5 × 23 cm; 115 p., 65 ill., 2 maps).

"When Egypt Was A World Power. State and Society during the 18th Dynasty. Historical sources, edited by Rudi Thomsen". A source book dealing with 18th Dynasty Egypt, intended for secondary schools. Introduction (p. 9-23). Internal Affairs (24-81), which constitutes the first part of the book, is divided into the following sub-headings: Pharaoh; Government; Economic and Everyday Life; Religious Affairs. Egypt and the Outside World (82-107); the second part, consists of: Campaigns; Trade and Tribute; What the Amarna Letters Tell us; An Unsuccessful Marriage Alliance.

At the end there are a list of sources and illustrations, proposals for papers, a bibliography and an index.

Torben Holm-Rasmussen

74737 Das Tier in der Antike. 400 Werke ägyptischer, griechischer, etruskischer und römischer Kunst aus privatem und öffentlichem Besitz. Ausgestellt im Archäologischen Institut der Universität Zürich vom 21. September bis 17. November 1974, Zürich, [Archäologisches Institut der Universität], 1974 (21 × 27 cm; 71 p., 64 pl., frontispiece, fig. on cover). Pr. Sw. Fr. 48

The first part of this exhibition catalogue is devoted to animals from Egypt, consisting of a description of 139 objects ranging from the Neolithic to the Coptic Period. For each item all relevant data and bibliographical references are given, while all are represented by a photograph (plates 1-24). The objects from Pharaonic Egypt mostly belong to one of the following categories: palettes, vessels (either shaped like an animal or decorated with animals), and statuettes in wood, bronze or faience (several amulets).

74738 TOBIA, Sami K. and Edward V. SAYRE, An Analytical Comparison of Various Egyptian Soils, Clays, Shales, and Some Ancient Pottery by Neutron Activation, *Recent Advances in Science and Technology of Materials*, 99-128, with 2 maps, 2 fig. and 7 tables.

In order to correlate the pattern of impurities in pottery to that in clay from probable sources samples of clay, mud and shale from twenty sites throughout Egypt have been analyzed. Although Nile mud appears to be identical all through Egypt other materials show considerable variation in composition, so that further investigations of this type may yield important results.

74739 TÖRÖK, L., Abdallah Nirqi 1964. Finds with Inscriptions, *Acta Archaeologica Academiae Scientiarum Hungaricae*, Budapest 26 (1974), 369-393, with 52 ill. (on 18 pl.).

Unter den Funden mit Inschriften aus Abdallah Nirqi gehören Inscr. 8 und 9 — in beiden Fällen eine Gruppe von Zeichen, die auf einem Vorratsgefäß vor dem Brennen angebracht wurden — in die vorchristliche Zeit. Alle übrigen Beispiele werden in die christliche Zeit datiert. *Inge Hofmann*

74740 TÖRÖK, L., An Archaeological Note on the Connections between the Meroitic and Ballana Cultures, *Studia Aegyptiaca* *I*, 361-378, with 3 fig.

Das Grab W. 130 auf dem Westfriedhof von Meroe sowie die Tumuli 47 von Ballana und 14 von Qustul enthielten Schmuckstücke (die ersten beiden Gräber Armreifen, das letztgenannte einen Ring), die in der Anfertigung so ähnlich sind, daß sie wahrscheinlich aus derselben Werkstatt stammen. Anhand der übrigen Beigaben behören die Grabanlagen in die Mitte des 4. nachchristlichen Jahrhunderts. Verf. schließt daraus auf eine politische Beziehung zwischen den nachmeroitischen "adligen" Familien, die auf dem Westfriedhof noch nach dem Erlöschen des Königtums in Meroe bestattet sind und den neuen Machthabern im Norden, den Prinzen, die in Ballana und Qustul begraben wurden. *Inge Hofmann*

74741 TÖRÖK, L., Bemerkungen zu Paul van Moorsel: Zur Diskussion: Was ist "Nubologie"?, *MNL* No. 14 (Février 1974), 59-60.

Verf. betrachtet vornehmlich die Methodik des Wissenschaftszweiges und kommt zu dem Ergebnis, daß die "Nubologie" nur zu einem kleineren Teil "eigene" Forschungsmethoden enthält, zum größeren Teil jedoch ein Komplex von Adaptationen allgemeinerer historischer bzw. kulturhistorischer Disziplinen sei. Ein weitgehender Spezialisierungsprozeß innerhalb der "Nubologie" ist unumgänglich und wünschenswert, solange das Bewußtsein gemeinsamer Arbeit erhalten bleibt. Sehe auch unsere Nummer 74741. *Inge Hofmann*

74742 TÖRÖK, L., Ein christianisiertes Tempelgebäude in Musawwarat es Sufra (Sudan), *Acta Archaeologica Academiae Scientiarum Hungaricae*, Budapest 26 (1974), 71-103, with 23 ill. on 8 pl. and 25 fig.

Das zur Diskussion stehende Objekt III A besteht aus dem in den Vorberichten über die Arbeiten in Musawwarat es Sufra als "Südtempel" bezeichneten Gebäude sowie einem kleinen Friedhof mit drei Gräbern. Diese gehören eindeutig der christlichen Epoche an, während das Gebäude bereits vor der Christianisierung Alodias als meroitischer Sakralbau bestand. Dieser dürfte jedoch relativ spät errichtet worden sein, wie aus sekundär verbauten Blöcken (möglicherweise von der nördlichen Wand des Kioskes II A) zu schließen ist. Verf. nimmt eine Bauzeit zwischen dem Ende des 3. und dem Ende des 6. Jahrhunders an (p. 92). Bei den Ritzzeichnungen aus der christlichen Zeit fällt die starke Heraushebung des Erzengels Michael auf. Das Gebäude III A kann nicht lange als christliche Kirche gedient haben; das Dach stürzte wegen des Vermorschens der Holzkonstruktion ein und riß dadurch einen Teil der Wände ab. *Inge Hofmann*

74743 TRAUNECKER, C. und A. BELLOD, Wandmalereien aus den Krypten der Tempel von Karnak. Erforschung und Fotografie im ultravioletten Licht, *Arbeitsblätter für Restauratoren*, Trier 7, Heft 1, Gruppe 19, Naturwissenschaftliche Untersuchungen (1974), 23-29, with 2 ill. and 1 fig.

The authors deal with the crypts in the Opet temple, where no inscriptions occur but only faint traces of wall paintings, and they describe the technics applied in order to make them visible.

74744 TRIGGER, Bruce G., La Candace, personnage mystérieux dans un royaume nubien dont l'écriture demeure hermétique, *Archéologia*, Paris No 77 (Décembre 1974), 10-17, with 8 ill., 1 fig., 2 maps and 1 plan.

Nach einem kurzen Abriß der nubischen Geschichte wird auf die Rolle der Kandake hingewiesen; Verf. schließt sich der allgemeinen Ansicht an, daß es sich bei ihr um die Königsmutter handle. Eine ausführliche Besprechung der Grabungsergebnisse von Arminna-West wird dargelegt und auf eine Stele mit meroitischer Kursivschrift verwiesen, auf der ein Amt beim König sowie eines bei einer Kandake vermerkt ist. Die Institution einer Kandake, die zum erstenmal in einer Inschrift der Königin Bartare im 2. Jahrhundert v.Chr. vorkommt, bestand demnach noch im 3. nachchristlichen Jahrhundert. *Inge Hofmann*

74745 TRIPPS, Manfred, Der ägyptische Brotträger im Deutschen Brotmuseum zu Ulm, *Antike Welt*, Küsnacht-Zürich 5, Heft 1 (1974), 39-42, with 4 ill.

Publication of a wooden statuette of a boy bearing a tray with loaves on his head. Comparing it with late bronzes the author dates the object in the XXVIth Dynasty. He suggests that it may have been part of a row of offering bearers.

74746 TRÜMPENER, Hans Josef, Ankünding einer soziologischen Arbeit über die Ägyptologie, *GM* Heft 9 (1974), 11-12.

The author describes a project to study the history of Egyptology from the viewpoint of a sociologist. *Dieter Mueller*

TURNER, E.G., see our number 74567.

74747 VALLOGGIA, Michel, Deux stèles égyptiennes de la Première Période Intermédiaire, *Genava*, Genève 22 (1974), 249-254, with 2 ill.

Publication of two funerary stelae of the First Intermediate Period, both probably from Upper Egypt. One (Musée d'art et d'histoire de Genève Inv. No. 15197) can be assigned on palaeographical grounds to the VIIIth Dyn., the other (Inv. No. 15198) to the Xth Dyn. *Dieter Mueller*

74748 VALLOGGIA, Michel, Les vizirs des XIe et XIIe dynasties, *BIFAO* 74 (1974), 123-134.

The author lists 15 viziers during the XIth and XIIth Dynasties, including those mentioned by Weil (*Die Veziere des Pharaonen-*

reiches, Strasbourg, 1908). Of each of them the known monuments are mentioned with their publication, followed by the date of their office.

The second part of the study argues that, as in the Old Kingdom, the title vizier was in some instances merely honorary, particularly with the princes of the Hare nome.

74749 VANDERSLEYEN, Claude, Sinouhé B 221, *RdE* 26 (1974), 117-121.

L'auteur analyse la genèse d'une faute et propose une correction purement graphique dans le nom des *Fnḫw* du passage en question pour fournir de nouveaux arguments à une juste appréciation de la valeur relative des divers manuscrits de Sinouhé. *Ph. Derchain*

74750 VANDIER, Jacques, La publication des textes du Musée du Louvre, *Textes et langages III*, 159-167.

After describing the origin of the Egyptian collection in the Louvre Museum the author presents a survey of its history, mentioning the more important acquisitions under various directors. The notes refer to some publications.

74751 VANDIER, Jacques, Le temple de Tôd, *Textes et langages III*, 259-265.

After a survey of early studies on the Montu temple at Tôd the author describes the results of the French researches before the war by Bisson de la Roque. After the war various French scholars have worked on the publication of the texts, which is still in an unfinished state.

74752 VAN DUYN, Janet, The Egyptians. Pharaohs and Craftsmen, London, Cassell, [1974] (15.5 × 23 cm; 176 p., 3 maps, 2 fig., 73 ill. [51 in colour]). Series: Cassell's Early Culture Series.
Pr. £ 2.50

A book for the general public, probably mainly intended for older children, without scientific aims. The author deals in fourteen chapters with chosen subjects from the history and civilization of Egypt, i.a. Tutankhamon's tomb, the country, Hatshepsut, the Zoser complex, early archaeologists, etc. The subjects are not dealt with in any chronological order.

74753 VARGA, E., Quelques notes sur une momie factice au Musée Hongrois des Beaux-Arts, *Studia Aegyptiaca I*, 379-388, with 4 ill.

A small mummy (length 73 cm) in the Museum of Arts in Budapest, supposed to contain the body of a child, was examined by X-raying and appeared to contain bones of an adult. The author mentions a number of similar instances and suggests that the embalmers, having made a mistake during the mummification of a child, replaced its body by bones of an adult in order to deceive the parents of the child.

74754 VARGA, Edith, Szépmüvészeti Muzeum Egyiptomi Kiállitás, Budapest, 1974 (88 p., 59 ill.).

"Museum of Arts. Egyptian Exhibition".
Guide to the reorganized exhibition of Egyptian antiquities at Budapest. With a preface relating the history of the collection, by V. Wessetzky. Not seen.

74755 VELGUS, V. A., Фокусники древнего египта и александрийские фокусники в Китае, *in*: *Основные проблемы африканистики. Этнография. история. филология.* К 70-летию члена-корреспондента АН СССР Д. А. Ольдерогге, Moscow, Издательство « Наука », 1973, 312-323.

"Ancient Egyptian Jugglers and Alexandrian Jugglers in China". The country Li-shan, mentioned by Chinese chroniclers of the 2nd and 1st centuries B.C. in connection with the arrival of jugglers or illusionists, has been identified by many scholars with the city of Alexandria for good reasons. This particular art profoundly influenced Chinese theatrical performances. Alexandrian illusionism was quite renown in the Hellenistic Period, and it rested firmly on much older Egyptian traditions, evidenced by e.g. the stories in the *papyrus Westcar*.

J. F. Borghouts

74756 VENOT, Christiane, Le cimetière MX TD de Mirgissa, *CRIPEL* 2 (1974), 27-49, with 6 fig. and 1 map.

Analyse eines "armen" Friedhofs, der wahrscheinlich in der Zeit Thutmosis' III. angelegt und 30 bis 50 Jahre benutzt wurde. Die Garnison in Mirgissa war recht klein; Frauen, Kinder und Hilfspersonal waren gleichfalls auf dem Friedhof MX-TD bestattet.   *Inge Hofmann*

74757 VENTURA, R., An Egyptian Rock Stela in Timna, *Tel Aviv* 1 (1974), 60-63, with 1 fig. and 2 pl.

Publication of a poorly executed rock stela (rather an inscription) on the cliff about 20 m above the Hathor shrine at Timna, discovered in 1972. The figure of Ramses III is depicted standing before and offering to Hathor. A partly lost line under the representation mentions, according to the author, the arrival of the Royal Butlers Ramesu and another whose name is lost

74758 VERCOUTTER, Jean, État des recherches à Saï, *BSFE* No 70-71 (Juin et Octobre 1974), 28-36, with 5 ill.

Bericht über die vier letzten Ausgrabungskampagnen auf der Insel Sai : ein ägyptischer Tempel aus der 18. Dynastie wurde freigelegt ; der am meisten verehrte Gott auf der Insel war Amun-Re, als dessen Begleiterin jedoch Nut und nicht Mut aufscheint, sowie der falkenköpfige Horus, der als "mächtiger Stier" und "Herr von Nubien" verehrt wurde. Sehr zahlreich sind Fragmente von Denkmälern mit dem Namen des Nehy, Vizekönigs von Nubien unter Thutmosis III. Aus der 18. Dynastie stammt weiterhin ein kleiner Friedhof mit wertvollen Beigaben, auf dem vermutlich eine bevorrechtete Priesterschicht bestattet wurde.

Der riesige Kerma-Friedhof im Zentrum der Insel enthielt auch Gräber der Pfannengräberkultur. Auch Funde aus der meroitischen, der X-Gruppen- und der christlichen Kultur wurden getätigt. *Inge Hofmann*

74759 VERCOUTTER, Jean, Saï 1972-1973, *CRIPEL* 2 (1974), 11-26, with 2 maps and 1 plan.

Während der Ausgrabungskampagne 1972-73 wurden die Arbeiten am Fort systematisch weitergeführt sowie die Ausgrabung der großen "Kerma"-Nekropole im Zentrum der Insel Saï fortgesetzt. Das Fort reicht von der türkischen Zeit des Mittelalters bis in die pharaonische der 18. Dynastie. Die Mauer aus der letzteren Epoche besitzt rechteckige Bastionen wie die Außenmauern in Sesebi, Amara und Soleb. Mauerblöcke eines kleinen Heiligtums zeigen eine Szene mit der Göttin Hathor. Nur wenige Fragmente stammen aus der meroitischen Zeit. Im Süd-Süd-Osten des Forts liegt ein Friedhof der pharaonischen Zeit, dessen Gräber nach dem Inventar hauptsächlich in die 18. Dynastie zu datieren sind. Er scheint allerdings noch während der 20. Dynastie benutzt worden zu sein, da sich ein Amulett mit dem Namen des Königssohnes von Kusch, Ramses-Nacht, fand.

Im Kerma-Friedhof wurden drei Grabtypen festgestellt, wobei der älteste Typ weder der C, noch der Kerma-Kultur zugeschrieben werden kann. Auch die Grabfunde zeigen einen Übergang zwischen der A-Kultur einerseits und der C- und Kerma-Kultur andererseits.

74760 VERGOTE, J., Une nouvelle grammaire du Moyen Egyptien, *CdE* XLIX, No 98 (1974), 301-308.

Article de recension de notre No. 71078.

74761 VERGOTE, Joseph, Le rapport de l'égyptien avec les langues sémitiques. Quelques aspects du problème, *Actes premier congrès de linguistique sémitique*, 49-54.

The author presents a summary of his earlier study of the relation between Egyptian and the Semitic languages (see our number 65502).

74762 VERGOTE, Joseph et George M. PARÁSSOGLOU, Les Psaumes 76 et 77 en copte-sahidique d'après le P. Yale Inv. 1779, *Le Muséon*, Louvain 87 (1974), 531-541.

Publication of Pap. Yale Inv. 1779, a sheet with the Sahidic version of *Ps.* 76 and 77. After a description of the ms. and a comparison with the text of the codex Brit.Mus. Ms.or. 5000 the authors give the Coptic text with a translation.

74763 VERNER, Miroslav, Abusír '74, *Květy*, Praha No. 31 (1974), 30-35.

Interview with Dr. Verner about the work on the mastaba of Ptahshepses.

74764 VERNER, Miroslav, Egypt — země faraónů. (Katalog výstavy fotografií Milana Zeminy, Praha, 1974.

"Egypt. Land of the Pharaohs (Catalogue of a Photo Exhibition of Milan Zemina)".
The catalogue contains a survey of the Czechoslovak Egyptologists' work in Egypt, chronological tables of the Egyptian history and descriptions of the photographs. *B. Vachala*

74765 VERNER, Miroslav, 10. Egyptologická expedice ČsEÚ v EAR, *Zpravy Čs. společnosti orientalistické*, Praha, 1974.

"The 10th Egyptological Expedition of the Czechoslovak Institute of Egyptology in the A.R. of Egypt". Not seen.

74766 VERNER, Miroslav, The Seal-Bearer Qenamūn, *ZÄS* 100, 2 (1974), 130-136, with 6 ill.

Publication of a wooden head-rest (Inv. Nr. 5985) and a wooden coffin (1085) from the Metternich collection. For the mummy in the coffin one may consult our number 74722.
The same name and title occur on the fragment of a stela that is the subject of our number 3671 (Baltimore, W.A.G. 22.101). It is probable that these pieces belonged to one man who lived in Thebes under the XVIIIth Dynasty before Akhnaton, not to be confused with Qenamon, the Chief Steward of Amenophis II.
M. Heerma van Voss

74767 VERNUS, Pascal, Deux statues du Moyen Empire, *BIFAO* 74 (1974), 151-159, with 4 fig. and 3 pl.

The author publishes two statues. First a headless, black granite statue of a squatting man from the private collection of Robert

Jongeryck, dated to the end of the XIIth Dynasty or somewhat later. The text is badly damaged. Then a similar statue, Cairo 90151, with a longer text mentioning as its owner a *Sbk-m-mr.i*. The author comments on his titles, which are fairly obscure. The piece is dated to the reigns of either Sesostris III or Amenemhat III.

74768 VERNUS, Pascal, Un édifice cultuel *Ḥwt-km-wr*, *GM* Heft 13 (1974), 31-36.

A passage from the *Pyramid Texts* (*Pyr*. 1657a-1659b) and a fragmentary biographical inscription of the early Middle Kingdom from Lisht (*PM* IV 84) treat *ḥwt-km-wr* as a structure that forms part of a funerary complex. *Dieter Mueller*

74769 VERNUS, P., Une formule des shaouabtis sur un peudo-naos de la XIIIe dynastie, *RdE* 26 (1974), 100-114, with 2 fig. and 2 pl.

Publication d'un petit monument quadrangulaire de la XIIIe dynastie décoré sur ses quatre faces de niches contenant alternativement une statuette momiforme tenant dans les mains des vases *ḥs* et un couple. Outre la formule de l'offrande funéraire et la titulature du défunt, on trouve sur ce monument, en rapport avec les statuettes momiformes, une copie de la déclaration ordinaire des ouchebtis telle qu'elle figure dans *CT* VI 2 a-h. L'auteur fournit des inscriptions du monument un commentaire détaillé. *Ph. Derchain*

74770 VERNUS, P., Sur une formule des documents judiciaires de l'époque ramesside, *RdE* 26 (1974), 121-123.

La formule *nty bwpwy p3 R' dit* de plusieurs papyrus judiciaires, signifiant "dont Râ n'a pas permis (qu'il assume telle fonction)", au delà de l'expression de la suppression simple d'une fonction retirée au criminel à qui elle s'applique, doit avoir eu aussi la valeur d'une imprécation magique, équivalente de la suppression du nom. *Ph. Derchain*

74771 Verzeichnis deutschsprachiger Dissertationen 1945-1973. Beilage zum Informationsblatt der deutschsprachigen Ägyptologie, Berlin Heft 8 (Juni 1974) (8 p.).

A list of nearly one hundred titles of dissertations, with mention of their publication if ever published.

74772 VIRCHOW, R., Ägyptenreise 1888. Rudolf Virchows Briefe an seine Frau, *Die Waage*. Zeitschrift der Chemie Gruenenthal, Stolberg im Rheinland 13, nr. 1 (1974), 1-20, with 14 ill.

Publication of some letters of the famous German scholar Rudolf Virchow to his wife written during his travels in Egypt and Nubia in 1888. Some of the ill. reproduce original photographs of Virchow, i.a. of Karnak and Abu Simbel.

74773 VITTMANN, Günther, Eine bemerkenswerte Schreibung des Namens der Göttin Nephthys, *GM* Heft 11 (1974), 49-52.

The author collects examples of the late spelling *nb.ty* for *nbt-ḥwt*, and compares Coptic ⲛⲉⲃⲑⲱ.
Cfr the "Nachtrag", *GM* Heft 17 (1975), 45.   *Dieter Mueller*

74774 VITTMANN, Günther, Was there a Coregency of Aḥmose with Amenophis I?, *JEA* 60 (1974), 250-251.

The view of Redford is quoted that juxtaposed cartouches without double-dated inscriptions provide no certain evidence of a coregency, but indirect evidence from the stela of Neferrenpet at Tura quarries indicates that if queen Aḥmose Nefertari is called 'King's Mother' in year 22 of her husband, her son may well have been associated on the throne, and Sethe's theory may thus be discounted.   *E Uphill*

74775 VITTMANN, Günther, Zur Lesung des Königsnamen, *Orientalia* 43 (1974), 12-16.

Suite à l'article de Priese, *MIO* 1968 (notre No 68492), et après examen notamment des attestations du même nom porté par d'autres personnes, l'auteur fait valoir qu'une origine égyptienne pure du nom de Piankhy ne pourrait donner la solution complète du problème. Le signe *'nḫ* est inconnu comme déterminatif; le comprendre ici comme idéogramme expliquerait les orthographes instables, mais exclurait la lecture étrangère. Seule la variante *p + y* préciserait la lecture Piye, à comprendre "le vivant" en kouchite; le cartouche complet rendrait la traduction égyptienne. Cette dernière jouerait sur la ressemblance fortuite mais frappante entre les aspects écrits du nom royal dans les deux langues. Le premier signe a d'un côté une valeur verbale, de l'autre la valeur d'article; le *y* final, rarement écrit dans ce nom dans ses autres apparitions, laisse transparaître une finale étrangère. Sur la stèle C 100 du Louvre, il faudrait comme ailleurs lire en conformité avec l'orthographe: il faut donc admettre tantôt l'habituelle traduction Piankhy, tantôt le nom originel Piye.   *J. Custers*

74776 VITTMANN, Günther, Zur Plastik des Mittleren Reiches: Sebekemsaf und Jui, *GM* Heft 10 (1974), 41-44.

The Vienna statue of Sebekemsaf is stylistically related to two statues of the vizier Jui, for whom a Middle Kingdom date is far more likely than the early XVIIIth Dynasty. A continuation of our No. 73762. *Dieter Mueller*

74777 VITTMANN, Günther, Zwei Königinnen der Spätzeit namens Chedebnitjerbōne, *CdE* XLIX, No. 97 (1974), 43-51.

Réexaminant sept documents portant le nom de *Ḥdb Nt irt bjnt* accompagné tantôt du titre *ḥmt njswt* (*wrt*) *mwt njswt*, tantôt de *ḥmt njswt* seulement, tantôt sans titre, et étudiant la provenance de chacun, l'auteur conclut qu'il faut distinguer deux reines de ce nom, dont l'une aurait pu être l'épouse de Necho et la mère de Psammétique II, enterrée à Sais, et l'autre fille d'Apriès et épouse d'Amasis, dont la tombe se trouvait à Saqqara. Cette dernière toutefois pourrait avoir été plutôt l'épouse de Nectanébo II, comme on l'avait admis jusqu'ici.

74778 VOGEL, Kurt, Ein arithmetisches Problem aus dem Mittleren Reich in einem demotischen Papyrus, *Enchoria* 4 (1974), 67-70.

The Problem No. 56 in Dem. Pap. Brit. Mus. 10520 explains the method of dividing 2/35 into 1/30 and 1/42 attested in the table 2:n at the beginning of the Rhind Mathematical Papyrus.
Dieter Mueller

VOLKOFF, Oleg V., see our number 74781.

VOLLMER, John, see our number 74443.

74779 VOLOTIN, N.I., Меры длины Египта и использования их в IV-XVII вв. на Востоке и Средний Азии, *Klio*, Berlin 55 (1973), 159-195, with 5 ill.

"The length-measures of Egypt and their use in the 4th-17th centuries in East and Middle Asia".
The author tabulates several lists of ancient Egyptian measures of length (no Egyptian terms are used, and sources remain unquoted everywhere), equated with Greek, Persian, and other measures. Sometimes the entries are enriched with non-Egyptian measures (like the Russian *wershok*) but converted subsequently to Egyptian units. One tabulation holds good from the beginning of Egyptian history until king Amenophis IV (p. 160-163). Under Akhnaton, length measures — important, of course, in the agricultural economy — were reduced with one tenth. The tabulated results (164-8) can be verified from the dimensions in Egyptian measures of Tutankhamun's tomb (after Carter; 170-1). For the author, there is little doubt that the king (a reformer par excellence) revised the current system to alleviate the burden of the heavy-taxed people (like Solon did in Athens). Other reforms took place under Psammetichus I (with a reduction of 1/25th; see the results on p. 172-5) and the

Ptolemies (again an overall reduction of 1/10th; 175-9). In the meantime, Akhnaton's new system had been adapted by the peoples of the Lebanon and Syria, slightly modified (overview on p. 180-5). And later on, when the older Egyptian linear measures had found their way into the Greek, Roman and Byzantine cultures, a Coptic system was devised (187-191), borrowed by the Arab dynasts. This system was transferred to Middle Asia, as can be verified from measurements of mediaeval public buildings in Samarkhand and Bukhara. *J.F. Borghouts*

74780 Voyages en Égypte des années 1597-1601. Bernardino Amico da Gallipoli. Aquilante Rocchetta. Henry Castela. Traduits de l'italien par Carla Burri et Nadine Sauneron. Présentation, notes et index de Serge Sauneron, [Le Caire, Institut français d'Archéologie orientale du Caire, 1974] (16.5 × 19.5 cm; XVI + 252 p., 1 folded map, 3 fig. [1 folded], fig. on cover) = Collection des voyageurs occidentaux en Égypte, 11.

The eleventh volume of the series contains parts of three books. The first, by Bernardino Amico, deals with the chapel near the Fountain of the Virgin at Matarîya (p. 5-9).
The second is the travel story of Rochetta from Ghaza through Cairo to Rosetta and Alexandria, in 1599. The exact descriptions are valuable.
The third is the description of a journey along the same route by Castela from Toulouse in 1600-1601.
The editor has added a foreword, notes, and extensive indexes (p. 225-252).

74781 Voyages en Égypte des années 1634, 1635 & 1636. Henry Blunt. Jacques Albert. Santo Seguezzi. George Chr. von Neitzschitz. Présentation, traduction et notes de Oleg V. Volkoff, [Le Caire, Institut français d'Archéologie orientale du Caire, 1974] (16.5 × 19.5 cm; 366 p., 1 folded map) = Collection des voyageurs occidentaux en Égypte, 13.

The first part of the volume (p. 1-75) is devoted to the travel story of Henry Blunt, a distinguished Englishman, who visited the Orient in 1634. The pages of his story on Egypt are translated, introduced and explained by notes. His description of Cairo is full of mistakes, that of the antiquities rather superficial. The second part (77-173) contains the books "État de l'Ægypte" by Jacques Albert (from 1634) and "Revenues d'Ægypte" by Santo Seguezzi (from 1635), both for a longer time inhabitants of Cairo. The editor presents information about the authors in the foreword and has added notes and indexes.

The last part (175-366) contains the travel story of von Neitzschitz, a German who several times visted the Orient and went from Alexandria to Cairo in 1636. His descriptions are vivid, but rather inexact; see e.g. his description of the Sphinx: "un rocher formé par la nature comme la tête d'un homme", in which used to live "un oracle ou esprit devin diabolique" (p. 244-245). Indexes to part 3 on p. 349-364.

VYHNÁNEK, Luboš, see our number 74722.

74782 van der WAERDEN, Bartel L., Science Awakening. II. The Birth of Astronomy. With Contributions by Peter Huber, Leyden, Noordhoff International Publishing — New York, Oxford University Press, [1974] (17.5 × 25 cm; XVI + 347 p., frontispiece, 34 ill., 26 fig.). Pr. bound fl. 98

Revised and English version of our number 66505. Chapter 1, on the astronomy in ancient Egypt, has improved with the help of Klaus Baer. It now contains a section on the Late Period originally dealt with in Chapter III. Discussion of Egyptian planetary tables in chapter 8, p. 308-323. On p. 324 a summary of Parker's article on two astronomical papyri in the Carlsberg Collection (our number 62458).

74783 WAGNER, Guy, Le temple d'Herakles Kallinikos et d'Ammon à Psôbthis-El Qasr, métropole de la Petite Oasis (Notes de voyage à l'Oasis de Baharieh, 18-25 Janvier 1974), *BIFAO* 74 (1974), 23-27.

Notes on the temple of Herakles and Ammon at el-Qasr in the Oasis Bahrîya. The remains of the building, at present covered by a village, yield mainly Greek inscriptions, but also a sphinx with a fragmentary hieroglyphic text.
For Greek dedications to Herakles, see the same author, *BIFAO* 73 (1973), 183-189, and an addition in *BIFAO* 74 (1974), 21-22, with 1 pl.

74784 van de WALLE, B., Le cinquantième anniversaire de la Fondation Égyptologique Reine Elisabeth (1923-1973), *BiOr* 31 (1974), 194-197, with 4 ill. on 2 pl.

Survey of the history of the Fondation Égyptologique Reine Élisabeth, its aims and activities during the first fifty years of its existence.

74785 van de WALLE, B., Une famille de médecins de la XIXe dynastie (Complément à *RdE* 25,58-83), *RdE* 26 (1974), 123-124.

L'auteur montre que le médecin Amenhotep (No 6 de la liste de Jonckheere) est le grand-père de *Ḫꜥj* (No 66), fils de *'Iwnj* dont on peut assurer qu'il avait des relations avec le corps médical.
Ph. Derchain

74786 van de WALLE, B., Le mastaba de Neferirtenef, *BSFE* No. 69 (Mars 1974), 6-19, with 5 ill.

Discussion of the reliefs of the mastaba of Neferirtnef, originally at Saqqâra and since 1900 in the Musées Royaux d'Art et d'Histoire at Brussels. The author studies the titles of its owner, who has been connected with some Sun Temples of the Vth Dynasty, and those of his wife *Wṯst-k3w*, as well as his funerary cult. Since the tomb chapel is rather small only a restricted choice of the possible scenes has been carved on its walls, among which the author describes the hunting and fowling scene (one of the oldest examples known to us and evidently a copy of that in the funerary temple of Sahure), a family scene, and the representations of aspects of the agriculture.

74787 van de WALLE, Baudouin, La publication des textes des musées : Bruxelles (Musées Royaux d'Art et d'Histoire), *Textes et langages III*, 169-180.

The author briefly describes the history of the collection and draws up a list of the more important antiquities arranged in chronological order, each followed by the relevant publications.

74788 van de WALLE, B., Jacques Vandier. (28 octobre 1904-15 octobre 1973), *CdE* XLIX, No 97 (1974), 113-114.

Obituary article. Compare our number 73828.

van de WALLE, Baudouin, see also our number 74093.

74789 WALTERS, C. C., Monastic Archaeology in Egypt, Warminster, Aris & Phillips, [1974] (17 × 24.8 cm; X + 354 p., frontispiece, 2 maps, 29 plans, 44 fig., 49 ill.); series: Modern Egyptology Series; rev. *JEA* 61 (1975), 303-305 (Alan B. Lloyd); *Rivista* 50 (1976), 243-247 (Tito Orlandi).

Although this study of the material side of Egyptian monasticism until c. 1200 A.D. is outside the scope of the *AEB* it may be consulted with profit by egyptologists for the study of the continuity of the material culture.
After an introduction on early Christian Egypt and the beginnings of monasticism, both the Anthonian and the Pakhomian type, there follow chapters on the evolution of these types of monasteries, on ecclesiastical and non-ecclesiastical architecture, on painting, stone- and woodwork, aspects of daily life such as diet (e.g., ovens, corn mills, wells, water tanks, salt, wine, etc.), clothing, occupations and latrines, and a chapter on burial customs.
Appendix A contains a list of the principal monastic sites each with some archaeological information and a bibliography;

74790 WÅNGSTEDT, Sten V., Demotische Steuerquittungen aus Edfu in der Berliner Papyrus-Sammlung, *Festschrift Ägyptisches Museum Berlin*, 323-334, with 27 ill. on 5 pl.

Publication of 26 Demotic tax receipts from Edfu, preserved in the Berlin collection. They date from the year 22 of Augustus to the year 22 of Tiberius and relate to one family, of which the author draws up a genealogical table. Various kinds of taxes are mentioned.
The author gives of each text a photograph (plus a facsimile), a transliteration and a translation with a few notes.

74791 WARD, William A., The Semitic Biconsonantal Root *sp* and the Common Origin of Egyptian *čwf* and Hebrew *sûp*: "Marsh (-Plant)", *Vetus Testamentum*, Leiden 24 (1974), 339-349.

The author discusses the relation between Eg. *twf(y)*, "marsh (-plant)" > "papyrus" (actually *twf*, Coptic ⲭⲟⲟⲩϥ < *čawf*) and Hebrew סוּף. The latter has recently been explained as "border, end", derived from a Semitic root *sp*, which also occurs in Eg. *sp.t*, "bowl". For a parallel development the author refers to *ph*, "arrive" — *phwy*, "end" — *phw*, "marshes of the Delta". It is unlikely that the Egyptian *twf* and Hebrew סוּף are borrowed in one direction or the other, but both are according to linguistic changes from a Canaanite **sp > *sawp*.

74792 WÂSIF, Fathy Melek, Soundings on the Borders of Ancient Sais, *Oriens Antiquus* 13 (1974), 327-328.

Brief report on a small excavation at Sais, by which a Late Period mud-brick building was found and a number of objects from daily life. Most interesting was the discovery of a group of erotic figurines (couples drinking together, musicians, and couples in various positions of coitus).
A later sounding brought to light the granite head and torso of a royal statue.

74793 WATERMANN, Rembert, Osteoarchäologische Sammlungen am Nil und am Niederrhein, *Medizinische Monatsschrift*, Stuttgart 28 (1974), 119-124, with 1 table, 1 plan and 6 ill.

General article about osteo-archaeological collections, with sections on the skeletons deposited in tomb 30 (Hekaib) of Qubbet el-Hâwa, Aswân.

WEILER, Ingomar, see our number 74006.

74794 WEINSTEIN, James, A Fifth Dynasty Reference to Annealing, *JARCE* 11 (1974), 23-25, with 1 fig.

Two relief scenes of the Vth Dynasty are known where the technique of annealing (heating a material in order to soften it for further processing) is represented: in the tomb of Ti at Saqqâra (ed. H. Wild, pl. 173) and in that of Wepemnofret at Gîza (Selim Hasan, *Excavations at Gîza 1930-1931*, fig. 219). The latter scene is extensively studied and its terminology discussed.   *J.F. Borghouts*

74795 WEINSTEIN, James Morris, Foundation Deposits in Ancient Egypt, *Dissertation Abstracts International A*, Ann Arbor, Mich. 34, No. 4 (October 1973), 1902-A.

Abstract of a doctor's thesis University of Pennsylvania, 1973 (Order No. 73-24,237; 513 p.).
The author discusses in chapter 1 the various rites of the foundation ceremony. In Chapters 2-7 the foundation deposits are systematically examined by chronological periods, each chapter being divided into an analysis of the archaeological material and a corpus of the deposits.
Chapter 8 is devoted to the question of human foundation sacrifice in Egypt, while the last chapter presents a summary of the evidence for the relation between the archaeological material and the foundation ceremony.   *L.M.J. Zonhoven*

74796 WEINSTEIN, James M., A Statuette of the Princess Sobeknefru at Tell Gezer, *BASOR* No. 213 (February, 1974), 49-57, with 1 ill. and 1 fig.

Publication of a fragment of a statuette (feet and part of the base only) found at Tell Gezer in 1971 and, according to the inscription, representing the king's daughter Sobeknefru. The stratum in which the piece has been found dates from the late 13th to early 12th century B.C., the statuette itself from the Middle Kingdom, since Sobeknefru was the daughter of either Sesostris I or Amenemhat III, probably of the latter. The author discusses other instances of statuary from the Middle Kingdom discovered in Palestine and suggests that they may have reached the country only some time afterwards; they then do not reflect any economic or political relations with Egypt.

74797 WEIPPERT, Manfred, Semitische Nomaden des zweiten Jahrtausends. Über die *šȝsw* der ägyptischen Quellen, *Biblica*, Roma 55 (1974), 265-280 and 427-433, with 1 fig.

A review article of our number 71204.

74798 WENDORF, Fred, Romuald SCHILD, Vance HAYNES, Rushdi SAID, Achilles GAUTIER and Michal KOBUSIEWICZ, Archaeological and Geological Investigation in the Egyptian Sahara: The 1974 Season, *Newsletter ARCE* No. 89 (Spring 1974), 20-28.

After a summary of previous results a description of the research activities into the prehistory of the Sahara in 1974 at Bir Torwafi and Gebel Nabta in the Egyptian Sahara is given.
L.M.J. Zonhoven

WENDORF, Fred, see also our number 74293.

74799 WENIG, Steffen, Arensnuphis und Sebiumeker. Bemerkungen zu zwei in Meroe verehrten Göttern, *ZÄS* 101 (1974), 130-150, with 10 fig., 7 ill. and 4 pl.

Der in Ägypten unbekannte Gott Sebiumeker ist wohl als Schöpfergott des meroitischen Pantheons nicht nur in Musawwarat es Sufra mehrfach belegt, sondern aufgrund ikonographischer Details als eine der Statuen vom sog. Isis-Tempel in Meroe nachzuweisen. Zusammen mit Arensnuphis bildet er ein Paar, das sich möglicherweise in Gestalt eines männlichen Löwenpaares manifestieren kann. Beide Götter sind im Innern des Apedemaktempels von Naga, nahe dem Eingang, dargestellt, und die beiden Kolossalstatuen von Argo scheint man nicht mit ihnen identifizieren zu dürfen. Sebiumeker und Arensnuphis, für den gleichfalls meroitischer Ursprung angenommen wird, hatten im Tempel Wächterfunktionen. Während Sebiumeker seine Attribute, vornehmlich die Doppelkrone, unmittelbar von Horus, mittelbar von Atum entlehnte, soll der meroitische Arensnuphis im Verlauf der 25. Dynastie mit dem ägyptischen Jägergott Onuris identifiziert worden sein. Die Gleichsetzung ging so weit, daß nichts Meroitisches, auch nicht der Name, erhalten blieb. Verf. hält 'Irj-ḥms-nfr für eine ägyptische Übersetzung des meroitischen Namens oder eines Epithetons, wobei der Name "der gute Gefährte" sehr gut zur Rolle des Arensnuphis als Gefährte des Sebiumeker passen würde.
Sehe jetzt auch: Inge Hofmann, Nochmals zur Herkunft des Arensnuphis, *GM* Heft 22 (1976), 31-37, und E. Minkowskaya, Über den Gott Arensnuphis, *Studia Aegyptiaca II*, Budapest (1976), 79-87.
Inge Hofmann

74800 WENIG, Steffen, Das Grab des Soldatenschreibers Ḥwj. Untersuchungen zu den memphitischen Grabreliefs des Neuen Reiches II, *Festschrift Ägyptisches Museum Berlin*, 239-245, with 1 pl. and 5 fig. including 4 plans.

Sequel to our number 72764.

Publication of three relief fragments from the Memphite tomb of a Huy, one in Berlin (Inv. No. 2087), one found North of the pyramid of Teti (cfr Quibell and Hayter, Excavations at Saqqara. Teti Pyramid, North Side, Le Caire, IFAO, 1927, pl. 19,1) and one (unpublished) from a magazine in Saqqâra. Moreover, the author mentions a group statue of Huy and his wife, also found by Quibell and Hayter. The three reliefs are suggested to belong to one tomb on stilistic and iconographic grounds. The author also discusses the position of the tomb, which may be in the neighbourhood of Kagemni's tomb, and its date, probably the reigns of Eye or Horemheb.

74801 W[ENTE], E. F., Egypt, History of. II. From the beginning of the 18th Dynasty to c. 330 B.C., *Encyclopaedia Britannica*. Volume 6, 471-481, with 1 map.

In this second part of the lemma on the history of ancient Egypt (for the first part see our number 74357) the author presents a survey of the history of the New Kingdom, with a section on its society and culture, and of the Late Period until the Conquest by Alexander the Great.
For other references to the history of ancient Egypt see the above edition. Micropaedia. vol. III. *L. M. J. Zonhoven*

WERNER, A. E., see our number 74131.

WERTIME, T. A., see our number 74524.

74802 WESSETZKY, Vilmos, Die Ägyptologie in Ungarn, *XVIII. Deutscher Orientalistentag*, 42-44.

Survey of the egyptological studies in Hungary.

74803 WESSETZKY, Guillaume, Données relatives à l'interprétation des représentations égyptiennes de poissons, *Bulletin du Musée Hongrois des Beaux-Arts*, Budapest 42 (1974), 3-12, with 7 ill.

The author first discusses two palettes in the shape of a fish in Budapest, one from the late Prehistoric or the Archaic Period (Inv. No. 60.4.E.) and one from the New Kingdom representing a *tilapia* (Inv. No. 60.5.E).
He then discusses the problem why Kebehsenuf in the Late Period was sometimes represented as a fish, pointing at the possible influence of the word kbh, "pure water", which may have conveyed the notion of purity. On the same spot, over Osiris on his couch, where on a sarcophagus from el-Gamhûd preserved in the Cairo Museum a fish is depicted, occurs on another sarcophagus from the same place now in Budapest (Inv. No. 51.1992) the *ba*-bird, indicating that fish and bird here constitute the same symbol.

On the stela of *Nfr-ḥȝwt*, from the time of Tuthmosis III (Inv. No. 51.2143) the adorant is bearing at a yoke, apart from young gazelles and a bird, two fishes, the latter symbolizing the fertility of the Nile.

A Hungarian version of the same article (Adatok az egyiptomi halábrázolázok értelmezéséhez) on p. 107-110.

74804 WESSETZKY, Vilmos, Egyiptomi élet — és örökkévaláság jelképek Arnechamani meroei uralkodó jelvényein, *Idö és történelem*, 205-208, with 1 fig.

"Ägyptische Ewigkeits- und Lebenssymbole am Ornat des Meroitischen Königs Arnekhamani".

Nach der Verlegung des königlichen Friedhofes nach Meroe traten immer mehr einheimische Elemente in der Kunst und Religion in den Vordergrund. Das zeigt sich z.B. in der Ikonographie des Königsornates, wo altägyptische Ewigkeits- und Lebenssymbole, Skarabäus, Frosch, Herz, Widder, etwas stilisiert dargestellt sind. *V. Wessetzky*

74805 WESTENDORF, Wolfhart, "Auf jemandes Wasser sein" = "von ihm abhängig sein", *GM* Heft 11 (1974), 47-48.

The metaphorical expression "to be on someone's water" (*Sinuhe* B 74-75) alludes to the inferior position of someone whose water supply is dependent upon the good will of anyone in control of the upper part of an irrigation canal; it therefore means "to be dependent" rather than "to be loyal". *Dieter Mueller*

74806 WESTENDORF, Wolfhart, Das Eine und die Vielen. Zur Schematisierung der altägyptischen Religion trotz ihrer Komplexität, *GM* Heft 13 (1974), 59-61.

The "multiplicity of approaches" which characterizes the religion of ancient Egypt does not preclude the existence of, and search for, an underlying system. *Dieter Mueller*

74807 WESTENDORF, W., Horizont und Sonnenscheibe, *Studia Aegyptiaca I*, 389-398, with 1 fig.

Horizon (ȝḫt) and sun-disk (itn) are originally complementary realizations of two eternities, ḏt and nḥḥ, but when the sun-god became liberated from the categories of time and space the male-female scheme failed: horizon and sun-disk became both realizations of one eternity, viz. ḏt. The author discusses the consequences of this development in religious texts and representations.

74808 WESTENDORF, Wolfhart, Koptisches Handwörterbuch. Bearbeitet auf Grund des koptischen Handwörterbuchs Wilhelm

Spiegelbergs. Lieferung 5, Heidelberg, Carl Winter Universitätsverlag, 1974 (17 × 24.5 cm; p. 321-400); rev. *BiOr* 33 (1976), 31-33 (Werner Vycichl); *Mundus* 12 (1976), 129-130 (Alexander Böhlig); *Orientalia* 44 (1975), (H. Quecke); *WZKM* 68 (1976), 186-187 (H. Satzinger). Pr. DM 48

Sequel to our number 72768.

The fascicle contains the words ϢΠΙΗΤ to ϨϮΤ.

74809 WESTENDORF, Wolfhart, Papyrus Berlin 10456. Ein Fragment des wiederentdeckten medizinischen Papyrus Rubensohn, *Festschrift Ägyptisches Museum Berlin*, 247-254, with 1 pl. and 1 fig.

Preliminary publication of the papyrus fragment Berlin P 10456, years ago found by Rubensohn's excavations on Elephantine (1906-8) and mentioned by Möller as "disappeared", but recently rediscovered. The sheet contains a series of receipts against coughing, from the Ptolemaic Period. The author discusses orthography, vocabulary and grammar, and offers a photograph, a transcription (by Ulrich Luft), and a provisional translation with comments. The receipts, though new to us, are of the usual type, proving that the medical knowledge had not perished after the New Kingdom.

74810 WESTENDORF, Wolfhart, Zweiheit, Dreiheit und Einheit in der altägyptischen Theologie, *ZÄS* 100, 2 (1974), 136-141.

Verfasser unterscheidet bei der Zweiheit drei Systeme. Ein polares (Gegensatz-Paare), ein ausgleichendes und ein ungleichmässiges. Die Dreiheit ist nur eine verdeutlichende Sonderentwicklung der Zweiheit. Im Rahmen der Einheit bespricht Westendorf das ägyptische Modell und die christliche Trinität. Vgl. unsere Nummer 73288. *M. Heerma van Voss*

74811 WILDUNG, Dietrich, Wilhelm Spiegelberg (1870-1930). Verzeichnis seiner Schriften, *Enchoria* 4 (1974), 95-139, with 1 pl.

A bibliography of W. Spiegelberg, previously accessible only on microfiche (see our number 73800). *Dieter Mueller*

74812 WILDUNG, Dietrich, Zwei Stelen aus Hatschepsuts Frühzeit, *Festschrift Ägyptisches Museum Berlin*, 255-268, with 18 fig. and 2 pl.

Study on Berlin Stela 15699 (published *Urk.* IV, 143-145) and Berlin stela Inv. No. 3/71. The first piece pictures Tuthmosis II, the queen-mother Ahmose and Tuthmosis' wife Hatshepsut. The stela may come from Edfu and date from the early reign of

Hatshepsut. After her accession to the throne as sole king she changed the original title of Ahmose "king's sister" into "queen-mother".

The second stela, here published, pictures the "king's [sister]" Ahmose in front of Hathor of Dendera, guest in Edfu, and a destroyed king (Hatshepsut) in front of Horus of Edfu in the upper register, and two priests Wadzmose and Montu on both sides of the Hathor emblem in the lower register.

The author draws up a list of representations of the emblem on stelae (with drawings), of which Berlin 3/71 is the earliest example, proving an early occurrence of a Hathor cult in Edfu.

74813 WILDUNG, Dietrich [et alii], Aufbau und Zweckbestimmung der Königsliste von Karnak, *GM* Heft 9 (1974), 41-48, with 2 ill.

The author approves a theory proposed by G. Maspero who explained the list of kings in Karnak as an enumeration of rulers represented by a statue in the precinct of the Great Temple of Amun. He suggests that these monuments were removed by Thutmosis III to make room for his Festival Hall, and replaced by a relief listing their names. *Dieter Mueller*

WILDUNG, Dietrich, see also our number 74670.

74814 WILSDORF, Helmut, Bemerkungen zu den mineralogischen Pharmazeutika der Kopten, *in*: *Studia Coptica*. Herausgegeben von Peter Nagel, Berlin, Akademie-Verlag, 1974 (= Berliner Byzantinistische Arbeiten, 45), 77-100, with 6 pl.

Of interest to Egyptologists may be the statement that the medical knowledge of the Coptic monks does not derive from ancient Egyptian medicine, and the thorough discussion of the chemical composition of five minerals and metals, known from both ancient Egyptian and Coptic: alum (*ibnw*; ⲱⲃⲉⲛ), lead (*dḥty*; ⲧⲁϩⲧ), natron (*ḥsmn*; ϩⲟⲥⲙ), reddle (*prš*; ⲡⲏⲣϣ) and salt (*ḥmȝt*; ϩⲙⲟⲩ), and some other substances.

L.M.J. Zonhoven

74815 WILSDORF, Helmut, Nach 110 Jahren. Zum Gedenken an Georg Steindorff. *12.11.1861 in Dessau. †28.8.1951 in North Hollywood, *in*: *Studia Coptica*. Herausgegen von Peter Nagel, Berlin, Akademie-Verlag, 1974 (= Berliner Byzantinistische Arbeiten, 45), 11-17.

A biographical article, written on the occasion of the 110th anniversary of Georg Steindorff's birthday.

WILSON, John A., see our number 74188.

WINDBLADH, Marie-Louise, see our number 74574.

74816 WINTER, Erich, Erfahrungsbericht über ein seit 20 Jahren verwendetes Ordnungssystem der Hieroglyphenzeichen der Spätzeit, *GM* Heft 14 (1974), 55-64.

The author illustrates the principles governing the arrangement and structure of his private list of Ptolemaic signs.
Dieter Mueller

74817 WINTER, Erich, Das hieroglyphische Schriftsystem vor allem der Spätzeit. Stand und Aufgabe, *GM* Heft 14 (1974), 9-15.

A short paper on current tasks in the exploration of the hieroglyphic writing system especially of the Graeco-Roman Period.
Dieter Mueller

74818 WINTER, Erich, Philae, *Textes et langages III*, 229-237.

Proceeding from its description in the *Description de l'Égypte* the author discusses the publications on the temple of Philae, stressing the importance of work done by Junker. The more important historical texts are mentioned, and the recent complete publication of the inscriptions (cfr our numbers 58345 and 65266) is discussed, of which two more volumes are in preparation. The last pages are devoted to the salvage of the building. At the end mention of its Demotic and Greek graffiti and their publications.

74819 WINTER, E., Wem war der Tempel von Bigge geweiht?, *Studia Aegyptiaca I*, 399-406.

In addition to the lemma "Bigga" in *LdÄ* 1, col. 792-793, the author argues that the temple on Bîga was dedicated to Osiris and Isis, as the inscriptions on its remains demonstrate, and not to Hathor-Tefnut as one has supposed in connection with the Hathor-Tefnut legend. A sanctuary of this goddess on the island has completely disappeared.

74820 WINTERS, Robert K., The Forest and Man, New York-Washington-Hollywood, Vantage Press, [1974] (15 × 23 cm; 393 p., 5 maps, 6 fig., 26 ill.).

In this book on the impact of the forest and its products on civilizations and national policies one long chapter (p. 36-83) is devoted to ancient Egypt, with notes to it on p. 338-342.
The author follows a chronological order, dealing with pre-history, the 3rd, 2nd and 1st millennia B.C. successively, and discussing the use of wood in house, tomb and boat constructions, of charcoal in copper mining, the occurrence of frankincense and myrrh, flagpoles, etc. Although a specialist his results are nowhere conspicuous, while the author does not quote the study of J.M.A. Janssen (our number 918).

74821 WOOD, Wendy, A Reconstruction of the Triads of King Mycerinus, *JEA* 60 (1974), 82-93, with 1 plan, 3 diagrams and 3 pl.

An analysis of the five triads recovered from the valley temple of Mycerinus by Reisner, 1908-10. These show the king with Hathor and the personifications of the 4th, 7th, 15th and 18th Upper Egyptian nomes, while the fragments indicate an original set that was larger and more complete. They are all made from greywacke probably from the Wâdi Hammamât. The writer disputes the accepted interpretation of these as equivalents of the food-bearing women in Old Kingdom reliefs, suggests there were only 8, not over 30 of them, and locates them in the portico chapels. They would thus represent only those provinces in which the cult of Hathor had been established with royal patronage.
E. Uphill

YOUNG, W.J., see our number 74541.

74822 ZANDEE, J., Das Alte Testament im Lichte der Ägyptologie, *in*: *Vruchten van de Uithof.* Studies opgedragen aan Dr. H.A. Brongers ter gelegenheid van zijn afscheid (16 mei 1974), [Utrecht], Theologisch Instituut Utrecht, 1974, 145-157.

Some concepts and institutions attested in the Old Testament are compared with similar beliefs and practices in Ancient Egypt. *Dieter Mueller*

74823 ZANDEE, J., Een egyptische inscriptie uit het Oude Rijk, *Mededelingenblad Vereniging van Vrienden van het Allard Pierson Museum*, Amsterdam 8 (1974), 1-2, with 3 ill.

Publication of a limestone block probably from a tomb of the VIth Dyn. Five incomplete lines of text contain some titles and laudatory epithets of the owner, whose name is not preserved. The block was bought from a dealer in Cairo, and is now in the Allard Pierson Museum in Amsterdam (Inv. No. 8752).
Dieter Mueller

74824 ZANDEE, J., Egyptological Commentary on the Old Testament, *in: Travels in the World of the Old Testament.* Studies presented to Prof. M.A. Beek on the Occasion of his 65th Birthday. Assen, van Gorcum, 1974, 269-281.

A selection of 28 passages from the Old Testament with parallels from assorted Egyptian texts. *Dieter Mueller*

74825 ZANDEE, Jan, Sargtexte, Spruch 78 (Coffin Texts II 19-23c), *ZÄS* 100, 2 (1974), 141-144.

A translation of *CT* Sp. 78, accompanied by a brief commentary. Continuation of our No. 73817. *Dieter Mueller*

74826 ZANDEE, Jan, Sargtexte, Spruch 79 (Coffin Texts II, 23d-27c), *ZÄS* 100, 2 (1974), 145-149.

A translation of *CT* Sp. 79, accompanied by a brief commentary. Continuation of our preceding number. *Dieter Mueller*

74827 ZANDEE, Jan, Sargtexte, Spruch 80 (Coffin Texts II 27d-43), *ZÄS* 101 (1974), 62-79.

A translation of *CT* Sp. 80, accompanied by a brief commentary. Continuation of our preceding number. *Dieter Mueller*

74828 ZANDEE, J., Sargtexte, Spruch 81 (Coffin Text II 44), *ZÄS* 101 (1974), 80-81.

A translation of *CT* Sp. 81, accompanied by a brief commentary. Continuation of our preceding number. *Dieter Mueller*

74829 ZAUZICH, Karl-Theodor, Die Bestätigung einer Rekonstruktion (P Loeb 62 + P Berlin 15558), *Festschrift Ägyptisches Museum Berlin*, 335-340, with 1 folded fig. and 1 pl.

Pap. Loeb 62, published by Spiegelberg (Die demotischen Papyri Loeb, München, 1931, pl. 34) has repeatedly been studied, i.a. by Nims (our number 60527). The author has succeeded to find the missing part in the lower left corner, which is P. Berlin 15558. It proves the restoration by Nims to be largely correct.
Zauzich gives a facsimile of the complete text with transliteration and a translation with notes, as well as a photograph of the Berlin papyrus.

74830 ZAUZICH, Karl-Th., Die demotischen Dokumente, *Textes et langages III*, 93-110.

The discussion of the non-literary Demotic texts deals with the documents after their main characteristics, dividing them into 28 categories, e.g. deeds of renunciation, letters, oaths, graffiti, lists and accounts, ostraca, etc. At the end the author adds remarks on the requirements for further study.
A bibliography of 107 numbers, alphabetically arranged after the authors' names, on p. 105-110.

74831 ZAUZICH, Karl-Theodor, Drei neue Fragmente zu Pap. Carlsberg 9, *Enchoria* 4 (1974), 157-158, with 1 pl.

Three small fragments discovered by the author in Berlin complete Col. II, 14-20 and Col. III, 1-8 and 9a-10a of Pap. Carlsberg 9. *Dieter Mueller*

74832 ZAUZICH, Karl-Th., Entzifferung der karischen Schrift, *Akten des XIII. Internationalen Papyrologenkongresses*, 489-497.

Report of the author's decipherment of the Karian script with the help of Egyptian-Karian bilingual texts, particularly the names. For further results compare our number 72801.

74833 ZAUZICH, Karl-Theodor, Spätdemotische Papyrusurkunden III, *Enchoria* 4 (1974), 71-82, with 1 pl.

The Demotic papyri Berlin P. 6857 and 30039 form part of one document concerning the sale of a house in Soknopaiou Nesos in A.D. 45. The Greek and Demotic versions of the text are re-published with translation and commentary.
Dieter Mueller

74834 ZAUZICH, Karl-Theodor, Teephibis als Orakelgott, *Enchoria* 4 (1974), 163.

The first line in four demotic texts from the Coll. Michaelides published by U. Kaplony-Heckel (our No. 72362) is to be read *i Dd-ḥr-pȝ-hb*, introducing requests for oracles addressed to the local god of Kasr-el-Agouz.
Compare our number 74596.
Dieter Mueller

74835 ZAUZICH, Karl-Th., Textveröffentlichungen der Museen: Berlin, *Textes et langages III*, 131-139.

Survey of the publications of texts in the three Berlin collections. The texts are divided into three categories: hieroglyphic inscriptions, hieratic texts and ostraca, and Demotic texts. For each of them the author first mentions the publications of collections of texts, followed by references to single texts arranged after their museum numbers.

74836 ZAUZICH, Karl-Theodor, Zu einigen demotischen Glossen im Papyrus Jumilhac, *Enchoria* 4 (1974), 159-161.

The marginal notes in Demotic accompanying some of the vignettes in Pap. Jumilhac specify where those illustrations really belong. The author suggests several new readings.
Dieter Mueller

74837 ZIMMERMAN, Michael, New Approaches to the Study of Ancient Disease, *Expedition*, Philadelphia, Penn. 17, Number 1 (Fall 1974), 24-30, with 8 ill.

General article about the results for the history of diseases to be gained from the study of mummies of various origins, particularly from ancient Egypt. The author, member of the staff of the Dra' Abû el-Naga' expedition, examined the mummy fragments from the tomb of Nebwenenef.

74838 ZIVIE, Christiane, Giza, Saqqara ou Memphis?, *GM* Heft 11 (1974), 53-58.

The author stresses the necessity to distinguish clearly between the Gîza cemetery, the Saqqâra necropolis, and the territory of the Memphite nome, and illustrates with several examples the confusion that may be caused by a careless use of these terms.
Dieter Mueller

74839 ZIVIE, Chr., Princes et rois du Nouvel Empire à Giza, *Studia Aegyptiaca I*, 421-433.

As a special aspect of the subject of her thesis (see our number 73823) the author here studies the texts relating visits of young royal princes to Gîza, mostly from the XVIIIth Dynasty. From their contents she concludes that not the "sportsmanlike" events but a pelgrimage to the remains of their great "ancestors" was the genuine reason for erecting the stelae, and that the Sphinx was the representative of these earlier kings.
The thesis itself has now been published: Christiane M. Zivie, Giza au deuxième millénaire, [Le Caire], Institut français d'Archéologie orientale du Caire, 1976 (= Bibliothèque d'étude, 70).

ZIVIE, Christiane, see also COCHE-ZIVIE.

NECROLOGIES

74840 el-AMIR, Mustafa: *BSFE* Nos 70-71 (Juin et Octobre 1974), 9 (anonymous).

74841 BARNS, John Wintour Baldwin: *BSAC* 21 (1971-1973), 1975, 219-222 (Emil Maher); *BSFE* No. 69 (Mars 1974), 4 (anonymous); *JEA* 60 (1974), 3 (Hugh Lloyd-Jones) and 243-246, with portrait (W.V. Davies).

74842 BONNET, Hans: *ZÄS* 100, 2 (1974), VI (Elmar Edel).

74843 CHEVRIER, Henri: *BSFE* Nos 70-71 (Juin et Octobre 1974), 7-8 (anonymous).

74844 HAYCOCK, Bryan: *BSFE* No. 69 (Mars 1974), 4 (anonymous); *JEA* 60 (1974), 3 (M.F. Laming Macadam); *MNL* No. 14 (Février 1974), 2-3 (P.L. Shinnie).

74845 OTTO, Eberhard: *BSFE* Nos 70-71 (Juin et Octobre 1974), 8 (anonymous); *Informationsblatt der deutschsprächigen Ägyptologie* 9, 1 (Januar 1975), 3 (Reinhard Grieshammer); *Saeculum* 25 (1974), 291-292 (Joachim Krecher); *SAK* 2 (1975), V-VI (Wolfgang Helck); *ZDMG* 126 (1976), 1-4, with portrait (Hellmut Brunner).

74846 SAAD, Ramadan : *BSFE* Nos 70-71 (Juin et Octobre 1974), 9 (anonymous).

74847 SCAMUZZI, Ernesto : *Aegyptus* 54 (1974), 203-205, with bibliography (Silvio Curto).

74848 TERRACE, Edward L.B. : *Newsletter ARCE* No. 88 (Winter 1974), 1-3 (anonymous).

74849 WOLF, Walther : *ZÄS* 101 (1974), V-VI (Martin Krause).